George Aldrich

Walpole As It Was and As It Is

Containing the complete civil history of the town from 1749 to 1879, together with

a history of all the church organizations; also, a history of one hundred and fifty

families that settled in the town previous to 1820

George Aldrich

Walpole As It Was and As It Is

Containing the complete civil history of the town from 1749 to 1879, together with a history of all the church organizations; also, a history of one hundred and fifty families that settled in the town previous to 1820

ISBN/EAN: 9783337261023

Printed in Europe, USA, Canada, Australia, Japan

Cover: Foto ©ninafisch / pixelio.de

More available books at **www.hansebooks.com**

AS IT WAS AND AS IT IS,

CONTAINING THE

COMPLETE CIVIL HISTORY OF THE TOWN
FROM 1749 TO 1879;

TOGETHER WITH

A HISTORY OF ALL THE CHURCH ORGANIZATIONS;

ALSO,

A HISTORY OF ONE HUNDRED AND FIFTY FAMILIES THAT SETTLED IN
TOWN PREVIOUS TO 1820, WITH BIOGRAPHICAL SKETCHES
OF A LARGE NUMBER OF ITS PROMINENT CITIZENS,
AND ALSO, A CENSUS OF THE TOWN
TAKEN APRIL, 1, 1878.

BY GEORGE ALDRICH.

"He that is not proud of his ancestors, either has no ancestors to be proud
of, or else he's a degenerate son."

———

PRINTED BY
THE CLAREMONT MANUFACTURING CO., CLAREMONT, N. H.
1880.

LIST OF PORTRAITS.

Rev. Henry W. Bellows, D. D., Frontispiece—see page   200

Hon. Henry A. Bellows, ...   202

Luther Burt, ...   221

Henry Burt,.   222

Josiah G. Graves, M. D.,.   .   .   .   266

Foster Hooper, M. D.,   .   .   .   279

Aaron P. Howland, ...   288

Hope Lathrop,.   310

Jonathan Livingston, ...   314

Aldis Lovell, Esq., ...   315

Bolivar Lovell, Esq., ...   316

Oliver Martin, ...   322

Winslow B. Porter, M. D.,   .   .   .   344

PREFACE.

In the spring of 1878 the author and compiler of the following pages thought that a census of the inhabitants of the town of Walpole with their names, ages and place of nativity, together with short biographical notices of some of the prominent men that had lived in town, and, also, a brief history of its early settlement, would be of some value and interest to the townspeople and meet with a ready sale. Acting upon such supposition the census of the town was taken during the following summer, and material was gathered sufficient to make a pamphlet of 150 pages octavo, which would complete the original design of the undertaking.

In the following winter, when the work was well nigh completed, Josiah G. Bellows Esq., Rev. William Brown, Dr. Abel P. Richardson and Curtis R. Crowell generously lent their time in reading what had been written, and feeling impressed with the importance of the undertaking to the town at the present time, and to future generations, thought it best to elaborate what had been written and furnish matter for a bound volume to embrace a more general and complete history of the town. To follow their suggestions with a mere local sale for the work would result in a loss of time, money and labor in the undertaking to the author. In this dilemma he was left the alternative of publishing the work as it was or appealing to the generosity of the town for assistance. The latter course was taken and the subject was presented to the town at its annual March meeting in 1879, and resulted in a unanimous vote for raising and appropriating $500 to be expended in printing and binding a work of four hundred octavo pages ; the undersigned to furnish the matter and receive for his compensation a stipulated sum from the towns-people for the work after publication. At this stage, the labor of adding 250 pages and rewriting much of the original matter was commenced and prosecuted with much labor, expense and perplexity, till its completion.

In writing and compiling the following pages all available information has been made to contribute matter both historical and personal, touching the history of the town ; such as the various histories of Vermont and New Hampshire afforded, together with the valuable history of Charlestown, from which the Selectmen of that town generously allowed the writer to make copious extracts.

The Historical Monograph written by Rev. Henry W. Bellows, D. D. has been an invaluable source of information from which the writer of this work has largely drawn ; the language from which has sometimes been slightly altered ; (not for the better) to conform to the present work. Files of old newspapers, once pub-

lished in town, have also been of invaluable aid, from which some curious facts
have been obtained.

That portion of the work which relates to the general history of the town and
the various churches and religious societies is believed, in the main, to be complete. No attempt has been made to furnish the entire genealogy of *all* the families in town, only those who became permanent settlers before 1820, and of those
a *general* history, with biograpical notices of the prominent men that have lived
in town, are only given, rather than merely a genealogical record ; for to secure
a full and exhaustive genealogy of some of the families would require years of
time and patience.

Of some of the oldest and most numerous families in town it is believed that
no family records are in existence, and their history is made up imperfectly from
what has been gleaned from stray leaves of baptisms, deaths and marriages found
in the old church and town records. In many instances appeals have been made
from time to time to persons to furnish matter in relation to their families, which
have as often been neglected, till at last what knowledge has been gained has
been furnished from outside parties. Such persons, if their family record is imperfect or not given at *all*, need not complain. No doubt many of the descendants of the old families will be surprised to learn for the first time the names
of their grand parents and the number of their uncles and aunts.

No doubt many errors of a minor nature will be found, for they are unavoidable
in a work of this kind ; but those that know the unreliable nature of information obtained generally from persons, will spare the author unnecessary criticisms.

Acknowledgments are due to Col. David Buffum for information in relation to
the general business transactions in town for the last sixty years, which has always
been cheerfully given ; and also to Josiah G. Bellows, Dr. Abel P. Richardson,
Rev. William Brown, Curtis R. Crowell, Alfred W. Burt, Henry Burt, Willard
T. Blanchard, David C. Thompson, Miss Katie J. Foster, Mrs. Mary A. Wilder
and her mother Mrs. David Russel, and others, for rendering valuable assistance.

Particular acknowledgments are due to Mr. Francis B. Knapp for his general interest manifested in the author's undertaking and his labor of love, patience, just
criticisms and valuable suggestions made when reading the manuscript before its
going to press.

With the foregoing remarks this volume is presented to the people of Walpole,
believing that the pledge given is amply fulfilled, and, also that it has the merit,
if nothing more, of rescuing from oblivion and recording in permanent form
some of the many traditions and incidents of the town's early history, which are
now held only in the memories of its oldest citizens, who are fast passing away.

G. A.

CONTENTS.

FROM 1724 TO 1750.

Introduction—Shad and salmon—Wigwams—Gov. Belcher—John Wentworth—His son Benning—State boundaries—Equivalent lands—Indian fight at Great Meadows—Capture of Nehemiah How—Settlement of John Kilburn and family—Shooting of David Rugg—His Burial—Charters—Settlements of Charlestown, Hinsdale, Chesterfield, Keene and Westmoreland.

FROM 1750 TO 1760.

Col. Benjamin Bellows procures a charter of the township—The charter—Wentworth's calf pasture—Kilburn's claim—First Town meeting—Town Records—General Benjamin Bellows commenced keeping the records at the age of fifteen—Men of straw—The Indian Philip—His treachery—Murder of Flynt and Twitchell—Anxiety of the settlers, Gov. Shirley forewarns the settlers of impending danger—Kilburn's fight with the Indians and his heroic defence, Exhuming of bones supposed to be Philip's—Joshank—Noshank's story.

FROM 1760 TO 1770.

First public business—Settling Jonathan Leavitt—His Letter of acceptance—Unsettling him—Building the first meeting house—Laying out the first road—Deer reeves—Settlement of Thomas Fessenden—His letter of acceptance—Description of the early settlement of Walpole—Sympathy for those in affliction—Story of the lost child.

FROM 1770 TO 1780.

Public schools—Col. Bellows gives to the town 100 acres of land for a Grammar School—Aaron Hodskins kills a wolf—Wolves, bears and catamounts—Wentworth's land grants—Gen. Bellows repairs to the scene—His influence —French's epitaph—The town represented at Exeter by Col. Webber—His instructions—Interesting document—Death of Col. Bellows—His will—Battle of Lexington, Gen. Ben. and Col. John hasten to the scene—Walpole in the Revolutionary War.

FROM 1780 TO 1790.

Theodore and Thomas Bellows vote illegally—Thomas defends himself—Gov. Wentworth becomes alarmed and writes to the Gov. of New York—Land grants—Trouble ahead—Causes of the troubles—Interesting account of the same—Building the old Town House.

FROM 1790 TO 1800.

Appearance of Walpole village in 1793—Printing office—Joseph Dennie—Farmer's Museum—Brilliant corps of writers—Heavy frost in 1796. The Crafts Tavern—Drinking bouts—Abraham Hall—Joseph T. Buckingham—The old bell—Cold Weather.

FROM 1800 TO 1810.

Settlements on Derry Hill—Cider—Famous law suit Norman vs. Burt and Wiers—Burt & Wiers vs. Norman—Crean Brush—Small pox—"Political Observatory"—Settlement of Pliny Dickinson—His letter of acceptance—Old Iron cannon—Stolen three times—West street, village bridge and brick store built.

FROM 1810 TO 1820.

Spotted fever—Hydrophobia—Walpole in the War of 1812—Clearing of Boggy Meadow—Cold season.

FROM 1820 TO 1830.

Cider and cider brandy—Purchase of Boggy meadow by Jonathan Mason—His barn—Its dimensions—Cattle shows—Barter trade—Prices of articles—Shoe making—Moving the old meeting-house—Exciting times—Sheep Husbandry—Foot rot—Number of sheep in town at time, 16,000.

FROM 1830 TO 1840.

Death of Christopher Lincoln and Elisha Angier—Catastrophe at Cold River—Three lives lost—Financial crash of 1837.

FROM 1840 TO 1850.

Shade trees—Reed's tannery Burned—Bankruptcy—Burning of the Brick store.

FROM 1850 TO 1860.

Hail storm—Second conflagration of stores—Purchase of the new cemetery—Consecration of the same—Bellows family gathering and erection of monument—Second planting of shade trees.

FROM 1860 TO 1870.

Walpole in the Rebellion, full account—Indebtedness of the town—Bank robbery—Sanatary Commission—Free bridge—Shirt manufactory—Tobacco culture—North Walpole and Drewsville.

MISCELLANEOUS.

Church History—Education—School Committees John Pratt the Prophet—Military—Music—Protest—Mortality Delegates to Exeter—List of representatives—Votes given for all the candidates for governors—Revolutionary soldiers—Town Officers—Early Settlers—Walpole as it is—Appendix, &c.

HISTORY OF WALPOLE.

A little more than one hundred and twenty-five years ago the territory which is now included in the present town of Walpole was one unbroken, gloomy forest, which shaded the deep, rich soil that the summer sun had not warmed for centuries. What is now called " Derry Hill" was thickly wooded with a heavy growth of beech, birch and maple. " Boggy Meadow" and the table lands east were heavily timbered, mostly with stately white pines, towering, in many instances, to one hundred and fifty feet or more, while on the river bank monstrous elms and buttonwoods luxuriated in the deep, mellow soil.

" Fall Mountain" * also was covered with a heavy growth of white pines, which had, perhaps, withstood the blasts of centuries ; while on the south and east the yellow pine covered the area to a considerable extent.

Old, decaying trees, which had fallen in every conceivable direction ; fantastic forms of withered limbs and old standing trees, denuded of their bark, contrasted strangely with the freshness of a later growth. Reptiles sported in the slimy pools of the lowlands or crawled unharmed over piles of decaying timber.

The rattlesnake lay coiled asleep in some sunny nook, or was noiselessly drawing his hideous form over mouldering vegetation, in quest of some luckless frog. The huge, ungainly, black bear, unsuspecting of danger, was shuffling from

* Now known as " Kilburn Mountain," so christened by Dartmouth students, some twenty-five years ago.

place to place, seeking some esculent root from the marsh, or craunching the mast that had fallen from the oak or the beech. The red deer and stately moose cropped the uncut herbage of the openings in summer, and browsed on the tender twigs of deciduous trees in winter.

The smaller streams were filled with speckled trout, which had never been lured by the sportsman's fly, the Boggy Meadow's and sedgy swamps, on a summer's evening, were overhung by clouds of mosquitoes and the exhalations that arose from decaying vegetation sowed the seeds of malarial disease and death. The night was made dismal by the moan of the catamount or the howl of the grey wolf, seeking the destruction of innocent life. Silence reigned by day unbroken, save by the continuous roar of the " Great Falls," or, broken perhaps, morning and evening, by the tattoo of the male partridge cheering his mate.

The red man was the sole human occupant of the soil, and was as wild as the savage beasts around him,—a predatory vagabond, in constant warfare with his own race ; seeking the destruction of the settlers, or leading them into a captivity worse than death; the bark of the white birch his canoe ; strings of shells his ornaments, his calendar and his coin ; huts made of bended saplings and evergreen boughs, roofed with the rind of trees, his habitation ; leaves of the forest and skins of wild beasts his bed; his religion, if any, the adoration of nature; His morals not much above the instinct of intelligent animals; disputing with them the occupancy of the thickets, and dividing with the squirrel and bear the fruits of the hills—such was the scene that greeted the vision of the first settlers.

Annually, in the months of May and June, shad and salmon, in great numbers, set out from the ocean for the head waters of the Connecticut and its tributaries. Shad, unable to pass the rapids at the Great Falls, were crowded into the basin below and far down the river, while the salmon, more agile in their movements, were able to surmount the rapids and fulfill their summer mission of depositing their spawn, and returning again in the fall to the ocean. The shad, less fortunate, after a time became discouraged at their futile attempts to run the rapids, fell back, and ascended some of the larger tributaries. Their number was immense. From time immemorial the Great Falls had been the best fishing ground to be found in all New England. Tradition says that there were once Indian *wigwams* on or near the site where now stand the railroad station near cold river and the dwelling near by, extending below more than one fourth of a mile, the Indians being a sub-tribe of the five nations called the Abenaquis or Abenakees, meaning the *pines*. There were also other wigwams of the same tribe on a small brook in Westmoreland, on land now owned by Robert E. Green, about half a mile south of Walpole town line which is called *Wigwam Brook* to this day. In the narrow defile between Fall mountain and the river was the Indian path where they used to travel from the white settlements in Massachusetts below to Canada, in their marauding expeditions. The blossoming of the *shad tree (Amelanchier Canadensis)* was the signal for all the Indians for many miles around to gather about the falls for the purpose of shad and salmon fishing. Imagination can see them now, perched upon the rocks, spearing the twenty-pound salmon or scooping with their nets multitudes of shad, or, perhaps, crossing and recrossing in their bark canoes the basin below, while the old squaw was doing the drudgery about the huts, the papoose, half naked, wallowing in the filth, and the dusky maiden loitering about in the shade of the stately elms, stringing her ornaments and wampum. 'Twas here, it may be, they held their orgies and concocted their hellish designs on the white settlers. The ploughshare of civilization has unearthed Indian skeletons, spear heads, arrow heads, heaps of clam shells and numerous other Indian relics, which, together with the rude carvings on the rocks at the Falls, are indubitable evidences of there having been a famous wigwam in this vicinity in pre-historic times.

The Indian, naturally morose and sullen in his disposition, and having been driven from time to time from the graves of

his fathers and his fishing and hunting grounds by the en-
croachments of the whites, needed but little to incite him to
plunder and the most cruel barbarity; consequently he was
found continually harassing the frontier settlements, in small
predatory bands, burning the habitations of the early settlers,
destroying their cattle, killing men, women and children, or
forcing them into a captivity worse than death.

The tales of those atrocities were the first lessons taught the
children of the early settlers. The grey haired veteran with
his grandson upon his knee recounted to him, the hundredth
time, the Indian tales of by-gone times. The child drank in
every word, and became so much excited that his thoughts by
day and his dreams by night were but one continued picture
of murder and pillage. Thus he became thoroughly schooled, at
manhood, with all the wiles of Indian warfare. Under such circumstances it seems almost incredible that any one could have
the courage, hardihood, or even temerity to plant himself in a
howling wilderness, far removed from any friendly habitation
and nearly in the jaws of hostile Indians ; yet, notwithstanding,
in 1749, John Kilburn is found, with Ruth, his wife, Mehitable
his daughter (Hetty) and John, his son, snugly settled down
in a small log hut on the fertile interval, about one-fourth of a
mile south of Cold river, a little to the north of east of the residence of Mrs. Joseph Wells, on the east side of the highway
passing her house. Ezra Kilburn, the grandson of John, senior,
told the author of these pages, some thirty years ago, that
the exact spot where his grandfather's hut stood was where
is now growing the *sprout* of an old appletree planted by his
grandfather, near the location described above : while others
say that his abode was south west from Abenaque springs.

In order that the reader may fully understand the true condition of affairs in relation to the grants made on Connecticut
river it will be necessary to go back a few years antecedent to
the first settlement.

In 1724, the government of Massachusetts erected a strong
fort for the protection of her western settlements, just opposite
the town of Hinsdale N. H. (now in Vermont), which territory

was then supposed to belong to Massachusetts. This was fort Dummer. With that exception there were no forts nor settlements north and west in Vermont; all was one gloomy wilderness on both sides of the Connecticut north to the Canadas.

Incidents trivial in themselves often result in important changes in nations, as well as in the lives of individuals, as the following narrative will show. At this time (1728) Massachusetts and New Hampshire had but one Governor, but each Province had separate Lieutenant Governors and Assemblies. William Burnett was at this time Governor, and was succeeded two years later by Jonathan Belcher, a native and merchant of Boston; a man of elegant manners and large fortune. Having made a short visit to New Hampshire, and returned to Massachusetts, he made a discovery which resulted in a serious misunderstanding between himself and Lieutenant Governor Wentworth, Benning Wentworth's father. It was this; prior to his appointment as Governor, Wentworth, not knowing whether Governor Shute, who had been long absent, would return and resume the chair or Belcher be appointed in his stead, and being eager for office, had written complimentary letters to both. This act Belcher considered dishonorable on the part of Wentworth, and he carried his indignation and resentment so far that in a subsequent visit to Portsmouth, he declined an invitation to dine with the Lieutenant Governor, at his house. He also cut off the emoluments incident to his office and dismissed from office all his friends and relatives. Wentworth soon died, but his son Benning and his brother-in-law, Theodore Atkinson, took up the cudgel of resentment, and, being backed by their friends and influential connections, formed a strong party in opposition to Belcher, which finally resulted not only in the dismemberment of the territory claimed by Massachusetts but in the appointment of a separate Governor for the province of New Hampshire, in the person of Benning Wentworth, in 1741, and Theodore Atkinson was made Secretary.

From 1733 to 1740, the warfare between Wentworth and Governor Belcher increased in warmth, one feature of the quarrel being the settlement of the boundary line between Massachusetts and New Hampshire.

John Tomlinson supported the Wentworth party and obtained a royal order constituting a board of commissioners, to be selected from the councillors of the provinces, with power to settle the contested line. This board met at Hampton N. H. Aug. 1737, and in a few days the Assemblies of both provinces met in the neighborhood; that of Massachusetts at Salisbury, and that of New Hampshire at Hampton Falls. After a long session and angry disputes the Commissioners agreed on a result which established the eastern boundary line as it now is, but left the southern boundary undetermined. It was seen by all parties that this protracted dispute could only be settled by a Royal decree; consequently petitions were submitted by each party to the English Monarch who ordered a Commission, to run and establish a line between the provinces.

This was done in 1738, commencing three miles north of the mouth of the Merrimac river, on the Atlantic ocean, and following a curved line on said river to Pawtucket falls, and from thence due west to "His Majesty's other Governments." This line gave New Hampshire a territory fifty miles long and fourteen broad more than she expected, which was very gratifying to Wentworth, but mortifying to Belcher. In the mean time a large number of grants had been made by Belcher on both sides of the Connecticut, as far north as No. 4, now Charlestown. The grantees soon ascertained that their titles were worthless and prayed to be reannexed to Massachusetts, where they had supposed they belonged; but their prayers were not answered. It was ordered by the general court of Massachusetts in 1735, on petition, that townships should be laid out on Connecticut river from the Great Falls on the east side south to lands granted to Josiah Willard and others, in as many townships of six miles square as the territory would admit, in one tier, and on the west side, commencing at the same point, to the "Equivalent Lands" in as many townships of an area of six miles square as the territory would contain.

New Taunton, now Westminister, was one of those towns and was considered then No. 1.

These " Equivalent Lands" were grants made by Massachusetts, but on running the line between Massachusetts and Connecticut, in 1713, they fell within the limits of Connecticut. Massachusetts wishing to retain them, set off a portion of what she then considered her own territory, to Connecticut as an equivalent. The whole area comprised 107,793 acres, in four different localities; 43,943 acres were in the vicinity of Westmoreland N. H. and Brattleboro Vt. In 1716 these lands were all sold at Hartford Ct. by auction, and brought a trifle more than one farthing per acre,—the money thus obtained was applied to the use of Yale College.

In 1735 Governor Belcher obtained leave of the Massachusetts Assembly, for services rendered by his brother Andrew, in the Canada expedition of 1690, to survey and lay out, in two pieces, 1000 acres of the unappropriated lands of the province : and accordingly 'two plots' of land on Connecticut river were laid out by "Thomas Hinsdale and chairman on oath." One of these 'plots' was laid out on the east side of Connecticut river, in the vicinity of Cold river, and the other on the opposite side. It is said that a plan of the town granted to Willard, Bellows and others in 1736 is on file at the state house in Massachusetts. Whether this last grant embraced the first is not known. The name of the town was originally Great Falls, and afterwards *Bellowsborn* prior to the time that Col. Benjamin Bellows obtained his grant in 1752. The name *Bellowstown* shows pretty conclusively that some person bearing the name of Bellows must have owned land in the vicinity of the falls prior to Col. Bellows' settlement. In 1736, several towns were laid out bordering on Connecticut river, among which were Westminister, Vt. No. 1, Walpole, No. 2, Goldenstown, (now Rockingham, it is inferred), No. 3, and Charlestown, No. 4. The same year a grant was made by Massachusetts to John Flynt and others. The above nos. were changed a few years later and made to correspond to the several forts. Chesterfield was made No. 1 ; Westmore-

land, No. 2; Walpole No 3; and Charlestown No. 4. The
plots of these townships known as 1, 2, 3, and 4 were accepted
by the General Court of Massachusetts, Nov. 30, 1736. The
following persons were appointed to call the first meetings of
the proprietors of the above named townships, viz. Samuel
Chamberlain of Westford for No. 1, (Chesterfield,) Nathaniel
Harris of Watertown for No. 2, (Westmoreland,) John Flynt
for No. 3, (Walpole) and Thomas Wells for No. 4, (Charlestown.) It does not appear that the grantees of No. 3, ever occupied the township; if they did at any time, most likely they
were driven away by the Indians. There are some reasons to
suspect that the Flynt, subsequently killed by the Indians,
was the grantee above mentioned.

In 1745 a body of French and Indians, the latter twelve in
number, attacked the garrison at the Great Meadow (now Putney Vt.) on the 12th of October, at noon. A brisk fight was
carried on for an hour and a half and one Indian was killed,
but the fort was defended with so much courage and determination, that the enemy withdrew. In lieu of victory, they
killed and drove off most of the cattle. Nehemiah How, who
was cutting wood about eighty rods from the fort, was taken
by the Indians and no attempt was made to rescue him. As
they were leading him away by the side of the river, on the
west side, they espied two men approaching in a canoe when
they fired and killed one of them, David Rugg, and the
other, Robert Baker made for the opposite shore and escaped. The Indians scalped Rugg and mounted the scalp on
a pole and carried it through Charlestown, in triumph to
Crown Point. This David Rugg was the identical man (without much doubt,) who, tradition says, was hoeing corn on Boggy Meadow and was shot by the Indians from the west bank
of the river, and was buried on what is now called Rugg Meadow, near the river just opposite the lower farm-house.

The same year, also, a dispute arose respecting the boundary
line between Massachusetts and New Hampshire and Col.
Benjamin Bellows of Lunenburgh was appointed surveyor, on
the part of Massachusetts, to mark the line. This appoint-

ment brought Mr. Bellows in contact with Benning Wentworth, then Governor of the province of New Hampshire.
The Governor being anxious to settle the western portion of
the state, and perceiving Colonel Bellows to be a man possessing resolution and other qualities for a pioneer life induced
him to accede to his wishes and make a trial in Walpole.

The condition of the settlements bordering on Connecticut
river, about the time Col. Bellows came to Walpole, is briefly
told. In 1744 England declared war against France, and, in
consequence, their respective colonies in America became involved in the struggle. The war lasted till 1763. The French
in Canada incited the natural cupidity of the Indians living in
the vicinity (the St. Francis tribe), by offering bounties for
captives and white men's scalps, to more than their usual
activity in harassing the border settlement. During the period of thirteen years there was scarcely a family to be found
in the beautiful valley of the Connecticut which did not
mourn the loss of some near and dear relative by the tomahawk or fire-arm of the savages. A narrative of all the depredations committed by the Indians during this period would fill
volumes.

There was a strong fort at Charlestown which was settled
in 1740, one opposite to Hinsdale, built in 1724, (Fort Dummer,) and two at Hinsdale, Hinsdale's and Bridgman's. Hinsdale was settled in 1683, resettled in 1739, and incorporated
in 1763. Westmoreland (Great Meadows) was settled in 1741.
Putney and Westminister built two forts on Putney Meadows
for mutual protection. One was built in the center and the
other and larger one on the site of the house lately owned and
occupied by Col. Thomas White. It was sufficiently large to
build fifteen dwellings within its inclosure. Some of those
forts were built of heavy hewn timbers and were inclosed with
palisades. They afforded ample protection to the inhabitants
when within the gates. Keene and Chesterfield were both
settled before Walpole; the former in 1739, and the latter in
1736. Keene however was laid out in 1731.

From 1750 to 1760.

Gov. Wentworth, as an inducement to Col. Bellows, offered him his choice of the unappropriated townships on the Connecticut. After looking about for some time, for various good reasons, he (Col. B.) concluded to locate on No. 3, afterwards Walpole. In 1752 Col. Bellows, Theodore Atkinson, Col. Josiah Blanchard and sixty-seven others, grantees, purchased the township above mentioned and obtained a Charter. Following is a copy of the charter:

"George II. by advice of Benning Wentworth, Governor, granted unto his loving subjects, inhabitants of New Hampshire, and his majesty's other governments, in equal shares whose names are entered on this grant, to be divided among them in sixty seven equal shares, all that tract of land in said province of New Hampshire described &c., &c. And the same is incorporated as Walpole, and the inhabitants thereof are enfranchised and declared entitled to the privileges of other towns in said province, and as soon as there shall be fifty families resident there, shall have the liberty of holding two fairs annually, and shall also have a market opened and kept one or more days in each week, as may be thought advantageous. The first meeting of said town shall be held the third Wednesday of March next (1752) and Benjamin Bellows is appointed moderator of such meeting, and to call the same.

"To hold said land upon these conditions, namely, every grantee shall within five years, cultivate five acres of land for every fifty acres of his share, and shall continue to improve and settle the same by additional cultivation, on penalty of forfeiture of his share.

"That all white and other pine trees, fit for our royal navy, be preserved for use, and none be cut or felled without his majesty's special license upon same forfeiture and punishment of any acts of parliament now or hereafter enacted.

"That before division of land, a tract or center of township shall be marked in town-lots, one of which shall be allotted to each grantee of the contents of one acre, yielding and paying therefor to us, etc., for ten years, *one ear* of *Indian* corn annually, on first day of January, if lawfully demanded.

"Every proprietor, settler, or inhabitant shall yield and pay to us, etc., yearly, after the expiration of ten years, one shilling, proclamation money, for every hundred acres he so owns, setfles or possesses, and so in proportion for greater or less tracts, which said money shall be paid to our council-chamber, or to officers, appointed to receive it.

(Signed by) "Benning Wentworth.

"In testimony, etc., Feb. 13th, 1752, and twenty fifth year of George's reign.

"Recorded by Theodore Atkinson, Sec."

Nine years after the date of the charter, the grantees represent that, by reason of the Indian wars it has become impracticable for them to comply with its conditions; therefore the time is lengthened from year to year until the conditions of the charter are fulfilled. This document is dated March 12, 1761, being the first year of George the III.

The immediate cause for Col. Bellows' leaving Lunenburg, according to the "Memorial Monograph" of Rev. Henry W. Bellows, D. D., was "That he had become embarrassed by being bound for others, and, in the great scarcity of money, was unable to meet the demands of his creditors." He says, "That he was pursued by the sheriff to the state line, and, once fairly over it, stopped and held a parley with the sheriff, stating that he had no disposition to avoid his obligations, but a jail was a poor place in which to find the means of meeting them, that he would soon return and liquidate his debts." It is most certain that he soon satisfied his creditors, for he soon returned to Lunenburg to look after his interests there.

Benning Wentworth was strongly attached to the Church of England, and in the granting of charters, he reserved in every township five hundred acres of land, the income of which went into the treasury of that church as a missionary fund. A lot, also, was reserved for the first settled minister.

The Governor not having a very definite idea of the surroundings in the vicinity of the Great Falls, and supposing the land lying in the immediate vicinity to be the most valuable for his purpose, on account of the shad and salmon fisheries, and to make the matter doubly sure, consulted Col. Bellows about the propriety of locating his plot of five hundred acres east of the Falls. The Colonel very *honestly* told him that a plot in that vicinity would be of very little value to him,—that it might make a "*good calf pasture*, but nothing better." It is presumed that the Governor suspected the Colonel of a little sharp practice by undervaluing this plot, therefore he decided to *pitch* his missionary lot on the top and sides of Fall Mountain. This lot has since become a part of the town of Langdon; but is called the "Governor's calf pasture" to this day.

Rev. Thomas Fessenden, of this town, in writing to Jeremy Belknap, Jan. 29th, 1791, says that "One family settled here in the spring of 1749, under the Bay claim; but the Hampshire proprietors began in 1742, and that Col. Benjamin Bellows moved his family here in 1753. The family at that time consisted of himself, wife and five children.

His children were Abigail, born Dec. 21, 1736, died three years later at Northampton, Mass. The others were Peter, born Jan. 6th 1739; Benjamin, born Oct. 6th, 1740; John, born Nov. 3d, 1743; and Joseph, born June 6th, 1744. It would seem by the above account that Col. Bellows built his habitation in 1752. This habitation was built on or near the spot where now stands the horse barn of Thomas Bellows, Esq., a little north of his dwelling. It was built sufficiently commodious and strong to be called a fort, and shaped like the letter L, being about one hundred feet in the arms and twenty feet broad, strongly built of logs and earth, and surrounded by a palisade.

On opening the town records is found, in compliance with the letter of the charter, the doings of the first town meeting, which was held on the third Wednesday of March, 1752. According to the provisions of the charter Col. Bellows was the first moderator. The meeting was without *warrant*, nor does it appear that any meeting of the grantees was ever called, as was customary in other towns. The record is as follows:

' "At a meeting held at Walpole In the Province of New-hampshire agreeable to Charter on the third Wednesday of March, A. D. 1752, Benjamin Bellows being appointed Moderator,—first voted and Chose theodore Atkinson Esq. Joseph Blanchard Esq," and "Benjamin Bellows Seleetmen for sd year Insuing," "Secondly Chose Benja. Bellows Town Clark, then desmissed said meeting" Attest Benjamin Bellows Town Clark." The record of the meeting in 1753, is precisely like the foregoing. In 1754, the first part of the record is the same as the foregoing except Sam Johnson is chosen moderator, " Secondly Chose Benjamin Bellows Sam Johnson " and " Robert Powker Selectmen, 3d chose Col. Willard Town Clark." The name of Col. Bellows seems to have been scratched out and Col. Willard's name substituted. " Fourthly, chose Enoch Cook Constable, Fifthly, chose Enoch Cook *Scrayer* of *hie* Ways."

The first three records appear to have been made at the same time and at one sitting, and probably were, from the fact that seven years later each settler was assessed one shilling, to purchase a " town book to be kept for the use of the town." When obtained, most likely the records were transcribed into the new book from some loose memoranda. The records for the first three years were undoubtedly in the handwriting of Col. Bellows ; but after that time were in the handwriting of his son Benjamin, although signed and attested by the father, till Benjamin Bellows, jr. was chosen town clerk in 1759, when he was only nineteen years of age. Thus it will be seen that Benjamin, jr. commenced keeping the records of the town when only fifteen years old.

Benjamin Bellows, jr. was town clerk from 1759 till 1795, a period of thirty-six years, with the exception of two years, 1778-9, when Amos Babcock, and in 1782-3, when one N. Goddard were chosen. The town made a bad move in making the change, for both were evidently poor scholars, and Goddard was a miserable penman, while on the other hand Mr. Bellows' records show much culture for those days, in spelling, grammar and legibility of handwriting.

Theodore Atkinson and Joseph Blanchard, who appear on the records as selectmen the first two years, the former living in Londonderry, and then secretary of the province ; and the latter (a brother-in-law of the Col.) living in Dunstable, attending to his multifarious business transactions probably, were not ambitious enough to find their way through the snows of March, guided by blazed trees, to attend a town meeting, in the then infant town. Sam Johnson and Robert Powker, who appear as selectmen the next year, died yearlings, for they do not appear in the records again. The same year Col. Willard is recorded as chosen town clerk, a man who had the infant town of Winchester on his hands, and consequently had no rights as a citizen in Walpole. Enoch Cook, who was chosen constable and also a surveyor of "hic ways" the same year, together with Johnson and Powker as selectmen, it is more than suspected, were *mere men of straw*, as there were but four families in town five years later.

In 1755 Benjamin Bellows Esq., is chosen moderator, selectman, town clerk and town treasurer, and Mr. John Kilburn and Daniel Twitchel appear on the records as selectmen. Why John Kilburn, an actual resident of the town, with the paucity of men at that time, was not chosen to some office before, seems to be significant. At this remote time a *true* explanation is out of the question; but it may be that the most friendly feeling did not then exist between Mr. Bellows and Mr. Kilburn.

A plausible explanation of the above is suggested by a statement made in a letter written to the author by George Kilburn, Esq., of Lonsdale, R. I., the great grandson of John, senior. He says "all the older members of our family talked about a charter held by my great grandfather, granted by the state of New York, by which he became the rightful owner of the whole township of Walpole." "This was fully attested by Josiah Bellows, 2d., the son of Col. John." He further says: "Josiah Bellows, 2d. told me, in 1823, that Col. Bellows offered to divide the township with my great grandfather; but he bravely replied "No! I bought the whole and paid for it, and it is all mine, and I will have all or none." "This," he says, "was well understood by all the older members of our family." If, as above stated, Mr. Kilburn procured a charter from the state of New York, and owned the township, it was hard for him to lose his title; but under the circumstances the title appears to have been void, as New York never held jurisdiction on the east side of Connecticut river; although New York might have claimed it. He was not alone in his loss; hundreds of others suffered from a similar cause.

Be it as it may, they both had mutual sacrifices to make, and common dangers to meet, which toned down their animosity (if they had any) to forgetfulness and mutual good will. Kilburn had lived in town some two or three years, before Col. Bellows came to settle, without communication with friend or foe; although he had often sought intercourse with the Indians they had studiously avoided him. During this time he had no rest day nor night. He was not only exposed to the inclemency of severe storms in his rude hut, and all the hardships and privations incident to frontier life, but was living, day by day and night by night, in constant fear of the tomahawk or scalping knife. During the day he did not dare to go a few rods from his cabin without his gun; and at night his bed was the cold ground; a bear skin for his covering, and a cartridge box for his pillow; nor did he dare camp two nights in the same place while the Indians were lurking in ambush, ready to strike the deadly blow at the first opportunity. Many times the Indians, during his absence, visited his cabin, in the dead of night, and stole everything they could find and carry away.

Some time between 1751 and '5, a company of Indians came down the river, landed above the falls and invited Kilburn to trade with them. He visited their boats, bought some skins and made some presents of flints, flour and fish hooks. For a while the Indians continued to hunt and encamp about the neighborhood, and, as no mischief was done, the settlers felt more secure, from day to day, the sight of wigwams becoming familiar to their eyes and the sound of their guns an every day occurrence to their ears.

In the spring of 1754, some say '55, a large Indian, by the name of Philip, who could speak a little broken English, visited Kilburn's cabin, in a friendly way, pretending to be on a hunting excursion, and in want of provision. He was generously supplied with flints, flour and other articles and dismissed. Soon after it was ascertained that this same wily, treacherous scoundrel had visited all the frontier settlements with the same plausible story and was suspected by all as a wolf in disguise.

Gov. Shirley, of Albany, a few days later sent word by a

friendly Indian, that five hundred Indians were collecting in Canada, whose purpose it was to wipe out by wholesale butchery the entire population of the advance settlements on Connecticut river.

The inhabitants of the town were thrown into the greatest state of excitement and misery on hearing of the foray of the savages into Charlestown, at an early hour on the morning of the 30th of June 1754, before the families had risen, and of their taking and carrying into captivity, James Johnson, his wife and three children, together with his wife's sister (Miriam Willard) Ebenezer Farnsworth and Peter Labaree. One Aaron Hosmer eluded them by secreting himself under the bed. The narrative of this capture, and of the sufferings of the captives, is one of the most thrilling of the kind on record. [See History of Charlestown.]

It appears from a letter written by Col. Bellows to Col. Joseph Blanchard, who had command of a regiment in the lower part of the state, that Col. Bellows' concern for the general welfare of the inhabitants had ripened into the most intense anxiety, as an extract from the letter plainly shows. He says: "The people are in great distress all down the river and at Keene and at Swanzey, and the few men sent will not more than supply one town, and the people cannot secure their grain nor hardly keep their garrison, etc." The letter was dated at Westmoreland, and it appears he had been down the river for the purpose of adding strength to his garrison by more men, for in a P. S. he says "I have got no further than Westmoreland when I wrote this, and got all the men safe there B. B." This letter is dated Aug. 31st, 1754. It would appear from it and other sources that Col. Bellows drew men and supplies for his fort at the public expense. Col. Bellows' fort had been, with others in the chain of defences, supplied with a heavy iron cannon by the royal government for public protection. He had also, caused a lookout to be constructed from the top of his fort into the forks of a large elm tree standing near by, which commanded an extensive view in all directions. There was, also, another fort on the river bank, west of Mrs.

Joseph Wells' residence, to protect the settlers in going back and forth from the upper part of Westminster, which was settled early. Kilburn had built a palisade around his dwelling and made other provisions for his security, the best his scanty means would permit. Here he lived with his family in the most dreadful suspense, sometimes bordering on despair, debating with himself the alternatives of leaving his home, his cattle, his crops and his all, or braving the prospective danger. Driven almost to phrensy, and with stoical indifference to his fate, he chose to brave the impending trial. Such dreadful suspense did not last long, for some time between March 1755 and the following August (the exact time not being precisely known), two men, named Flynt and Daniel Twitchel, who had been chosen one of the selectmen, the March previous, went back on to the hill east, to procure some ash timber for oars, and were both shot by the Indians ; one was scalped, the other was cut open and his heart taken out, cut in pieces and laid on his breast.   Flynt was buried on the spot ; Twitchel, having friends, was carried away and buried elsewhere.   The exact spot where Flynt was buried is about one and a half miles from Walpole village, on the Drewsville road, about fifteen rods from the corner of the first woods, and four rods west of the highway.

The solemn impression this occurrence made on the minds of the settlers was not soon effaced.   It is said "the guardian spirit of Twitchel continued to hover over his friends, warning them of the wiles and hostile intentions of the Indians, as long as his murderers were permitted to live."   A remarkable rock in Connecticut river where he used to fish with never failing success was for a long time held in religious veneration, and to this day, such is the propitious influence of the presiding spirit, that few of the votaries of angling who come to worship on the Twitchel rock return without taking from the limpid stream a "generous fry."   This rock can be seen at low water a little south of Cold River station.

For some time after Col. Bellows settled in town he had to go to Northampton to mill, going down with his corn in boats, in spring, and returning with his meal and other stores, necessary not only to feed his own family and hired help, but many families that resorted to his fort for protection, and all other comers and goers who wanted to appease their hunger or stop over night. As soon as he could procure proper help and material he built himself a mill on a small stream, now called " Blanchard's brook," at the beautiful falls about eighty rods from where the travelled road crosses the stream in going to Drewsville. From this mill it is said he supplied the early settlers of Langdon, Alstead and Lempster with meal, for several years. They transported their meal on their backs, in some instances ten or twelve miles, when it became so heavy that " a peck seemed to weigh a bushel."

The time is now approaching when is to be related an occurrence which for coolness and heroism puts into the background any narrative of the kind on record; where two men, two boys and two females defended themselves against *four hundred* bloodthirsty savages, *six long hours*, and held their ground. This occurrence commenced about noon on the 17th of Aug., 1755, two miles or so north of Walpole village, near the residence of Willard T. Blanchard, and as the traveller approaches his residence let him pause, for he is on historic ground! There was at that time a foot path from Col. Bellows' mill to his fort. This path ran past Blanchard's house, and from thence over the then wooded plain to the fort. Just east of Blanchard's house, before one descends to the brook, was where hostilities commenced.

The narrative of this eventful day was first published in the ' Cheshire Gazette,' a newspaper published in this town in 1826, and is said to have been written by Dr. Ebenezer Morse, long a resident of Walpole, and who lived contemporaneously with some of the oldest settlers, and whose opportunity to gather correct information in relation to those early times was unequalled. His narrative is here quoted entire. He says : " Kilburn and his son, John, in his eighteenth year, a man named Peak and his son, were returning home from work about noon, Aug. 17, 1755, when one of them discovered the red legs of

the Indians among the alders 'as thick as grasshoppers.' They
instantly made for the house, fastened the doors, and began to
make preparations for an obstinate defence. Besides these
four men, there were in the house Kilburn's wife and his
daughter Hetty, who contributed not a little to encourage and
assist their companions, as well as to keep a watch on the
movements of the enemy. In about fifteen minutes the Indians were seen crawling up the bank east of the house,
and as they crossed a foot path, one by one, *one hundred and
ninety-seven* were counted; and about the same number remained in ambush near the mouth of Cold river.

The Indians had learned that Col. Benj. Bellows and his
men were at work at his mill about a mile east, and it would
be best to waylay and secure them before disturbing those who
had taken refuge in the log house. Bellows and his men (about
thirty in number) were returning home with each a bag of
meal on his back, when their dogs began to growl and show
symptoms of an enemy's approach. He well knew the language
of his dogs and the native intrigue of the Indians. Nor was
he at a loss in forming his opinion of their intention to ambush
his path, and he conducted himself accordingly. He ordered
all his men to throw down their meal, advance to the rise,
carefully crawl up the bank, spring on their feet, give one
whoop and instantly drop into the sweet ferns. This manœu-
vre had the desired effect; for as soon as the whoop was given
the Indians all arose from their ambush in a semicircle around
the path Bellows was to follow. This gave his men a fine
chance for a shot, which they improved *instanter*.

The first shot so disconcerted the plans and expectations of
the Indians that they darted away into the bushes without
firing a gun. It is said, that they ran down the steep bank
west, and that the impetuous Peter (the Col.'s oldest son) followed them, and it required much earnest persuasion to induce
him to return to the company. Bellows finding their number too numerous for his ordered his men to file off to the
south and make for the fort. The Indians next appeared on
the eminence east of Kilburn's house, when the same " old
devil," Philip, who had visited him the summer before, came
forward, and, screening himself behind a tree, called out to those
in the house to surrender, 'Old John, young John' says he,
'I know you, come out here—We give ye good quarter!'
'Quarter!' vociferated old Kilburn, with a voice of thunder
that rang through every Indian's heart and every hill and valley, 'You black rascals, begone or we'll quarter you!"

Who would have anticipated this more than Spartan reply from four men, when called upon by as many hundreds to deliver up their arms.

Philip then returned to his companions and after a few minutes' consultation the *war* whoop commenced as if (to use the expression of an ear witness) "all the devils in hell had been let loose." Kilburn was so lucky as to get the first fire before the smoke of the enemy's guns obstructed his aim, and was confident he saw an Indian fall, which from his extraordinary size and other appearances must have been Philip. The Indians rushed forward to the work of destruction; and probably no less than *four hundred* bullets were lodged in Kilburn's house at the first fire. The roof was a perfect " riddle sieve." Some of them fell to butchering the cattle, others were wantonly destroying the hay and grain, while a shower of bullets kept up one continued pelting against the house.

Meanwhile Kilburn and his men were by no means idle. Their powder was already poured into hats for the convenience of loading in a hurry, and everything prepared for a spirited defence or a glorious death. They had several guns in the house which were kept hot by incessant firing through the port holes, and, as they had no ammunition to spare, each one took special aim to have every bullet tell. The women, with true Grecian firmness, assisted in loading the guns, and when their stock of lead grew short they had the forethought to suspend blankets in the roof of the house to catch the balls of the enemy, which were immediately run into bullets by them and sent back to the savages with equal velocity. Several attempts were made to burst open the door, but the bullets within scattered death with such profusion as soon compelled them to desist from the rash undertaking. Most of the time the Indians endeavored to keep behind stumps, logs and trees, which evidently evinced, that they were not insensible to the unceremonious visits of Kilburn's bullets."

" All the afternoon one incessant firing was kept up, till nearly sundown, when the Indians began to disappear; and as the sun sank behind the western hills the sound of the guns and the cry of the war whoop died away in silence. This day's rencounter proved an effectual check to the expeditions of the Indians and induced them immediately to return to Canada; and it is within the bounds of reason to conclude that this matchless defence was instrumental in rescuing hundreds of our fellow citizens from the horrors of an Indian massacre."

Thus did our intrepid Leonidas, not with *three hundred*, but with only *three* followers, repulse the congregated forces of the Canadian savages.

Seldom has it fallen to the lot of any of our forefathers, by personal courage and valor, to reap a more brilliant crown of laurels than that won by Kilburn on that memorable day. Only one of this invincible band of heroes was wounded. Peak, by exposing himself before the port-holes received a ball in his hip, which, for want of surgical aid, proved fatal the fifth day. During the whole of the Indian and French war that continued till 1763, the Indians never afterwards made their appearance in Walpole.

Kilburn lived to see the town of Walpole populous and flourishing, his fourth generation on the stage, and to reciprocate with them all the comforts and enjoyments of civilization. He possessed an honest heart, manifested in his upright deportment a Christian temper, and died in the expectation of seeing that country where wars and fighting never come. A substantial, plain, unpolished stone, indicative of the character which he maintained, points out the spot in Walpole burying ground where sleep his mortal remains, with this inscription.

" In memory of
John Kilburn who departed
this life for a better, April 8, 1789,
in the 85 year of his age.
He was the first settler of this town
in 1749."

His son "young John" for the last time revisited the field of his youthful exploits in 1814. After that he resided in Shrewsbury Vt., with his children till he died, which was in 1822.

The people at the fort could distinctly hear the incessant firing at Kilburn's all the afternoon, and their anxiety for the fate of his family was intense, but no one dare venture his life for their assistance. After the firing had ceased, and the black mantle of darkness had shrouded the woods, the daring Peter Bellows anxious to learn the fate of Killburn's family, with almost breathless silence crept through the woods alone late at night to Kilburn's cabin, and was the first person admitted to learn the fate and congratulate Kilburn for his heroic and noble defence.

Many years after the "Kilburn Fight" a relative of the Blanchards (our townsmen), living in the State of New York, became acquainted with a very old Indian whose name was Joshark Noshark, a former chief of the St. Francis tribe of Indians, who was then living in the same place. His memory was not impaired in the least. He said he was at the "Kilburn Fight," being a young man then but nineteen years of age. He gave a full and minute description of all the scenes that transpired on that ever memorable day, and described minutely all the surroundings,—the falls, the mountain, the mineral spring and the red and yellow paints which he said his tribe often procured to decorate themselves when they visited the fishing ground, which they did every season.

He said that Philip was killed in the early part of the fight and was buried south of the falls together with many others of his tribe. Philip was buried in a separate place and was covered first with dirt, and then a large flat stone was laid over the grave, after which more dirt and then leaves were strewn over to prevent the whites from finding him. He gave as a reason that Walpole was not afterwards molested that his tribe believed the "Great Spirit" frowned on their conduct towards Kilburn, after having been so generously treated by him.

At the time the Cheshire Railroad was being built several Indian skeletons were exhumed and among them one answering the description given of the size of Philip, and also the stone resting on the grave. It is said that one Dr. Robbins procured what was supposed to be Philip's bones and wired them together, and that these are now in the possession of his family.

Kilburn did not live long on the meadow; but seven or eight years after the 'Kilburn fight' he located on the farm now owned by Oliver J. Hubbard, where he lived till he died. On his removing to his new home, he said: "I shall defend *this* home as long as I live against foes of every kind." Frederick Kilburn, John senior's great grandson, who is now nearly three score years and ten, is the only descendant of the name now living in town. He has two married daughters and one grandson, residents of the town. This grandson is Thomas Bellows Buffum, the great-great-great-grandson of John Kilburn sen., and the great-great grandson of Col. Benjamin Bellows. Thus it is seen, after the lapse of more than one hundred years, that the mingled blood of the first two settlers of the town, is coursing the veins of one of their descendants.

The descendants of Kilburn, as far as known, are all respectable, thriving people, and they are quite numerous. [See Kilburn family.]

Although the Indians did not again make their appearance in Walpole, still they continued to lurk about and harass the settlers in towns in the vicinity. In 1757 they killed Lieut. Willard in Charlestown, and captured a few persons in Winchester.

The same year a party of settlers went up from Westmoreland several miles above to hoe corn on a small island a short distance from the south line of Walpole; on attempting to return by way of the forts on Putney meadows, and approaching the west bank of the river, a large dog belonging to one of the party ran up the bank, when his actions spoke as loudly as words that Indians were in ambush. The party feeling alarmed, with speed, silently crossed to the east bank and hurried home speedily. The next day they ascertained that a large body of Indians were in ambush ready to destroy them on their ascending the bank. The dog saved them.

Col. Bellows buried his first wife (Abigail Stearnes) Nov., 1757. She was the first tenant of the burying ground. The next year, in April, he married the widow Mary Jennison, of Lunenburg, by whom he had five children; viz., Abigail, Theodore, Thomas, Mary and Josiah, all born between 1759 and 1767. This widow Jennison was the mother of all the Jennisons who ever resided in town. [See Jennison family.]

The Col. was very strict in his regulations and would allow none of his men to leave the fort after dark. It is said, however, that his son Ben, being then eighteen, was one night put on the watch; but his appetite for watermelons overcame his fear and parental restraint, and induced him to leave his watch and go to the meadow to procure the coveted fruit. While looking about he discovered unmistakable signs of Indians, when he betook himself to the bank of the river, the enemy being between him and the fort. There he remained all night and the next day, afraid to stir. The anxiety of the family in the mean time was the most intense; still they did not dare search for him. To the great joy, however, of the family, he returned next day safe and sound, his appetite for watermelons being appeased to satiety.

Col. Bellows appears to have been a factotum of a peculiar kind, for he is not only found at the head and tail of all the town business; but in surveying and laying out towns in the vicinity, procuring a charter for the town of Keene, for which he received 122 Spanish milled dollars, and calling and presiding over the first town meeting. Very likely, too, he was engaged in clearing up the land, hunting up settlers, and in all the multifarious business incident to pioneer life.

FROM 1760 TO 1770.

The first business of a public nature done in Walpole, besides choosing town officers, was to assess each settler 12 shillings lawful money to be worked out on the highway at 3 shillings per day, if worked out before the first of Sep., if not, 2 shillings thereafter. This was in 1761. At the same time they assessed each settler 7 shillings to pay for preaching, and voted that "Benjamin Bellows, Esq. provide seats and other conveniences for the purpose."

At a legal meeting of the Inhabitants held at the Fort in Walpole, Dec. 22d, A. D., 1760, the town voted to give Mr. Jonathan Leavitt a call to become their minister, and at the same meeting they also voted to give him the following encouragement and salary. The stipulations as recorded in the Town records, read thus:

"Voted to give Mr. Jonathan Leavitt Seventy five pounds Sterling money of Great *Britton* as an encouragement to settle in the work of the ministry in said Town, the one half, that is thirty seven pound ten Shillings Sterling in three months after his Ordination and the other half in nine months after his Ordination, as also the Right in the Town that is Reserved for the first settled minister in said place to be his provided he accepts and settles in Said place."

They also vote to give him " for a *Salory* provided he settles in the work of the ministry in this Town of Walpole, namely to begin as thus for his first Year Thirty Seven pound ten Shillings Sterling money of Great *Britton* and to rise three pound fifteen Shillings Sterling money each year annually to be added to said *Salory* till it amount to the sum of Sixty pound Like money there to stay at sixty pound Sterling till there be Eighty Ratable *poles* in said Town Inhabitants belonging to said Town, then rise fifteen Shillings on Each *pole* that shall be added to said town till it makes the sum of seventy five pound Like money for Each year and then to *stope* and be the yearly *Salory* so Long as he the said Mr. Jonathan Leavitt shall continue to be the minister in Said Town," " 5ly Agreed and Voted that Each settler in and belonging to said town that is an Inhabitant and belonging to said Town, pay the sum of two pound five Shillings Sterling money of Great Brittain for the Use of and settlement of Mr. Jonathan Leavitt and his first Years *Salory* that is one pound ten Shillings toward his settlement and fifteen Shillings Toward his first Years *Salory* and it is agreed and voted that May'r Benjaman Bellows make up the rest of the sum of one hundred and Twelve pound ten Shillings Sterling being the money Voted for the settlement of Mr. Jonathan Leavitt and his first Year *Salory* if he accepts and settles in said Town."

On the succeeding February Mr. Leavitt made the following reply:

" Walpole February, 20, 1761.

" Being called upon by you the Inhabitants of this Place to settle among you in the work of the *Gosple* ministry and viewing it as my Duty, Do now in the Fear of God Depending on him by his Grace and spirit to assist me in the Faithful Discharge of this so Great a Truth comply with your call, Relying upon it that you will Do all on your part and in your Power to assist Strengthen and incourage me so long as God shall continue me with you. I say relying on this I do engage to settle among you provided that there shall nothing appear between this & the time of Ordination to forbid it, in which time I expect that you will Lay out the right of Land through this town of Walpole which by Charter is given to the first settled minister in the Place. And in Testimony of this solemn engagement I here unto set my hand.

Jonathan Leavitt."

The terms of Mr. Leavitt's settlement and salary were very liberal for those days when there were so few to pay, there being but twelve or fifteen families in town, at that time, all told. The purchasing power of money was then three fold as great as at the present time.

Mr. Leavitt was ordained on the 10th day of the following June, and Serg't Israel Calkins was paid two dollars for his services in going for a minister to attend Mr. Leavitt's ordination. Nothing more is heard of him till April, 1764, when the settlers call a town meeting for the purpose of hearing the minds of the inhabitants on some difficulties that had arisen between Mr. Leavitt and his parishioners.

At this meeting they "Voted that they think it best that the Rev. Jonathan Leavitt be no longer minister in this town."

The town chose a committee consisting of Nathaniel Hovey, Abraham Smith and Edmund Jackson, to wait on Mr. Leavitt and invite him to hear the minds of the parishioners. A consultation was held between the committee and Mr. Leavitt and it was mutually agreed by the parties that a council should be held on the 20th day of May to settle the difficulties. Before the time arrived for holding the council Mr. Leavitt and the town concluded on a settlement and no council was held.

It will be seen by the following communication from Mr. Leavitt that he releases the town from all obligation to him in any way after the 27th day of May 1764.

"Walpole May 7, 1764. These may certify that I the Subscriber have this Day agreed with Misrs Benjamin Bellows, Nathaniel Hovey and Abraham Smith, a Committee Legally Chosen by the Inhabitants of Said Town to agree and settle with me, that from and after the Twenty Seventh Day of this Instant may that then my Yearly Salory Shall cease and from and after that time I Do Discharge the said Inhabitants of Walpole from any Demand I now have or might have against said town by Virtue of the votes and agreement made with me upon my Settling in Said Town and upon my receiving the pay of the Present Years Salory which is Completed the Said Twenty Seventh Day of this Instant May then that to be in full of all Demands I now have or might have against

said Town, as Witness my hand in Presents of Jeremiah
Phelps, Jonathan Leavitt, Asa Baldwin."

Mr. Leavitt seems to have been in bad odor with his people,
which caused the inhabitants to act very unanimously and
with promptness, and Mr. Leavitt to submit to their decision
with as quiet grace as possible.

Ministers were not so easily dismissed in those days and had
there not been something more than common to agitate and
arouse the feelings of his charge there would have been a division of sentiment.

One of the reasons for his summary dismissal, it is said, was
that the parson was detected in leading home a runaway
slave of his, a *woman*, by a rope round her neck and attached
to the pommel of his saddle. Col. Bellows, hearing of the
outrage, declared "That such cruelty should not be tolerated,"
that he "settled parson Leavitt and he would unsettle him."
What became of Mr. Leavitt is not known. The town, after
his dismissal, immediately hired one Jonathan Moore who
preached for them some time.

It appears that the moral and religious welfare of the inhabitants was paramount in their minds, for they had stated
preaching long before any meeting house was built. Sometimes meetings were held at one Ephraim Baldwin's when not
at the fort.

Many meetings were held to see what could be done towards
providing a place for public worship; finally it was "voted to
build a meeting house fifty-six feet in length by forty-two in
breadth, and that each settler work four days or pay twelve
shillings towards putting up a frame. It appears that each
settler was to pay an equal sum, poor or otherwise, and that
Col. Bellows was to "make up the rest" however much it
might be. The meeting house was located just in front of
John W. Hayward's wood house and the pulpit was over
where now is a well of the purest water to be found in town.

For more than twenty years the town records are filled with
"votes" to do something about finishing the meeting-house till
the number of inhabitants in town demanded a more com-

modious structure. How far it was completed is not known, but it is certain that it never was finished. Every annual town meeting three or four men were chosen, called Tythingmen, who were a kind of Sunday police. It was their duty to see that order was observed in and around the church on the Sabbath, and also to see that no one labored in their fields or travelled on the highway unnecessarily. Such officers were chosen in town down nearly to the nineteenth century.

In 1762, a road was laid out from Charlestown line to Westmoreland line, and, as it was the first road recorded in the town records, and much of it is in use at the present time, a description, as recorded, may not prove uninteresting.

The description is as follows :

" A Description of a Road Layed out by the Selectmen of Walpole through said Walpole from Charlestown to Westmoreland beginning at Charlestown Line where the Road is now made Running as the Roads is now Cut four Rods wide to Cold River meadows to where the fence Stand between Maj. Bellows and Mr. John Kilburn then Running upon the North Side of Mr. Kilburns meadow Land two Rods wide to Cold River—then wide enough a Cross Said River for a Good Bridge then two Rods wide to the Hill then up the hill upon the plain where the path now is four Rods wide to Maj. Bellows and so East of his Corn house and so to the old Road till it Comes to the meeting house and thence by marked Trees on the East of Ephraim Baldins house and so Strait by the Rev. Mr. Leavitts house and so where the Road is now Cut to Mr. Abraham Smiths then as near the Line of Lotts Between the third and fourth Range of Lotts as the land will admit as it is marked to Westmoreland being about a South Point Liberty for altering a Few Rods on Either side to make the Road Better if the Land will admit said Road to be four Rods wide all but Cold River meadow and the River as that to be as above Described."

In the above description it is stated that the road, after passing Ephraim Baldwin's, who is supposed by certain circumstantial evidence to have lived somewhere on the east side of the road south of John W. Heyward's, passes by Parson Leavitt's. Now where did Parson Leavitt live? Parson Leavitt and wife would not be likely to live in a hovel, for it is said they were the most dressy people in town at that time.

The house where Henry Allen now lives is *probably* the oldest house in the village, and, as tradition is silent about the original ownership, may it not be probable that Allen's was the Parson's house?

At this time, and many years following, a kind of officer was chosen annually called a "*Deer Reave.*" Sometimes three or four men would be chosen to fill that office in different parts of the town. The curious might ask for what object such officers were chosen. Deer were plenty at that time and afforded delicious and cheap meat to the early settlers, and they wanted them protected from slaughter, at certain seasons of the year, and Deer Reaves were chosen for that purpose. If a person was caught killing deer during the season prohibited by law he was fined heavily.

In 1766, it appears by the records, the inhabitants of the town had for some time been agitating the subject of settling a new minister and that Mr. Thomas Fessenden had been preached to them as a candidate.

A meeting of the inhabitants was called to see what action the town would take on the subject.

Following is a copy of the proceedings of a meeting called in Sept., taken from the records.

"Province of New Hampshire."

"Walpole, Sept. 26, 1766."

"At a Legal Meeting of the Inhabitants of said Walpole held at the Meetinghouse in said Town Firstly, Chose Benjamin Bellows Esq. Moderator. Secondly, Voted to give Mr. Thomas Fessenden a call to settle in the work of the ministry in said Walpole. Thirdly, Voted to give as an Encouragement to the said Mr. Thomas Fessenden one hundred and fifty pounds Lawful money Dollars at Six Shillings Each, as a settlement and said Bellows is to pay one third of said settlement, and it is *Purposed* that the settlement be in two payments half said sum in six months from his Ordination and the other half one year from his Ordination.

"Fourthly, Voted to give said Mr. Fessenden as a yearly Salary for the first year Fifty pounds like money, and for the second year fifty-three pounds and so rise three pounds a year for five years then to stand at Sixty Five pounds a year till there be one hundred settlers in Said Walpole or *familys* to make up the hundred Inhabitants Properly called *familys*, than to rise to Eighty pounds Like money as above paid and there to Continue at that sum yearly so long as he the said Mr. Thomas Fessenden shall be our minister and the People have Liberty to pay said Salary if they see Cause in good winter wheat that is *Marchantable* at four Shillings Per Bushel, Good Rye at three Shillings per Bushel, and Good Indian corn at two Shillings p'r Bushel, Good Beef at two pence p'r pound or Good Pork at three pence p'r pound the Pork being *hoggs* that weigh Eught *schore* and upwards all which is to be Delivered at the house of the said Mr. Fessenden at the above prices."

In the November following Mr. Fessenden presented his acceptance to the call of the town in the following communication.

"Province of New Hampshire."

"Walpole, Nov. 1, 1766."

"Gentlemen:

After mature and Serious Consideration of a copy of Votes passed at a Legal meeting of the Inhabitants of Walpole Transmitted to me and attested by the Town *Clark* Containing an invitation of me to settle in the work of the Gospel Ministry in said Town with Proposals for my Encouragement and support therein—Must Confess the hand of Providence appears in the unanimity Subsisting and that your Proposals and offers are in themselves Generous. But the tender and manner of payment Does not in all things appear agreeable to your Design and the nature of the work you invite me to engage in. I would therefore to my acceptance of your Invitation Subjoin the following Explanation and amendments. Upon your acceptance of which this is my answer in the affirmative.

1st. That the settlement be payed as there proposed 2d. That by families, inhabitants and settlers you mean the same thing as it is there stated. 3d. That half the Salary be in money as more Grain and meat than is needful for me to spend will Oblige me in order to provide for my household to turn *Marchant* so Divert me from my Studies and Proper Calling and in the same Proportion Deprive you of my labor.

Upon these terms I accept of Your Call Trusting that you will Communicate to me in Temporals as you see me need as I Communicate to you in Spirituals hoping and Praying that harmony and Love may subsist between us to the Furtherance of

Each others present best good and our future Happiness and Joy."

> "I am with sincerity in the Common Savior your well wisher and firm friend.
>
> THOMAS FESSENDEN."

"To the Inhabitants of the
town of Walpole."

Mr. Fessenden was not unreasonable in requiring one half of his salary to be paid in money, and the inhabitants saw the point was well made, and had the good sense to arrange matters more satisfactory to Mr. Fessenden.

He was ordained the minister of the town, Jan. 7, 1767, but the town records are silent in relation to the proceedings on the occasion.

It is inferred that during this decade there was no store kept in town, of any importance, for in an old ledger that once belonged to Aaron Burt of Northfield, Mass., are found accounts against sixteen Walpole men. In 1762, a large invoice of nails and hinges are charged to Benjamin Bellows the same year he built his new house.

In 1768 the town 'vote' to have three schools and vote 15 pounds to support them in winter, and the next year vote 24 pounds for schooling, and to form three districts.

An account of the manners and customs of this decade is found in a communication to the "Cheshire Gazette," a paper before referred to, in 1826, the substance of which was communicated to Dr. Morse by a Mrs. Watson of Pennsylvania, who lived in Walpole in 1762, then but eight years old; but whose recollections, though old, were as vivid and strong as in earlier life. It runs thus:

"It seems that a Mr. John Fanning, the father of the narrator, left Stonington, Ct., with a view of establishing himself on Otter Creek, Vt., but, owing to the difficulties of travelling in new countries, advanced no further than Walpole. In 1762, the family took passage in a sloop of their own as far as Hartford, where they purchased a wagon and two horses, to convey them up the east side of the river. The country, as far as Chicopee river, is represented as remarkably fine, both as respects the fertility of the soil and the improvements of the settlers.

Hatfield was then but a small town, having been recently destroyed by the Indians.

This calamity is said to have been forewarned by some of the inhabitants having, as they supposed, heard a few nights previous, the approach of tribes of savages, and the sound of their snow-shoes. The fields of grain were immense and without any division fences.

At Sunderland the road then travelled was mountainous, which rendered it necessary to leave some of their articles and purchase a yoke of oxen to help them along. They next passed a small village called Keene, and came to Walpole, No. 3. There they purchased a lot of land, now (1878) owned by S. J. Tiffany, built a house of square timber, cut down the trees and cleared the land, so as to raise a good crop of corn the same year. The roof of the house was covered with bark, and the gable ends remained open some time, which enabled them to hear the barking of foxes, the howling of wolves, and the cries of the panthers, while sitting before the fire. The latter resembled the voice of a woman in distress, and (seemed) intended to decoy people into the woods, where the salutations of these roving gentry were apt to prove troublesome, unless prevented by the use of fire-arms.

The flesh of the deer and bear afforded the settlers many a delicious repast. The approach of the latter was often unceremonious, and sometimes rude to strangers. Wild turkeys were trapped and shot, and quails and pigeons caught in nets, in great abundance. The brooks were filled with trout and dace, and the river abounded in salmon and shad; one of the latter was taken near the falls which had a rattlesnake's head in its stomach.

An intercourse with the animal creation was carried to an unusual length. A brood of young raccoons were taught to suck the cat, and play about the house, like kittens, only much more mischievous. The effect of this wild mode of living was exemplified in the case of a Mrs. Prichard, who was lost in the woods and subsisted, like wild beasts, on berries and the bark of trees, twenty one days. She started, during a thunder shower, from a place called "Jennison's Hill," with a child of two years old, to visit a neighbor's house. Leaving the track, to avoid a large snake, she lost her way, and was not seen again for just three weeks, when some men discovered her at the mouth of Cold river. She fled at the sight of men, like a deer, but was overtaken and brought back to a house. Her clothes were completely torn off. After recovering her senses in a degree, she stated that her child died the third day, and she buried it under a log. She said she heard the Indians' guns, and saw them several times in pursuit of her (probably her friends, who spent several days looking for her), but she secreted herself so as to elude their vigilance. She was living in Westminister a few years ago in a state of mental alienation.

' The country was pretty much cleared of Indians, but the hardships of the primitive settlers, and their frequent encounters with wild beasts and savages, furnished a fruitful topic of conversation, with which to spend the evenings, and regale their distant friends who visited them.

A man by the name of Root was delightfully serenaded by a bear and two cubs at the foot of a tree, while he lodged on the limbs above.

A Mrs. Wheeler, of Keene, was one of seven women who bravely defended a fort, without any other weapons than *boiling soap*. The men had gone into the woods with all their guns, when the Indians made their attack. By keeping up a well directed fire of that hot article in the face and eyes of the assailants, as they approached the port holes, the women finally succeeded in routing the enemy.

At this time, (1762,) there were about twelve or fifteen log-houses in the town. The meeting-house was unfinished; there was not a carriage in town, the travelling being performed on foot or horseback; sometimes three or four children were carried in this way at a time, beside a wife, on a pillion, and upsetting a load of this magnitude was not an uncommon occurence.

Col. B. Bellows was the most considerable man in town; his eldest son, Peter, was settled in Charlestown, where the people used often to go to attend meeting. A remarkable trait in the character of the first settlers was their punctuality in attending public worship. Mr. Leavitt, the minister, like other clergymen of that day, wore a large wig, full powdered, and when he entered the meetinghouse, the whole congregation rose to do obeisance to the man in black, who, in his turn, always responded with a formal bow. Powder was not worn on the hair by those who were contented with the use of the eel-skin, which was considered as adding dignity to the wearer, in proportion to the size and length of the *queue*.

Officers of the militia wore cocked hats. Of the ladies Mrs. Leavitt took the lead in dress; at church she wore a full suit of lutestring, without any bonnet, holding a fan to shade the sun from her face, as was the fashion "down country."

Next to her were the daughters of Col. Bellows, and their

two half sisters, Jenisons. They wore plain Quaker bonnets of
black silk; white or colored ones were not seen. To improve
their figures the ladies quilted their petticoats with wool, to
make their hips show off to advantage, which contrasted with
the smallness of the waist, painfully compressed with long
stays. Home-made durants, camblets, and serges, full of gay
flowers of artificial needlework, were fashionable articles.
Stockings, of their own knitting, and high-heeled shoes with
buckles, were indispensable. It was thought an improvement
to beauty and elegance to expose the petticoat before, through
a screen of lawn apron, the gown being left to swing open.
The hair was all combed back, leaving no curls nor ringlets
about the face. Instead of following the modern fashion of
covering the *back* part of the head, their bonnets were so much
pitched forward, that the cap and back part of the head were
exposed.

A large portion of *pin money* was derived from the sale of
golden thread, ginseng, and snake root, which were procured
by their own hands. Dr. Chase was the only physician."

The article closes with "To be continued," but no continuance can be found

Sympathy for those in affliction was more intense in the
early days of the settlement of the town than at the present
time. It was a time when joys and sorrows were shared in
common, for many miles around, by the entire community.
Boundary lines between townships were not taken into consideration. Such fraternal feeling was strikingly exemplified in
1770 when a child, a son of Isaac Cady, got lost in Alstead.

The following narrative of the circumstance is copied from
Rev. Mr. Arnold's History of Alstead.

"In 1770, Jacob Cady, two and a half years old, son of
Isaac Cady, was one day missing. The region around was one
vast wilderness, and thickly inhabited by beasts of prey. Jacob, peculiarly dear to his mother, left her one afternoon to go
to his father chopping in the woods at a little distance. But
when the father returned home at night the child was missing.
The anxious family flew immediately in search of their little
boy, and the more they hunted and called, as the thick darkness of night gathered around them, the more their anxiety increased and their hopes desponded. The night was spent in
anxious search and awful suspense, but all their care and toil

were vain. The light of morning returned, and yet their child was lost. But the day was now before them, and parental affection does not easily relinquish its object. The neighbors, though distant and few, were friendly and kind. Some immediately joined with the afflicted parents in ranging the woods and others carried information to the neighboring towns. But the day declined, and hopes which were for a time enkindled sunk in despondency as the darkness closed upon the light. Fires were kindled at distances from each other, suited to direct their search and attract the attention of the child, and numbers spent the night in fruitless attempts for his recovery. As the light of another day gilded the horizon and invited their renewed exertions multitudes were collected from Charlestown, Walpole, Marlow, Keene and all the neighboring towns (400 or 500 persons in all), to lend their assistance to make one united effort, and, if possible, to relieve the anxiety of these bereaved parents. Hope was again revived, and earnest expectations were entertained as the bands went forth to scour the woods with critical and careful attention to every nook, and to every circumstance that might show signs of the lost child. In their faithful searches among the rocks, forest trees and fallen timber, at one time, they discovered tracks of a child and those of a bear, or some wild animal very near them. Eager and trembling were the pursuers. Soon, however, all indications of discovery disappeared, and as the day began to decline they relinquished their object as hopeless, and many returned to the house of Mr. Cady. "Alas!" said the mother, under the burden of fatigue, a want of sleep and a spirit sinking in despair, 'if I could know that the child was relieved from suffering, even by the devouring beasts, I could be still. Could I see a fragment of his torn limbs, I would say no more. But can I lie down to rest not knowing but my little Jacob is wandering and starving in yonder gloom?' (The house overlooked two deep forests) 'Can a fond parent forget her child or cease to look for the little wanderer? Even the sleep of night would be disturbed by the visionary dreams of his suffering state and the seeming cries for a mother's aid.'"

Such artless eloquence as this could not fail to move those generous feelings and noble sentiments which our fathers inherited. It was sufficient to put in lively exercise that compassion and benevolence, that spirit of enterprise and perseverance for which they were so much distinguished. "Gen. Benjamin Bellows and Capt. John Jennison of Walpole, Capt.

John Burroughs of this town, Mr. Abner Bingham of Marlow and a few others who had not left the house immediately determined to renew the search. And even the prospect of approaching night only served to hasten their steps and nerve their weary limbs. They agreed on the following signals, and set off in pursuit. If they should discover any signs of the child, *one gun* was to be discharged; if he should be found dead, or to have been destroyed, *two guns* were to be discharged; and if found alive, the discharge of *three guns* would give notice. With anxious, though enfeebled solicitude did the parents and those at the house listen to catch the first sound that might burst upon the ear from the still expanse of the south. No sooner had their eager attention begun to subside than the first signal was heard. Every countenance instantly glowed with a fluctuating crimson, which told the emotions of joy that struggled alternately within. But these emotions soon gave way to a deadly paleness, and fearful apprehension when the second discharge was heard. Is the child dead? was the secret inquiry of every look. Now all were breathless to hear, and afraid they should not. But soon the *third* discharge broke the dreadful suspense, and burst the veil of uncertainty that hung over the scene. The change that so quickly succeeded, the joy that kindled in every breast, glowed in every countenance and sparkled in every eye, can be more easily imagined than described. The child was found asleep, east or south east of Warrens' pond, and restored with peculiar satisfaction and joyful triumph to the embrace of its delighted parents, by General Bellows of Walpole."

From 1770 to 1780.

The town at this time contained probably less than four hundred inhabitants, for in 1767 when the first state census was taken there were but three hundred and eight, and only one over sixty years of age. The settlements were confined principally to the territory south of Cold river, as far as where the village now is, and east as far as the valley; a few families, however, were settled in other portions of the town.

This year and the next (1771) the town, as seen by the records, is manifesting a very laudable ambition in raising money for the support of schools and building school-houses in three different districts. No. 1 school-house was built where Josiah

G. Bellows' house now stands; and when the old brick school-house was built, on what is now the corner of West and Elm streets the old house was removed to the west side of "Washington Square," where it now stands and is the residence of Moses Q. Watkins. For a long time an old woman by the name of Lathwood and her maiden daughter resided there; the daughter was very gross, weighing some 250 pounds. The young people used to call frequently on them to hear the mother address her daughter as her "dear little lamb."

No. 2 school-house was near Cold river, and No. 3 was near where it now is. An old resident of the town, now living, states that when a boy he went to school there, and the number of pupils, was "rising of eighty."

In 1772 the town vote "that the constable warn out of town every person that comes in, that has no estate in town," and it was made one of the duties of that functionary many years thereafter, to comply with the vote. In those days our modern tramps would have fared hard. At this time the town paid four pence an hour for working on the highways, and in 1775 the town vote "thanks to Col. Benjamin Bellows for his generous gift of a lott of a hundred acres of land in the town of Walpole, for the use of a *grammar school forever.*" This one hundred acres is remembered in his will two years later, with this clause; "provided the town will clear and put under improvement *sixty* acres of the land in six years." The town, in subsequent years, voted from time to time to clear up a certain number of acres, but the Revolutionary war having then commenced, and thirty-three men, out of a population of 658, having already gone into the service, and the multifarious duties incident to those who remained at home, pressing so heavily upon them, probably, prevented the town from meeting the provisions of the bequest; consequently it reverted. The school was to have been kept in the house above mentioned.

At this time the town vote "to pay forty shillings to any person who kills a wolf in the *town.* Mrs. Geo. D. Kingsbury's grandfather (Aaron Hodskins) killed one and received the bounty, the first money he ever had which he could call his

own. With the money he bought a saddle and a pair of steers.
That kind of "gentry" was quite numerous at this period;
they used to congregate in large numbers in the somber hem-
lock woods that once covered the "Valley" and serenade the
early settlers that lived on the side hill south. Bears and catamounts were not unfrequently seen and killed. The grandmother of a lady living in town went to the turnip patch one
day to get some turnips, when she discovered a large bear
helping himself to a vegetable dinner. She immediately ran
for the house, much excited, and told the men what she had
seen. They rallied her on being so much frightened at a mere
dog, but she declared it was a bear. One asked if the animal
had "a long tail or a short one"; she said "a short one,"
whereupon the men sallied forth, discovered his bearship's
whereabouts, and arming themselves with muskets, clubs and
pitchforks, with numerous dogs, followed Bruin into the edge
of Westmoreland, and after an exciting contest dispatched him,
and had a jolly time over bear steak.

It is related that Col. Bellows, when hunting small game on
Fall mountain, came in contact with a huge bear, which he immediately dispatched, but soon after another "put in an appearance," which soon shared the same fate, when he began to think
that kind of game was becoming too numerous. Immediately
a rustling was heard in the bushes near by, and on turning his
eyes in the direction of the noise he beheld a pair of round
eyeballs fiercely glaring at him above the brakes. He instinct-
ively recognized the new customer as a large catamount, a different kind of "varmint" from the clumsy bear, to deal with;
but the Col's courage was not lessened on that account. He
brought his gun to his shoulder, with not a little trepidation,
however, knowing well the disposition of the animal when
wounded, and, aiming at the eyes, fired, and in a second all
was silent. The Col. not caring to investigate the result of
the discharge too closely, at that time, beat a hasty retreat to his
house. Returning immediately with his men he found that
his last shot was fatal. The meat of the bear furnished a delicious repast in those days and it is presumed the Col's family

did not lose the rare opportunity of dining on bear steak. To kill a catamount in those days, and also to-day, single-handed, is considered a great triumph of courage.

On the 19th of April 1775, was fought the battle of Lexington, and messengers were immediately dispatched from the scene of strife to every town of any importance in New England bearing the news. As soon as the news reached Walpole General Benjamin Bellows, his next brother, Col. John, and Thomas Sparhawk mounted their horses and started for Lexington followed by a large number of townsmen. On arriving at Keene in the afternoon of the next day after hearing the news, they rode to the house of Capt. Wyman and made inquiry for him, and being answered that he started for Concord in the morning at sunrise at the head of a company of thirty men, they exclaimed, "Keene has shown a noble spirit," and hastened onwards. There were thirty-five that went from Walpole on this occasion, and they were out about eleven days on this expedition.

Walpole was not behind other towns in the state in furnishing men and means for the service and use of the Continental army; nor were the families of soldiers neglected at home, for the town records bear evidence of money's being raised from time to time for the use of such families, and committees were appointed to see that they were made comfortable. In 1778 the town "voted to raise sixty pounds to be expended for soldiers families who had gone to the war." The pay of the soldier was ten pounds for one year's service or wheat at five shillings per bushel. In 1779 the town voted one thousand pounds to procure five soldiers for the Continental army; but it took that year twenty-three hundred and ninety-three pounds of the money so raised to purchase one hundred and four pounds in gold. Continental money, as it was called, continued to depreciate till the close of the war, when it was hardly worth having; even in 1781 it took twelve thousand pounds in government *scrip* to equal one hundred pounds in gold or silver coin.

The exact number of men that went into the Continental

service cannot be ascertained from any available source, but it
is said most of the able-bodied men in town served a longer
or shorter period.

General Benjamin Bellows, though he rose from the lowest
office in the militia of the state to be a Brigadier General, never was long in the field. He was mostly engaged in raising
troops for the regular United States service and was one of the
principal men in the state sought for when any aid to the National Government was wanting. "Twice he marched his own
regiment to Ticonderoga, first in October 1776, for a service
of twenty-five days; and again, June 28th 1777 to reinforce
the garrison there besieged by the enemy, when, according to
the pay-roll, the time of service was only twelve days. Finally, he carried his regiment, September 21st 1777, to reinforce
the Northern Continental army at Saratoga under the command of Gen. Gates at the time when Burgoyne surrendered."
"The historian says after a battle 'severe and bloody' the victory of the Americans was complete." Gen. Gates detached
strong bodies of his troops in various directions to cut off the
retreat of the enemy. Burgoyne retired by Saratoga creek to
the Hudson, at which point he was met by the New Hampshire
militia, under the command of Colonels Webster, Bellows, and
Morey. At this place the enemy halted, and Burgoyne observed that "it was vain to contend with the owners of the
soil." Therefore he and his army laid down their arms and
surrendered themselves prisoners of war. In Gen. Bellows'
account with the government is a charge for a horse killed in
his service, but it is not stated whether killed under the Colonel
or not. Most likely many of the men from this town were
with General Bellows at this time for it is said, "all the men
from Walpole went to Saratoga." General Bellows was highly
complimented by Gen. Gates for the services he rendered him
with his men from Cheshire county, on that occasion. Our
late esteemed townsman Mr. Lyman Watkins (now deceased)
used to seek every opportunity to draw what information he
could from the old Revolutionary soldiers in relation to the
events that occured during their service. Following is one of

the many stories he had treasured up. He says among the
Walpole men in the above named battle was one Crane and one
Hall, who went out with General Bellows as scouts and fell in
with Indians and captured one hundred and fifty in the first
day of their service. Crane had a dreadful encounter with an
Indian armed with a cutlass which in the struggle he grasped,
cutting his fingers in such a way as to be unable to open his
hand ever after. Munn Hall* of Walpole, is reported to have
said to Burgoyne at the surrender, "We've got you for breakfast, and we'll have Lord Cornwallis for dinner."

Thomas Bellows in speaking of the men who went to Saratoga from Walpole remembered the names of twelve, among
whom were Ephraim Stearns, Farnham, Messer, Lawrence
Massey, etc. Although his memory was very remarkable, he
never was able to recall to mind the name of the twelfth one.
After hesitating a moment he would say, "No matter, 'twas a
black man any way." This black man was a blacksmith who
had a shop on a farm near where the old meeting-house used
to stand, now owned by B. E. Webster, "General Bellows
claimed to have seen some Indian service, and used to wear,
on high military occasions, a belt of wampum, as a trophy of
victory over the savages." Quite a number of Walpole men
brought trophies from Saratoga which were preserved by later
generations as objects for the curious to look at. Samuel Wiers
had some harnesses, a powder-chest and a hatchet, which could
be seen some thirty years ago, when in the possession of his son
John H. Wiers who lived on the first farm in Westmoreland,
on the river road.

Some of the Walpole soldiers captured a boat belonging to
the enemy that contained barrels which they supposed were
filled with rum; but what was their chagrin when on boring
into one of them they found it contained *pork*.

Aug. 16th, 1777, was fought the battle of Bennington, which
decided the fate of Burgoyne. During the day the booming
of the cannon was distinctly heard on the Walpole hills and
in the valleys. Moses Burt, grandfather to our townsman

* Munn was a nickname, his real name was Jonathan Hall, Jr.

Henry, was with another man, stooking wheat in his field when he heard the reports of cannon reverberating from mountain to mountain. He and his men immediately set out for the seat of war (see Burt family.) Rodger Woolcott also heard the firing and left for the scene of conflict the next day. Most of the surrounding towns had to keep an eye on tories in their midst ; but Walpole seems to have been free from them. With the exception of General Bellows, Colonel Christopher Webber appears to be the only man that gained military distinction during the Revolutionary struggle.

In 1776, Dec. 9, at a legal meeting called for the purpose the town chose Capt. Christopher Webber to represent it in the General Assembly to be held at Exeter, and also chose at the same time a committee consisting of Capt. Goldsmith, Amos Babcock, Samuel Trott, Barnabas Delano and John Marcy to give Mr. Webber instructions. Following are the instructions which were presented to the town in due time for their adoption.

" We the Freeholders and Legal Inhabitants of the Town of Walpole Vested with the Priviledge of Chosing a representative at a meeting Duly Warned the ninth of this month having made Choise of your Captain Christopher Webber of this town to act in that Capacity for us in the General Assembly to meet at Exeter 18th of this Instant in all such affairs as shall be thought necessary for the Public Good Do without any Design to Deminish from the Trust reposed by us in your Wisdom and Integrity or to Infringe the Liberty of others to act for themselves, Make use of our unalienable right to Instruct you in what we your Constituants in the Present Poster our Public affairs apprehend will be most for the Publick in Consequence of your Close adherence to these our Instructions we fully Impower you to Act for the well fair of this State and as your Constituants, the Present Internal Situation of our affairs in our View is such as to Call for our utmost Exertions to preserve our Union by removing every Ground of Uneasiness and by Presuing such Measures as the Present times and seasons Seems to Require Union at Home is the more needful now to give Energy to our Exertions for our External Safety and Defence against our Insidious and Inveterate Enemies. However the Wisdom of the Last Assembly might think it necessary at the recommendation of the Continental Congress to form Such a plan of Government as they Did to Continue During our Present Contest with Great Brittain a Submission to which so far as known we have not and Do not refuse to Yield yet we think the Great Charge that hath since Commensed in our State from Dependance when a Possability of Reconcilliation with Great Brittain remained to that of Independence wherein Nothing but the will of the Conqueror must be our Law if we are Subdued will Justify us in our Present Sentiments of the Absolute necessity of so far Reconsidering what has been Done as to proceed Immediately to Create and Establish a Lasting Constitution of Government for this State as the only thing that will give Quiet to the Uneasy Satisfaction to our Friends and Prostrate the hopes of our Foes. What we request of you Sir is in our belief to Use All Your Influence that the Present Assembly as soon as may be prepared the way for the Compleat Organization of Government by Issuing Precepts to every Settled Incorperated Town through the State to Send Representatives if they see Cause Expressly for the Purpose of Forming a Constitution of Government and to Impower and Instruct them Accordingly we would have the Design of this meeting fully and Perticularly Inserted in the Precepts reserving to the People the Power of ratifing Said Constitution when Formed and a Plan of it returned to them if they Approve of it Making Such Alterations in it as the Majority by their representatives shall think best. We Amagine the Vast and Lasting Importance of the Transaction of Setting up Government Renders it Very Proper that a Fast be Appointed through the State that all by Prayer may Seek Direction from the Great Governor of the World that we may have such an Equal Form Established as to secure the Civil Moral rights of His Majesty and the Just Dues of Rulers and People as his Subjects Assertained and Preserved Further as the Infringement of the Liberty of the Press that Great Butt of Arbitary Power is a high Insutt of a Free People we would have you Labor to have that member or members Discovered and made Publick who forbad the Printer from Printing a Late Pamphlet set Forth by the Committees of a number of Towns in the Northwesterly Part of this State. If these our reasonable Requests should not be complyed with while we allow others to Judge for themselves we as accountable to god and Posterity for what we Do at this Juncture think it not Best for you to act upon Publick Business but retire Leaving a Copy of these ourInstructions as your Reasons for so Doing.

Wishing you Success we are your Constituants the Inhabitants of Walpole

Dec. 12th A. D. 1776

To Capt Christopher Webber

JOHN MARCY,
BARNABAS DELANO,   } Committee.
SAMUEL PRATT,
AMOS BABCOCK.

The above instructions were duly submitted to the town and were accepted *"with amendments to make it grammar."* It would be interesting to know whether the foregoing copy is the original or in the *amended* form.

Mr. Webber did not obey the *instructions* and the inhabitants were much excited over it, and he received many angry threats of bringing him to the bar of the town to answer for his misdoings. Whether he doggedly refused to obey the wordy instructions, or whether he was so obtuse in understanding as not to comprehend their signification is not known. Be it as it may his reputation did not suffer in consequence of his delinquency for he was returned to Exeter the next year by a rousing majority.

Col. Bellows died July 10th, 1777, and his civic mantle fell on his son Benjamin, by whom it was never tarnished. The colonel left to his nine children, by his will, a very large landed estate in Walpole and other towns in the vicinity. It appears by his will that he had given to his children a princely estate before he made it, the number of acres of land it is impossible to state; but by his will he bequeathed to each of his children the number of acres which follows, viz., to Peter, he gave seven hundred acres in Rockingham and six hundred acres in Walpole, in the north part; to Benjamin, four hundred acres in the south part of the town, to John, eight hundred in two lots, to Joseph, seven hundred in Rindge, Mason and Fitzwilliam, besides unenumerated lands in Lunenburg Mass.; to Abigail, one hundred and thirty acres with buildings; to Molly, five hundred acres in Westminster, Vt.; to Josiah, five hundred acres in Walpole, and thirty-three acres in Westminister, Vt. He also gave seventy acres in Keene to Mary Willard, fifty acres in Walpole to John Jennison and one hundred acres to the town, for a grammar school. He also gave one-ninth part of all his lands in Rockingham, to each of his nine children; the number of acres is not given. Thus it is seen that when Col. Bellows died he was in possession of, from six to eight thousand acres of land enumerated and unenumerated. He also gave his children one thousand and fifty pounds in money, together with numerous oxen, cows, horses, and also household furniture, taken together amounting to a large sum.

In person Col. Benjamin Bellows was tall and stout, weighing, a short time before his death, three hundred and thirty pounds: but still he continued, until late in life, looking after his extensive farming interests; riding about his farm on a strong sorrel horse, from place to place, with his son Josiah, mounted behind, ready to slip off as occasion required to let down the bars. He lived in a style that necessitated much activity and forethought to satisfy the daily demands of his own household, to say nothing of the numerous strangers and public men who were hospitably treated and cared for, as they called when going and coming. A large oaken table, in the kitchen under the house, was always spread for his workmen. He maintained a separate table for his own family. He raised his own stores, and killed an ox or a cow every week, which was consumed by the family. He made four hundred barrels of cider annually and put down twenty barrels of pork every winter. Eggs were brought in by the half bushel, and salmon was so common that his hired men stipulated that they should not have it oftener than three times a week.

In 1779, the town "voted to Taich Possession of the Publick Wrights of land in sd Town and Improve the same." The land to which allusion is above made is the "Governor's calf pasture" heretofore mentioned. Accordingly, the land, or a portion of it, was leased to one John Prentiss of Langdon, for a series of years, the betterments of which were sold to the town afterwards.

FROM 1780 TO 1790.

The first year of this decade the town call upon Thomas and Theodore Bellows to answer to the charge of voting illegally. One who ever knew the 'Squire' in after life would hardly believe that he could ever have been caught in a trap of the kind. The town does not appear to have pushed the matter farther than a gentle remonstrance, while the 'Squire' vindicated his act satisfactorally to himself on the ground of representing his property.

During the decade between 1770 and 1780 a great deal of excitement was produced among the settlers on both sides of the Connecticut river, embracing all the towns from Massachusetts line, north, as far as the New Hampshire grants extended. Benning Wentworth, soon after becoming governor of the province of New Hampshire, commenced granting townships to settlers under a royal commission which he had obtained from the Crown of England. All the lands west of Connecticut river had been granted, by letters patent, to the Duke of York. In 1749 Wentworth made a grant to certain citizens of the township of Bennington Vt.,—which name is derived from his own. Quite a number of other grants followed. It seems that he had some apprehension that trouble might grow out of such measures, for he entered into a correspondence with Lieutenant Governor Colden, then acting governor of New York, reciting his acts, and asking his (Colden's) views on the subject. Wentworth received no reply from Colden; but in 1750 he received a reply from Gov. George Clinton stating that New York claimed all land west of Connecticut to the east side of Delaware bay, by letters patent from Charles the II. Wentworth, who was proud and arrogant, and had, during life, generally been successful in carrying out his plans, continued to grant charters till 1764, when the number amounted to one hundred and thirty-eight, at which time the matter of jurisdiction between New York and New Hampshire was submitted to the British Crown. The decision was made in favor of the claims of New York.

After the decision was made New York became arrogant and grasping in turn and not only claimed jurisdiction but the right of *soil* also, assuming the ground that all grants made under the authority of New Hampshire, were null and void. The settlers and claimants, a numerous and powerful body, were determined to resist such assumption and support their titles. Those conflicting claims led to bitter disputes between the two parties, so vehement in their nature, at times, as to threaten bloodshed. The settlers would have quietly submitted to the jurisdiction of New York, had they been permitted to hold their lands; but when suits of ejectment were brought and declared against them in the New York courts the officers who attempted to dispossess them of their homes met with such resistance as compelled them to retire.

On the part of the people holding titles emanating from New Hampshire the irritation at length became so great as to lead them to the fixed and determined resolution not to come under the jurisdiction of the state of New York, but to assume and exercise a distinct jurisdiction. The Green Mountain boys had no idea of surrendering lands for which they had given a valuable consideration, and New York, by grasping at too much, at length, lost the whole. Their determination to govern themselves was clearly foreshadowed in a convention held at Dorset as early as 1776. In 1778, a constitution having been formed, the first legislature met at Windsor Vt. Most of the settlers, on the New Hampshire grants in New Hampshire were from the state of Connecticut, and were more assimilated in their manners and feelings to the people of Vermont than to those in the eastern part of New Hampshire, consequently, when the legislature met at Windsor, fifteen towns in Grafton county, together with Cornish in the present county of Sullivan, through their agents, applied to the Vermont assembly for admission into Vermont as part of the state. When their petition was first presented, the Assembly was inclined to have nothing to do with it, but the agents were so persistent, and a portion of the representatives so determined on their admission, that the assembly

passed a resolution to refer the consideration of the petition to
the several towns for instructions, which should be presented
to the next assembly, which was to meet the following June.
When the assembly met it was found that thirty-seven of the
forty-nine towns represented were in favor of their admission.
The assembly did not inquire into the matter any further, but
proceeded to pass a resolution by a small majority, admitting
the sixteen towns with power to send representatives; and also
resolved that other towns wishing to join them might do so by
securing and producing a vote of the majority of the towns applying for admission. The assembly soon found that it had
taken a false step through the misrepresentation of those who
had the matter in charge. It was represented to the assembly
that the state of New Hampshire would not notice the movement, and also that the petitioning towns were unanimous in
their votes to be annexed; whereas, in some towns, a bare
majority was procured in the most unscrupulous and underhanded way.

In the following August, Meshech Weare, the then Provincial President of the State of New Hampshire, wrote to Governor Chittenden of Vermont, setting forth the claim of New
Hampshire to her jurisdiction over those seceding towns, and
animadverting severely on the course Vermont had pursued.
The sixteen towns informed the governor of New Hampshire
of their proceedings and requested a correspondence on the
subject; but no information is obtained that any reply to their
overtures was ever made to them. The seceding towns justi-
fied their course on the following grounds; that the original
grant of New Hampshire was limited by a line drawn sixty
miles from the sea; that the lands west of this line were annexed to the province merely by royal authority and as that
authority ceased at the declaration of independence, the inhabitants of those lands had reverted " to a state of nature " and
might form such political connections as were most convenient.

At the autumnal session of the Vermont assembly only a
part of the sixteen towns were represented. They requested
to be organized into a new county or to be annexed to the one

adjacent in Vermont. The assembly had just learned that
Congress, to which President Weare had communicated the
proceedings of the Vermont assembly, was opposed to such
encroachment on the territory of New Hampshire, consequently those sixteen towns received no favor from the assembly,
and, moreover, the assembly began to realize that the course
it had heretofore taken would have an adverse effect on the
admission of the State into the Union, the consummation of
which was very much desired by the people of that State. The
representatives of the seceding towns, on being so summarily
repulsed, withdrew in disgust together with a considerable
number of towns on the west side of the river also, leaving
the assembly with a bare quorum to do business. These with-
drawing towns organized and agreed to call a convention at
Cornish on the following ninth of December.

This convention, when assembled, concocted various schemes,
which were to be tried, and, if not successful, it was in favor
of forming the county adjacent to Connecticut river, which
was to include the whole region between the Masonian line on
the east, and the Green mountains on the west, into an independent state, and locate the capitol somewhere on Connecticut
river in the vicinity of Hanover; but as will be seen the whole
proceedings of the convention proved abortive. Matters at
this time had become pretty well mixed up, and the most intense excitement prevailed on both sides of the river, Vermont
sharing the greatest amount of perplexity. It required the
most astute wisdom and caution on the part of her leading
men to know what course to pursue, under such perplexing circumstances. One party was bound to dismember New Hampshire, another to annihilate Vermont, a third party adhering to
the State of New York, while a fourth was desirous of forming
a new state out of all the western New Hampshire grants.

Among the resolutions passed at the Cornish convention
was one which gave the Vermont assembly great uneasiness,
the substance of which was this; "That the State of New
Hampshire should extend her protecting wing over *all* the
western New Hampshire grants." This resolution was present-

ed to the assembly of New Hampshire and in due time adopted, with the promise that they would abide the decision of Congress in relation to the disputes that were pending in relation to the boundary line. Thus it is seen that New Hampshire had given the cold shoulder to her Vermont friends.

The assembly of Vermont, at its session in February 1779, after discussing the union that had been formed, and wishing to conciliate New Hampshire, which she felt had been wronged, passed a resolution "That the said union be and hereby is *dissolved* and made totally void, null and extinct, and that the governor be and hereby is, directed to communicate this resolution (accompanied with the proceedings of the assembly in relation to the seceding towns) to the president and council of the State of New Hampshire." The papers were transmitted to the president and council of N. H. by Ira Allen. Thus it is seen, Vermont was placed in a humiliating position, well nigh losing her existence as a state. Her only hope was that Congress would interfere and make her the fourteenth state in the union. Vermont had now divorced herself from the entangling alliance which she had formed with the sixteen New Hampshire towns, and it would seem that by her exercising patience and discretion, after awhile, those perplexing troubles might be brought to a settlement; but agitation and strife had gone so far, and the several parties were so persistent in their views that peace and quiet were out of the question. The question of settling the boundary line, and the troubles which were incident to it, had been submitted to Congress by both parties, and some movements had been made to that end; but Vermont was adverse to its proceedings, for reasons which will be hereafter mentioned. The Revolutionary struggle was still pending, and Congress was absorbed in measures pertaining thereunto, but it cannot be denied, according to the public transactions in relation to the affiair, that a dilatory disposition was manifested in pushing the matter to a settlement. But in the meantime resolutions of an advisory nature had been sent to Governor Chittenden and others, leading the people to believe that something would be done in due time. Such a sense of uneasiness prevailed throughout the whole region embraced in the New Hampshire grants, and hope had so sickened on account of the delay of Congress, that the people once more took the matter into their own hands. The most palpable reasons for the people's so doing were, first, that Congress, in dealing with the matter, had wholly ignored the existence of such a municipality as the State of Vermont, and had treated her agents only as men, and not as accredited delegates of an organized state. The people of Vermont had been active during the Revolutionary war, and patriotic, and their exertions in the northern frontier towns had been a potent barrier to the common enemy, the British. Under such circumstances the treatment they had received by Congress, was almost sufficient to cause them to relinquish all efforts for liberty in the common cause. The Vermonters not only felt deeply grieved but manifested a decided aversion to Congress. In the second place the settlers in the south-east corner of the state of Vermont had long been waiting with painful anxiety for some decision, hoping it would be favorable to the claims of New York, for in that portion of the state the inhabitants were mostly New York adherents. New York had virtually lost all jurisdiction over the eastern portion of the state, and the New York adherents had no inclination nor disposition to affiliate with those who had formed a state government; nor was there any protection offered to them by the state of New Hampshire. They were in a condition where no just legal remedy nor protection could be obtained. No wonder, then, that they should make the first move, hoping in some way to better their condition. Not only the New York adherents, but a large majority of the settlers living on the western grants, were in favor of some change in their municipal regulations, believing, that any change in their condition would redound to their benefit, for as they viewed their unstable and unhappy position, nothing could be worse, but precisely what that change should be no one had a definite idea, since, by a resolution of Congress passed on the 27th of Sept., 1780, the further consideration of the question respecting the jurisdiction of the New Hampshire Grants had been postponed, and the prospect of a settlement seemed no nearer a consummation than at the beginning. At this juncture a few leading men from three counties, by previous agreement, met at Charlestown, New Hampshire, Nov. 8, 1780, for interchange of views, and also to initiate some movement to better their condition. The New York adherents were foremost in this movement. At this informal meeting there was so much unanimity of sentiment that it was determined to call a more general convention at Walpole on the fifteenth day of the same month. The convention, when assembled, appointed a committee of the most influential men in the convention to confer with the delegates from the different towns represented, and report the substance of the information gained, and also the sentiments of the delegates. General Benjamin Bellows was chairman of this committee.

The report of the committee recited, in substance, that a *union* of all the grants was necessary to insure peace and good order throughout the territory. This convention was in session two days, and, as there were not delegates present from all the towns embraced in the New Hampshire Grants, it was thought advisable to call another convention to be held at Charlestown, N. H. Jan. 16th, 1781, and that an invitation should be extended, by means of printed circulars, to every township within the limits of the grants, to send delegates. So far every thing had gone on smoothly in relation to the consolidation of the grants; but when it became generally known that a convention of *all* the towns comprising the New Hampshire Grants was to be held at Charlestown, the 16th of January, all the discordant elements were aroused. The leading New Hampshire men were boisterous and exultant over their success so far in the contemplated movement for the consolidation of the grants. They were busy in the intervening time, between the announcement and the holding of the convention, in circulating documents and exercising all the influence that could be brought to bear to further their scheme.

In the meantime those who had been New York adherents,

were active in propagating their views, which were to unite all of the territory west of the Masonian line to the top of the Green mountains into a municipality; the leading men, no doubt, indulging in visions of a seat in the gubernatorial chair of a new state, or of holding some high office of dignity and emolument.

The adherents of the Vermont government looked upon the movement of both parties with feelings of disgust and indignation. They felt like a man about to die being forced to leave the accumulations of a lifetime to his bitterest enemies. However, they had men for leaders who knew how to pull down as well as to build up. Their energies at this time were directed in contriving some way to undermine the machinations of their adversaries. For this purpose they worked secretly, but with a determined purpose. At length the time for holding the convention had arrived and it was found that forty-three towns of the New Hampshire Grants had sent delegates, and the meeting was organized by the choice of Hon. Samuel Chase as Chairman and Bezaleel Woodward as Clerk. A committee was chosen, Benjamin Bellows of Walpole being chairman, to draft a statement embracing facts in relation to the unhappy condition of the people living on the New Hampshire Grants, and also to recommend such measures as they thought would be conducive to their welfare. The report is very long, able and exhaustive in relation to the subject that called the convention together; and it closes with a recommendation to form and consolidate a *union* of the grants and, also, to confer with the assembly of Vermont at its next session on the subject of an union. Also, an invitation was extended to those towns which were not represented in the convention to join them. This report was accepted and adopted by a large majority.

Thus far the proceedings of the convention had been one of unanimity of purpose, but during the session on the second day the sentiment of the convention underwent a radical change. Instead of confering with the Vermont assembly a resolution was passed that all the grants on the west side of

Connecticut river should be annexed to the government of New Hampshire, which virtually annihilated the state of Vermont. The New Hampshire delegation were in high spirits over their achievement, and had a long and late jollification during the night succeeding the passage of the resolution, never dreaming what the morrow might bring forth.

Ira Allen, one of Vermont's most able and astute schemers, had been employed by the governor and council of Vermont to attend the convention, and had also, been accredited from Sunderland as a delegate; but did not arrive until after the convention had been in session two days, and then did not present his credentials; but nothwithstanding his influence was potent through the night with some of the leading men of the convention in changing the whole aspect of affairs the next day. When the convention assembled the next morning a motion was carried to recommit the report to a committee for emendations, that it might be in a suitable form for publication. When the committee submitted the amended form of the report for adoption it was found that a clause had been inserted in it recommending the grants on the east side of Connecticut river to consolidate with Vermont, which was a great surprise to those not in the secret. The question on the adoption of the report in the amended form was put and carried by a very large affirmative vote. This change of front was the work of Ira Allen during the night previous.

Twice, now, through the intrigues of the leading men of Vermont, New Hampshire had been dismembered of their jurisdiction, and twice Vermont had well nigh become annihilated by the proceedings of unscrupulous men in New Hampshire and no good result had been the consequence.

There were twelve men in this convention belonging to the council and assembly of the state of New Hampshire, Benjamin Bellows of this town being one of the number, who were not inclined to remain silent and see the dismemberment of their state accomplished in such an underhanded manner, and consequently they withdrew, leaving with that body a short but vigorous protest against such proceedings.

When the convention closed its session at Charlestown it adjourned to meet at Cornish on the first Wednesday of February 1781. When met plans were discussed in detail on measures to be submitted to the Vermont assembly for their adoption, in relation to the courts, the appointment of officers and everything necessary to be done in conformity to the new relations they were about to assume. The Vermont assembly was now in session and the Charlestown resolutions on annexation were presented for consideration. At the same time a petition was submitted from towns lying west of the Green mountains, now belonging to New York, for annexation also. Both applications were considered and acted upon in the following manner. "That the legislature of the State do lay a jurisdictional claim to all lands situated east of the Connecticut river north of Massachusetts and south of latitude forty-five, and that they do not exercise jurisdiction for the time being." A like claim was also recommended to extend to the " Hudson river, east of the center of the deepest channel in said river to the head thereof, from thence east of a north line, being extended to latitude forty-five, and south of the same line extending to Massachusetts ; embracing all the lands and waters in the place where this state now exercises jurisdiction, and not to exercise jurisdiction for the time being."

One of the provisions made by the Vermont legislature was that if two-thirds of the towns embraced in the grants desired annexation in the manner prescribed, then representatives from the annexed towns could take their seats, and the consummation of the consolidation would be ratified. The assembly adjourned to meet on the first Wednesday in April, and when met it was found that the necessary two-thirds were ready to join, including thirty towns on the east side of Connecticut river. One or two representatives, as the case might be, from each of the above towns, were qualified and took their seats at the adjourned session of the legislature, at Windsor, in April. Lieut. John Graves was the representative from this town. Vermont had now the "inside track" and although she had been very circumspect in her proceedings, yet, ere long, she

had reason to suspect that she had purchased an *elephant*, as
will hereafter be seen.

Immediately after the accession of representatives from the
east side of Connecticut river, the legislature commenced passing a series of acts in order to conform to the new order of
things, which were drawn up in such a manner as not only to
strengthen the confidence in those towns which had joined
but to allay animosity and inspire respect for the movement
in the towns that had not.

The assembly which had held its session at Bennington in
June 1781, in order to soothe the ill will which had been en-
gendered on account of holding the session at that place, and
to further a semblance of fairness, resolved to hold the next
session at Charlestown, the following October.

The representatives from towns on the New Hampshire side
of Connecticut river were as follows: Acworth, Peleg Sprague;
Alstead, Nathaniel S. Prentiss; Bath, Elisha Cleveland; Canaan, Thomas Baldwin; Cardigan, Sawyer Bullock; Charlestown, Dr. William Paige, Capt. Samuel Wetherbe; Chester-
field, Samuel King, Silas Thompson; Claremont, Benjamin
Sumner, Matthias Stone; Cornish, Wm. Ripley; Croydon,
Moses Whipple; Dresden, Bezaleel Woodward; Enfield, Bela
Turner; Gilsum, Ebenezer Deroy; Grafton, Russel Mason;
Gunthwaite, John Young; Hanover, Jonathan Wright, Jona-
than Freeman; Haverhill, Timothy Bedel Esq., Joshua How-
ard; Hinsdale, Daniel Jones; Keene, Isaac Wyman, Ezra
Stiles; Landaff, Absalom Peters; Lebanon, Elisha Paine,
Elihu Hyde; Lempster, Elijah Frink; Lyman, Nathan Hodges;
Lyme, Jonathan Child, Ebenezer Green; Marlow, Samuel Can-
field; New Grantham, Abel Stevens; Newport, Benjamin
Giles; New Stamford, Israel Mead; Orford, Davenport Phelps,
Eben Fairfield; Piermont, Thomas Russel; Plainfield, Francis Smith; Richmond, Silas Gaskell; Saville, Moses True;
Surry, Wolston Brockway; Walpole, John Graves, Jonathan
Hall; Westmoreland, Jonathan Cole, Archelaus Temple. At
a town meeting held in Keene, March 20, 1781 they "voted
not to unite with the Grants," but still the town was represented.

It has been said that Congress had had the matter of settling
the various claims under consideration for some time, and had

passed certain resolutions on the 7th and 20th of August, in relation to the matter; and the tenor of correspondence between some of the leading men of the nation, in relation to the boundary affairs, taken together, were not calculated to inspire the Vermonters with much confidence in the hope of being admitted into the union with a part of two states attached to her skirts. The Vermonters even went so far as to deny the power of Congress in the premises at all; and, moreover, if they felt disposed to submit to the suggestions of Congress to limit their boundary to the west bank of Connecticut river, they knew of no honorable way to shuffle off their late accessions, inasmuch as they had pledged their honor to protect them; therefore, they resolved to hang together and wait further developments. They were in a condition, that they could not accede to the resolutions of Congress if they would, and were in such a frame of mind that they would not if they could.

Courts were established by the Vermont government on the east side of Connecticut river and sheriffs appointed. When disputes were referred to the courts for settlements the parties sought the one they preferred; but when executive officers like sheriffs and constables attempted to exercise their functions and authority a collision was the consequence. Small clouds could be seen rising in the political atmosphere portending a storm at no distant time. Belknap, in his history of New Hampshire, says:

"Majorities in towns attempted to control the minorities and these were disposed not to submit, but to seek protection from the government with which they had been connected. At the same time and in the same place, justices, sheriffs and constables, appointed by the authority of both states, were exercising jurisdiction over the same persons. High words, party rage and deep resentment were the effects of those clashing interests."

Such a state of things could not last long without an outbreak, which was precipitated in the town of Chesterfield where a large majority of the people were adherents of the Vermont government. It appears that a small *coterie* of the

citizens of Chesterfield had assembled at the house of one
Nathaniel Bingham for the purpose of selecting some suitable
persons who would serve for Justices of the peace, and send
in their names to be appointed by the New Hampshire assembly, as the town had no civil nor military officer holding a commission under the laws of her State. This was in the fore
part of November, 1781. In the course of the evening, Samuel Davis, a constable holding a commission under the laws of
Vermont, came into the room with five other persons. Mr.
Bingham, probably well knew his (Davis's) business and accord-
ly treated him with coldness and indifference. Such treatment
exasperated Davis and high words followed between them.
Finally, Bingham told him he was busy with his company and
gave him to understand that his presence was not wanted.
Davis took the hint and left, not, however, before telling Bingham that he had a precept for one of the company. On the
12th instant, Bingham and one John Grundy, jr., who was
one of the company, were arrested for resistance to a properly
constituted officer of the state, and lodged in Charlestown
jail. The prisoners immediately drew up a petition to the New
Hampshire assembly, which was then in session, and caused it
to be delivered, praying for their release. The assembly
acted upon it the next day after its reception, and on the 27th
passed a general Act covering the whole ground where conflict of jurisdiction of the two States might occur, and also for
the mode of procedure by the executive and judicial officers appointed by the State of New Hampshire.

Col. Enoch Hale, who was then sheriff of Cheshire county,
a man of resolution and force of character, but whose education was nothing to boast of, was called upon to perform the
unenviable duty of releasing Bingham and Grundy from
Charlestown jail. He repaired to Charlestown without a posse,
and only armed with the laws of the State of New Hampshire.
When he arrived at the jail he was refused admission by the
jail-keeper. He made some attempts to break down the door,
but did not succeed. The next day he was arrested by a
Vermont sheriff and put under £500 bail or stand commit-

ted to appear at the next County court to answer for his attempt to break into the jail at Charlestown, N. H., for the purpose of releasing Nathaniel Bingham and John Grundy, Jr., prisoners. Although Mr. Hale's pride was somewhat *humbled*, in not being able to consummate his purpose, yet his resolution had undergone no abatement of force, for he immediately applied for and obtained a *parole* to visit General Bellows of Walpole, for the purpose of confering with him in relation to the kind of movement to be made, in order that he might obtain his freedom.

Mr. Hale returned to Charlestown immediately after his interview with General Bellows, and obtained the liberty of the jail yard and settled down, patiently waiting for something to turn up favorably in his behalf, at the same time consoling himself now and then with a mug of flip at the tavern kept by Abel Walker.

Soon after Mr. Hale's visit at Walpole General Bellows addressed a spirited letter to President Weare, setting forth the facts as above stated and deploring the humiliating position New Hampshire would be reduced to if she did not maintain her jurisdiction. He also advised him to raise a force *out* of the county of Cheshire, sufficient to maintain her authority in the western section of the state. President Weare, on the receipt of General Bellows' letter, called the Committee of Safety together and communicated to them the purport of the above named letter. The committee immediately issued orders to the brigadier generals of the state to call out the militia under their commands for the release of Col. Hale and others confined in Charlestown jail.

The sheriff of Washington county in Vermont being advised of the measures the Committee of Safety were taking in New Hampshire, took measures to call out the militia of Vermont in order to oppose force to force. Capt. Phineas Hutchins, Capt. Hooper (Levi) and Capt. Bundy of this town were called upon to resist the laws of their State. Matters had now ripened into a condition in which a collision of armed forces seemed inevitable, but wiser counsels prevailed. The public officers of both states wrote frank and considerate letters to each other; both parties deploring a collision and counselling conciliatory measures till such times as the heat of passion had subsided and wiser counsels could prevail.

Although both parties had counselled peaceful measures, still New Hampshire, through the Committee of Safety, was one day giving orders to the militia to march, and the next day countermanding the same. Commissioners were sent from Vermont to Exeter to see if some plan could not be devised for the settlement of the difficulties. The Washington county sheriff, one Dr. Paige, was one of the three commissioners and on their arrival, he was immediately brought before a committee of the House of Representatives, and interrogated in relation to the position he held with the two conflicting governments, when it was found that he held the commission of sheriff under the laws of Vermont, and had exercised the functions of his office in Cheshire county, whereupon he was arrested and committed to jail in Exeter to await his trial at the next session of the Superior Court. He was not allowed bail, being held as a hostage for Hale. Several other persons were arrested about the same time for the part they had enacted growing out of the conflict of jurisdiction. In several cases outspoken people, belonging in New Hampshire, and living in towns where the majority were in favor of Vermont, were obliged to flee from their homes and families and seek shelter in the neighboring towns.

Following are two letters, one written by Joseph Burt of Westmoreland and the other by Benjamin Bellows of this town, portraying the troubled condition of society at that time.

" Honored Sir :

This moment two men from Chesterfield, who made their escape from the mob, who, after they had rescued Samuel King from the officer, returned to Chesterfield and apprehended Lieutenant Robinson, and two others, whom they determined to treat according to the custom of Vermont; that is by whipping them. Whether they will realy venture upon this business is very uncertain to me. But they have actually driven many of the good subjects of the State from their homes in this cold night.

Mr. Bingham's son is one of the men that have come to my house for shelter, who I have this account from, who expected to have found his father here with another man who made their escape. They have not been here and I am some concerned for them. The triumphs of the Vermonters are great and say that New Hampshire dare not come like men in the day time, but like a thief and steal a man or two away. Your honour cannot be insensible of our situation.

I would not wish to dictate, but pray that something may be done that shall be for the relief of the good subjects of this part of the State. I thought it my duty to inform your honor, as it is not likely that any other person will be informed that will write to you by the post."

I am sir your honor's
most obedient and humble servant,
JOSEPH BURT.

Hon. President Weare Esq.

Westmoreland, Jan. 1st, 1782, at 12 o'clock at night.

N. B. You will excuse the writing; being called out of bed in a cold night."

Benjamin Bellows to President Weare.

"Walpole, Jan. 2, 1782.

Sir. I have often troubled you with a narrative of our distresses and difficulties in this part of the State. Notwithstanding, I presume you, and the rest of honorable committee of safety, will exercise your wonted indulgence, while I give account of some new difficulties arising upon the officers attempting to convey one Samuel King, of Chesterfield, to Exeter, which rescue you will have an account of before this reaches you. Upon the return of the mob, after proper refreshments at said King's, they sought for all those persons who were any way concerned in assisting the aforesaid officer; some of whom they got into their hands and have abused in a shameful and barbarous manner, by striking, kicking and all the indignities which such a hellish pack can be guilty of; obliging them to promise and engage never to appear against the new State again, and that is not all; they swear they will extirpate all the adherents of New Hampshire, threatening to kill, burn and destroy the persons and property of all who op-

pose them; that the friends of this State cannot continue at
said Chesterfield with their families, but are obliged to seek
an asylum in other towns among the Hampshire people. I
have two respectable inhabitants of said Chesterfield now
sheltering themselves under my roof, who, I have the greatest
reason to think would be treated by them in a barbarous manner were they in their power, as they have stove in doors and
broke up houses in search of them. I am credibly informed
that there is in said Chesterfield about one hundred persons
who support said King, * * and say they (New Hampshire) can do nothing only in a mean and underhanded way;
in short, they defy all the authority and force of the State, and
are determined to support and maintain their ursurped authority, maugre all attempts that have or shall be made to curb or
restrain their usurpations. The wrath of man and the raging
of the sea ,are in Scripture put together, and it is in He alone,
who can rule the latter and restrain the former.

I hope and trust the Author of Wisdom will direct the honorable Committee to such measures as will ultimately tend to
the pease and happiness of this part of the State, and especially those adherents of New Hampshire, who are in a sense suffering for righteousness' sake.

I am with all esteem and respect
Your most obedient and humble Servant,
BENJAMIN BELLOWS."

It appears by the foregoing letters that a troubled state of
political affairs existed at this time of which the present generation can form but a very imperfect idea. From diligent
search there is no evidence of any outrage having been committed in this town. Probably one reason for the quiet demeanor of the citizens was the controlling influence of General Bellows and his kindred over the town's people, although at
one time, as has been seen, a majority was in favor of the new
State, many of whom were leading families—the Hoopers,
Hutchinses, Halls and Graveses, were among them.

General Bellows and others living in Cheshire County, were
informing President Weare of the condition of affairs, and appealing to the New Hampshire government for immediate action in sustaining her laws and jurisdiction. The committee
of safety was vacillating in its course and no one knew what

to expect. Through information gained by Ira Allen, the government of Vermont was informed that New Hampshire, before making any hostile movements, was to seek the advice of Congress, through an agent appointed for that purpose. Whiton, in his "Sketches of New Hampshire" says that the government of New Hampshire issued a proclamation requiring the revolted towns to subscribe within forty days an acknowledgement of the jurisdiction of the State of New Hampshire, and ordered the militia to hold themselves in readiness to march against them in case of refusal. After repeated vacillating movements on the part of New Hampshire, it was finally decided to raise an armed force of one thousand men, to be sent into Cheshire county to support civil authority there. Vermont now began to see her position through different lenses from those she had been wont to use. She clearly saw that if she pursued and maintained the course she had it was a mere question of time when the problem would be settled by the intervention of Congress, or by an attempt to maintain jurisdiction by the arbitrament of the sword. She clearly foresaw that the longer she continued in her present attitude the more remote would be her chances of being admitted into the union; that an attempt to try Col. Hale on New Hampshire soil would result in disaster; and more than all she had become weary of fighting foes within and without her borders. At one time the idea was entertained of taking Col. Hale to Bennington for trial; but the way was not clear in that direction. Finally it was thought that no good could grow out of detaining him longer and some plan must be devised to get him out of the way.

In a letter to President Weare, Mr. Hale graphically describes the manner in which he was released from his confinement. The letter is quoted in full, and cannot but interest the reader, as showing the character of the man.

"Walpole, January ye 11, 1782.

Sir:—"I once venture to trouble your Hon'r with a few lines, as I think it my duty to give the Earliest Intilligence in my Power of the Conduct of the People in our unhappy County. Sir, as General Bellows has Rote I shall Omit many things that I should otherwise have mentioned. Could only wish to mention the perticular circumstances of Esq. Giles being Resqued from me a second time—and to give the True Character of the Inhabitants of the Town of Charlestown, where we are under the disagreeable necessity of Holding Two Courts in a year without the least help from them or any Town in that Quarter, Respecting juriors, &c.—and have to undergo the further mortification of well know Combinations Consulting the *ocer-through* of our Courts and the Imprisonment of the officers of the same,—but any further on that head I forbear.

Sir :—I have had great opportunity of hearing the People in that Part of the County finding fault with Every member of our General Assembly—when they have thought the Militia was coming up, they said, why should the People all suffer for the Rash Conduct of some of there Civil officers, and seamed to condem the measure, they had taken—but when theAssembly seamed to comply with their own wishes, they must still find fault and said, why do they make night work of it—let them come like men by day light and they would not met any difficulty—but still I find that what don't sute the will Can Never sute there hand—it happened on the 10th instant that I took Esquire Giles about Twelve miles up the River, and Brought him down to Charlestown in open day light and on my arrival, just at Evening, the People Collected and arrested him out of my hands in a most Extroydinary manner, and all deaf to my Commands for assistance Notwithstanding many were Present that had been our pretended friends—they soon after held a Consultation for taking me and carrying me to Bennington, but fearing that would not so well sute they sent there Judas to advise me, as a friend to make my escape immediately, to avoid going to Bennington. I gave for answer, that if that was there intention I would Tarry all Night. But in the morning I had a second message, that they would be ready for me in half an hower. I gave for answer that that would be time enough for me to take breakfast which I then called for, and after breakfast I had a third message, that if I did not make my Escape they would Catch me before I got three miles, for which he should be very sorry. I gave for answer, that I should have the Less way to com back—but if I was not molested I meant to set out for home soon—but finding that all these strategies would not Prevent my Taking breakfast and leaving Town in an open and Public manner, they then Rallied all there force that was Near at hand to the amount of about forty men and a Pretended Dep'ty Sheriff at there head, but for a front Gard they Raised some of there most ablest women and sent forward with some men dressed in woman's appareil, which had the Good luck to Take me Prisoner,—Put me aboard of one of there Slays and filled the same with some of there Principal women and drove off nine miles to Willan Tavern, (probably Wightman's) in Walpole; the main body following after with acclimations of Joy, where they Regailed themselves and then set me at liberty, nothing doubting but that they had intirely subdued New Hampshire.

Sir, you Pardon me for Righting this Extroydinary letter. I should not have done it, had I not been desirous that Plain facts of there Conduct might be known. Som go in fear, and all Good subjects of New Hampshire Grone under ther burthen —it has become a serious matter and a Remedy much wanted —and in full belief that the wisdom of the General assembly will be sufficient to direct them I Rest assured and remain your Honour's most Obedient and most Humble Servant.

ENOCH HALE.

Hon'ble Mesech Weare Esqr.,"

After the Col. had somewhat unburdened himself in writing the above " *Extroydinary* " letter he seems to feel that his position in the community is an important one as the following letter written the next day will fully show.

" Marlborough, January ye 12, 1782.

Sir :—I am now returning home to see my family which I have not seen since the 26th of Nov'r : I may Not Expect to Tarry long with them as the outrages in our unhappy County increase with so much rapidity. I am willing, however to spend the remaining Part of the winter in the Servis of my Country, if I might be able in any degree to Relieve the distressed among us. Sir, I had forgotten in my letter of the 11th instant to inform your Hon'r that I never received any order from the Hon'ble Committee of Safety, as mentioned in the acts of the General Assembly of the Twenty-Eight of November, last past which has been a great hindrance in my progress; for after outrages had been committed I might have secured several of the Perpitrators of the same had all our good subjects been fully Convinced that my authority had been suffi-

cient, which I think would had a very great Tendency to
check these that have been so son of Resque in Prisoners.
     I am Sir, with much Respect,
          your Honour's most obed't Humble Servant,
                              ENOCH HALE.
Hon'ble Meshech Weare Esq'r."

The next move of the Vermonters was to dissolve the bond
of Union that existed between them and their New Hampshire
and New York adherents.   Gov. Chittenden of Vermont
wrote a confidential letter, to General Washington, Dec. 14,
1781, portraying fully the condition of affairs with candor,
frankness and much solicitude.   General Washington replied
to him with equal frankness, Jan. 1, 1782.   The correspondence was not official on either side.   Gen. Washington, knowing the sentiment of Congress in relation to the dispute, gave
the governor no comfort in his letter that Congress would
waver in the position that had been taken by that body on the
7th and 20th of August previous. This letter, coming from the
source it did, and the potency of the arguments adduced in
relation to the best mode of settlement, could not help to have
a weighty influence on Gov. Chittenden's future course and
proceedings.   The legislature of Vermont met according to
adjournment on the 31st of Jan. 1782, and proceeded with
the customary routine of business till the 11th of Feb., when
the question whether the union of the grants should be continued was brought before the assembly.

The resolutions of Congress on the 7th and 20th of August,
and the correspondence between Governor Chittenden and
General Washington were discussed in detail, *pro et con*, after
which a committee was appointed to bring in a resolution and
bill in conformity with an informal expression of the sense of
the assembly, which on the 23d were submitted to that body.
A vote was then taken whether the union should be *dissolved* or remain, which resulted in an affirmative vote.   Thus
an union from which no good had ever resulted, but much
evil, was forever severed.   The Vermont adherents on the east
side of Connecticut river were very indignant, and did not

cease to make trouble whenever and wherever an opportunity presented, for two or three years after.*

The Revolutionary war still continuing the town is very active in furnishing men and means to satisfy the demands made upon it. At this time (1781) seven men are wanted, as the town's quota, which it was not an easy matter to procure.

Although the inhabitants were sorely pressed on every side, in order to make their ends meet, still they are holding meetings several times a year to see about moving or finishing their meeting house, sometimes undoing what was done at meetings previously held, and at other times not being able to do any thing but adjourn, on account of the diversity of opinion. This matter continued to agitate the people, till at length the number of inhabitants outgrew the size of the meeting-house, when the question came up about building a new one. This subject absorbed the minds of the inhabitants for a year or more, and, after holding several meetings and discussing the subject, finally, in 1786, the town got a majority vote to build a new house, when a long time was spent in coming to an agreement where it should be located. Finally the town agreed to locate it on the hill near the house of Antipas Harrington, who lived on land now owned by Benj. E. Webster. To raise money for the purpose of building, it was agreed to sell pews by "Public Vendue," and it was stipulated that any person bidding off a pew should give bonds to a committee chosen for the purpose, for the payment of the same. The building of the meeting-house continued to absorb the attention and tax the resources of the town till it was completed.

The feasibility of building a bridge across Connecticut river, was considered visionary by the "knowing ones" when the subject was mentioned, and in those days it might have been considered a Herculean task, but Col. Enoch Hale, a citizen of Rindge, moved to Walpole in 1784, obtained a charter from the Legislature for a toll-bridge and erected in 1785 the first bridge that ever spanned Connecticut river. It was built just

* Abridged from History of Charlestown.

below the principal fall at Bellows Falls and connected Walpole with Rockingham. The "experiment," as many regarded it, attracted a great deal of attention at the time, and gave Col. Hale a wide-spread reputation. It remained the only bridge on the river till 1796. Its length was three hundred and sixty feet and its height above the water about fifty feet.

The next year (1786) the town voted to "set off to the town of Langdon all the land north of Mr. Atkinson's north line, from the east line of Walpole to Connecticut river, being about a mile and two hundred rods in width, reserving to Walpole "all the Public Rights to be forever freed from all taxes." The next year a petition was presented to the Legislature to re-annex that narrow portion from the Falls to the line of Charlestown to Walpole, which was granted. The probable reason for so doing was that the people living on the west side of Fall mountain would be better accommodated to remain in Walpole, than to belong to the town of Langdon.

The town in 1784 made an effort to sell the Public Rights above mentioned to pay Mr. Fessenden's salary for the "year ensuing," and appointed a committee to make the sale; but having some doubts about the right to sell, the town vote to "save the committee harmless."

From 1786 to 1790, no particular business worthy of note was transacted by the town except an effort was made to collect a minister tax of those belonging to the Baptist denomination, which proved impracticable, and the town withdrew the suit and paid the cost.

FROM 1790 TO 1800.

The first United States census was taken the first year of this decade and the town was found to contain 1248 inhabitants. The meeting-house was now completed, and it will be seen by the names of those who purchased pews, that the descendants of nearly one-half of those men are still living in town, either as children, grand-children, or great grand-children. Following are the names of those persons who purchased pews in the meeting-house with the number of pews purchased affixed to their names :

FIRST FLOOR. Geo. Sparhawk, 1; Isaac Bundy, 1 ; Roger Walcott, 1 ; Benj. Bellows, 13 ; Daniel Whipple, 1 ; David Hogg, 1 : Samuel Trott, 1 ; Asahel Bundy, 1 ; Jonas Hosmer, 1 ; Ephraim Stearns, 1 ; Asa Gage, 1 ; Thomas Bellows, 1 ; Joseph Griswold, 1 ; Minister's pew, 1 ; Thomas Fessenden, 1 ; John Jennison, 2 ; Amasa Allen, 3 ; Roger Farnham, 1 ; John McFarland, 1 ; Abraham Holland, 1 ; John Dennison, 1 ; John Graves jr., 1 ; Jona. Royce, 1 ; John French, 1 ; Levi Hooper, 1 ; Josiah Goldsmith, 2 ; Christopher Webber, 1 ; John Bellows, 2 ; Thos. Sparhawk, 2 ; Const. Gilman, 1 ; Nathaniel Baker, 1 ; Nathan Bundy, 1 ; Eliphalet Fox, 1 ; Nathan Dennison, 1 ; Nicanor Townsley, 1 ; John Flint, 1 ; Jona. Jennison, 1 ; Thomas Parker, 1 ; Sylvanus Titus, 1 ; Manoah Drury, 2 ; Levi Hubbard, 1 ; Dr. Kittredge, 1.

UPPER FLOOR. Daniel Merriam, 1 ; James Eastman, 1 ; Elisha Fullam, 4 ; Benj. Flood, 1 ; Amos Butterfield, 1 ; Daniel Denison, 1 ; Nicanor Townsley, 1 ; Col. Bellows, 2 ; Benj. Bellows, 1 ; Peletiah Hall, 1 ; Manoah Drury, 3 ; Jonas Hosmer, 1 ; Timothy Eaton, 1 ; Abraham Holland, 1 ; Const. Gilman, 1 ; Jona. Hall jr., 1 ; Isaac Bundy, 1 ; John Jennison, 1.

It will be seen that Gen. Benjamin Bellows purchased fourteen out of the seventy-four pews, showing clearly that he had no niggardly spirit about him. Manoah Drury comes next, being the purchaser of five, and Elisha Fullam, four, a person of whom no trace is discovered.

The Revolutionary war being ended, the constitutions of the United States and the state being adopted, and the boundary line being settled, the people began to feel more hopeful and cheerful, and perhaps it would be interesting to take a view of the appearance of the village in 1793 and perhaps somewhat earlier. It is said Col. Bellows intended the village of the town should be located near his own house, but from some cause or other, settlements had crept down the river to such an extent that a small village had grown up without any ulterior intent, the settlements being confined mostly to Main street. Beginning at the old parson Fessenden house, (now Justin Farr's) and going south, the first house that was met with

at that early period was Thomas Sparhawk's, on the site of
Mrs. Benjamin Grant's. About opposite, a little east of Thomas C. Sparhawk's, Samuel Trott lived, whose name is met with
frequently in the town records as a town officer. The next
was the Mead house so called which used to stand just in front
of Mrs. Ephraim Holland's, and where Thomas Collins Drew
lived when first married, and opposite was the first school
house built in town, now the residence of Moses Q. Watkins.
The next building was a tannery, just north of the residence of
Levi Foster, belonging, it is said, at one time, to David Stevens,
and afterwards to Daniel W. Bisco, whose house stood where
Foster's garden now is. Opposite, about where H. A. Hitchcock's house now stands, was a bakery. The house where H.
Allen now lives is supposed to be the oldest in the village ;
but by whom built is not known. About opposite was the
old Johnson tavern, now occupied as a dwelling by F. A.
Wier. One Caleb Johnson built it and the next building
south, which was long occupied as a store, then as a hatter's
shop and for some years as a shoe manufactory, and finally by
H. A. Hitchcock for furniture &c. Opposite was a tailor's
shop where one George Cochran carried on tailoring business.
The Wentworth House, owned by John Crafts, was in existence at that time and called the "Crafts Tavern." The next
building opposite and now owned by George H. Holden, was, in
1793, the famous bookstore and printing office. If the amount
of business done at that time, holds any comparison with the
catalogue of books advertised for sale in the newspaper of that
date, it must have been a business of more than ordinary magnitude for a country town. The business was carried on by
Isaiah Thomas and David Carlisle, jun. They did quite an extensive business in book publishing. Here was printed and
published the first American novel which was honored with
republication in England. It was written by Royal Tyler of
Brattleboro, Vt., and was entitled, "The Algerine Captive, or
The Life and Adventures of Dr. Updike Underhill, six years a
prisoner among the Algerines." The work was published
by David Carlisle, jr., in 1797. In 1801 a 12mo. work of three

hundred and eighteen pages was published, by Thomas &
Thomas, entitled "The Spirit of the Farmers' Museum and
Lay Preacher's Gazette," embracing all the poetry and spicy
gems and anecdotes contained in the Museum during several
years' publication. It is a literary curiosity, a copy of which
is in the possession of Mrs. Oliver Martin. The next building
south was Gen. Amasa Allen's store, business being then done
there under the firm name of Allen & Crafts. The building is
now owned by the Blake heirs. On the site of David Buffum's
brick store once stood an old two story wooden building,
which for many years was occupied for a store. It was burned
in 1859 and rebuilt in 1860. Further south, a few rods, the
ground was occupied by a building now the residence of Mrs.
Wm. Farnham, where Major Samuel Grant for many years
carried on the business of a saddle and harness maker, and
which afterwards was converted into a drug store, and kept for
many years by Deacon Thomas Seaver, till about the time it
was moved away. There was probably no other house on the
east side of Main street, till the foot of the hill south of the
Unitarian meeting house was reached, except where Mrs. Prentiss Foster now lives, which was built and occupied by Gen.
Benjamin Bellows. South of the Crafts Tavern, which was in
1793 advertised for sale by Samuel Mead, of Alstead, who had
married the widow Crafts and was guardian of her children,
stood a large building called the Great White Store, near
where B. F. Aldrich's house now stands, and a little west stood
a dwelling once occupied by a son of the ventriloquist, Potter.
The Abel Bellows house was built by Dr. Geo. Sparhawk, the
next by Amasa Allen, the next, which once stood where Dr.
W. B. Porter's residence now is, by David Stevens. It was
moved back west about forty years ago, and now is owned and
occupied by Mrs. Asa Titus. This house once went by the
name of the "Cochran house." The Wm. Buffum house was
once owned by Ebenezer Crehore and it is supposed he built it;
at any rate a deed shows that it was owned by him in 1786.
The original shape of all of these four houses was nearly the
same, with "gambrel roofs." Col. John Bellows built the

house which the Rev. H. W. Bellows now owns, and occupies as a summer residence. Up Prospect St. there were a few dwellings scattered along. The first was known as the Drew house and occupied by Thomas C. Drew; the next was the house now occupied by the Misses Maynard. It was then a one story house. The house where A. K. Maynard now lives was built very early, but by whom is not known. Jona. Livingston occupied it very early in the present century. The Caleb Bellows house now occupied by Moses J. Hale, was built as early as 1793, by Benj. Bellows, for his son Caleb. The next house was owned and occupied many years by Pliny Dickinson, though previously occupied by Eliphalet Fox. The house opposite, where Mr. Barnes now lives, was once owned and occupied by Oliver Sparhawk, who for many years had charge of the singing in the old church, and was also, at one time, a merchant in town. The next house was built by Stephen Mellish early in the present century. The old house was torn down in 1876, and John Selkirk has since erected a new house on the site. On the site of the house now occupied by Isaac M. Graves a house was burned some twenty-five years ago, which, for many years, was owned and occupied by James Campbell, who for a long time was Register of Deeds for the county of Cheshire which then embraced Sullivan county; and the old woodshed now standing on the premises was the Register's office. Gamaliel Huntington resided on the east side of the road. There might have been more than the Apollos Gilmore and the Pressy houses standing on the road before the meeting house was reached, but those enumerated were the principal ones in 1793. Near the meeting house (south) stood two houses, one occupied by Thomas Parker and the other by Antipas Harrington. A few houses may have been built west of Main street in 1793. If any the John Livingston house where John C. Brown now resides, the Mead house now owned by Oliver Martin and the Stephen Rice house where Mrs. Stoddard now resides were among the number. On the east side of Main street, on the site of the High School building, stood a distillery owned and run by Col. Caleb Bellows, where a large quantity of potatoe whiskey was made annually. The road from the village to the meeting house at or soon after '93 was shaded on either side by beautiful forest trees among which the Lombardy Poplar was conspicuous; but vandalism and the hand of ruthless time have swept them mostly away. Whether there was a post office at this early date it would be difficult to ascertain, as the early records at Washington were burned in 1836, but it is most certain there was one, as the Museum printed at this time (1793) speaks of receiving news by *mail*. Comparatively it must have done a small business, for, in the post office at Keene, two years later, when Asa Bullard was post master, the receipts for the first quarter of 1795 were only $1.36, and Keene was then a larger place than Walpole.

In 1793, Apr. 11, the publication of the famous " Farmer's Museum " was commenced by Isaiah Thomas and David Carlisle, (Carlisle was a native of the town and a freed apprentice of Thomas), with Joseph Dennie for editor. At the commencement the paper was called " The New Hampshire Journal and Farmer's Museum." The size of the sheet was eighteen by eleven inches, the paper was coarse and dingy, and the type inferior and old fashioned. Like other newspapers of that day, at its *commencement*, there were no elaborate original articles in it. Snatches of news, a few deaths and marriages, some foreign intelligence, a few lottery and other advertisements some poetical effusions, an essay or so, 'Spectator fashion, and some racy anecdotes made up the bill of fare. A few years later, however, the last page was surmounted with an engraving of a flower pot, and underneath was printed in large capitals " The Dessert." In 1796, Dennie became its conductor, and from that time he gathered around him one of the most brilliant corps of writers ever engaged to advance the fortunes of a similar undertaking in America. It numbered among its authors, each continually furnishing a department, the witty lawyer Royal Tyler, a man of acute mind and well directed powers; David Everett, Thomas Green Fessenden, Isaac Story and others whose abilities may be traced in its elegantly arranged folio pages. " The inventions of the pa-

per were endless." Poem, essay, criticism were served up with
the skill of a French cook compounding his hundreth varia-
tion of omelett. There were the "Farrago" the "Lay Preacher," the "Shop of Colon and Spondee," Peter Quince," "Simon Spunky," "The Hermit," "The Rural Wanderer," "Peter
Pendulum," "The Desk of Beri Hesden," and every trick of
alliteration to catch the negligent reader." *The Farrago* was
a series of essays full of warm apprehensions of the poetic
beauties of life and literature. The *Lay Preacher* was a series
of essays founded on texts of Scripture. The " Museum " like
all other things went into a decline, while poor Dennie was
calling on the public to subscribe and authors to write (for
fame), as if both were under equal obligation. The paying
days of American authorship had not yet dawned. Books,
even small duodicimos, were published by subscription with
humiliating "proposals" by sensitive authors. A notice to
" Readers and Correspondents " in the Museum, Dec, 4, 1797,
indicates its height of popularity, which is curious to contrast
with the claims of publishers eighty years later, by the million,
with the area of reading enlarged to Mexico and the Pacific:—
" The constant swell of our subscription book suggests a theme
to our gratitude and a motive to our industry. The Farmer's
Museum is read by more than *two thousand individuals* and has
its patrons in Europe and on the banks of the Ohio."

When the Museum was first started it was neutral in politics,
but in 1800 its political complexion was of the Federal stripe.
Its publication was suspended twice for a short time and was
revived for the last time in 1827, with A. Godfrey as editor, and
remained in Walpole eighteen months or so, edited by Nahum
Stone, from May 2, 1828, when it was removed to Keene, having then changed its political complexion, advocating Democratic principles. It is still published under the name of
' Cheshire Republican.' It was removed to Keene Nov. 14, 1828.

In the spring of 1794, there was a heavy frost destroying the
entire apple crop, the apples then, it is recorded, *being as large
as bullets*.

About this time Maj. Asa Bullard came to Walpole, and for

some years thereafter kept the once famous Crafts Tavern.
His house was the resort of a *coterie* of wags, wits and literati
from all the surrounding country; such men as Royal Tyler
of Brattleboro, Vt., who afterwards was Chief Justice of the
State; Samuel Hunt afterwards member of Congress; Samuel
West of Keene, a brilliant advocate, together with Jo' Dennie
of this town, Editor of the 'Farmer's Museum'; and Royal
Vose, who, also, was afterwards member of Congress.

The foregoing persons all belonged to a literary club who
wrote for the 'Museum.' There were others who occasionally
joined the above named coterie, such men as Jeremiah Mason,
Dr. Heilliman, Alpheus Moore, Dr. Spaulding and Maj. Bullard, who not only provided the good things for the inner man;
but was not the least among the party in merry making. The
old tavern, in those days, at those gatherings, was turned into a
literary pandemonium; wine drinking, late suppers, card playing,
joke cracking and the like formed the programme for frequent
meetings during the year; and the " wee hours of the morning were the only acknowleged signals for breaking up. The
good cheer of Maj. Bullard's house was known far and
wide, and all travellers wanting a good time made it a point to
stop at the Major's. Those wags were not content with cracking jokes on one another; but their shafts of ridicule extended to parson Fessenden, who was a diminutive man in size, and
wore a "cocked hat" and small clothes, which made him resem-
ble the "Jack of Clubs," and in consequence they dubbed him
" Old Palm," as the "Jack of Clubs" played an important
part in their favorite game "Palm Loo." Jeremiah Mason,
who afterwards became a distinguished lawyer in New England, was then a young man, just commencing practice here.
He was very tall, being some six feet seven inches in stature
and mal-formed, his legs being proportionately longer than his
body, and when seated in one of the old fashioned sleighs with
a high back his appearance was that of a small boy. On going over the hills to Keene one day, it is said, to attend court,
he met a burly teamster who was not disposed to give him
his part of the road. High words passed between them, and

finally the teamster threatened to whip him and was about to
put his threat into execution, when Mason began to elevate his
person from beneath the buffalo-robes to defend himself, and
as he rose up, up, up, the frightened teamster exclaimed "I
guess that'll due stranger, I'll turn out myself 'foré there's any
more on yer." In those days there was another set of men
living in town who used to, on all public days, congregate at
the Major's house and drink something stronger than wine,
and for amusement roll ten pins. They prided themselves on
their courage, bravado and strength; and after drinking till
their courage was wrought up "to the sticking point," if any
of the parties had any old unsettled 'score,' this was the time
for settling it by a free fight, when, in some instances, all parties became involved. On some of those occasions one Abraham Hall, whose avoirdupois was four hundred and twenty
pounds at the age of sixty, sometimes put in an appearance as
peace-maker, by taking the belligerents by the nape of the neck
and holding them asunder till their pugnacity cooled off. He
is said to have been the most powerful man, physically, that
ever lived in town. On one occasion he was driving a team of
oxen with a heavy load down a steep hill, when one of the bow-
pins came out and left one ox free to himself. At this juncture Abraham took the yoke upon his own shoulders and
"played ox" to the foot of the hill. On another occasion he
went into the woods with a team to haul home a stick for sled
runners. In felling the tree it rolled down a bank. The team
made several futile efforts to haul it up, Abraham grew impatient, unhitched his team and without help shouldered the log
and brought it on to level ground.

Such drinking bouts as above related were not wholly confined to old 'soakers' of that day, for Joseph T. Buckingham,
who afterwards became a famous journalist, relates, in substance, in his autobiography, that when sixteen years old, he
worked in the printing office of David Carlisle, six months,
in 1796, and that those days were the most unhappy ones of
his life. He says: "Before I was in the office two hours, I was
called upon to treat the whole crowd, on brandy, wine, sugar,

cheese, eggs and crackers." When they were told that he was not in the habit of drinking he was reproachfully taunted for not having manhood enough about him to get *drunk*. Drinking bouts were frequent in the office, nights, in which he was forced to participate, and when his money, which was but little, was all gone, he, being the youngest, had to do the errands for the rest, which paid his portion. He at length became so thoroughly disgusted with his life in Walpole that he left and went to Greenfield, Mass., where he found life more agreeable.

In 1795, the town purchased a bell for the meeting-house, which remained in the old tower till 1826, when the house was moved into the village. It was subsequently put into the tower of the new meeting-house where it remained for many years, and was rung at noon and at nine in the evening for many years, by Apollos Gilmore, who attributed his longevity, in a measure, to the healthful exercise. The old bell, which is still young in voice, speaks to us occasionally from the tower on the Town House.

> Full many a time its "ding a dong"
> Has called the farmer with its song,
> With quickened steps, that measured long,
>   Home to dinner.
> How many times its iron tongue
>   Has called the sinner!
>
> How many times that ancient bell
> Has sounded forth its doleful knell
> To mourning homes no one can tell;
>   But many a score.
> Its cherished tones long may they dwell
>   In memory's store.

In the "Museum," date June 20, 1793, is an account of a hurricane which passed over the northeast corner of the town, and exceeded in violence anything of the kind ever known in this vicinity. Five barns were entirely ruined and many others moved from their foundations. The dwelling of Col. Webber, (now the Geo. Jennings place) who lost two barns, was much damaged in the roof and windows. The windows of other

houses were much broken by the hail. Orchards were uprooted, flax and winter grain were wholly destroyed; spring
grain and grass were damaged and the wooden fences all laid
flat. The force of the wind was such as to lift naked
rafters from a new building, although firmly spiked down.
The closing year of this decade is said to have been unusually
cold during the winter. Snow fell about the middle of November and continued on the ground till late in spring. On
Mar. 30th it was three feet deep, in the woods. Such was the
condition of Walpole at the close of the eighteenth century.

From 1800 to 1810.

The town now contained 1743 inhabitants. The settlers on
Derry hill had made some progress in clearing up the land and
getting their homes in a comfortable condition to live in. A
man by the name of Reed was the first who settled there but
he did not remain long. Wm. T. Ramsay was the first permanent settler, who settled, in the early part of the last decade,
on what is now called the Harry Jennison place. He was the
grandfather of our townsman Wm. T. Ramsay. His brother-
in-law Jehoiada Moore felled the first tree on the farm now
owned by Alfred Watkins.

The settlers who followed Ramsay were John and George
Barnett, Thomas Moore, George Cochran, Matthew Dickey,
Daniel Marsh, and Manoah Drury, all from Londonderry,
(formerly Nutfield) in this state. This little colony, were
Scotch-Irish, their ancestors having immigrated from the
north of Ireland, except the last two. They were families
of frugal and industrious habits and sparing economy. By
their patient industry, in a few years, the forests were cleared,
and what is now impoverished land produced an abundance
for man and beast. Thomas Moore found his way to Derry
hill by marked trees. Derry hill formerly belonged to Theodore Atkinson and extended north on the Alstead line as far
as the Mark Webster place. A large tract of land in the
S. E. corner of the town, came into the possession of Gen.
Benjamin Bellows by his father's will, and afterwards passed

into the hands of Samuel Grant, by the marriage of the general's daughter. The tract in the vicinity is known at this time by the name of Carpenter's hill, although Davis Carpenter for whom the place was named was not among the first settlers. According to an ancient map of the south part of the town John Merriam, Josiah Goldsmith, who built what was formerly known as the Carpenter tavern, Pope and Darling who settled on the W. H. Scovill place, Barnabas Willey, who settled on the place first south of No. 8 school house, one Wright, who settled still farther south, and Ebenezer Crehore, were the first settlers. A little later one Adams, Joseph Mason, sen., and Capt. John Flynt settled there, Flynt on the farm now owned by Gilbert Stevens and Crehore on the farm now known as the Proctor place.

When those farms were first settled they were very productive, yielding immense quantities of hay, grain and potatoes. Whether the first potatoes raised in town were raised on Derry hill, is uncertain; but the first raised in New England, came from the seed brought from Ireland to Londonderry, by the immigrants to that place.

The third New Hampshire turnpike was completed in 1803, which opened better facilities for the transportation of the surplus products of those farms, and, for a time, business was quite prosperous on those hills.

About this time the apple orchards in town, which had been early set out, produced apples in abundance, which were made into cider. Every man had his orchard and every tenth man his cider mill. Every well-to-do farmer put into his cellar yearly from twenty to fifty barrels of cider which was all drunk on the premises. Col. John Bellows had an orchard of thirty acres,—the largest in town. In 1805, there were 4,800 barrels of cider made and every drop was drunk in town.

Neighbors who occasionally called on each other were always regaled with a mug of cider, and the boys and housemaids were pressed into the service of tending the spigot. When formal calls were made every man had to bring forth something stronger, or else he was stamped a niggard. Every well-

to-do citizen, in those days, had his sideboard, which was well
stored with various stimulating drinks.

At this time a famous lawsuit was pending in the courts between one Mrs. Norman as plaintiff and Samuel Wiers and
Moses Burt as defendants. A short time before the Revolutionary war broke out, an educated Irishman, Crean Brush by
name, and lawyer by profession, came to this country leaving
behind him in the care of relatives, an orphan daughter by
the name of Elizabeth.

After his arrival in America he married again, a widow,
who also had a daughter. Soon after he made his advent
into Westminister, Vt. His courtly manner, dash and ability soon won for him lucrative places of honor and trust in
Cumberland county, and, also in the State, although he was a
rank Tory both in sentiment and action. For several years he
ran an unscrupulous career in New York and various parts of
New England, and in the mean time got possession, by purchase or otherwise, of an almost baronial estate—some fifty
thousand acres of lands located in New Hampshire and Vermont.

Among the numerous tracts of land found in his possession
after his death was one lying in the south west corner of this
town, on which Samuel Wiers and Moses Burt had located in
its early settlement.

Brush committed suicide before the Revolutionary war
closed; and after his death it was found that he had bequeathed his landed estate in America, in equal shares to his wife, her
daughter and his own, Elizabeth. On his daughter's arriving at
maturity she married an Irishman by the name of Thomas
Norman, and soon after set sail for America to lay claim to
her property. On arriving she purchased the shares of her
mother-in-law and her daughter, thus becoming sole heir. She
soon found that her property in Vermont, through the instrumentality of Gen. Ira Allen, had been confiscated and irredeem-
ably lost; but she commenced a suit for the recovery of her
property in Walpole against Wiers and Burt, who by some
way were in possession. The suit was in court some twenty

years and was the theme of conversation in town and county
for a long period. In 1802 Wiers died and was buried on the
premises; people at that time believing that by such action
the heirs of the deceased party could hold the land. The suit
was continued by his son, John H. Wiers who was administrator
of his father's estate. After a while both parties became wea-
ried at the "law's delay," when the prosecution made overtures
to the defendants for a settlement, on the basis of an equal division of lands and costs. The case was then on trial. Mr.
Burt went to see Mr. Wiers the evening before the case was
decided, being anxious to settle the matter on the above mentioned plan, telling Mr. Wiers that "half a loaf was better
than no bread"; but Mr. Wiers was adverse to any settlement
only on the principle of "whole loaf or nothing;" Mr. Burt
was greatly disappointed, he having, during the continuance of
the suit, borrowed large sums of money to carry it on, and for
which he was then paying twelve per cent. He considered if
the suit went against them he would be well nigh ruined.
The next day the suit was decided against the defendants.
The defendants now, after having seemingly lost their *all*, became plaintiffs in a suit for the recovery of betterments, and,
after another long and tedious suit, recovered. Both parties
were thoroughly beaten, Mrs. Norman receiving less than a
thousand dollars, after paying expenses, out of her father's
enormous estate.

From 1798 till 1802 or 3 the small pox raged in town, the
extent of its ravages being throughout New England. Several times during those years an article was inserted in the town
warrant " to see if the town would build a pest house," but the
town invariably voted the proposition down. The inhabitants
were also reluctant in giving permission to have their families
vaccinated. Thomas Jefferson and some of the leading men
at Washington tried vaccination in their own families, which
proved efficacious, after which a general circular was issued, to
the people of the United States, setting forth its harmless effect on the patient and its potent effect in preventing the spread
of the dread disease. The physicians and some of the lead-

ing men of Keene also issued a similar circular, after which the inhabitants of Walpole, less fearful, allowed their families to be vaccinated and in a short time the small pox found no food to live upon.

In 1803 a new newspaper, called the "Political Observatory," and printed by David Newhall, was published here. The proprietors were Thomas C. Drew, Elijah Burroughs, Amasa Allen, Alexander Watkins and Jonathan Royce. Its first editor was Stanly Griswold, grand-father of our townsman H. W. S. Griswold. The paper was very ably conducted, supporting the Administration of Thomas Jefferson, while the Museum, at this time, advocated the principles of the Federal party which had held political sway in town from the time of the adoption of the United States Constitution. Thomas C. Drew, Elijah Burroughs, Amasa Allen, Alexander Watkins and Jonathan Royce cast, it is said, the first votes in town in opposition to the Federal party.

In the number of the Political Observatory of the 20th of October, 1804, is published an account of a heavy fall of snow, which covered the fall crops to the depth of three feet. Orchards were nearly ruined, one man estimating his individual loss at $ 300. The same year, Amasa and Oliver Allen's store was robbed of goods to the amount of $ 600, for the thieves of which they offered a reward of $ 500.

In 1805 several town meetings were held to see what could be done about supplying the pulpit, as parson Fessenden, on account of the infirmities of age, was no longer able to discharge the duties incumbent on him as the minister of the town. On the 18th of February a meeting was called for the above named purpose. It appears by the town records that Mr. Pliny Dickinson had been preaching to the old parish some time, as a candidate for settlement, and the town voted to give him a call to preach as a colleague of Mr. Fessenden, and to pay him $ 500 annually, "so long as he should be the minister of the town." They also voted to give Mr. Fessenden $ 175 a year for his future support. A committee was appointed to wait on Mr. Dickinson and inform him of the vote of the town. The offer did not meet with favor with Mr. Dickinson, he wanting $ 600 a year salary. The town did not accede to Mr. Dickinson's amendment and voted to defer further action till March meeting. It is infered that the town had become tired of delays, for a reconsideration of the vote to defer further action till March meeting, was moved and carried, and a new committee was appointed to wait on Mr. Dickinson and get an *immediate and final* answer. The matter had now come to a crisis;—it was "now or never" with Mr. Dickinson and he concluded to send to the meeting the following reply and acceptance.

Gentlemen:

Having received a *recent* communication from your committee, and having endeavored by seeking light and direction to discover the path of duty in respect to the call which you have been pleased to present me, I feel ready and inclined to bring the business to an immediate close. As in my former communications I expressed some doubts with respect to the permanent sufficiency of your offer, I would here observe that my confidence in your judgment as to the increasing expenses of living, your generous readiness in the late subscription, and the many public and private assurances of your liberal intentions, conduce me to make trial of your present encouragements,—in the meantime, however, I beg leave to promise myself, that I shall not be more ready to *receive* than you will to *grant* future assistance, I lately proposed; provided my future circumstances require additional aid. Persuaded I am, that you never think it a *hard* thing for one who sows to you in *Spiritual* things, to reap a sufficiency of your *carnal* things.

With these proposals before me, I, under a serious sense of most solemn duty, invoke the benediction of Jehovah, and publicly declare my acceptance of your call.

Pliny Dickinson.

The town voted to accept the above answer and he was settled colleague of Mr. Fessenden.

Parson Fessenden had been the minister of the town thirty-eight years, and had, by his public and private ministrations become endeared to almost every family in town. The old esteemed him for his learning and pleasant 'chat,' while the

young revered him for his age and sanctity. Many are the
stories told of his ministry and his congregation; how the
young people were wont to repair to their pews at the nod of
General Bellows, how the people sat and listened to his prosy
sermons on cold wintry days, without fire, till his sermons reached their fifteenthly, when a general review was had and then
completed with a summary; how the damsels would vie with
each other in singing the loudest under the direction of their
famous leader, Oliver Sparhawk, and how the pew seats would
rattle after the benediction, when all would repair to the tavern opposite, kept by Alexander Watkins, to warm up; how
the *worshippers* would form a semicircle round a blazing fire
in his large drawing-room and sip *flip* from a huge mug indis-
criminately, for "the stomach's sake," and how Uncle Alex.
would add an extra stick of fuel to the fire for every mug of
flip sold. In those days, it was not considered derogatory for
the 'cloth' to take a little something to give nature a jog, and
parson Fessenden was no exception to the fashionable rule,
which was done openly with his parishioners.

In 1807, the mail stage from Boston passed through Walpole three times a week to Hanover, thus affording a mail from
Boston every other day.

At this time the old heavy iron cannon which was given to
the early settlers by the king of England and used at Col.
Bellows' fort, was left unguarded on Main street. A party
from Keene, wishing to use it for a Fourth of July celebration, came to Walpole one night and surreptitiously took
it away. The whole population of the town became aroused
and very indignant at being over-reached in such a dastardly
manner, and determined to have redress in a legal way, and
accordingly arrested the delinquents and brought them to
trial in the County Court, Chief Justice Smith then presiding. The court decided that said cannon was not the property of the town of Walpole, and the defendants were discharged. Thereupon, the cannon was immediately loaded
to the muzzle and drawn in front of the Court house and discharged. Roger Vose was counsel for the plaintiffs, and on

hearing the report, immediately rose and addressed the Court, thus: "May it please your honor, the case is already *reported!*"

The irritation of the Walpoleans knew no bounds and they determined to have redress by taking the law into their own hands, and accordingly, on the eve of the fourth of July, 1809, they secured the services of a stage driver to go to Keene, with a heavy wagon, ostensibly for the purpose of purchasing grain. It had previously been ascertained that the cannon was hidden in a granary there. He bargained for some grain, and on pretence of wishing to start early the next morning, on account of the heat, and not wishing to disturb the clerk so early, procured the key to the granary.

Everything thus far had progressed to his liking, and he started towards Walpole to meet his comrades, and on arriving at Ash swamp, was met by a cavalcade of about thirty stalwart fellows, mounted on spirited horses, commanded by an officer of high rank, when he reported progress. They left their horses on a cross road fringed with bushes leading from Court to Washington St., and stealthily moved to the granary. The weight of the cannon, on its being moved, shook the surroundings like a "miniature earthquake, which awoke those persons living in the immediate vicinity, who soon discovered what was going on. The town bell was immediately rung and an alarm of fire was raised. The men in the granary for a time labored without success, while the people of Keene were seen flitting about from place to place, not knowing exactly what to do. At length, by a desperate effort, the old cannon was loaded, and the whip was put to the horses, headed towards Walpole. At break of day the old ordnance once more *spoke* to the people of its adoption, amid the cheering of a hilarious crowd.

In the meantime a party of citizens of Keene, mounted on horses, pursued the returning cavalcade, but, fortunately, by design or mistake, they took the wrong road, thus probably avoiding a desperate conflict. But the story of the old cannon is not yet completed, for afterwards the people of Westminster clandestinly took it for the purpose above mentioned to be

used the next day. When the people of the town found their
old favorite again missing they immediately summoned about
eighty stalwart fellows, none of whom weighed less than one
hundred and sixty pounds, and started, with the selectmen at
their head, for Westminster for the purpose of retaking it at all
hazards. They left the travelled road, and cautiously approached the village on the east side where there was a high
board fence, completely hiding the party from the Westminster folks. The Vermonters were busily engaged in loading
and firing, and at every report, would shout, looking towards
Walpole: "Do you hear that Walpoleans?" After our boys
had heard the same question put three or four times they si-
multaneously put their shoulders against the fence and in an
instant it was prostrate, the men shouting at the same time, in
answer: "Yes, we do hear it! and without parley, pounced
on the cannon, and wrested it from the Vermonters and
brought it away in triumph. The man who held the swab,
was reluctant in giving it up, whereupon one of the strongest
Walpoleans, seized one end and swung the Vermonter so high
in air that he was forced to relinquish his hold. It was afterwards taken by men from Alstead and, on firing it, being loaded heavily, with green grass for wadding, it *spoke* for the last
time, and its fragments were gathered and converted into im-
plements of peace at a neighboring foundery.

Several years before and at this time quite an extensive
business was carried on in town in the manufacture of potash.
In different parts of the town, the location of the asheries is
frequently discovered on moving the soil. One large estab-
lisment was near the residence of Allen Dunshee, and was
carried on by Joseph Bellows, who is found doing various
kinds of business in town about this time, such as mercantile
and public house keeping.

In 1806, West street was built and the old brick store, and
the year following a bridge was built across the Connecticut
river on the site of the present village bridge, which is said to
have been the third on the Connecticut. It was built by a corporation and the superstructure was on wooden piers. At its

completion the citizens had a great jollification, on the land just west of the bridge, playing ball, wrestling and drinking *blackstrap*. Before commencing their games a substantial crop of mulleins had to be cleared away, the land at that time bearing nothing better, and being considered of but little value.

FROM 1810 TO 1820.

At the commencement of this decade the town contained nearly the same number of inhabitants as at the present time, viz., 1894. Most of the early settlers, who had borne the heat and burden of the day, had now been gathered to their long homes; but many of their children remained on the old homesteads, in the full vigor of their days. The virgin soil produced plentifully, and all had the home comforts of life and ease. The drift of life was even and the occurrences worth recording were very few, and any little event that occurred varying from the general routine of life, was the theme of conversation for many months.

At this time, and for two or three years previous, the New England States, had witnessed the rise and spread of a singular disease, which was called the "spotted fever," but afterwards took the name of "malignant fever." This town was not exempt from its ravages and many homes were made desolate. The first indication of an attack was not infrequently a sudden pain in the extremities, quickly spreading over the whole system, and often terminating fatally in less than twenty-four hours. The disease was not thought to be contagious. In the spring of 1812 several children died of it. Among the number were two daughters of Wm. Watkins, Clarissa, aged sixteen, and Olive, aged fourteen, who were said to have been the most beautiful young ladies in town, a great stroke of affliction to the surviving parents. The following March, 1813, seven persons died of the disease, in as many days. Among the number was Daniel Carlisle, aged thirty-nine. The majority of the remainder were adults. The number that died of this disease in town cannot be definitely ascertained but it was large. The disease then called spotted fever is supposed to be the same as that now known as cerebro spinal meningitis.

In 1815, Mr. Amasa Tiffany, who lived in what is now called the Mead house, opposite the residence of Geo. W. Grant, had a cur dog which became rabid and bit David, a promising son of John Livingston. After an interval of a few days the boy, who was about eight years of age, began to show symptoms of hydrophobia, which increased in violence till he died. His death caused a deep gloom to shroud the family and neighborhood for a long time, and, years afterwards, the story of his death and sufferings was as familiar as household words among the inhabitants, it being the only case of hydrophobia ever known in town.

In 1812, war was declared by this Government against England, which lasted about two years, the scenes of strife being principally on the ocean and great lakes or removed far from the vicinity of New England, the people of this town did not participate to a very great extent. A company, however, went from this town to Portsmouth in the fall of 1814, consisting of the following persons, viz: Josiah Bellows, 3d, Captain ; Nathaniel Chapin, clerk ; Stephen Tiffany, corporal ; and James Priest, fifer. The following were privates, viz., Daniel Hubbard, Elisha Angier, Ephraim Holland, Ziba Lovell, Israel Brown, John Griggs, David Perkins, Samuel Ruggles, Abel Page, Ransom Lawrence, Willard Johnson, Nathan Conant, Benj. Miller, Gordon Beckwith, Thomas Nichols jr., William Wellington, Ebenezer Watkins, Frederick Scoville, Alfred Priest, James Sturtevant, John Bundy, John Marshall, Edmund P. Davis, Samuel A. Wightman and John Graves, servant. Those belonging to Capt. Warner's Company were Aaron Baker, Sergt., Wm. Lyman, 2d Lieut. The privates were Elijah Cooper, Prentiss Foster, Samuel Grant, Charles Kingsbury, Levi Leonard, Samuel Nichols, Luther Ripley, Charles Titus, George Way and Amasa Wheeler. This company was in service but a short time, and the trophies brought home and the laurels won were very few.

During the existence of the war, many articles of necessity

rose to fabulous prices, only being equalled by the prices during the late rebellion, it is said.

About this time, or a short time before, Josiah Bellows, David Stone and Josiah Bellows 3d, purchased the Boggy Meadows—a thousand acres—on speculation, and employed Thomas Cunningham and others to cut off the timber, which found a market in Hartford, and sowed a large part of the land to winter rye, in the fall of 1815, which probably was the largest field of grain ever seen in town, and the sowing that year proved a fortunate circumstance, as the next year, 1816, was the coldest season ever experienced in this vicinity, and, in consequence, the corn crop was a perfect failure. 1816 is well remembered by the old citizens as the cold season or " poverty year." The *mean* mercurial temperature was about 43°. Snow fell in June, and August was the only month exempt from frosts. The early frosts of September cut off the unripe corn, which some persons vainly tried to save by early husking and spreading. There was a heavy crop of English grain, otherwise the inhabitants would have suffered a partial famine.

FROM 1820 TO 1830.

Two thousand and twenty inhabitants were found in town by the census of 1820, the largest number at any period in the history of the town thus far. The soil produced abundantly and everybody found enough to do, but the prices paid in money for labor were comparatively small. Most of the business done at the stores and workshops was a barter trade. Everybody had enough to eat and drink, but to get money for labor and produce was a difficult matter. The orchards were annually loaded with common fruit, which was made into cider and sold for fifty cents per barrel, to be converted into cider brandy at the old distillery which once stood about fifty rods south of the Lucius Slade place. The distillers paid for their cider in cider brandy at thirty-three cents per gallon. Cider mills were located in different places all over town, and their groans in autumn, in crushing apples, could be heard half a mile distant, while the boys who scraped the nuts in cold weather,

cursed the day when the making of cider was discovered.
Cider brandy was cheap, nearly every family had a supply of it,
and it was thought by some that it was the great *panacea* for
all the ills and ails of life, and consequently a great deal of it
was used as a common beverage, which accounts for the unusual number of red faces and brandy noses seen about this
time.

In 1822, Jonathan Mason a wealthy citizen of Boston, Mass.,
purchased what is called the Boggy Meadow farm, eight hundred acres, for $15,000. It originally extended as far north as
what is now called the 'Track' farm, which was included in it;
east as far as the farm of Josiah W. Batchelder; south as far
as the southern limits of the land now owned by Henry J.
Watkins; and west to the river.

In 1823 Mr. Mason built a large barn on his place, which
was for many years considered the largest farm building in
these parts. It was sixty feet square in the centre, with a lean-
to on all sides, which made the entire building one hundred
feet square. It took eleven thousand five hundred and fifty-
nine feet of *square* timber for the beams and sills, and ninety-
seven and a half thousands of shingles to cover the roof. Recompense Hall and Joel Chaffin were the carpenters. It took
the united strength of three hundred men and five hours and
forty minutes time to raise it. It remained substantially as it
was first built till quite a recent period.

The annual cattle show was largely represented from this
town, in sheep, cattle, hogs and farming products—horse trot-
ting was reserved for a later and more *enlightened* day. There
were no Devon, Aderney nor Durham cattle in town—all were
natives. Stages from every quarter stopped at the old Crafts
tavern, in passing through on their stipulated daily trips, and
the passengers either supped, dined or were cared for in some
other way there. The Jehus vied with one another in the style
and care of their teams or the crack of their whips. At this
time David Stone was postmaster, and although an immense
amount of mail matter had to be overhauled at the post office
here, (it being then and many years after a distributing office)

still the amount of mail matter lodged in the office for town distribution was very meagre, it being all contained in a letter box the size of which was about three feet by two. Comparatively, there were a large number of stores in town, where goods were sold in exchange for farmer's products, such as butter, cheese, pork, lard, beef, and, also, productions of the household, such as mittens, socks, frocking, tow cloth, etc. Large quantities of such commodities would accumulate in the store of the merchant during the season, which the farmer considered his special privilege with the merchant with whom he traded, to transport to market in winter, one or two loads of such products, and load back with such articles as the merchant needed to replenish his store, for which the farmer received in payment a few dollars in money and the rest from the store. Many farmers who could procure a horse and *pung* were sure to make one or more trips to Boston during the winter, for the purpose of exchanging their own and neighbors' products for such articles as were needed for family use. They generally carried their own food, such as baked beans, doughnuts, cooked spare-rib, and brown bread, and, also, the oats for baiting their teams. So great was the number of such teams at times, that the more popular innkeepers found it difficult to accomodate them. After caring for their teams they resorted to the bar-room of the inn, where they always found an inviting fire in an open fireplace, when they would, after taking a little *flip*, draw forth from their buckets their home cooked viands and make their suppers, after which a little more flip, and sometimes with story telling it would be flip, flip, till the dying embers admonished them of the midnight hour. Generally the most the landlord got out of it was the profit on the flip and their lodging.

Most of the heavy goods of the merchants were purchased in Hartford, Conn., and brought up the river in *scows*; every trader, who sold groceries, and most of them did, kept all kinds of liquors for sale. They, together with the tavern keepers, sold immense quantities of spirituous liquors. New England rum appears to have been a favorite beverage. A man

now living in town states that "*fifty hogsheads* were sold annually at his store," and such a quantity was but a fraction of
what was sold in town.   A barrel was always "on tap," to be
drunk by customers, free, when they bought a small bill of
goods, at the store.   Blackstrap was only three cents a glass.
Being so cheap, men could, and did, for a few coppers, become
suddenly *rich*, in their imaginations, to be followed in a few
years, it may be, by the loss of a farm and abject poverty.
A large codfish, in many cases was suspended near the rum
barrel, on which hung a label requesting the pilferers to confine
their depredations to that *one* until the bones were bare.   It is
supposed the cod fish was eaten to create a thirst and relish
for a little more blackstrap.   In all the advertisments for the
sale of goods in country stores at that time *New England* rum
was printed with the largest type.   Happily for New England
a temperance reformation commenced before the close of this
decade.

Following are a few of the prices that various commodities
were sold at, not varying much for a number of years ; corn,
50 cents per bushel ; oats, 25 cents, do.; young beef, 2½ cents
per pound ; butter, 12½ do.; cheese 6 to 7 do.; pork, 4½ to
5 do., in Boston.   Board, among farmers, was $1.00 to $1.25 per
week ; at hotels, in the country, $1.50 to $2.00 do.; and rock
maple wood was $2.00 per cord.   Farm labor was from $10 to
$15 per month for six or eight months in the best of the season.
School teachers received from $1.00 to $1.50 per week of 5½
days, for females, in summer ; male teachers, in winter, were
paid, on an average, about $13 per month and board.   Some
of them had to 'board round' at that.   Plenty of good female
help could be procured from $1.00 to $1.50 per week.

In 1826 a new newspaper was started in town, which lived but
one year.   It was called "*The Cheshire Gazette.*"   In size and
general appearance it was quite respectable.   It was under the
editorial management of one Francis Parton.   The Farmers'
Museum was published here in 1823 and 4 by Hale and Moore
and then suspended till about 1827, when it was revived by
Nahum Stone and continued to be published in town till Nov.

14, 1828, when it was removed to Keene. Since its removal
to Keene it has had several different owners, editors, and
names. Mr. Stone was a shoemaker by trade, and when Mr.
John Prentiss, who for many years was editor and publisher
of the New Hampshire Sentinel, first learned that it was the
intention of Mr. Stone to establish himself in Keene he fa-
cetiously remarked, well knowing the hazard of such an en-
terprize, " I hope Mr. Stone will not lose his *awl*."

As early as 1815, an enterprise was commenced in town
which subsequently was prosecuted to a considerable extent.
It was the manufacture of sale shoes for the Southern market, and was commenced by Jonathan H. Chase, at the south
part of the town, on the premises now owned by one of
the Houghton brothers. Mr. Chase removed there, about
1815–16 from a portion of the town called "Lane's Mills,"
his first purchase in town ; and commenced the tanning business ; and, not finding a local sale for all his leather, he conceived the idea of manufacturing 'brogans,' thus using his
surplus leather. At the outset the business was conducted in
a small way, the work then being all *sewed*; by which it may be
infered that pegged shoes and boots did not obtain at that
time. Mr. Chase's shoes were consigned to his brother-in-
law J. B. Kimball, of Boston, who was of the firm of J. B.
Kimball & Co., and sold on commission. It was not long before pegged work came into general use, when the business
was prosecuted with energy, employing a large number of
workmen in town and out. During that decade, Jared Miller
was manufacturing boots and shoes for George Carlisle, a
Walpole man, who had established himself in Cincinnati, Ohio.
Mr. Chase having purchased the old Johnson tavern and store,
the latter as a place of business, removed his family and effects
to the village, in 1834, or about that time, and, in conjunction
with his two sons, Charles E. and Aaron K., continued the business for several years. In the meantime other shoe firms
were in operation which gave the town the appearance of a
miniature Lynn. Many of the shoemakers were young, unmarried men, who were a roistering, improvident set of fel-

lows, spending all their earnings and sometimes more, dressing in an extravagant style, wearing the highest priced Saxony broadcloths and other expensive material to match. Their wages were graded by their dexterity and application to business. The prices paid for bottoming 'brogans' ranged from twenty to twenty-seven cents per pair, and an expert workman could bottom from five to eight pairs per day. The business continued brisk till the financial crash of 1837, when it declined. The manufacture of boots and shoes, however, for the western market, was carried on by Amherst K. Maynard & Co., till within a recent period.

The following singular document is found in the town records of 1826. One singular fact in connection with it is that many of the names appended were afterward, if not then, some of the most thorough going orthodox church members living in town. Stephen R. Bradley's name is found among the number, who it is said, paid Mr. Dickinson's salary one year, from his own purse, after the disruption of the church and society:

"We the subscribers respectively, do hereby certify and declare, that we are *not* of the religious persuasion of the Rev. Pliny Dickinson, who is settled as a minister in the town of Walpole. In witness whereof we have hereunto set our hands this 31st day of January, A. D. 1826."

Abijah Bugbee, Asahel B. Hodskins, Joshua Marsh, John S. March, Clark Huntley, Reuben Dodge, Elisha White, Daniel Corlis, Daniel Clark, Stephen S. Johnson, Henry Jennison, David Thompson, Willard Hodskins, Jona. Emerson, Jesse Priest, John B. Sparhawk, Walter Sparhawk, John Moore, William Arnold, Jacob Tuttle, Daniel Marsh, Ezra Hixon, Edmund A. Marsh, Robert Barnett Frederick Johnson, Luther Fay, Benj. Davis, Hiram Watkins, Anson Lawence, Joseph Osborn, Stephen R. Bradley, Geo. Sparhawk, William Guild, Ethan Griswold, Moses Fisher, David Aldrich, Danforth Clark, Loren W. Clark, Geo. Flint, John Allen, Abial Williams, James Cresty, Charles Watkins, James Davis, David Cushing, Wm. Wellington, Nehemiah Wheeler, Jona. Cross, Luke Thurston, Samuel Morrison, James Stowell, Wm. Danforth, Josiah Simonds, Bela Frink, James H. Fuller, Mason Fay, Daniel Pratt, Geo. Bundy, Cyrus Dickey.

Oct. 6th 1826, the town " voted that the meetinghouse in the town may be moved on to lands south of the brick school-house and on the west side of the common in Walpole village on condition that the individual or individuals who may remove it shall give good and sufficient security to the town that the house shall be removed in one year from the first of December next and completely finished in good order, with the privilege of altering the steeple if they wish, and also procure for the town a good and sufficient deed of so much land situate as aforesaid as shall be convenient for setting said house and the building of sheds, and all this free of any expense to the town."

The following persons signed a bond, each man, putting a *seal* opposite his name, to the town for *ten thousand dollars*, that they would cause the meeting-house to be removed according to the above stipulations or forfeit the bond.

Thomas Bellows, Abel Bellows, Daniel W. Bisco, Jona. Cutler, Samuel Grant, Wm. Gage, Nathl. Holland, Jacob N. Knapp, Christopher Lincoln, Ebenezer Morse, Isaac Redington, David Stone, Josiah Bellows, Charles Stratton, George Watkins, Masey Adams, Dexter Anderson, David Mead, Daniel Gilbert, Samuel Mead, Elijah Kilburn, Leonard Bisco, Wm. Mitchell, John Carlisle, Hubbard Bellows Lovell Farr, Frederick Vose, Stephen Rice, Walton Mead, Daniel Brooks.

The house was moved by Col. Edward Glover of Alstead, and every piece was marked when taken down and put in its place when rebuilt. The Colonel often remarked in his old age that it was the most profitable job he ever undertook in his life. He was paid one thousand dollars for removing it.

Following is the protest of the legal voters of the town who were opposed to the removal of the meeting-house. It gives not only the names of those who were opposed to the removal, as showing the animosity prevailing, but the names of a large minority of the legal voters living in town at that time, eight of whom only are known to be living April, 1879. It is found in the Cheshire Gazette of Feb. 18, 1826, and is headed

PUBLIC NOTICE.

We, the subscribers, being inhabitants of the town of Walpole, and proprietors of the public meeting-house in said town, having taken into serious consideration the great and lasting damage and inconveniences, which in our view will be the consequence of the last vote of the town, to give liberty to certain individuals to remove said meeting-house into Walpole village, in case the said vote is carried into execution—do therefore most solemnly protest against the removal of said meeting-house. AND FURTHERMORE, We do hereby forbid the removal of the same into said village by any person or persons whomsoever.

Walpole, Feb. 7, 1826.

George Sparhawk, James Howland, Edward Baker, George Bundy, Roger Wolcot, Wm. Anderson, Manoah Drury, Isaac Jennings, Philip E. Bundy, James H. Fuller, Benj. Davis, Stephen Prentiss, William Guild, John B. Sparhawk, Samuel Morrison, Jeremiah Kittredge, Edmund A. Marsh, Thomas C. Drew, James Stowell, Willard Hodskins, Roger Fenton, Caleb Farnham, Marvin Royce, Henry Cram, J. Kittredge, jr., David Cummings, Z. W. Lovell, Levi Fay, Nehemiah Wheeler, Levi Powers, Mason Fay, Luke Thurston, Josiah Simonds, Ethan Griswold, Bela Frink, Gardner Watkins, Luther Knowlton, Reuben Dodge, John Royce, John Marshall, Elisha White, Geo. W. Bellows, John Ingalls, David Corlis, Ira Wales, Luther Fay, Asel Griswold, Mathew Towle, S. S. Johnson, Joseph Bond, Abner Mead, Nathan Bundy, Israel Brown, William Young, James Watkins, Wm. Bond, Joseph Cobb, Asahel B. Hodskins, Eli Hosmer, John Goodenough, Thomas Moore, John Emerson, Elijah Drury, Mathew Dickey, Adams Milliken, Lewis Gilmore, Cyrus Dickey, Alpha Fish, Elisha Royce, Robert Barnett, John Barrett, Wm. M. Barnett, Obadiah Redding, Clark Huntley, Levi Hall, Frederick Scovill, Cleveland Redfield, Jonathan Emerson, Robert Cochran, Levi Kimball, Levi Leonard, Sampson, Drury, Ralph Watkins, Calvin Carpenter, John Cross, jr., Horace Jennings, Henry S. Allen, Ezariah Dickinson, Caleb Miller, Thomas Allen, Jonathan Cross, Nehemiah Royce, Daniel Merriam, James C. Cristy, Charles Watkins, Samuel Mason, John Morrison, Jonathan Cummings, Adolphus Fletcher, Stephen Britton, jr., Aaron Emery, James Davis, Jonathan Fletcher, Abijah Bugbee, David Aldrich, Jona. Blanchard, Sylvanus L. Titus, Moses Fisher, Stephen Tiffany, Stephen Johnson, Anson Lawrence, Nathan Smith, Ezra Hixon, Oliver Jones, Francis Bundy, Aaron Hodskins, Joshua March, David C. Thompson, John S. March, Ebenezer Gilbert, George Flint, Silas Williams, Danforth Clark, William Farnham, Loran W. Clark, Abiah Kidder, David Clark, Asa Gilbert, Daniel Marsh, Arvin Priest, David Thompson, Isaac

Fisher, Samuel Martin, David Fisher, David Hodskins, Alva
Walker, Henry Slade, Charles Howland, Solomon Haskell,
Aden Henry, Alva Stearns, John Moor, William Thompson,
Henry Jennison, Holland Burt, Job Giddings, Solomon God-
frey, Emery S. Wyman, William Wellington, Roger Farnam,
William Sanford, Elias Burbank.

SHEEP. Merino sheep were introduced into this town as
early as 1800, or about that time, by Joseph Bellows, who was
a grandson of the founder of the town. The first buck was
purchased from an importation from Spain, made by Consul
Jarvis of Vermont. It is said that Bellows paid as high as
$1500 for one buck. The farmers about town immediately
commenced improving the quality of their wool, by infusing
the blood of the merino with the blood of their old Irish flocks,
till about 1825, when two brothers, by the name of Searles, imported a flock of Saxony sheep into Boston, a few of which
found their way into this town. In 1827, the Searles brothers
imported another flock into New England, in the care of one
Kreauchman, a German, one hundred of which were leased to
Maj. Samuel Grant and William Jennison, who had formed a
copartnership. By the terms of the lease the company was to
have one half the increase. Maj. Grant then owned a large
farm in the south-east corner of the town, known as the "Seven
Barns," and Maj. Jennison owned the farm which Wm. T.
Ramsay now owns, both of which were admirably adapted to
sheep husbandry.

John F. Kraetzer, a lad then about sixteen years of age—a
German by birth, came to Walpole with the one hundred sheep,
as shepherd, and cared for that portion allotted to Maj. Jennison, for several years.

Young Kraetzer was wont to utilize his time when not
otherwise engaged with his sheep in knitting socks in true German style. About the same time Grant and Jennison purchased a buck of the Searles brothers for which they paid
$110, which was considered a great price at the time. He was
known to the farmers by the euphonic name of "Old Hanuch." A
disease known as the "*foot rot*," was brought into town by some

of the above mentioned flock, that were infected; a disease, which has spread all over New England. The most careful and assiduous care was bestowed on those sheep, for they were very tender and susceptible to climatic changes, the lambs in many instances had to be cared for before a fire within the house. The fleece of those Saxony sheep was very fine, but light, not averaging more than two and a half pounds per head. The wool brought from sixty to eighty cents per pound, when ordinarly washed, but when perfectly cleansed, it brought $1.00 and more per pound. Sheep husbandry had now become a passion with most of the farmers in town,—the flocks in many instances being wholly Saxony. The fever reached its maximum between 1830 and 1840, when there were sixteen thousand sheep in town; and as late as 1854, the number was twelve thousand seven hundred and seventy one, since which time it has decreased. The Boggy Meadow farm kept one thousand, Maj. Grant one thousand; to which he fed the hay contained in seven well filled barns and from one to two thousand bushels of potatoes, yearly. Asahel B. Hodskins, Isaac F. and Thomas Bellows, Charles Watkins, Luther Burt, William Jennison and many others had flocks varying from three to five hundred each. Within the last thirty years the French merino has taken the place of the Saxony, and to-day probably not one pure blood Saxony sheep could be found in town.

From 1830 to 1840.

The census of this year, 1830, disclosed the fact that the town had gained fourteen inhabitants, making the number 2034. In October of the same year, as a party were returning from Keene, where they had been to attend Court, Christopher Lincoln of this town was thrown from a wagon, at the foot of the hill near Wm. Arnold's, and received such injuries that he died on the eleventh of the same month. Five years later, Sept. 3d, when a two horse wagon load were returning from Keene, where they had been to a regimental muster, Elisha Angier was killed by running off a small bridge, a few rods east of the residence of Wm. Wellington. The places where those accidents occurred are not more than one hundred rods apart. Both left widows and large families of minor children.

In the spring of 1844, May 2d, a very high wind, accompanied with rain and sleet, prostrated some valuable timber lots in the south part of the town, blew down a number of barns, unroofed sheds, levelled wooden fences, &c., &c. The velocity of the wind was such that a person could not without effort stand against it.

The financial crash of 1837 paralyzed all kinds of business in this town, as it did elsewhere. Many young men were idle, and those who obtained work worked for very small wages. Good field laborers were glad to work for from fifty to seventy-five cents per day. Business men struggled on between hope and despair till 1842, when they sought relief in bankruptcy. No less than thirty men in this town paid their honest dues by that means.

The same year, Mar. 14th, ("Town-meeting day,") three stages with mail and passengers, started on their accustomed trips north, in the morning, and on arriving at Cold river it was found so much swollen by the backing of water from the Connecticut, that the bridge was almost afloat. One of the drivers Wm. Simonds, hazarded the experiment of crossing the bridge. Just as his leaders reached the north bank, the bridge floated away, taking the coach and all on board with it, and at the same time dragging the horses from the bank into the water. There were four passengers in the coach, three of whom were females and they, together with the driver, were precipitated into the river, which, at that time was filled with cakes of ice. The name of the man who was in the coach, was Swain—a messenger, conveying money to the bank at Bellows Falls. He had $5,000 in a small trunk to which he clung, and also to one of the females till she was crushed by the ice, when he made for the west bank of the Connecticut as best he could on floating cakes of ice. All three of the females were lost, a Mrs. Dunham, Mrs. Chesley and her sister. The next driver, a Mr. Putnam, on seeing the catastrophe immediately returned to the village with his coach for help, while the third driver passed

round, and over the upper bridge, (there were two bridges
then,) and went on his way. Help was immediately obtained,
half the men in town repairing to the scene. Simonds, the driver, was still in the water when help arrived, clinging to an over-
hanging bough. Slabs were procured and thrown upon the ice
forming a perilous foothold, when Mr. F. A. Wier and others
pulled him ashore in an insensible condition, but he soon revived. The body of one of the women was taken from the
water at the time; but the other two were not found till the
following summer, one being found on the Vermont side of the
Connecticut opposite the residence of Thomas Bellows, and
the other near Boggy meadow. The coach and three of the
horses were lost, and the town, in consequence of the disaster,
suffered heavy damages.

From 1840 to 1850.

In the fall of 1843, at the time of the last regimental muster,
in town, a company belonging to this town, known as the " Saucy Six," broke down, uprooted and destroyed the beautiful
shade trees, which the citizens of the village had set out a few
years before and had taken unwearied pains to care for.

The citizens were highly incensed at such a high handed
piece of vandalism, and thereupon hung the captain of the
company, in effigy, on the nearest tree, and also took legal
measures to punish the perpetrators, but failed for the want
of statute law to sustain an action. At the next session of the
legislature, however, a stringent law was passed for the protection of shade trees. The act of destroying those trees was
justly censured at the time, and has ever been considered one
of the most uncalled for and lawless acts of which our staid
townsmen have been guilty. About that time (1843), or perhaps a year later, the old meeting-house was remodeled into a
town house, substantially as it is in its present form.

In Sept., 1847, a large building standing just over the brook
north of the residence of Levi H. Foster, and owned by Harvey Reed, was consumed by fire. The lower part of the building was occupied as a tannery, where Reed carried on an ex-

tensive business; while the upper floor was occupied by the French brothers, as a carriage manufactory. The loss was heavy and without insurance, as the company in which the building was insured had failed a few weeks before. In Sept., 1849, the old brick store which was built in 1806 was burned. The building was a large block, three stories high, with room on the ground sufficiently large for three commodious stores, all of which faced to the east. The building was occupied at the time by Philip Peck, dry goods and groceries, Tudor & Rockwood, do., and W. G. Wyman, variety store. There were three other buildings just west of the store, one of which was a dwelling, the others mechanics' shops, which were burned at the same time. The cause of the fire was unknown.

Another store built substantially like the one now occupied by E. K. Seabury, and another wooden store just north, facing the east, and also a dwelling and grocery store on the burnt district west, were immediately rebuilt. In 1855, a fire broke out in the new dwelling, just west of the stores above mentioned, and extended to the stores, and the former burnt district was all burned over the second time. In the course of two years or so buildings were put upon the burnt district as they stand at the present time. The last conflagration was caused by an overheated stove funnel, improperly adjusted, running through a partition. The house was occupied at the time of the fire by Thomas C. Ball and family. The losses were partially covered by insurance.

SAVINGS BANK. In July, 1849, a charter was obtained for a savings bank in this town, which went into operation in 1850. The first President was Otis Bardwell. In 1852 David Buffum was chosen President and continued to hold the office till the bank went into liquidation, in consequence of the robbery in 1868. (See bank robbery.) In 1850 David Buffum was Sec'y. and Treas.; in 1851 Edward Crosby; 1856, John W. Heyward, and in 1858 Benjamin F. Aldrich, who held the office till 1864. The deposits amounted to $108,045.58, besides $3,841.58 surplus, at the time the bank was robbed. During the existence of the bank the trustees made some poor invest-

ments in railroad bonds, which were likely to cause a loss to
the depositors, to the amount of $2,500; but the trustees man-
fully assumed the loss till such time as the difficulty was bridg-
ed over.   The names of the trustees at the time were David
Buffum, Frederick Vose, Jesseniah Kittredge, Aaron P. Howland, Edwin R. Wells, Benj. B. Grant, Ephraim Holland, Lyman Watkins, Thomas Bellows and Abel Bellows.

FROM 1850 TO 1860.

In the summer of 1850, June 20th, a violent hail storm passed
over the village, which was confined to a narrow belt in its immediate vicinity, and was unprecedented in the amount of rain-
fall and destruction of property, in so short a time, in this
region.   According to the account of an eye-witness, who was
not in the habit of telling marvellous stories; two clouds
from opposite directions, black and gloomy in appearance, began to approach each other a little past noon, when the heav-
ens suddenly became very dark.   Soon the rain and hail began to pour in torrents, accompanied with a strong wind.   People hurried to close the blinds on their dwellings and were
met by fragments of broken glass and hailstones as large as
partridge eggs.   In less than thirty minutes three large streams
of water came rushing down the hill east of the village, which
had the appearance of small rivers.   Mad brook immediately
rose to an unprecedented height and volume.   Trees a foot in
diameter were borne along with rapidity by the swollen cur-
rent together with an indescribable miscellaneous *debris*.   Three
cows belonging to the villagers were taken from the rubbish,
one of which was dead and another was minus one horn.   The
stream rushed madly on, taking every thing with it as far as it
spread, till it reached the railroad culvert, which was not large
enough for such a volume of water to pass.   The water soon
rose to the top of the embankment, which could not withstand
the pressure of the accumulated water, and it gave way, the
water driving before it about one hundred feet of the embankment, together with the heavy masonry, of the culvert.   Some
of the blocks of stone which were carried quite across the river

would have weighed one or two tons. Those stones could have been seen a few years since at low water near the west bank of the Connecticut imbedded in the sand. There was not a supply of glass in town sufficient to replace what was broken and many villagers had to go to Keene to purchase it. Young orchards suffered severely, many of which were ruined by bruises from hailstones. The roads, also, were badly torn and washed, and some bridges were carried away.

In 1852 the town purchased of the heirs and widow of Josiah Bellows the beautiful oak grove west of the old cemetery extending to the travelled highway, for the purpose of enlarging the grounds which had then become well nigh filled. A committee was appointed by the town to survey and lay it out, of whom Benjamin B. Grant was chairman. With his proverbial energy he caused the plot to be tastefully laid out and a map of the same to be made. On its completion a large number of the town's people gathered under the shade of the beautiful oaks in the cemetery and listened to the consecrating discourse delivered by Frederick N. Knapp, which was one of the most appropriate and chaste efforts ever made in town. Subsequently the sexton, who had charge of the grounds paid little attention to the map or the laying out, allowing the town's people to locate their lots where fancy dictated, till there was so much irregularity that it was difficult to know where people owned lots and where they did not. In 1873 the town appointed a committee who caused a new survey to be made and a new map to be projected which enables one at a glance to find any lot desired.

In 1853, a committee of the descendants of Col. Benjamin Bellows, issued a circular to their relatives for the purpose of raising a fund to erect a monument in commemoration of their ancestor who was the founder of the town. In time the circular was duly responded to with a sufficient guaranty to warrant the erection of a suitable monument. Benjamin Bellows Grant, A. Herbert Bellows, Frederick Vose, David Buffum, Isaac F. Bellows, Philip Peck and Fred. N. Knapp were the committee to whom was intrusted the furtherance of the plan. In 1854, the monument was completed and erected. It is beautiful in design and proportion. It consists of a granite base, about six feet square, surmounted by a marble obelisk twenty feet high. On the west side, in a circle, is carved a beautiful emblematic device representing a powderhorn, sickle, tomahawk, etc., and on the east is the representation of a partly unrolled parchment with seal, on which are inscribed these words, " Charter of Walpole, 1752." On the south side is the following inscription, viz. " Col. Benjamin Bellows, a wise, courageous, and honest man, by a large hospitality, by faithfulness and ability in public trusts, by bravely protecting, prudently counselling, and liberally aiding the frontier settlers, gained the respect and love of his contemporaries, and made himself a pattern for those who seek to be founders of communities.' On the north side is the following.

TO THE MEMORY OF

BENJAMIN BELLOWS

THE FOUNDER OF WALPOLE

WHO DIED 10 JULY 1777

AGED SIXTY-TWO YEARS

THIS MONUMENT WAS ERECTED

IN THE YEAR 1854

BY HIS DESCENDANTS

At the time of the completion of the monument, a large number of the descendants of the Col. and their friends gathered in town to celebrate the Centennial of the town's settlement and for the interchange of fraternal feelings. Rev. Henry W. Bellows, D. D. of New York, a great-grandson of the founder, delivered the Historical Address on the occasion, in his usual happy style, which evinced much labor, patience and research. The address together with the doings of the meeting, were subsequently published in a pamphlet of about one hundred and twenty octavo pages and distributed among the relatives and friends of the Bellows family. The book is of much historic value, and from it the compiler of this work has largely drawn.

SHADE TREES. In 1855 or 6, Benjamin B. Grant and Thomas G. Wells, and perhaps some others, under the protecting act of the legislature, replanted "Washington Square" and all the principal streets in the village with forest shade trees, principally elms and rock maples, the most of which are now standing and growing vigorously, affording an agreeable shade in summer and beautifying the village to an extent which is unsurpassed in most country towns. The act was duly appreciated at the time by the village people and will continue to be as long as the spreading branches protect from the hot summer sun those who seek their grateful shade. Perhaps some great-great-grandson, of antequarian proclivities, will be seen one hundred years hence, with his tape line measuring the size of the present growing trees, who may be heard to exclaim, "My great-great-grandfather planted these trees, one hundred years ago!"

WALPOLE IN THE REBELLION.

Previous to 1861, the two political parties in this town had been vehement rivals for political ascendancy. The exertions annually made at the March and other elections, by both parties, to carry the town, and the amount of money expended for the purpose, became a proverb for strife and animosity. The Democratic party honestly believed that the course that the Republican party was pursuing was wrong, while on the other hand the Republicans believed themselves to be in the right, and as there was no way to settle the dispute except at the ballot box, the Republicans felt at ease, because they were in the ascendancy in town, county, state and nation.

After the war commenced this feeling would have, in a great

measure, died out had it not been for indiscreet expressions used by a few individuals of each party, which, as the case might be, were construed as being the sentiments belonging to the *whole* of either party. But, notwithstanding, when men were called for to volunteer for the defence and maintainance of the Union, one party was as fully represented in the ranks as the other.

On the 12th of April, 1861, Fort Sumter was fired upon by Southern forces under the direction of Jefferson Davis and the flag of the union dishonored. The Fort was evacuated on the 14th, and within twenty-four hours thereafter, President Lincoln called for seventy-five thousand men to put down the Rebellion. The news spread like a prairie fire over the Northern States, and the people were under the greatest excitement and in a condition of not knowing what to do, as no military organization was complete in this State at that time. However, John M. Pike, Bellows Emerson, Quincy A. Emerson, Edward R. Pratt and George R. Tower, immediately enlisted into the 1st and 2d New Hampshire Militia as volunteers from this town. Pike and Pratt were in the first battle of Bull Run. Another call was made by the government, May 3rd, 1861, for sixty-four thousand volunteers for the Army and eighteen thousand for the Navy. To this call James Stack, Albert D. Scoville, Geo. M. Snow, Wesley J. Barnett, Warren D. Fay, William Flynn, Lewis Hooper, John B. Hooper, Eugene Henderson, George Weymouth, Charles Hinds, John E. Mitchell, John L. Houghton, and William Gage, responded. Further on the number of regiment and time of enlistment will be noticed.

The first town meeting that was called, when any business was transacted for war purposes, was held Oct. 9th, 1861. At that time the town voted $500 to be expended for soldiers' families. The townsmen had but little idea of the magnitude the conflict would assume, and rested quietly on the statements made by public men that the war would be closed in *sixty days*. In the meantime the women were active in devising some means for alleviating the sufferings of the soldiers, which, practically, at this time, amounted to but little ; but when the

Sanitary Commission was organized their help and exertions were all-powerful in mitigating the sufferings in body and mind of the wounded and sick soldier. Many soldiers, who had heretofore enlisted had died, while others had returned home, broken down with exposure and hardship, and the novelty and excitement incident to a soldier's life had well nigh died out, which had nearly put a stop to the enlistment of volunteers.

In 1862, Aug. 6th, the town held a meeting for the purpose of doing something in a pecuniary way to induce men to enlist into the service, as a draft would most likely be made if volunteers were not forthcoming. The town voted a bounty of $100 to every man that enlisted from the town. This was to fill the quota for three hundred thousand volunteers. The conditions were that the men who enlisted should be mustered into the service before the 15th of the month. According to the records no one seems to have enlisted before the 15th, in conformity to the above vote. On the 2nd of Sep. the town voted to pay $100 bounty for three years men from the 15th of August. Under this call the following persons enlisted into the New Hampshire 14th, Reg. vol., namely: John J. Johnson, Chandler A. Wilber, A. Mason Adams, Charles H. Jennison, Austin H. Wolf, Clement G. Lane, Charles A. Green, Jonathan Turner, Charles H. Gilbert, Wm. A. Barker, Ellery C. Benson, Chas. H. Brown, Willard E. S. Bragg, Amasa T. Bundy, Wilson W. Colburn, Bellows Emerson, John S. Farnsworth, Benjamin Gates 2d, Frank B. Graves, Henry H. Hooper, Alfred G. Keyes, John F. Kraetzer, Otis P. Kraetzer, Edward H. Livingston, George Perigo, Henry Reason, George A. Sherman, Thomas Tahan, Elnathan R. Templeton, Albert T. Wilkins and Geo. L. Wetherby.

On the 11th of Sep. 1862, the town "voted to pay a bounty of $200 each, for filling the quota of nine months men called for." At the same meeting it was "voted that if both quotas required could be filled by volunteers, an additional sum of $50 should be paid the nine months men as bounty."

In the spring of 1863 volunteering had nearly ceased, the

enemy were pressing hard and more men must be had. A draft appeared the only alternative and consequently the President of the United States issued a proclamation for a conscription of three hundred thousand men on the 8th of May, in the above mentioned year.

Fifty-two men was the quota of this town, and volunteers could not be obtained. An enrolment of all the men between the ages of eighteen and forty-five was made, and probably at no time in the town's history could there be found so many men who wished they had been born a few months earlier or a few months later. When the draft was completed, it was found that many of the uncoveted prizes had fallen to those who were not in a situation to comply with the demand. The drafted men had a choice of three ways to pursue, one was to *go*, the second was to procure a substitute, which would clear them from any future draft, and the third was to pay a commutation fee of $300 to the United States Government, which would clear them only for the pending conscription. On the following 18th of July three hundred thousand more men were called for. And now politics were out of the question—every man was now for himself. No young men were inclined to shoulder the musket, and fathers who had young sons were willing to do almost any way rather than have them expose themselves to the hardships of a soldier's life. Money was of no account, if substitutes could be procured, at the expense of the town, for those who were liable to go. There was but one party at the town meetings held for several months about this time, and the meetings were so frequent that they ceased to attract much attention except from those who were directly interested.

In the month of Sept. 1863, 16th day, the town held a meeting and " voted to pay to each drafted man, that was accepted, the sum of $ 200; and also to drafted men's families the same amount as to the families of volunteers," Nov. 16, same year, at another meeting the town voted $ 100 bounty to volunteers, in addition to the bounty offered by the United States Government, and on the 28th, " voted to borrow the sum of $ 15,000 to obtain volunteers to fill the town's quota, and Henry Allen was appointed special agent to procure the men. At a meet-held in Feb., 1864, the town voted to raise $1,200 for the re-en-listment of *veterans*—how many the record does not disclose. At March meeting, 1864, " Voted to raise by taxation the sum of $ 800 to continue the State aid to the families of soldiers." At the same meeting " voted to pay the veterans who have re-en-listed, the sum of $ 300 each." At the same meeting also "voted to raise $ 1,200 to pay the bounties of veterans who re-enlisted June 7, 1864." And further, at the same meeting, the town " voted to pay each man who had been accepted in the service of the United States $ 300 ; and that the selectmen be author-ized to procure a sufficient number of volunteers to fill any quota that may be assigned to the town at any subsequent *call*, and to pay such bounties as may be necessary to procure such volunteers previous to any draft's being made, said bounty not to exceed the sum of $ 1,000 per man, and'that the selectmen be authorized to borrow on the credit of the town *any* amount of money sufficient to carry this vote into effect." At the same meeting the town "voted to raise by taxation $ 1,200 to re-enlist-ed veterans and to men that had been drafted." At an adjourned meeting held the 18th of the same month, " voted that the se-lectmen be authorized and directed to fill any quota of the town, by obtaining volunteers for that purpose, and also, that the selectmen be instructed to borrow on the credit of the town such sums of money as are necessary to pay the bounties to such volunteers."

Jan. 21, 1865, the town " voted to pay men, citizens of the town, volunteering for one year, $ 167 ; for two years, $ 300 ; for three years, $ 400 : and that the selectmen borrow money to pay bounties." Feb. 19, the above vote was re-considered and the town " voted to raise each man, citizen of the town, $ 500 for one year, to fill the quota of the town under the late call for three hundred thousand men." This was the last town meeting called and held for war measures ; as the backbone of the rebellion was broken the following April.

Following are the names of those persons, actual residents

of the town, who enlisted into the service of the United States during the rebellion, as nearly as can be ascertained:

Pike, John M., en. May 3, 1861, N. H. 1st Reg.; discharged Aug. 9, '61; re-en. into the Vt. 8th Cavalry.

Emerson, Bellows, en. May 3, '61, N. H. 1st; re-en. Sept. 22, '62, N. H. 14th; dis. for disability at Poolsville, Md., Feb. 5, '63.

Emerson, Quincy A., en. May, 31, N. H. 2nd Reg.; dis. Jan. 1, '64; re-enlisted.

Pratt, Edward R., en. May 31, N. H. 2nd Reg.; dis. July 23, '63. He was at the first battle of Bull Run.

Tower, Geo. R. en. May 31, N. H. 2d Reg.; dis. July 16, '61.

Stack, James, en. Sept. 17, N. H. 2nd Reg.; dis. Jan. 1, 64; re-enlisted Jan. 1, 1864.

Holbrook, Samuel F., en. Jan. 1, 1864, N. H. 2nd Reg.

Scovill, Albert D., en. Aug. 24, '61, N. H. 3d Reg.; dis. Jan. 1, '64.

Snow, Geo. M., en. Oct. 23, '61, N. H. 5th Reg.; dis. July 7, '62, dis'y.

Barnet, Wesley J., en. Nov. 28, '61, N. H. 6th Reg.; died Jan. 14, '62.

Fay, Warren D., en. Nov. 28, '61, N. H. 6th Reg.; died Jan. 16, '62.

Flynn, Wm., en. Nov. 28, '61, N. H. 6th Reg.; re-en. Jan. 3, '64,

Hooper, Lewis, en. Nov. 28, '61, N. H. 6th Reg.; dis. Jan. 3, '64, re-en. Jan. 3, '64, N. H. 6th, Pro. Corp., killed in action May 12, '64.

Hooper, John B., en. Nov. 28, '61, N. H. 6th Reg.; dis. June 3, '64; re-enlisted.

Henderson, Eugene, en. Nov. 28, '61, N. H. 6th Reg.; dis. Jan. 3, '64; re-enlisted, wounded July 30, 1864.

Weymouth, Geo., en. Nov. 28, 61, N. H. 6th Reg.; dis. Feb. 5, '63.

Hinds, Charles, en. Nov. 28, '61, N. H. 6th Reg.; the record does not say when discharged.

Mitchell, John E., en. Dec. 7, '61, N. H. 6th Reg.; dis. Jan. 14, '63.

Houghton, John L., en. Nov. 28, '61, N. H. 6th. Reg.; dis. Jan. 14, '62.

Wilber, Chandler A., en. Sept. 22, '62, N. H. 14th; dis. for disability, Nov. 10, '62; re-en. Mar. 15, '64, N. H. Cav.

Johnson, John J., en. as Capt., Oct. 9, '62, in the N. H. 14th Reg.; honorably dis. Nov. 3, '63.

The following twenty-nine persons all enlisted the same day, Sept. 22, 1862, in the N. H. 14th Reg.

Adams, A. Mason, resigned April 1, 1863.
Jennison, Charles H., discharged July 8, '65.
Wolf, Austin H.,   "   "
Lane, Clement G.,   "   "
Green, Chas. A.,   "   "
Turner, Jonathan,   "   "
Gilbert, Chas. H.,   "   "
Barker, Wm. A., died Jan. 28, 1863, at Washington, D. C.

Benson, Ellery C., discharged July 8, 1865.
Brown, Charles H.,   "   ".
Bragg, Willard E. S., died of disease Aug. 19, '64.
Bundy, Amasa T., discharged July 8, '65.
Colburn, Wilson W.,   "   "
Farnsworth, John S.,   "   "
Gates, Benjamin 2d., died at Washington, D. C., Dec. 14, 1863.
Graves, Frank B., discharged July 8, 1865.
Hooper, Henry H., died Dec. 14, 1863.
Keyes, Alfred G., discharged Sept. 19, 1864, wounded.
Kraetzer, John F.,   " 1864 ; disability.
Kraetzer, Otis P., died Nov. 3, 1863, from wounds received.
Livingston, Edward H., died of disease at Poolsville, Md., Feb. 18,'63.
Perigo, George, killed at Winchester, Va., Sept. 19, 1864.
Reason, Henry, discharged July 8, 1864.
Sherman, Geo. A.,   "   "
Templeman, Elnathan R., discharged July 8, 1864.
Wilkins, Albert T., deserted Oct. 15, 1862.
Wetherby, Geo. S., killed at Winchester, Va., Sept., 19, 1864.
Hubbard, John L., en. Oct. 28, '62, in N. H. 15th Reg.; dis. Aug. 13,'63.
Bixby, John M.,   "   "   "   "
Carpenter, Edward,   "   "   "   "
Griffin, Dennis,   "   "   "   "
Hyde, Patrick,   "   "   "   "
Lawrence Charles,   "   "   "   "
Bellows, Geo. H., en. as Maj. in the N. H. 17th Reg., Oct. 23, 1862 ;
     mustered out April 17, '63.
Moultrup, Chas., en. Dec. 31, '64, N. H. 18th Reg.; dis. July 29, '65.
Pratt, Isaiah,   "   "   "   "
Wright, Lucius B., en. as sergeant, Oct. 18, '62, N. H. 16th Reg.;
     mustered out Oct. 20, 1863.

Following is a list of persons who were in the service and
credited to Walpole, but enlisted in regiments out of the state,
for which reason a full report cannot be given.

Burns, Owen, enlisted April, in the N. H. Cavalry.
Irish, Henry G., enlisted 1861, N. H. Cav.: dis. Feb. 15, '64, disability.
Lawrence, Leonard, Vermont 4th, and died.
Faxon, John,   "   "
Livingston William, enlisted Vermont Cavalry died.
Weymouth, Edward, enlisted Vermont 9th.
Tole, Patrick, enlisted Vermont 4th.
Smith, Ferdinand, enlisted N. H. 5th.
Bellows, Geo., enlisted N. Y. 8th.
Bellows, Edward, enlisted N. Y. 8th.
Titus, Charles, enlisted Mass. 6th.
Tower, Perley, enlisted N. H. 6th.

Isham, Charles, enlisted N. H. 2nd.
Kraetzer, Julius, enlisted Mass. 15th.
Graves, Frederick, E. R. enlisted U. S. A.
Emery, Curtis, enlisted N. Y. Cavalry.
Mellish, Walter, enlisted N. H. 2nd.
Graves, Ira R., enlisted N. Y. 16th.
Keyes, John W., enlisted Vermont 4th.
Newton, Hubbard B., enlisted N. H. Cavalry.

The six following persons furnished substitutes, viz., Oliver J. Hubbard, Benj. F. Aldrich, O. H. P. Watkins, Samuel D. Learned, Charles Fisher, James M. Paul, and Geo. P. Porter.

Of the personal reminiscences of those who enlisted and participated in the late rebellion from this town, there are but few worthy of mention. There is but one, according to the Adjutant General's Report, that actually enlisted from this town, who is known to have deserted, and he was not a native citizen. Most of them returned with an honorable soldier's record.

One of the Irish boys, it is said, being impatient of restraint in a *free country*, gave his superiors considerable trouble. Probably *rum*, furnished by myriad *land sharks*, had more to do in the above instance of insubordination than natural dispostion. Lewis Hooper appears to have emulated his grandfather (Levi) in doing his duty as a soldier. He was one of the first to enlist in town, although his age would have saved him from military service. After serving out his first term of enlistment he came home to visit his family and friends, after which he re-enlisted as a veteran, Jan. 3, 1864. He was promoted to corporal, and was killed in action, May 18, 1864. His son John B. was with his father during his whole term of service.

Two promising young men, Wesley J. Barnett and Warren D. Fay, the former the son of John Barnett, and the latter the son of Dana Fay, citizens of the town, both enlisted Nov. 28, 1861, into the N. H. 6th regiment. They were both dutiful, quiet unassuming boys, and those who knew them best would have supposed that they would have been the last ones to engage in such a life of turmoil and danger. They did not live, however, long enough to see much service, for they both died of measles, in the following January, Barnett on the 14th, and Fay on the

16th. They were both brought home and buried under the branches of the spreading oaks in the new cemetery, where yearly, when the summer sun opens the bud of the rose and violet, their graves are bedecked with the choicest of flowers, by living friends, as tokens of love and remembrance. Their premature deaths were a terrible stroke of affliction at the time, to their parents and relatives, and long years can only mitigate their sorrows.

Another young man, Edward H. Livingstone, who had been the stay and staff of his mother, enlisted in the N. H. 14th., Sep. 28th, 1862, with twenty-eight others at the same time. He contracted malarial fever, while stationed at Poolsville, Md. and died there, Feb. 18th, 1863. His body was brought to Walpole and buried in the old cemetery, where a suitable marble slab marks his last resting place. He was the only son of an aged mother, who mourns his death as only a mother can. Although many years have elapsed since his death, still she often visits his grave in summer, nothwithstanding her age is three score and thirty, and drops a silent tear as a token of her tender and abiding affection.

Wm. A. Barker and Benjamin Gates 2nd, both died of disease, the former leaving a wife and several small children and the latter a widow. John F. Kraetzer, and three of his sons, Otis, Henry and Julius, enlisted. The father at the time was considerably past middle life. He was for a time engaged in various hospitals caring for the sick and wounded—an excellent nurse. Otis was shot, and died from his wounds, and Henry died of disease. For account of other deaths see list of soldiers from this town.

Subsequent to the draft all demands made upon the town for men till the close of the war, were answered by the town's furnishing money to procure men for the service. The prices paid were regulated by the law of supply and demand, ranging from $400 to $750.

The indebtedness, of the town in 1862, was $5,300; and in 1866 it was $46,000; and it is safe to say that $40,000 of this indebtedness was incurred in consequence of the war. In

1869 the town debt was funded to the amount of $36,000, and it will soon be liquidated.

There were one hundred and eighty-five persons credited to this town in all, volunteers and substitutes, as going into the service, of whom seventy-five were actual residents. Eight of the three months men reenlisted; nine died of disease; four were killed outright; eight wounded; six missing; while fifty-three of the *substitutes* are known to have deserted, and five volunteers were discharged on account of disability.

Hubbard B. Newton enlisted from this town into the New Hampshire 14th, Reg., but, for some reason not known, he never received any bounty, nor was he credited to Walpole. He was subsequently transferred to the 1st Rhode Island Cavalry. At Mountville he was taken prisoner, in 1862, and marched to Richmond, hotly pursued by the Union forces, to recapture their men. He was on the march and *ran* three days and three nights before arriving at the place of his destination, which was Libby Prison; where he remained thirteen days, receiving its *hospitalities*, when he was paroled. After the battle of the Rapidan, on the retreat of the Union forces, he was shot in the right arm, producing a compound fracture, and taken prisoner again. A rebel soldier had charge of him and one other prisoner, and when they encamped for the night Newton complained of thirst, when the escort left his prisoners and went a short distance to a spring to procure water, but when he returned he found no one to drink—"the birds had flown." Newton and his comrade wandered about three nights before they entered within the Union lines. In the daytime they kept hidden, only venturing forth now and then to procure a little mush and milk of the friendly negroes. He served his country three years and was honorably discharged.

Benjamin Lawrence enlisted at the same time Newton did, and into the same regiments, but was not credited to this town. He was detailed as a regimental blacksmith; but his mercurial nature could not brook confinement to horses' feet and camp life; so he mounted his steed and went into the ranks, though not obliged to do so. At the battle of Mountville he was taken prisoner at the same time Newton was, and shared the same fate. At the battle of Aldie he was in the regiment of Col. Duffy (*Duffie*) who went into the fray with six hundred men and came out with *twenty-seven*, although subsequently sixty were picked up. The regiment was surrounded, and, in endeavoring to fight their way out Lawrence came in contact with a rebel soldier, who called upon him to surrender, and instead of obeying the rebel's command he pointed his pistol at him and made several unsuccessful efforts to fire, but his cartridge did not explode. In the meantime the rebel had approached within six feet of him holding his pistol levelled at his head. Lawrence now saw it was a case of life or death with him; whereupon he flung his pistol at the soldier's head, at the same time exclaiming "there take that, you —— !" His pistol struck the pistol of the rebel and gave it an oblique cant and at the same time it exploded, the ball entering Lawrence's body in an oblique direction just above the hip. He fell from his horse and was left for dead upon the field. In a state of unconsciousness he lay on his back during the day, with the hot sun pouring its rays into his face, till he was blacker than his sable neighbors. At night he revived and crawled to a shanty near by, where he was humanely cared for till the Union forces took him to a hospital; but surgical aid was of no avail; the bullet could not be extracted. He recovered sufficiently to be able to return to Walpole, where he lingered till Aug. 30, 1865, when he died from the effects of the wound received, aged thirty-six,—as brave a soldier as ever entered the ranks from Walpole.

SANITARY COMMISSION.

Soon after the late Rebellion broke out there was a general movement made by ladies of the northern states for the comfort and amelioration of the condition of the suffering soldiery, in which the women of this town participated in an humble degree. This movement at length culminated in the establishment of the U. S. Sanitary Commission, of which Rev. Henry

W. Bellows D. D. of New York was President. Of the number
who at *first* volunteered their services from this town was Rev.
Frederick N. Knapp (See Knapp). Joshua B. Clark went as superintendent of the soldier's home, Waldo F. Hayward as superintendent of supply department, Peter Reynolds went as relief agent, stationed at Washington, D. C. and at Brashear City,
La. Thomas B. Peck filled the position of clerk on sanitary
claims and Dr. Geo. A. Blake was general Agent and Hospital
Inspector. He is thus spoken of by the Sanitary Commission.
" In the department of the Gulf the work of the Sanitary Commission was admirably administered by Drs. Crane and Geo.
A. Blake, who continued at New Orleans until the close of the
war, doing most efficient service. Dr. Newbury sent down cargo
after cargo of vegetable food to Dr. Blake, who distributed it
among the garrisons at isolated points on the Gulf, the Red
river and to posts in Texas." One experience of Dr. Blake
in his connection with the Sanitary Commission is worth recording, and is as follows: The Dr. started from New York,
bound for New Orleans, on board the steamer Locust Point,
the second day of July 1864. At one o'clock a. m. of the
third she collided with the steamer Matanzas off Barnegat, New
Jersey, the latter vessel striking the former, diagonally, abaft
the engine, causing it to go down in seven minutes after the
collision. There were many lives lost and every person on the
port side of the Locust Point was lost save the Dr., who caught
a settee, which was the first floating material he could lay his
hands on, and with it plunged overboard, receiving a black
eye by contact with it as he struck the water. He, being of
rotund make-up and light bone, with the help of his frail craft,
managed to float one hour and twenty minutes; not, however,
without receiving an occasional ducking on account of the
careening of the settee through the motion of the waves, when
he was picked up by the crew of the Matanzas and landed in
New York, minus his baggage and $300 in bank notes, saving
only his watch and the clothes he had on, which consisted of
his shirt, pants and vest. He managed to get some temporary
clothing and money of friends in New York, when he went to

Boston and bought a suit of clothing and started again for New Orleans with better success.

SAVINGS BANK ROBBERY.

In Nov. 1864 the savings bank of this town, which was incoporated in 1853, was robbed of about $52,000 in money and securities of various kinds, a large share of which belonged to Col. A. Herbert Bellows. David Buffum was president and Benj. F. Aldrich, treasurer. The bank office was in B. F. Aldrich's store. The feat was accomplished on the 21st of November, by entering the store through a window. The parties glued some paper on one of the panes in order to deaden the sound of breaking glass. By pressing against the pane it was broken and noiselessly removed, after which the inside fastening was taken out which made an entrance easy. It was conjectured that the treasurer's movements had been "shadowed" for some months in order to ascertain what disposition he made of the safe key before retiring at night.

This key was made up of three pieces, one of which was left in his desk drawer, one was put into his business safe and the other was kept in his pantaloons pocket on retiring from business at night. The burglars had learned these important facts, as subsequent proceedings on their part plainly showed. They procured the piece the treasurer kept in his pocket, in the first place, by stealthily entering his house by means of round forceps, applied to his door key and entering his sleeping room and taking his pantaloons, which were found on his door steps the next morning. With false keys they entered his safe and drawer and were soon prepared to enter the bank safe, which they did, and extracted from its contents what they wanted.

Nothing was taken from the store save a few pieces of flannel goods which were left on the steps of a neighboring building, probably with the purpose of misleading persons as to the direction the burglars took on leaving.

Much excitement prevailed in the village the next day, and many crude and unjust speculations were made implicating some of the most worthy citizens of the town in the robbery.

Although $5.000 reward was offered no clue to the guilty parties was obtained till the following February, when information was received from Washington that some of the stolen bonds had been sold to some bankers in Scranton, Penn. Col. A. Herbert Bellows, on receiving such information, immediately started for Pennsylvania, and obtained such intelligence as warranted him in employing detectives in New York, on his return, to work up the case. The detectives obtained a cue which led them to suspect that one Mark Shinborn, a German Jew, who lived at Saratoga, was connected with the robbery. They immediately repaired to Saratoga but did not find Shinborn at his home on his farm, a few miles from the village. On calling at the Post-Office in the village they found that he had recently been there and had taken a letter from his box. On further inquiry it was ascertained that he had gone to a minstrel performance. He was a very dressy fellow, and wore, at the time, a hat of singular pattern which would not be likely to escape notice.

Shinborn knew one of the detectives and it was arranged that this detective should keep out of sight, by standing on the sidewalk, when the performance closed, at which time it was proposed to arrest him. The other two stationed themselves, the one at the entrance door from the sidewalk and the other at the entrance door to the auditorium of the theatre. The play being over, he escaped the eye of the first detective, in passing out; but on arriving at the second door he was recognized by detective number two. Whereupon, at a signal, number three sprang forward and the two closed in with him and had him in irons *instanter*. He contrived to get a letter from his pocket, which the detectives fortunately saw and took from him before he had time to destroy it, which, on opening, was found to contain two of the stolen bonds, and some coupons, which had been sent to Philadelphia to be sold, but were returned. This was sufficient evidence to warrant his being brought to Keene, where he was held for trial.

It was noticed by some parties that he was the same person who had been seen with one Geo. White, who was then keeping a public house in Stoneham, Mass., but who from his birth had resided in Westmoreland, N. H. Sufficient circumstantial evidence was found to warrant White's arrest, and he also was held for trial. At the trial Shinborn was found guilty and sentenced to the State prison, but the jury disagreed in White's case. They were both remanded to the jail, White to await another trial and Shinborn to await the sheriff's time to take him to Concord. In the mean time he got possession of a key to his cell door which he unlocked and walked out. An alarm was immediately given and he was pursued some distance, the pursuers, however, keeping at a respectful distance from him, he being armed with a revolver. Afterwards he was rearrested near Rome, N. Y. and taken to Concord; but he remained in prison but a short time. One night as he was returning from the workshop of the prison to his cell he broke from the ranks, and, running for the gate of the prison yard, he stooped and gave the lower part a smart pull when a portion of it came off, it having been nearly cut off previously by some unknown confederate outside. Through this opening he escaped and afterwards kept out of harm's way. White escaped, it was supposed, through the instrumentality of his wife, before the next term of court; but was subsequently arrested, tried, convicted and sentenced to the prison at Windsor, Vt. for participating in the robbery of a bank at Barre, Vt.

Soon after the robbery of the Savings Bank the directors thought it best to settle with the depositors and the concern was closed up with a loss of nearly ten per cent. A portion of the stolen securities were afterwards recovered.

VILLAGE BRIDGE.

The village bridge, which was built by a corporation in 1807, during a period of about sixty-two years was a toll bridge, the income of which was precarious, owing to natural decay and consequent repairs and the risk of damage or destruction by high water. Up to 1867 the old bridge had not received any serious damage by high water, although in a shaky condition. In the fall of that year the west end succumbed to the watery ele-

ment, taking away about one third of the superstructure and
wholly destroying the west pier and abutment, which were
soon re-erected by the corporation. The next year, in October,
the east portion went off. At a meeting of the proprietors
immediately after it was found that an assessment of seventy
dollars on a share must be made in order to repair the damage,
to the payment of which a majority of the proprietors manifested a strong reluctance. Mr. Horace A. Perry, one of the
stockholders, suggested the idea of relinquishing the entire
property to the towns of Walpole and Westminster, provided
that $ 3,000 should be raised by subscription, Walpole to raise
two thirds of the required sum; and that each of the towns, in
the same proportion, should raise by taxation a sum sufficient to
re-build the bridge and thereafter maintain it as a *free* bridge.

The matter was discussed at length *pro* and *con*, and the conclusion arrived at was that the suggestions were not feasible;
but Col. A. Herbert Bellows thought differently. He immediately took the matter into his own hands, in a measure, and by
unwearied patience, perseverance, hard work and much expense, carried out Mr. Perry's suggestions, and the result is a
free bridge to day. Some of the heavy tax payers in the east
part of the town and the west part of Westminster were
somewhat disturbed at the time; but not many could be
found, in either town, to day, who would care to have a toll
bridge instead.

RECENT INDUSTRIES.

In 1850 Mr. Silas M. Bates moved from Watertown, Mass.,
to this town and commenced the manufacture of shirts. The
business was carried on by Mr. Bates, in conjunction with his
wife, in a safe, economical but small way, till his wife died,
when other parties continued the business in the same small
way, for several years. In 1864 a copartnership was formed
by Silas M. Bates and Benj. F. Aldrich, under the style of
Bates & Aldrich. Mr. Aldrich had previously been in the
mercantile business in town, and had, by economy and industry,
accumulated a handsome fortune for country life. The com-

pany purchased some buildings on Turnpike street suitable for their business and commenced the manufacture of shirts in earnest. To facilitate their business, they purchased a large steam engine, which not only furnished motive power sufficient for their own use, but for running a saw and grist mill, planing machine, shingle machine and some half dozen other machines for the cutting and fashioning of lumber for various purposes. The lumber business was carried on by Lyman Ellis & Co., to whom Bates & Aldrich furnished the power for a stipulated yearly rent. For a few years an immense quantity of lumber was cut up and disposed of, and a large number of hands employed.

Bates & Aldrich employed some sixty females and half a dozen males in their factory, besides a large number of seamstresses living in and out of town. They paid their help liberally, the monthly pay roll was heavy, and a great share of the employes' earnings was spent in town. At length Mr. Ellis became financially embarrased, and, in order to utilize the rented steam power, Bates & Aldrich had to assume his debts and form a copartnership with him.

The business went on, apparently in a prosperous condition, till the June of 1876, when Mr. Aldrich, who knew the financial condition of the firm, suffered a small note to go to protest, which brought about a settlement with the firm in bankruptcy. The firm of Bates & Aldrich paid fifty per cent. Aldrich, thirty, and Bates, twenty, of their indebtedness. The last two mentioned embraced their individual indebtedness. Their liabilities were over $200,000. It was a severe blow not only to Bates and Aldrich, but to their employes and the general business of the town. The failure was mainly caused by the shrinkage of values, not only the manufactured goods, but on the material from which the goods were made, of which the firm had bought heavily a short time before the failure occurred.

Tobacco Culture.

About a dozen years ago the farmers of the town, or many of them, conceived the idea of becoming suddenly rich by tobacco culture, and fabulous prices were paid for help and fertilizers, to insure a crop. As high as fourteen dollars per cord was paid for manure. The fertile river farms, which were wont to yield a gladening harvest of yellow corn, were converted into green fields of the destroying "weed." Manures were bought fifty miles distant and brought into the vicinity on the cars, by rail; but such a state of things did not last long; the fever left about as suddenly as it came on, the farmers finding their yearly balance to be on the wrong side of their accounts. Although a very few realized a fair profit on their outlay, most of them made so little that the culture at this time is generally abandoned, and the farmers are returning again to the custom of their fathers and gladdening the sight of the beholder with broad fields of yellow corn. At one time 100 tons of tobacco were grown, but at this time not more than twenty are.

NORTH WALPOLE.

It appears from what information can be gathered, that but few settlements were made in this locality at an early period, although it might seem that the fishing grounds in close proximity would induce an early and populous settlement. As late as 1820 there were but few habitations in the vicinity on the east side of the river.

Solon Olcott, the Chapin brothers, Levi and Jonathan, who were natives of Westmoreland, an Englishmen by the name of Atkinson, who owned the locks at the Falls, and one Sylvanus Johnson, with their families, were the only persons remembered as living in the extreme north part of the town as late as 1823; the last mentioned being a very early settler. He was born and lived many years among the Indians, and his white friends had to use many persuasive arguments to induce him to leave them, so much had he become attached to their mode of life. He had a family of four children, two boys and two girls. One of the boys, Sylvester, was drowned; the other, John, with his sisters, lived to a ripe old age, all an unmarried life, on the paternal homestead, which was located near or on the spot where Marshall A. Davis now resides.

Old Sylvanus was very eccentric, never forgetting his early life with the Indians. It is said it was his custom for many years, in summer, to erect a wigwam on the top of Fall mountain, where he used to spend several weeks of enjoyment in the forest solitude, always declaring the Indian's mode of life preferable to civilization. Just east of the bridge, at the Falls, for many years, stood a large dwelling, on a slight elevation, called the "Tucker mansion," where a man by that name, and his family, resided, who owned the river bridge. This mansion was built by a man by the name of Geer, the daughter of whom Tucker married. At the time the railroads were built, (1849,) that dwelling was demolished and the eminence was graded down to serve the purposes of the corporations. Soon after the completion of the several railroads North Walpole began to grow, and the growth has steadily increased, principally from Irish immigrants, till now. The hamlet at the present time contains nearly four hundred inhabitants. Within the past year, (1878) a store and post office have been opened, both of which are kept by Daniel Lockwood, Esq., who claims the honor of naming and being the first postmaster in North Walpole. A commodious Roman Catholic church and parsonage have been completed the present year, (1878), and the place bids fair ere long to become populous.

DREWSVILLE.

Col. Thomas C. Drew, from whom the name of Drewsville was derived, removed there from the south end of Main St. in the village, about 1810. Before that time very few families resided in Drewsville. A man by the name of Jones and one or two other families of less note together with Uri Fairbanks, of whom Mr. Drew purchased one square mile of land, comprised about all the families residing there as late as 1800. No other reason can be assigned for the non settlement of that portion of the town till so late a time than the unfertile aspect of a portion of the soil. Mr. Drew probably foresaw the prospect of a business community's springing up in the place, at no distant day, by utilizing the then good water power in the immediate vicinity. He had manufactured brick which he intended to use in building a house on land now owned by Mrs. Lyman Watkins. The brick were made on land now owned by the Holland heirs just north of the bridge on Mad brook and were already drawn on to the contemplated location of his house; but owing to some unpleasant occurrence between Drew and some of the leading men of the village, he resolved to abandon his project of building in the village and immediately removed his brick to the east part of the town and erected the commodious building now owned by Thomas Taunt, and occupied as a hotel. After its completion it was opened for the accommodation of the public by Mr. Drew, and thereafter, till his death, he continued to keep it open. As a house of public entertainment it was favorably known, and many a jolly hour was spent by the Colonel, with such men as Gov. Henry Hubbard, Aldis Lovell, Esq., and others of like kith, who were in the habit of occasionally congregating there.

Mr. Jacob Putnam, the father of our townsman, Henry, about 1812, put the machinery into a factory which was located near the bridge and was burned. Subsequently a cotton factory was erected, which shared the same fate, and lastly another woolen factory was built on the same site of the former two, which was burned in 1860. Thomas Taunt was the proprietor.

Moses and Aaron Southard, twin brothers, commenced trade there very early and having amassed a competency in a few years, sold out and removed to Coös county in this State. Subsequently the firm of Butterfield & Walker went into business, and failed about 1828 or '30. After which Bellows & Crosby were in trade for a short time. Wm. Bellows a son of Josiah sen, and Edward Crosby a son of parson Crosby of Charlestown were the firm. A man by the name of Heaton was also in trade there between 1820 and '30 and failed. Samuel Nichols was in trade there for a long period and also Hope Lathrop, who moved to Drewsville in 1819. The latter was postmaster for some years and also deputy sheriff.

John P. Maynard came to Drewsville from Holden Mass., in 1836 and commenced the business of pulling wool and tanning sheepskins, which business is still carried on by his son, Augustus F. There were three woolen mills running in Drewsville at the same time, as late as 1840. Faulkner and Hartwell at that time did a large business in the manufacture of sash and blinds, in the building now occupied by Joseph Fisher.

After the burning of Taunt's factory in 1860 the boarding house, owned with the factory property, was converted into a hotel with additions, which was kept by Taunt for several years and was the rendezvous for social gatherings of all descriptions. It was burned about four years since, (1876.) The freshet of Oct. 1868 swept away a gristmill and carding machine establishment belonging to Charles Fisher, which was a severe loss to him.

Col. Drew gave the common and cemetery at Drewsville to the town. It is said that more business was done in Drewsville at one time (from 1820 to '30,) than in Walpole village. Col. Drew (see biography) was a leading spirit there for more than thirty years, but when the infirmities of age began to chill his ardent nature, the place began to show symptoms of decay, and has never recuperated

The Church.

It appears by the old church record that a church was formed as early as 1757 ; but it does not appear who the members were, till after the ordination of Thomas Fessenden. Reverend Jonathan Leavitt was ordained pastor June 10th, 1761, and dismissed June, 19th, 1764—the cause of his dismissal, as heretofore stated, not being wholly known. In 1767, Jan. 7th, Thomas Fessenden was ordained and a church was formed, the same day, consisting of the following members, viz. Thomas Fessenden, Col. Benjamin Bellows, John Graves, John Parmenter, William Smead, Jonathan Hall, James Bundy, Joseph Barrett, David Dennison, John Marcy, Samuel Holmes, Samuel Trott, John Kilburn jr., Timothy Delano and Nathaniel Harvey, with the wives of ten of the above-named, making the number twenty five in all. Eight years later the church

numbered one hundred. During the active pastorate of Mr.
Fessenden, of thirty eight years, the number admitted to the
church, by letter and profession, was three hundred and sixty
five, and during that time he solemnized two hundred and
ninety nine marriages. The church was called "The First
Congregational Church of Walpole," and the religious tenets
of its members were not unlike those of the Puritans, only,
perhaps, a little modified. This church in olden times was denominated "THE STANDING ORDER." The members were very
strict in the observance of the Sabbath and the Sanctuary, and
in looking after the misdoings of each other with assiduous
care and concern, as will appear by the following transactions of
the church. It appears that one Isaac Johnson was in the
habit of taking a little too much "for the stomach's sake," and
James Bundy felt disturbed. The transaction reads thus:
"Nov. 18, 1769, James Bundy complained of Isaac Johnson
for intemperate drinking—supported. Voted that he be suspended from spiritual privileges until he makes satisfaction."
He appeared, made confession, and was restored to fellowship.
On another occasion, "Oct. 11, 1770," Nathan Bundy complained of Isaac Stowell, "as guilty of falsehood and theft,
wherein, he also himself, was an accomplice—Voted to suspend both till it appears which is criminal" "They afterwards
make satisfaction and are restored."

In 1772 they "Voted one shilling per *pole* to provide for the
Lord's table, and those who refuse to pay the church tax be
suspended."

Every member of the church, who committed any irregular-
ities inconsistent with its dicipline, whatever its nature, or
whether male or female, was required to make *open* confession
at the preparatory lecture before communion.

For thirty eight years Mr. Fessenden preached to his devoted parishioners and broke the bread of life to them, without
bickering or dissension to disturb the tranquil flow of harmony and good will between himself and the people. He mingled with his people in their joys and sorrows for nearly two
generations. For sixteen years, in sunshine and rain, heat and

cold, mounted on his trusty old horse, and clad in old fashioned style, wearing a cocked hat and small clothes, he climbed Prospect St. *fifty two* or more times a year and punctually fulfilled his stipulated engagements to his patient congregation.

Mr. Fessenden at length became superannuated, when the town settled with him a colleague, in the person of Pliny Dickinson, May 6, 1805. The ministers who officiated at the Ordination were from the surrounding towns. As the names of the towns where they all resided are not in the record they cannot here be given. The order of exercises was as follows: Perley Howe made the introductory prayer, Sylvester Sage, of Westminster, preached the sermon, Aaron Hall, of Keene, made the consecrating prayer, Stephen Farrar gave the charge, Allen Pratt of Westmoreland, gave the right hand of fellowship and made the concluding prayer. After Mr. Dickinson's ordination, he took rooms with Col. Caleb Bellows, and soon became enamored with his daughter Mary, who reciprocated his feelings. The Col. objected to their marriage on account of the disparity of their ages, Mr. Dickinson being much older. But a few years difference in age was of but little concern of theirs and at length the publishing of their banns was drawing near. Mr. Bellows was informed of their intention of being published at a certain time, and repaired early to the meetinghouse in order to be in season to forbid the *bands*. It was the custom for the Town Clerk, in those days, before meeting was opened, to announce, by crying aloud, the intention of the parties desiring to be married. Nicanor Townsley was then Town Clerk, and no sooner had Mr. Bellows entered the church than he heard the last sentence of his daughter's publishment, when he rose excitedly and exclaimed " I forbid the bands!" " I forbid the bands!" For a few minutes all was silence. Of course that was an unhappy Sunday for Mr. Dickinson and the next Sunday he preached from the text: " I am a man of sorrows and acquainted with grief." The subject produced a nine day's gossip in the town, which finally died away and Mr. Dickinson married his Mary, lived happily, made a kind husband and an indulgent father to a large family, preached acceptably to his parish for twenty six years at $ 500 a year salary, and left, at his death, which occurred Aug. 27, 1835, a handsome fortune. The immediate cause of his death was being choked by the seed of a watermelon, at the dinner table, in Amherst, Mass., at the college commencement.

His connection with the society was severed finally in 1831, but virtually in 1826 when the meetinghouse was moved, the disturbances being of such a nature that his influence waned ever after. During his ministry of twenty six years two hundred and twelve persons were received into the church and two hundred and ninety eight marriages were solemnized. During the pastorates of Mr. Dickinson and Mr. Fessenden, which covered a period of sixty four years, twelve hundred and seventy seven persons received the ordinance of baptism.

Moving the meetinghouse caused a disruption in the church, which had been in existence from the early settlement of the town, and closed the society's connection with it, so far as pecuniary aid was concerned.

The meetinghouse was the property of the town. The ostensible motive for its removal to the village was that a larger number of families would be accommodated in the village than on the hill; but it is suspected the real underlying purpose was something else, which subsequent developments proved. Some of the leading men in the village signed a written obligation to the town that in case the town voted to move the meetinghouse they would shingle it and assume the expense of moving; which to a certain extent had an influence. In 1825 the question of removal came before the town in open meeting, and, being put, resulted in a majority of seventeen for removal, whereupon one hundred and fifty three legal voters, living in the south and easterly parts of the town, signed and published in the local newspaper a spirited protest. The protest was unheeded and measures were immediately taken to carry the voice of the town into effect. Probably the town never witnessed so much turmoil and angry feeling as that occasion produced. The feeling was intense, for it is found June 31, 1826, sixty six persons formally declare, " they are not of the religious persuasion of Rev. Pliny Dickinson, now minister of the town of Walpole." Probably this procedure of the parishioners was considered an effectual way of dissolving their connection with the town society. The dissenters immediately organized and formed a new society, which was called "The Independent Congregational Society," and took measures to prosecute the building of a new church on the site of the one removed. The church was completed the same year (1826) and the Rev. Mr. Dickinson preached there part of the time till 1831 when his connection with the society was dissolved as before stated. After the old meeting-house was removed Mr. Dickinson occupied the pulpit for a few months, when the society employed a man by the name of Thayer, a Unitarian. Mr. Dickinson was then called to supply the desk in the new house, which he did for a time, Stephen R. Bradley paying his entire salary from his own purse one year.

The new society was made up of all the discordant elements opposed to the removal of the old house, irrespective of the faith any one embraced. Aug. 31, 1831, Edwin Jennison, a native of the town, was ordained their minister—a sturdy Congregationalist in religious faith. A large majority of the society were Universalists and they soon became restive under the preaching of one not of their own faith. It is said annoyances of various kinds were continually occurring, till, at length, Mr. Jennison's situation became almost unendurable.

His orthodox friends, however, clung firmly and fondly to him; but they soon began to suspect themselves the victims of misplaced confidence in building the new church. The treatment Mr. Jennison had received, together with the helpless condition in which the minority found themselves, induced them to organize and form a new church and society, and also to build a new meeting-house. The parties forming a new church and society were few in number and feeble in purse, but resolute in purpose.

ORTHODOX CHURCH AND SOCIETY.

It has been seen that initiatory steps were taken to form a new church and society, which was accomplished Nov. 20th 1832, and it was called, The First Congregational Church and Society in Walpole. The original members were Wm. Jennison, Thomas Seaver, Geo. Kilburn, Orville Jennison, Calvin Blake and William Guild. The Rev. Z. S. Barstow, feeling that his brethren in faith had been circumvented, exerted himself in their behalf with the sister churches, and by his eloquence and persuasive manner raised money enough in a short time to warrant the commencement of the building of a new church edifice, which was completed in 1833, after which Mr. Edwin Jennison occupied the desk till March, 1835, when, being out of health, he relinquished his charge to one B. B. Beckwith, who was settled the same day of Mr. Jennison's retirement. Mr. Beckwith remained with the society less than ten months. The reason for Mr. Beckwith's dismissal does not fully appear; but it was said that he held to some views not consonant with the canons of the orthodox church.

Abraham Jackson was their next minister, who was settled Jan. 10, 1837, and was dismissed, at his own request, June, 5, 1845. Mr. Jackson during his eight years of labor gave general satisfaction to the church and society. He did not believe much in creeds, and during his ministry the old creed was somewhat modified; but within a few years it has been restored to its former reading. Mr. Jackson was quite liberal in his views for one of the orthodox faith, and after his dismissal preached for the Unitarians.

Aug. 6th 1845, Ezekiel H. Barstow was ordained, and continued to be their pastor till Dec. 30th, 1851, when he was dismissed, at his own request, and Alfred Goldsmith was installed the same day. Mr. Barstow was highly esteemed as a citizen of the town and was very acceptable as a preacher to most of the church and society; but there were some restless persons who desired some one else, and Mr. Barstow, knowing their wishes, determined to leave, and, although every member but one of the church and society, present at a society meeting, voted to have him recall his letter of resignation, still he remained firm in his determination. Mr. Goldsmith continued with the society till Mar. 7, 1853, when he was dismissed. The society was without a settled minister till Jan. 31, 1855, when Rev. John M. Stowe, of Hubbardston, Mass. was settled and remained till Feb. 4th 1862, a period of seven years. Mr. Stowe was universally respected by the town's people, and left town without an enemy. He was subsequently settled in his native town above mentioned. In 1877 as he was riding upon a load of wood which he was hauling to a needy friend, he was violently thrown to the ground and received such injuries that he died in a few days.

Rev. Gabriel H. De Bevoise, was the next minister; he was settled Aug. 31, 1865, and dismissed, Aug. 6, 1868. June 2, 1870, Rev. Wm. E. Dickinson from Amherst, Mass., was settled, and dismissed Mar. 31, 1875. During his pastorate (1874) the church edifice was raised and repaired, and convenient rooms were built underneath, for various society purposes, at a cost of about $ 6,000, of which sum the ladies of the society contributed $ 2,100, Benjamin F. Aldrich, $ 1800, Oliver Martin, $ 1500, and the rest was given by different individuals, in smaller sums. Edwin Hosmer presented a chandelier which cost $ 100

Rev. Thomas S. Robie supplied the desk from Sept. 18th, 1875 to Sept. 1876. Sept. 20, 1877, Fred Lyman Allen, of White River Junction, was ordained and settled and is the present pastor. During a period of more than forty years this church has had its times of sunshine and shade, and although its beginning was weak, it is now strong, and general harmony prevails.

WALPOLE TOWN CONGREGATIONAL SOCIETY.

This society was made up from a number of individuals, formerly belonging to the old town society before its disruption in 1826. Previous to 1830 one Mr. Thayer and others preached in the old meeting-house some three years, but were Unitarians in religious sentiment, and for that and some other

reasons the Trinitarians did not fellowship with them. The
society was no longer supported by a town tax, but by private
subscriptions, although the meeting-house was still the property
of the town.

A call was extended to Mr. Wm. A. Whitwell, in 1830, which
was accepted, and he was ordained, Feb. 3d, the same year.
He was the first Unitarian minister settled in Walpole, and
his stay was short, for it is found by the record, that in 1833,
May 23, Rev. Orestes A. Bronson was installed, who resigned
in March, 1834.

He (Bronson) afterwards adopted some other religious isms
and finally settled down a Roman Catholic. He was a man of
superior abilities and varied attainments, and, during the last
thirty years, has made considerable stir in literary circles by
his numerous writings and publications on various subjects.

Rev. Horatio Wood was installed Sept. 24, 1834, and resigned
June 22, 1838. At this time the *elite* of Walpole attended
church at the old meeting-house, where they were sure to be
entertained, if nothing more, by the superior choir music. Probably at no time in the town's history was church music so
exquisitely rendered as at that period. A rich treat was always
in store for those attended service there, which was continued
several years.

Wm. Silsbee was ordained July 1, 1840, and resigned Sept.
3, 1842. This year the Unitarian meeting-house was built and
a new society was formed, called " THE TOWN CONGREGATIONAL
SOCIETY." The church tablets were presented by Mr. Abial
Chandler, then of Boston, Mass., but afterwards a resident of
Walpole, who bequeathed a liberal sum to Dartmouth College at his death.

Martin W. Willis was ordained Dec. 6, 1843, and resigned
May 1, 1848. Mr. Willis was the first minister settled after
the completion of the new house.

The Rev. Wm. P. Tilden was installed Sept. 27, 1848, and
resigned June 1, 1855. Mr. Tilden will long be remembered
by the society for the goodness of his heart and his fidelity to
the best interests of the church and society. As a citizen he

always manifested a lively interest in the cause of general education and the promotion of temperance principles among the young.

Rev. Mr. Lathrop was installed Nov. 6. 1856, and preached about one year, when Mr. Ranney was hired one year to supply the desk. Chas. Ritter was installed Nov, 3, 1858, and left after preaching a little more than one year, the society being dissatisfied with him on account of some peculiarities not consonant with the bearing of a minister, after which the Rev. C. T. Canfield supplied the desk from Jan. 1, 1860, to the following June. Thomas Dawes was installed Dec. 15, 1861, and resigned Jan. 1, 1865.

The same year Nathaniel Seaver, Jun., was ordained Nov. 23, and resigned May 23, 1868. Russell N. Bellows supplied the desk from Oct. 18 the same year, and resigned Oct. 1, 1869. Geo. Dexter was settled June 10, 1870, and continued with the society till May 3, 1873, after which he left the ministry.

The next minister, the present pastor, Rev. William Brown, was installed Aug. 1873. The society shows no signs of weakness, and it has every reason to expect many years of prosperity in the future.

UNIVERSALIST SOCIETY.

In 1836 the "Independent Congregational Society," which had been in existence since 1826, dissolved, and those members believing in the doctrine of Universalism, being a large majority, immediately formed a new society, which was called, "THE FIRST UNIVERSALIST SOCIETY IN WALPOLE," and hired Rev. Daniel Ackley to supply the desk. How long Mr. Ackley continued to preach there the records of the society do not disclose, but for some two years or more; after which Rev. Charles Woodhouse and others occasionally preached there for some ten or twelve years. At length the society became weakened, the interest flagged, and preaching was suspended. For many years after the building stood empty, in a decaying, dilapidated condition, a fit habitation for owls and bats, and as a speaking monitor to professing Christians who will allow malice to usurp the throne of reason.

In 1869, the old proprietors being mostly dead, their heirs sold the old house by piecemeal, to the highest bidder. Thus ended an enterprise which began in a spirit of animosity and resulted in a pecuniary loss to the proprietors of 94 *per cent.* of their first investment, besides the loss of interest.

METHODIST EPISCOPAL SOCIETY.

In the summer of 1842 Walpole was made a Methodist station, in connection with Langdon, at the request of Increase S. Guild, and John P. Prouty was appointed preacher for the year. He moved into town in the fall of the same year and occupied rooms in the house of Mr. Lyman Watkins. His meetings were held in the town hall, and his labors proved successful. He was returned the next year and many converts were made. In 1844 Kimball Hadley was sent here by the conference and remained one year. Mr. Hadley was an able man and his people reluctantly parted with him. During the year the society commenced building a chapel, which was located on the west side of Washington square, where it now stands. In Nov. 1845, the chapel was completed and I. W. Huntley was the minister that year. In 1846, A. S. Tenney was sent here and remained two years. In 1848, Stephen Eastman was appointed to this station, and he also remained two years. The pulpit was supplied in 1850 by Dudley P. Leavitt, a young man of promise and greatly beloved by the brethren. His wife, Charlotte F., died Feb. 16, 1852, aged 23, and was the first tenant of the new cemetery. In 1851 Simeon P. Heath was stationed here for one year, and in 1852 Ira Carter for the same length of time. In 1854 Ozias S. Morris supplied the pulpit, kept the winter term of the high school, and represented the town in the General Court. In 1855–6 Henry Chandler and Hanson F. Forrestall supplied the pulpit respectively. In 1857–8 Philander Wallingford, from Claremont, supplied the desk to the satisfaction of all interested. Charles Lewis was the last minister sent here and lived but a short time after completing his labors for the year 1859. No church was formed till 1850. The first members, or some of the first, were Increase S. Guild, Uriah Newton, Anson Lawrence, Jacob W. Hale, Sanford Miller, and Hiram Hefflon. The society discontinued holding service after 1860, and rented their Chapel to a small number of Episcopalians who occupied the house some two years. In 1868 the chapel was sold to the Roman catholics, where occasionally they hold meetings.

At the disruption of the Methodist Society, a portion of its members worshipped with the Unitarians and the remaining portion sought fellowship with the Congregational Society.

THE UNITED RELIGIOUS CHRISTIAN SOCIETY.

About the year 1800, one Abner Jones, of Vermont, became dissatisfied with the tenets of the Freewill Baptists with whom he had been associated, and seceded from them, and commenced propagating sentiments of his own through Vermont and a portion of New Hampshire. The new sect were denominated "Christians." Edward B. Rollins, a convert to the new doctrine, came to Walpole in Oct. 1817, and, commenced holding meetings in private houses, barns, and at one time, it is said, in an old cider mill. He was a persuasive, powerful preacher and soon gathered around him a large number of followers. In the December following a church was formed. It appears by the church records, that in 1823 Jacob B. Burnham was their preacher, who it is said was a convert of Rollins. About this time some jealousies had crept into the church, which ripened into a division, one party adhering to Rollins and the other to Burnham. Following is the number and succession of pastors, the date of their pastorate not being obtained, viz. Edward B. Rollins, Jacob B. Burnham, Abiah Kidder, Jonathan Farnam, C. W. Martin, Wm. H. Ireland, Jared L. Greene, Seth Hinkley, David B. Murray, N. S. Chadwick, J. M. Woodward and Clark W. Simonds. Whole number of different members, two hundred and ninety seven.

The party adhering to Rollins built a house of worship on the "Flat," at the foot of what is called "March Hill." In

1826 those who followed Burnham, built a church, now standing at what is called the "Hollow." Every year for many years new converts were made, who were baptised in artificial pools made in the small brook in the vicinity of the meeting-house, where hundreds of people, from all parts, would congregate to witness the ceremony. For several years almost every family in that part of the town was represented in that church, and in some instances entire families. At one time the membership of the church was nearly or quite as large as any in town. The Rollins church was short lived. Mr. Burnham continued his pastorate till 1845 or '50 when he resigned the position which he had held so long, and commenced the practice of medicine. Preaching is still continued there, but it is evident that the noon of prosperity, in the church, is past.

EPISCOPAL SOCIETY.

The society at Drewsville, first known as "The First Protestant Episcopal Society of Walpole," was incorporated in 1816, and the first meeting was called in April, 1817, at the house of Thomas C. Drew. The meetings were held for a number of years in the hall of the public house belonging to Mr. Drew. The first Rector's name was Luman Foote. In 1836 the present stone chapel was built and consecrated, Bishop Alexander V. Griswold officiating. Thomas C. Drew gave the land whereon the edifice stands, with the proviso that it should never be used for other purposes. At the time of the consecration the original name of the society was changed to "Saint Peter's Church," by which name it is still designated. In 1867 the inside of the chapel was tastefully altered and repaired at a cost of about $2,000. At the present time the number of worshipers is not so great as in former times, but they are devoted and constant. The Rev. E. A. Renouf of Keene is now the Rector.

BAPTISTS.

Samuel Nichols, a merchant living in Drewsville, at the time the Episcopal chapel was built or immediately after, (1837) at his own cost built a small chapel for the Baptist denomination, where meetings were held for several years; but after a while the interest waned and the meetings were suspended. During the church's palmiest days it is said the membership was some thirty or forty. The building is still standing, but is used for a carpenter's shop. There are but very few, if any, Baptists in town at the present time (1878.)

EDUCATION.

In the early settlement of the town the people did not forget the education of their children, although money was scarce and the demands for it pressing. As early as 1768 the town established three schools, one near the meeting house, where one Ebenezer Swan taught, he being the first male teacher in town; one near Cold river, and the third in the "Valley." Two or three years later three school houses were built. In 1778, with a population of seven hundred inhabitants, 100 pounds was raised and the amount appropriated yearly has increased from that time till the present. In those early days the facilities for acquiring the simple rudiments of an English education were very meagre. As late as 1790 many of the children among the rural population received most of their education at home. The "New England Primer," the Psalter, Dodworth's spelling book, and the New Testament were the only school books used. There was no text book on arithmetic, but, to supply the place, the teachers used to give their pupils practical "sums," and explain the why and wherefore as best they could. Even "Dodworth's" spelling book was not introduced till 1770. Soon after the Revolutionary war, English grammar began to obtain in the common schools and about 1800 Morse's geography was introduced as one of the studies. It is said that poor children, in some instances, learned to write on *birch bark*. An instance is related of a poor boy, destitute of shoes, being then in his eighteenth year, and eager to acquire some education, made himself some *moccasins* from strands of swingletow, that he might go to school. His grandchildren now wear calf boots.

Early in the present century, about 1807, a brick schoolhouse was built in the village, on the corner of what are now called Elm and West streets. It had two schoolrooms on the first floor and a commodious hall on the second, where occasionally a select school was kept, called an academy. Wm. G. Field, a lawyer, residing in town, kept a select school there several years during the period from 1820 to 1830. In 1831 several persons procured an act of incorporation, built a building and established an academy, which building is now occupied by the village district high school. The first Principal was Charles H. Allen, a graduate of Harvard, of 1831, who opened the school in the fall of 1831, with a large number of students. After Mr. Allen Mr. Prichard was principal and then Mr. Packard. In 1837 Julius L. Janes was the principal, Abigail E. Janes preceptress, and Miss Ann Bellows teacher of music. The whole number of pupils during the year was 193. Mr. Janes did not remain long. After he left Mr. Henry F. Harrington had charge of the school for a considerable time and it is said was quite popular.

John Nichols, who was an eccentric character, one Seagrave, John N. Bellows, Fisher Rice, John Goldsbury, and S. H. McCollister, who has since become popular in the cause of education, were, among others, the principals till the time the property changed ownership. The school was not a success, although at the commencement a fair number of students attended. It was kept running, however, with varied degrees of success till 1854, when district number one obtained possession of the lot and building, built a new school house and established a graded school, under what is called the "Somersworth Act" which arrangement has continued unbroken to the present time.

Of the High School teachers, remembered are the following: Galen Graves, Francis B. Knapp, Burrill Porter, Geo. Brown, Abel P. Richardson, two by the name of Howard, Chas. C. Davis, John E. Russell and Curtis R. Crowell, the last of whom has held the position for eight years and is still the principal.

In 1814, the town appointed the first superintending school committee consisting of Pliny Dickinson, Oliver Sparhawk and

Ebenezer Morse, and has made yearly appointments ever since. This town has always manifested a lively interest in her common schools, doing as much and most of the time more than other towns, of its population, in the state. The number of scholars in town has greatly diminished within a few years. In 1841 the number was seven hundred and four, since which time it has diminished two sevenths, but more than one and a half times more money is appropriated now than then. The town has sent into the world's field more than twenty college graduates; thirty-nine physicians, ten lawyers, ten clergymen, one chief justice of the State, two judges and one member of Congress.

Library Association. The Walpole Library Association was first started in 1795 by Jeremiah Mason, who for a time resided in this town and practised the profession of a lawyer. Mason was the first librarian and Joseph Dennie the second. This association was kept up till 1849 when at the burning of the old brick store a portion of the books was destroyed, and soon after, the remaining portion was presented to the town. From that time till the present the town has annually appropriated one hundred dollars for the purchase of new books, excepting two or three years during the late war. Donations have been made occasionally, by liberal minded citizens, which have augmented its size, till now the number of volumes is nearly twenty five hundred. The books are mostly standard works on history, literature, science and agriculture. The library is cherished as one of the crown jewels of the town.

LIST OF SUPERINTENDING SCHOOL COMMITTEES FROM 1814 TO 1878:

1814. Pliny Dickinson, Oliver Sparhawk, Ebenezer Morse.
1815. Pliny Dickinson, Wm. G. Field, Abraham Holland.
1816. Stephen Johnson, Ebenezer Morse, Pliny Dickinson.
1817. Ebenezer Morse, Pliny Dickinson, Stephen Johnson.
1818. Pliny Dickinson, Roger Vose, Thomas Seaver.
1819. Pliny Dickinson, Oliver Sparhawk, Thomas Sparhawk.
1820. Pliny Dickinson, H. Crawford, Roger Vose.
1821. Pliny Dickinson, Roger Vose, Wm. G. Field.

1822. Pliny Dickinson, as principal visitor, Stephen Johnson
         and Oliver Sparhawk for No. 1; Wm. G. Field for
         No. 2; Henry Foster and Roger Vose for No. 3;
         and Joseph Mason and Ebenezer Morse for No. 4.

1823. Pliny Dickinson as principal visitor and Daniel Gilbert,
         Henry Foster, Joseph Bond, Wm. G. Field, Fred-
         erick Vose and Henry Fitch, associates.

1824. Pliny Dickinson, Frederick Vose, Wm, G. Field. (The
         duty of examining teachers was imposed on the
         committee this year for the first time.)

1825. Pliny Dickinson, Henry Foster, Aran Evans.

1826. Pliny Dickinson, Thomas Seaver, Frederick Vose.

1827. Pliny Dickinson, Wm. G. Field, Henry Foster.

1828. Pliny Dickinson, Wm. G. Field, Henry Foster, Aldis
         Lovell, Joseph Mason.

1829. Ebenezer Morse, Jacob B. Burnham, Frederick Vose.

1830. Jacob N. Knapp. From 1830 to 1834 the town voted
         to suspend visiting schools and no committee seems
         to have been appointed.

1835. Horatio Wood, B. B. Beckwith, Miles S. Gardner.
         The foregoing committee was requested by a vote
         of the town to visit schools and examine teachers.

1836. From 1836 to 1839 the town voted to dispense with
         the services of a Superintending Committee.

In 1838 the town voted to prohibit the introduction of any
         school books except those recommended by a coun-
         ty convention.

In 1839 the town voted to appoint a Superintending Commit-
         tee and have them examine teachers and visit schools.
         Abraham Jackson, Wm. Silsby, Henry F. Harring-
         ton, Joseph Mason and Wm. Guild Jr., were ap-
         pointed.

1840. Edward Livermore, John Nichols, Wm. Guild Jr.

1841. Edward Livermore, Abraham Jackson, Jesseniah
         Kittredge.

1842. Abraham Jackson, Ebenezer Morse, Jesseniah Kit-
         tredge.

1843. Ebenezer Morse, Abraham Jackson, Daniel G. Wright.

1844. Abraham Jackson, Martin W. Willis, Daniel G. Wright.

1845. Nathaniel G. Sprague, Frederick Vose, Martin W. Willis.

1846. Ezekiel H. Barstow, Martin W. Willis, Nathaniel G. Sprague.

1847. Ezekiel H. Barstow, Martin W. Willis, Farnum F. Lane.

1848. Ezekiel H. Barstow, Wm. P. Tilden, Thomas Bellows.

1849. Ezekiel H. Barstow, Wm. P. Tilden, Thomas Bellows.

1850. Ezekiel H. Barstow, Wm. P. Tilden, Thomas Bellows.

1851. Ezekiel H. Barstow, Wm. P. Tilden, Thomas Bellows.

1852. Wm. P. Tilden, Thomas Bellows, Alfred Goldsmith.

1853. Wm. P. Tilden, Thomas Bellows, Francis B. Knapp.

1854. Wm. P. Tilden, Thomas Bellows, Francis B. Knapp.

1855. Wm. P. Tilden, Thomas Bellows, Francis B. Knapp.

1856. John M. Stowe, Thomas Bellows, Frederick N. Knapp.

1857. John M. Stowe, John W. Knight, Thomas Bellows.

1858. John M. Stowe, John W. Knight, George Aldrich.

1859. John M. Stowe, John W. Knight, George Aldrich.

1860. John M. Stowe, John W. Knight, Geo. A. Blake.

1861. John M. Stowe, John W. Knight, Henry G. Wheelock.

1862. John W. Knight, Henry G. Wheelock, Jared L. Green.

1863. John M. Stowe, Jared L. Green, John W. Knight.

1864. John W. Knight, John W. Hayward.

1865. John W. Knight, John W. Hayward, Geo. H. Gilbert.

1866. A. P. Richardson, J. G. Bellows, A. Herbert Bellows.

1867. A. P. Richardson, A. Herbert Bellows, Geo. P. Porter.

1868. Abel P. Richardson, George Aldrich, George A. Blake.

1869. Abel P. Richardson, George Aldrich, George A. Blake.

1870. Abel P. Richardson, George Aldrich, George A. Blake.

1871. Abel P. Richardson, George Aldrich, George A. Blake.

1872. Abel P. Richardson, George Aldrich, George A. Blake.

1873. Abel B. Richardson, George Aldriah, George A. Blake.

1874. A. P. Richardson, George Aldrich, Samuel H. Porter.

1875. Abel P. Richardson, George Aldrich.

1876. William Brown.

1877. George Aldrich.

1878. Samuel H. Porter.

In looking over the columns of the "Cheshire Gazette," published in Walpole, by Francis Parton, in 1826 many articles of interest are found. Among the great number, the following may be of local interest.

"FOR THE CHESHIRE GAZETTE.

"I lately got sight of a little periodical publication, edited by Edward B. Rollins, called the "Bethlehem Star" and a twinkling star it is. Among the original matter that illumines its pages, is the account of the miraculous recovery of Mrs. Hadley and Mrs. Lamson, through the instrumentality of a man by the name of John Pratt, belonging to Walpole, N. H. who professed to have the gift of healing."

"Mrs. Hadley, of Bethel Vt. was taken sick with a violent fever and left in a helpless state, being unable to walk or raise herself up from the bed, for more than *ten* years, notwithstanding all the means used by the most skilful physicians. Sister Lamson was attacked with a scrofulous disease in the neck and right knee, so as to deprive her of the use of that limb. In this situation she was confined for more than *five* years, during which time she grew more feeble, and all prospects threatened her speedy dissolution. Brother Pratt, who had been sent for, informed them that he had received satisfactory evidence that the Lord had called him to lay his hands on the sick, and that they should be restored. Prayer and intercession were then made by brother Pratt and others, when, all of a sudden, sister Lamson arose upon her feet, clapped her hands with joy and walked around the house! The next morning sister Hadley obtained evidence that her *sins* were forgiven, when she instantly arose and walked into the other room crying *'glory to God?'* This remarkable event has revived several from a backsliding state, confirmed the saints in the faith of the Gospel, while gainsayers were put to silence and *confounded.* Mrs Hadley at present appears to enjoy perfect health; sister Lamson is entirely free from pain and the disease appears to be entirely removed."

From the Cheshire Gazette of the 30th of Dec. 1825, the

following *morceau* is taken; "Mr. Editor; I notice from various papers beyond the circulation of the "Bethelem Star" that the miraculous gifts of brother Pratt are daily becoming more and more a subject of notoriety, confounding gainsayers and giving the brethren great occasion to rejoice under copious showers of spiritual refreshings. Among the numerous instances in which he has been pleased to display his healing powers on our afflicted brethren, one lately occurred in this vicinity, which has not yet appeared in the Star, but which, from the singularity of the means used on the occasion, deserves to be laid before the public. The subject of his gracious interposition was a man about fifty years of age, who had for twenty years before been as *deaf* as an anvil, over which he and brother Pratt had both formerly interchanged the civilities of their professions. Various acoustics had been applied to no effect, and every day he was more inclined to turn a *deaf* ear to the exhortations of brother Pratt concerning his increasing maladies. This son of Vulcan remained *steeled* against the workings of the prophet's power, and no fervency of the good spirit was sufficient to *soften* the *temper* of the unregenerate. At this time the patient having some demands against the prophet locked him up in prison, "until he should pay the uttermost farthing.' But mark the powers of the righteous against whom the gates of prison shall not prevail. He groaned in his confinement, and lifting his hand towards heaven *swore*—when all of a sudden, his bands were loosed, his fetters fell from his feet, the prison doors flew open and the man of miracles walked out undisturbed, to the no small joy and astonishment of all true believers. And he departed straightway and being full of the 'good spirit' once more sought the face of his oppressor with a determination to display the full force of his Christian temper by 'heaping coals of fire upon his head' in the wonderful operation of opening his ears to understand the mystery of spiritual things. Hitherto he had opened the eyes of the blind, restored the lame to the full use of their limbs, raised from beds of sickness the decrepid and infirm, healed all manner of bruises and putrefying sores, and

decked the wrinkled brow of age with youthful bloom.   But
as yet his healing powers have been wholly confined to the sis-
terhood, whose maladies readily yielded to the soothing operation of 'laying on of hands.'   The constitution and temperament of his present patient and the situation of the mal-
ady were very different from any he had hitherto encountered.
The organ of hearing, protected by a petrous shell, in this instance *case hardened* by time and the constant percussion of the
hammer and anvil, would not as readily yield to the ordinary
applications.   Our prophet therefore wisely resorted to 'the
laying on' of *fists*; and after repeated applications of this sov-
ereign remedy to the regions of the auditories, and rebuking
the unclean spirit with various exhortations suitable to the occasion, lo! for the first time, the deaf began to hear the mer-
ciful dealings of the prophets, and feel the power of his influence.   The dividing of the Red Sea never *struck* the aston-
ished Egyptians with more *force* than did the man of miracles
the affrighted blacksmith.   And it is said that in commemoration
of that memorable event several drops of the same ocean were
seen to flow from the nose of the hopeful patient.   The cure
was perfect, and while history is read or the noble deeds of our
benefactors held in sacred remembrance, this miracle will be
handed down to posterity and remain a proud memorial in the
annals of John Pratt.

MILITARY.

That military organization was a feature in the town's history before the Revolutionary war commenced is known by
the facts that General, then Capt., Benjamin Bellows went to
Westminster with his *company* in 1775 to suppress the distur-
bance occasioned by the shooting of William French at that
place and, also, by the disciplined readiness of the men of
Walpole in starting for the scene of strife at Lexington, on
hearing the news of the collision between the British troops
and the Americans.

After the State Constitution was adopted in 1792, companies,
regiments and battalions were formed throughout the state,
and Walpole furnished her share of men to constitute the 20th

regiment. So far as is known an artillery company was the only uniformed one, except a portion of a mounted company (Westmoreland furnishing the other portion) called the Cavalry, up to 1826. The uniforms of the artillery were a blue coat and pantaloons trimmed with red, and, upon the head, a bell shaped leather cap with a black plume tipped with red. The ordnance was a six pound brass cannon, and each soldier wore a short sword strapped to his side. A portion of this company (drafted men) went to Portsmouth in 1814, under the command of Josiah Bellows 3d (see narrative).

The uniforms of the cavalry company were red coats trimmed with black, buff breeches with high legged boots and a hard, bell shaped leather cap, bearing a red plume tipped with white. Strapped upon the horse's back was a holster for a brace of pistols, a canteen and knapsack, while the soldiers wore a cutlass or broad-sword strapped to his loins. The music for the company consisted of clarionet, fife and bugle, without keys, played by Charles Chaffin of this town—now living. This company disbanded sometime between 1826 and 1830. In about 1826 a new company was formed consisting of about forty men besides the officers, and called the Walpole Rifle Co. Jonathan Cutler was the first captain of this company, David Buffum 2d, Charles Redington 3d, &c. Cutler made the rifles in a shop that stood on the site of Col. Buffum's store, and was a moving spirit in organizing the company. This company was uniformed in grey throughout, trimmed with velvet, with a black wool tuft on the shoulders of the coat. The 'pants' were faced with black velvet extending about eight or ten inches upwards from the bottom. Their caps were similar in shape to those above described except that the plume was black. This company made a very fine appearance when on duty and occupied on *muster* days the extreme left wing of the regiment, while the artillery occupied the extreme right. This company was in existence about fifteen or more years, when it was disbanded, owing to the growing disfavor for military organizations. Before 1840, for many years, every able bodied man between the ages of eighteen and forty five if not exempt by disability, was obliged, according to law, to do military duty in some military organization under a penalty of eight dollars fine annually, or imprisonment in the county jail till the fine was paid. The men were also obliged to furnish a gun, a knapsack, a cartridge box which would contain twenty four rounds of ammunition, and a canteen, at their own expense. Infantry (uniformed) companies were furnished guns at the expense of the state. In this town, besides the companies above noticed, there was a large number of persons who were liable to do military duty who had no military aspirations, but were obliged to meet the requirements of law in a company called the "Saucy Six." This company when called out made the occasion a time of hilarity, drinking and roistering, many of whom would dress most fantastically and give their officers much trouble, although they were liable to a heavy fine for any misbehavior. On training days, music and *rum*, (the latter by the pailful,) were furnished the soldiers at the expense of the company officers. The uniformed companies were generally furnished with a full military band, while the "flood-wood" companies had to put up with a fife and two drums. Drumming was an *art*, and drumming schools were taught in town eighty and ninety years ago. The honor of holding military office was deemed a matter of envied importance in the early history of the town, and the lucky one favored with a commission was ever afterwards, as seen by the town records, spoken of as Serg't A., Ensign B., Lieut. C. and Capt. D. Those titles were so much honored that they are perpetuated in marble in the old cemetery. The military spirit died out about forty years ago (1840); but there are indications at the present writing of history repeating itself. The last regimental muster in town was held east of the residence of Thomas Bellows, in the autumn of 1841, at which time the trees were uprooted on the common, as before mentioned.

Music.

The history of music in town affords very little material for the historian. The first mention that is made of it is found in the old church records, where Thomas Sparhawk is said to have been chosen to *set* the psalms, in 1771. According to tradition the "setting" of the psalms devolved upon the deacons, but sometimes deacons would be chosen who had no musical cultivation, when some other person was selected who had a musical *ear*. The setting consisted in reading one verse of a stanza by the deacon, and then giving the key or pitch of the tune to be sung, which was called "deaconing the psalm." In 1779 Roger and Eben Farnham were chosen to "set" the psalms. Church music for hymns and psalms was in its infancy at that time and the style of music that obtained can hardly be guessed at : but a little later Billings, Swan and Reed published tunes for lyric verse, many of which were called '*fugue*,' the different parts of the score of which follows in succession—the bass leading off in repeating the verse. One of those old tunes is so arranged that when a portion of a certain stanza is sung, ending in, "and bow before the Lord," a most ludicrous effect is produced, thus; "and bow, wow, wow before the Lord "

The town in 1788 "Voted to raise fifteen pounds for the use of Promoting Singing. To be Laid out in the Several Districts and if not Schooled out in each District, *it shall be in the rest in Proportion*." In a subsequent year fifteen pounds more was raised and a man was hired to teach singing and conduct the music on the Sabbath.

For several years Oliver S. Sparhawk conducted the singing in the old meeting-house on the hill. The first piano forte, or one of the first, ever used in town was of English manufacture, was made about 1790, and was owned by Col. Caleb Bellows long before attempts were made to manufacture such instruments in this country, to any great extent. It is a curiosity not only for its mechanical construction, but as showing the improvements since in such instruments. It may be seen in the village at the present time. From 1820 to 1850 pianofortes gradually were purchased from time to time, and at the last mentioned period, fifty could be counted in the village alone. When the piano-forte was brought into the parlor the spinning wheel vanished from the kitchen, and while perhaps some dozen ladies out of hundreds have achieved success as amateur players, the result to the rest has been a failure, their instruments serving rather as furniture for ornament than for utility.   Perhaps at no time did the cultivation of music obtain so generally as it did from 1835 to 1855, since which time a tacit indifference has been, for the most part, manifested in its cultivation.   An organ, which is said to have been the gift of Gen. Amasa Allen, was used in the old church from early in the present century, or before, till the disruption of the society, after which it was used by the Unitarian society till the purchase of the present one in about 1855.   One Samuel Johnson came here from Chester, Vt. and taught singing about 1836 or '7, and infused a new life into the music-loving people of the town which did not die out for several years.   There was a spirit of emulation between the church choirs to have good music, the result of which was that large congregations attended church on Sunday.   About the same time a brass band was organized consisting of the following members, viz. William and Ebenezer Guild, the former the conductor, Geo. C. Lincoln, Hubbard Wilder and brother, Wm. Daggett, Orin Wyman, Leonard B. Tinkham, Albert Wight, Henry D. Livingston, T. W. Farr, Geo. C. Reynolds and others.   This organization continued but a few years, owing to the vacancies which occurred yearly, with no musicians to fill them.   An anecdote is related concerning the band which is as follows: One of the bugle players, unfortunately, had weak lips, which rendered the tones of his instrument impure, as if passing through wool. Those tones disturbed one of the members who had a sensitive ear, and he procured an old rusty pair of shears, neatly done up with a note, and sent them to the unfortunate bugler, requesting him when he performed again to be sure and *shear his tones.*

MORTALITY.

No record of the yearly mortality of Walpole was kept till 1806, when Pliny Dickinson commenced and continued one

during his pastorate, which is very imperfect, when Thomas
Seaver continued it till he died. The pastors of the Congregational, and also, of the Unitarian churches, respectively,
did their duty in this matter. From 1860 to the present time
A. K. Maynard, and also the Town Clerk, have with great
care recorded all the deaths in town that came to their knowledge, although the ages of some of the persons are wanting.
From the foregoing named records some important facts have
been brought forth. From 1806 to 1850 a few yearly records
have been selected that are complete, which show the following
results: In 1806 the average length of life was 22 years; in
1812, 29; in 1814, 23; in 1830, 36; in 1846, 43; in 1847, 40;
in 1848, 44; in 1849, 41; in 1850, 40; in 1860, 47; in 1861, 70;
in 1870, 60; in 1872, 59; and in 1878, 59. The aggregate average age, for nine perfect records from 1806 to 1850 is $35\frac{1}{2}$
years. The aggregate average age from 1860 to 1878 inclusive is $52\frac{1}{4}$. Allowing the population of the town for the last
eighteen years to be 1900, the death rate has been $2\frac{3}{4}$ per cent
of the population yearly.

The causes which have contributed to the foregoing results
are conjectured to be as follows: First, the greater number of
births in the beginning of the century, and consequently the
greater number of early deaths from diseases incident to children. Secondly, the general ignorance prevailing at that time
of hygienic measures to prolong life. Thirdly, the customary
habit of the male adult population of drinking alcoholic drinks
to excess, which brought many to premature graves. On the
other hand, the causes which have contributed to greater longevity, later in the century, are more intelligent parents, a
better understanding of the laws of life and health and less
intemperance.

Following is an approximate list of persons who have died in
town whose days have numbered four score and ten years and
upwards. 1774, Phillippi Hall, aged 90; 1801, Dea. Benj. Foster, 94; 1802, Jona. Hall, 91; 1808, John Fletcher, 94; 1814, Aaron Graves, 93; 1816, Abigail Carpenter, 94; 1820, widow
Stearns, 90; 1821, widow White, 96; 1824, widow Robb, 95;

1824, widow Merriam, 96; 1831, Jerusha Alexander, aged nearly 100; 1833, Samuel Morrison, 91; 1837, Amy Wightman, 98;
1838 Sarah Carlisle, 99; 1840, Rhoda Jennison, 90; 1841, Mrs.
Butterfield, 90; 1842, Phillippi Hall, 91; 1845, Thomas Russell,
94; 1846, Dr. John Williams. 98; 1847, Dr. Geo. Sparhawk, 91;
1847, Dr. Abraham Holland, 96; 1850, Mary Nichols, 90, Molly
Stearns, 90; 1854, Moses Fisher, 91, Lucy Fay, 92, Jona. Fletcher, 100 y's 5 m. and 4 d.; 1857, Daniel Marsh, 92; 1861, Mary
Fisher, 91; 1862, Thomas Seaver, 90; 1867, Rebecca Wellington,
about 100; 1868, Jacob N. Knapp, 94; 1869, Mary Bellows, 96;
John Marshall, 95; 1870, Clarinda Adams, 92; Alvin Chickering, 92; 1878, Sally Ripley, 95, Mary Howard, 91.

DELEGATES TO EXETER.

In 1775 the town, not feeling disposed to bear the public
burdens of the Province without representation, sent the following named persons to Exeter to represent the town.

1775, Thomas Sparhawk six months and John Bellows the
remaining portion of the year; 1776-7, Christopher Webber;
1778. Ephraim Marsh; 1779, Josiah Goldsmith; 1780, John
Graves represented the town at Windsor, Vt.; 1781, Josiah
Goldsmith; 1782, Manoah Drury; 1784, Manoah Drury; 1785,
Levi Hooper; 1786, Amasa Allen; 1787, Amasa Allen; 1788,
Aaron Allen; 1789, Aaron Allen; 1790, Amasa Allen; 1791,
Amasa Allen.

LIST OF REPRESENTATIVES

to the General Court of the State of New Hampshire after the
Constitution of the State was adopted in 1792.

1792.	Thomas Bellows.	1800.	Joseph Bellows.
1793.	" "	1801.	Thomas Sparhawk, jr.
1794.	" "	1802.	Thomas C. Drew.
1795.	Thomas Sparhawk, jr.	1803.	Thomas Sparhawk.
1796.	" "	1804.	Thomas C. Drew.
1797.	Samuel Grant.	1805.	" "
1798.	Thomas Sparhawk, jr.	1806.	Amasa Allen.
1799.	Samuel Grant.	1807.	Thomas C. Drew.

1808.	Thomas C. Drew,	1839.	Stephen Stearns.
1809.	" "	1840.	Henry S. Tudor,
1810.	Josiah Bellows.	"	Wm. Bellows.
1811.	" "	1841.	Henry S. Tudor,
1812.	Stephen Johnson.	"	Ebenezer Morse.
1813.	Isaac Redington.	1842.	Stephen Stearns,
1814.	" "	"	Daniel Merriam, jr.
1815.	David Stone.	1843.	Edwin Hosmer,
1816.	Isaac Redington.	"	Henry S. Tudor.
1817.	Samuel Grant.	1844.	John P. Maynard,
1818.	Roger Vose.	"	Luther Proctor.
1819.	Josiah Bellows.	1845.	John P. Maynard,
1820.	" "	"	Luther Proctor.
1821.	Daniel W. Bisco.	1846.	Charles Sparhawk,
1822.	" "	"	Elijah C. Kilburn.
1823.	Josiah Bellows, 3d.	1847.	Samuel Nichols,
1824.	" "	"	Farnum F. Lane.
1825.	" "	1848.	Samuel Nichols,
1826.	Wm. G. Field.	"	Farnum F. Lane.
1827.	" "	1849.	Jacob B. Burnham,
1828.	" "	"	David Buffum.
1829.	" "	1850.	David Buffum,
1830.	James Hooper.	"	Jacob B. Burnham,
1831.	Leonard Bisco.	1851.	Jesseniah Kittredge,
1832.	" "	"	Thomas Bellows.
1833.	Frederick Vose.	1852.	Peletiah Armstrong,
1834.	Lem'l Starkweather,	"	David Fisher.
"	Thomas Bellows.	1853	David C. Thompson,
1835.	Leonard Bisco,	"	Aaron P. Howland.
"	Geo. Huntington.	1854.	Aaron P. Howland,
1836.	Leonard Bisco,	"	David C. Thompson.
"	Geo. Huntington,	1855.	Augustus Faulkner,
1837.	Geo. Huntington,	"	Ozias S. Morris.
"	Lem'l Starkweather.	1856.	Augustus Faulkner,
1838.	Samuel Grant,	"	Henry Mellish.
"	Lem'l Starkweather.	1857.	Henry Mellish,
1839.	Henry S. Tudor,	"	Thomas G. Wells.

1858.	Frederick Kilburn,	1868.	George Rust.
"	Henry A. Hitchcock.	1869.	Leonard B. Holland,
1859.	Frederick Kilburn,	"	George Rust.
"	Henry A. Hitchcock.	1870.	Benjamin E. Webster,
1860.	Augustus F. Maynard,	"	Sherman Watkins.
"	Oliver Martin.	1871.	Benjamin E. Webster,
1861.	Oliver Martin,	"	Sherman Watkins.
"	Augustus F. Maynard,	1872.	Christian B. Lucke,
1862.	John W. Hayward,	"	George Aldrich.
"	Major J. Britton.	1873.	Christian B. Lucke,
1863	John W. Hayward,	"	George Aldrich.
"	Major J. Britton.	1874.	Frederick Watkins,
1864.	Silas M. Bates,	"	Wm. G. Buffum.
"	Joshua B. Clark.	1875.	Frederick Watkins,
1865.	Joshua B. Clark,	"	Wm. G. Buffum.
"	A. Herbert Bellows,	1876.	Henry Burt,
1866.	A. Herbert Bellows,	"	John C. Brown,
"	John Hooper.	1877.	Henry Burt,
1867.	John Hooper,	"	John C. Brown,
"	Seth Huntley,	1878.	Allen Dunshee,
1868.	Leonard B. Holland,	"	Henry C. Rawson,

REVOLUTIONARY SOLDIERS.

Following is an imperfect list of those men that have lived and died in town, who, for a longer or shorter period, participated in the great and glorious struggle that gained for us our Liberties and Independence. The exact number who enlisted from this town cannot be ascertained, owing to the imperfect manner in which the State Adjutant General's report is compiled.

Col., Benjamin Bellows, Maj., John Bellows, Capt. Christopher Webber, 1st Lieut. John Jennison, 2nd Lieut. Levi Hooper, Ens. Ebenezer Swan, Lieut. Samuel Nichols, Ens. Joseph Lawrence, Ens. Joseph Facy, Surg. Martin Ashley, Moses Burt, Benj. Floyd, Jona. Fletcher, Jona. Hall jr., —— Crain, Joseph Fay, —— Fay, Daniel Marsh, —— De Bell, Ephraim Stearns, Samuel Salter, John Merriam, jr., Timothy Messer,

Roger Farnham, John Massey, Lieut. John Kilburn, Ebenezer Willington, John Martin, Joseph Mason, sen., John Howland, sen., Uzziah Wyman, Jonas Hosmer, Wm. Lathwood, James Campbell, Moses Mead, Joseph Bellows, Theodore Bellows.

Town Officers.

Following is a list of Town Officers from 1752 to 1879 inclusive.

1752.   Benjamin Bellows, moderator; Benjamin Bellows, town clerk; Theodore Atkinson, Joseph Blanchard and Benjamin Bellows, selectmen.

1753.   Benjamin Bellows, moderator; Benjamin Bellows town clerk; Theodore Atkinson, Joseph Blanchard and Benjamin Bellows, selectmen.

1754.   Samuel Johnson, moderator; Col. Willard, town clerk; Benjamin Bellows, Samuel Johnson and Robert Powker, selectmen.

1755.   Benjamin Bellows, mod.; Benjamin Bellows, town clerk; Benjamin Bellows, John Kilburn, Daniel Twitchell, select.; Benjamin Bellows, treas.

1756   Benjamin Bellows, mod.; Benjamin Bellows, town clerk; Benjamin Bellows, John Kilburn, Nath'l Powers, select.; Benjamin Bellows. treas.

1757.   Benjamin Bellows, mod.; Benjamin Bellows, town clerk; Benjamin Bellows, John Kilburn, select.; Benjamin Bellows, treas.

1758.   Benjamin Bellows, mod.; Benjamin Bellows, town clerk; Benjamin Bellows, John Kilburn, select.; Benjamin Bellows, treas.

1759.   Benjamin Bellows, mod.; Benjamin Bellows, jr., town clerk; John Hastings, Fairbanks Moor, select.; Benjamin Bellows, treas.

1760.   Benjamin Bellows, mod.; Benjamin Bellows, jr., town clerk; Benjamin Bellows, Nath'l Hovey, John Kilburn, select.; Benjamin Bellows, treas.

1761.   Benjamin Bellows, mod.; Benjamin Bellows, jr., town clerk; Benjamin Bellows, Nath'l Hovey, select.; Benjamin Bellows, treas.

1762. Benjamin Bellows, mod.; Benjamin Bellows, jr., town clerk.; Benjamin Bellows, Thomas Chandler, William Smead, select.; Benjamin Bellows, treas.

1763. Benjamin Bellows, mod.; Benjamin Bellows, jr., town clerk ; Benjamin Bellows, William Smead, Timothy Delano, select.; Benjamin Bellows, treas.

1764. John Graves, Mod. ; Benjamin Bellows, jr., clerk ; Benjamin Bellows, William Smead, John Graves, Select. William Smead, treas.

1765. Benjamin Bellows, mod.; Benjamin Bellows, jr., clerk ; Benjamin Bellows, William Smead, Benjamin Bellows, jr., John Marcy, Abraham Smith, Select.; Benjamin Bellows, treas.

1766. Benjamin Bellows, mod. ; Benjamin Bellows, jr., clerk ; Benjamin Bellows, William Smead, Samuel Trott, John Marcy, Abraham Smith, Select.; Benjamin Bellows, treas.

1768. John Graves, mod. ; Benjamin Bellows, jr., clerk ; Benjamin Bellows, John Graves, James Bundy, select.; Benjamin Bellows, treas.

1769. Benjamin Bellows, mod.; Benjamin Bellows, jr., clerk ; Benjamin Bellows, John Marcy, Asa Baldwin, select.; Benjamin Bellows, treas.

1770. Benjamin Bellows, mod.; Benjamin Bellows, jr., clerk ; Benjamin Bellows, Eliad Graves, Jonathan Hall, select.; Benjamin Bellows, treas.

1771. Benjamin Bellows, mod.; Benjamin Bellows, jr., clerk; Benjamin Bellows, Thomas Sparhawk, John Marcy, select.; Benjamin Bellows, treas.

1772. Benjamin Bellows, mod.; Benjamin Bellows, jr., clerk ; Benjamin Bellows, Thomas Sparhawk, John Graves, select.; Benjamin Bellows, treas.

1773. Benjamin Bellows, mod.; Benjamin Bellows, jr., clerk; Benjamin Bellows, Thomas Sparhawk, John Marcy, Lemuel Holmes, select; Benjamin Bellows, treas.

1774. Thomas Sparhawk, mod.; Benjamin Bellows, jr., clerk; Benjamin Bellows, jr., Amos Babcock, Lemuel Holmes, select.; Benjamin Bellows, treas.

1775. Benjamin Bellows, mod.; Benjamin Bellows, jr., clerk; Christopher Webber, Jona. Burt, Ebenezer Swan, select.; *Vacancy.*

1776. Benjamin Bellows, mod.; Benjamin Bellows, jr., clerk; Thomas Sparhawk, Benjamin Bellows, jr., Ebenezer Swan, select.; Benjamin Bellows, treas.

1777. Thomas Sparhawk, mod.; Benjamin Bellows, jr., clerk; Thomas Sparhawk, Ebenezer Swan, John Bellows, select.; Thomas Sparhawk, treas.

1778. Benjamin Bellows, mod.; Amos Babcock, clerk; Elisha Marsh, William Joyner, Aaron Allen, select.; John Graves, treas.

1779. Lemuel Holmes, mod.; Amos Babcock, clerk.; Lemuel Holmes, Christopher Webber, Aaron Allen, John Jennison, Sylvanus Titus, select.; John Graves treas.

1780. Benjamin Bellows, mod.; Benjamin Bellows, clerk; Thos. Sparhawk, Levi Hooper, select.; John Graves, treas.

1781. Elisha Marsh.; mod.; Benjamin Bellows, clerk; Thomas Sparhawk, Levi Hooper, John Graves, select.; John Graves, treas.

1782. Josiah Goldsmith, mod.; Benjamin Bellows, clerk; Thos. Sparhawk, John Bellows, Aaron Allen, Levi Hooper, John Jennison, select.; Samuel Trott, treas.

1783. Jonathan Hall, jr., mod.; Nathan Goddard, clerk; Jonathan Hall, jr., Aaron Hodskins, Isaac Bundy, select.; Amos Babcock, treas.

1784. Josiah Goldsmith, mod.; Benjamin Bellows, clerk; Jonathan Hall jr., James Lewis, Roger Farnham, Moses Stearns, Josiah Goldsmith, select. No choice of treasurer appears on the records for this year.

1785. Josiah Goldsmith, mod.; Benjamin Bellows, clerk; John Bellows, John Jennison, Roger Farnham, select.; Samuel Trott, treas.

1786. Josiah Goldsmith, mod. ; Benjamin Bellows, clerk ; John
       Bellows, Roger Farnham, Amasa Allen, select. ; Sam-
       uel Trott, treas.

1787. John Bellows, mod. ; Benjamin Bellows, clerk ; James
       Lewis, Abraham Holland, Jonathan Royce, select. ;
       John Crafts, treas.

1788. John Bellows, mod. ; Benjamin Bellows, clerk ; James
       Lewis, Jonathan Royce, John Dennison, select. ; John
       Crafts, treas.

1789. Abraham Holland, mod. ; Benjamin Bellows, clerk ; Thom-
       as Bellows, Thomas Sparhawk, Josiah Griswold, select.
       John Crafts, treas.

1790. Jonathan Royce, mod, ; Benjamin Bellows, clerk ; Thom-
       as Bellows, Thomas Sparhawk, Josiah Griswold, select.
       John Crafts, treas.

1791. Jonas Fairbanks, mod. ; Benjamin Bellows, clerk ; Thom-
       as Bellows, Thomas Sparhawk, Jonas Hosmer, select.
       No treasurer chosen.

1792. Jonas Fairbanks, mod.; Benjamin Bellows, clerk ; Thomas
       Bellows, Thomas Sparhawk, jr., Jonas Hosmer, select.;
       The choosing of town treasurer does not appear on the
       records by choice of the town nor by appointment.

1793. Jonathan Fairbanks, mod. ; Benjamin Bellows, clerk ;
       Thomas Bellows, Thomas Sparhawk, jr., Jonathan
       Royce, selectmen.

1794. Andrew French, mod.'; Benjamin Bellows, clerk ; Thomas
       Bellows, Thomas Sparhawk, Samuel Grant, select.

1795. Jonas Fairbanks, mod.; Nicanor Townsley, clerk ;
       Thomas Bellows, Thomas Sparhawk jr., Jonas Fair-
       banks, select.

1796. Jonas Fairbanks, mod. ; Nicanor Townsley, clerk ; Nicanor
       Townsley, Jonas Fairbanks, Jonathan Royce, select.;
       Thomas Bellows, treas.

1797. Andrew French, mod. ; Nicanor Townsley, clerk ; Nicanor
       Townsley, Jonas Fairbanks, Jonathan Royce, select.

1798. Amasa Allen, mod. ; Nicanor Townsley, clerk ; Nicanor
       Townsley, Noah Heaton, Eliphalet Fox, select.

1799. Amasa Allen mod.; Nicanor Townsley, clerk; Nicanor Townsley, Eliphalet Fox, Noah Heaton, select.

1800. Amasa Allen, mod.; Nicanor Townsley, clerk; Nicanor Townsley, Thomas Sparhawk, jr., Caleb Bellows, select.

1801. Amasa Allen, mod; Nicanor Townsley, clerk; Thomas Bellows, Aaron Allen, Jonas Fairbanks, select.

1802. Amasa Allen, mod.; Nicanor Townsley, clerk; Jonathan Royce, Alexander Watkins, Asa Sibley, select.

1803. Thomas Bellows, mod.; Nicanor Townsley, clerk; Jonathan Royce, Isaac Redington, Levi Allen, select.

1804. Jonathan Royce, mod.; Nicanor Townsley, clerk; Jonathan Royce, Isaac Redington, Levi Allen, select.

1805. Amasa Allen, mod.; Nicanor Townsley, clerk; Jonathan Royce, Isaac Redington, Joseph Fay, select.

1806. Amasa Allen, mod.; Nicanor Townsley, clerk; Jonathan Royce, Isaac Redington, Levi Allen, select.

1807. Asa Sibley, mod.; Daniel W. Bisco, clerk; Jonathan Royce, Isaac Redington, Levi Allen, select.

1808. Asa Sibley, mod.; Nicanor Townsley, clerk; Stephen Johnson, Isaac Redington, Levi Allen, select.

1809. Thomas Bellows, mod.; Nicanor Townsley, clerk; Stephen Johnson, Levi Allen, Joseph Fay, select.

1810. Thomas Bellows, mod.; Nicanor Townsley, clerk; Isaac Redington, Levi Allen, Stephen Johnson, select.

1811. Stephen Johnson, mod.; Nicanor Townsley, clerk; Stephen Johnson, Levi Allen, Silas Angier, select.; Daniel W. Bisco, treas.

1812. Thomas Bellows, mod.; Nicanor Townsley, clerk; Levi Allen, Daniel W. Bisco, Silas Angier, select.; Daniel W. Bisco, treas.

1813. Thomas Bellows, mod.; Nicanor Townsley, clerk; Levi Allen, Salmon Hooper, Daniel W. Bisco, select.; Josiah Bellows, treas.

1814. Thomas Bellows, mod.; Nicanor Townsley, clerk; Levi Allen, Salmon Hooper, Thomas Seaver, select.; Josiah Bellows, treas.

1815. Josiah Bellows 2nd, mod.; Nicanor Townsley, clerk ; Thomas Seaver, Salmon Hooper, David W. Bisco, select.; Isaac Redington, treas.

1816. Josiah Bellows 2nd, mod.; Nicanor Townsley, clerk ; Thomas Seaver, Salmon Hooper, John Barnett, select.; Issac Redington, treas.

1817. Josiah Bellows 2nd, mod.; Nicanor Townsley, clerk ; Thomas Seaver, Salmon Hooper, John Barnett, select.; Isaac Redington, treas.

1818. Josiah Bellows, mod.; Nicanor Towsley, clerk; Daniel W. Bisco, James Hooper, Josiah Bellows 3d, select.; Isaac Redington, treas.

1819. Roger Vose, mod.; Nicanor Townsley, clerk; Daniel W. Bisco, James Hooper, Josiah Bellows 3d, select.; Isaac Redington, treas.

1820. Roger Vose, mod.; Nicanor Townsley, clerk; Daniel W. Bisco, James Hooper, Josiah Bellows 3d, select.; Isaac Redington, treas.

1821. Roger Vose, mod.; Nicanor Townsley, clerk; Thomas Seaver, James Hooper, Josiah Bellows 3d, select.; Isaac Redington, treas.

1822. Roger Vose, mod.; Nicanor Townsley, clerk; Thomas Seaver, James Hooper, Josiah Bellows 3d, select.; Isaac Redington, treas.

1823. Roger Vose, mod.; Nicanor Townsley, clerk; Thomas Seaver, James Hooper, Josiah Bellows 3d, select.; Isaac Redington, treas.

1824. Roger Vose, mod.; Nicanor Townsley, clerk ; Stephen Johnson, Ebenezer Morse, Daniel W. Bisco, select.; Isaac Redington, treas.

1825. Roger Vose, mod.; Nicanor Townsley, clerk; William Buffum, Matthew Dickey, Martin Butterfield, select.; Josiah Bellows, treas.

1826. Henry Foster, mod.; William G. Field, clerk; William Buffum, Martin Butterfield, Matthew Dickey, select.; Josiah Bellows, treas.

1827. Josiah Bellows, mod.; William G. Field, clerk; Josiah Bellows, Daniel Brooks, John Dunshee, select.; Josiah Bellows, treas.

1828. Josiah Bellows, mod.; William G. Field, clerk; Josiah Bellows, Daniel Brooks, John Dunshee, select.; Josiah Bellows, treas.

1829. William G. Field, mod.; Josiah Bellows 3d, clerk; Josiah Bellows 3d, Stephen Stearns, Leonard Bisco, select.; Josiah Bellows 3d, treas.

1830. Josiah Bellows, mod.; Josiah Bellows 3d, clerk; Josiah Bellows 3d, Stephen Stearns, Leonard Bisco, Select.; Josiah Bellows, treas.

1831. Josiah Bellows, mod.; Walton Mead, clerk; Leonard Bisco, John Turner, Samuel Nichols, select.; Josiah Bellows, treas.

1832. Josiah Bellows 3d, mod.; Walton Mead, clerk; Leonard Bisco, John Turner, Samuel Nichols, select.; Josiah Bellows, treas.

1833. Josiah Bellows 3d, mod.; Walton Mead, clerk; Leonard Bisco, Daniel Brooks, Lemuel Starkweather, select.; Josiah Bellows, treas.

1834. Josiah Bellows 3d, mod.; Walton Mead, clerk; Leonard Bisco, Lemuel Starkweather, David Fisher, select.; Josiah Bellows, treas.

1835. Josiah Bellows 3d, mod.; Walton Mead, clerk; Leonard Bisco, Lemuel Starkweather, David Fisher, select.; William Buffum, treas.

1836. Josiah Bellows 3d, mod.; Walton Mead, clerk; Leonard Bisco, David Fisher, Joseph Mason, select.; William Buffum, treas.

1837. Josiah Bellows 3d, mod.; Walton Mead, clerk; Leonard Bisco, Samuel Starkweather, David Fisher, select.; Josiah Bellows, treas.

1838. Josiah Bellows 3d, mod.; Wm. Ruggles, clerk ; Lemuel Starkweather, Ebenezer Morse, Jonathan Emerson, select.; Leonard Bisco, treas.

1839.   Josiah Bellows 3d, mod.; Wm. Ruggles, clerk ; Lemuel
        Starkweather, Ebenezer Morse, George Bundy, select.;
        Ephraim Holland, treas.

1840.   Josiah Bellows 3d, mod.; Wm. Ruggles, clerk ; Henry
        S. Tudor, Jesseniah Kittredge, John P. Maynard, se-
        lect.; Ephraim Holland, treas.

1841.   Josiah Bellows 3d, mod.; Wm. Ruggles, clerk ; Ebenezer
        Morse, Daniel Merriam jr., John P. Maynard, select.;
        Ephraim Holland, treas.

1842.   Daniel Merriam jr., mod.; Wm. Ruggles, clerk ; Daniel
        Merriam jr., Leonard Bisco, David C. Thompson, se-
        lect.; Otis Bardwell, treas.

1843.   George Huntington, mod.; William Ruggles, clerk, Leon-
        ard Bisco, David C. Thompson, Stephen Tiffany, se-
        lect.; Otis Bardwell, treas.

1844.   Aaron P. Howland, mod.; Wm. Ruggles, clerk ; James
        Hale, Charles Sparhawk, David C. Thompson, select.;
        Jesseniah Kittredge, treas.

1845.   Aaron P. Howland, mod.; Wm. Ruggles, clerk ; Charles
        Sparhawk, George Bundy, Samuel Nichols, select.;
        Jesseniah Kittredge, treas.

1846.   George Huntington, mod.; Wm. Ruggles, clerk ; George
        W. Grant, George Bundy, Robert Barnett, select.;
        Jesseniah Kittredge, treas.

1847.   Aaron P. Howland, mod.; Wm. Ruggles, clerk ; Charles
        Sparhawk, Robert Barnett, James M. Burroughs, se-
        lect; Jesseniah Kittredge, treas.

1848.   George Huntington, mod.; Wm. Ruggles, clerk ; David
        Fisher, Peletiah Armstrong, Sherman Watkins select.;
        Jesseniah Kittredge, treas.

1849.   George Huntington, mod.; Williams Ruggles, clerk ;
        David Fisher, Pelatiah Armstrong, Sherman Watkins,
        select.; Jesseniah Kittredge, treas.

1850.   Geo. Huntington, mod.; William Ruggles, clerk; Oliver
        Martin, Sherman Watkins, Peletiah Armstrong, se-
        lect.; Jesseniah Kittredge, treas.

1851. Geo. Huntington, mod.; William Ruggles, clerk ; Warren Daniels, Harrison G. Smart, Henry A. Hitchcock, select.; Jesseniah Kittredge, treas.

1852. Geo. Huntington, mod.; William Ruggles, clerk ; Lyman Watkins, Isaac F. Bellows, Lewis Dicky, select.; David Buffum, treas.

1853. Geo. Huntington, mod.; Wm. Ruggles, clerk; George Bundy, Edward Crosby, Francis Locke, select.; Jesseniah Kittredge, treas.

1854. Daniel Merriam, jr., mod.; William Ruggles, clerk; Edward Crosby, Francis Locke, Elias Hardy, select.; Jesseniah Kittredge, treas.

1855. Aaron P. Howland, mod.; Wm. Ruggles, clerk; Edward Crosby, Eph. A. Watkins, John Hooper, select.; Jesseniah Kittredge, treas.

1856. Aaron P. Howland, mod.; Wm. Ruggles, clerk; Edward Crosby, John Hooper, Augustus F. Maynard, select.; J. Kittredge, treas.

1857. Aaron P. Howland, mod.; Wm. Ruggles, clerk; Augustus F. Maynard, John W. Hayward, Oliver Martin, select.; Jesseniah Kittredge, treas.

1858. A. P. Howland, mod.; Wm. Ruggles, clerk; Augustus F. Maynard, John W. Hayward, Oliver Martin, select.; Jesseniah Kittredge, treas.

1859. Aaron P. Howland, mod.; Harvey Ball, clerk; John W. Hayward, Francis Locke, Joshua B. Clark, select.; Jesseniah Kittredge, treas.

1860. Aaron P. Howland, mod.; Harvey Ball, clerk; John W. Hayward, Francis Locke, Joshua B. Clark, select.; Jesseniah Kittredge, treas.

1861. Aaron P. Howland, mod.; Harvey Ball, clerk; John W. Hayward, Alfred W. Burt, Lewis Thompson, select.; Jesseniah Kittredge, treas.

1862. Aaron P. Howland, mod.; John W. Lovejoy, clerk; Alfred W. Burt, Geo. H. Gilbert, Joshua B. Clark, select.; Jesseniah Kittredge, treas.

1863. John W. Hayward, mod.; John W. Lovejoy, clerk.; Geo. H. Gilbert, Benjamin Hitchcock, Henry Allen, select.; Jesseniah Kittredge, treas.

1864. John W. Hayward, mod.; Ransom L. Ball, clerk; Geo. H. Gilbert, Alfred W. Burt, Wm. W. Guild, select.; Jesseniah Kittredge, treas.

1865. John W. Hayward, mod.; Ransom L. Ball, clerk; George H. Gilbert, Alfred W. Burt, Wm. W. Guild, select.; Jesseniah Kittredge, treas.

1866. John W. Hayward, mod.; Ransom L. Ball, clerk; Alfred W. Burt, Wm. B. Mason, B. Sam'l D. Learned select.; Jesseniah Kittredge, treas.

1867. John W. Hayward, mod.; Ransom L. Ball, clerk; Samuel D. Learned, Wm. B. Mason, Joshua B. Clark, select.; Jesseniah Kittredge, treas.

1868. John W. Hayward, mod.; Ransom L. Ball, clerk; Benjamin E. Webster, Sherman Watkins, Charles Fisher, select.; Jesseniah Kittredge, treas.

1869. George Rust, mod.; Abel P. Richardson, clerk; Benjamin E. Webster, Sherman Watkins, Charles Fisher, select.; Jesseniah Kittredge, treas.

1870. George Rust, mod.; Abel P. Richardson, clerk; Charles Fisher, Frederick Watkins, Nehemiah Royce, select.; Benjamin F. Aldrich, treas.

1871. George Rust, mod.; Abel P. Richardson, clerk; Charles Fisher, Frederick Watkins, Nehemiah Royce, select.; Benjamin F. Aldrich, treas.

1872. John B. Russell, mod.; Abel P. Richardson, clerk; Charles Fisher, Frederick Watkins, Nehemiah Royce, select.; Benjamin F. Aldrich, treas.

1873. Curtis R. Crowell, mod.; Abel P. Richardson, clerk; Benjamin E. Webster, Nehemiah Royce, Wm A. Maynard, select.; Benjamin F. Aldrich, treas.

1874. Curtis R. Crowell, mod.; Abel P. Richardson, clerk; Nehemiah Royce, Wm. A. Maynard, Henry Burt, select.; Benjamin F. Aldrich, treas.

1875. Curtis R. Crowell, mod.; Abel P. Richardson, clerk; Henry Burt, Dares A. DeWolf, Albert F. Nims, select.; Benjamin F. Aldrich, treas.

1876. Curtis R. Crowell, mod.; Abel P. Richardson, clerk; Henry Burt, Dares A. DeWolf, Henry C. Rawson, select.; Thomas B. Buffum, treas.

1877. Curtis R. Crowell, mod.; Abel P. Richardson, clerk; Henry Burt, Dares A. DaWolf, Henry C. Rawson, select.; Thomas B. Buffum, treas.

1878. Curtis R. Crowell, mod.; Abel P. Richardson, clerk; Alfred W. Burt, John C. Brown, Benjamin E. Webster, select.; Thomas B. Buffum, treas.

EARLY SETTLERS.

How did the early settlers live? According to tradition the line of distinction, between the rich and the poor, the cultivated and uncultivated, was more distinctly drawn in the early days of the town's settlement than at the present time. With freedom to accumulate where there is a desire, and the results obtained by the fostering care of our common schools, there has been a general leveling up of the poorer class in the social scale, while improvidence and a want of thrift, on the part of those who were left with handsome fortunes, have caused a general leveling down of the latter class, so that to-day the line of damarkation is hardly seen, except in imagination. Luxuries in those early days were an exception to the rule. The poorer classes commenced life in a very primitive way, building, in the first place, a rude hut with unhewn logs, filling the open spaces between with clay and mud, and forming the roof with the bark of trees or rived splints. The interior, in many instances, consisted of one room only, which served as parlor, dining-room, kitchen and dormitory, at one end of which was built a rough stone chimney, the fireplace being sufficiently commodious to use wood four feet in length; over which, generally hung a fowlingpiece, powderhorn and shot bag, ready for use at a moment's warning. Some of those cabins were without flooring. Some families, more punctilious than others in the observance of decency, would partition the room with suspended blankets and the skins of animals. After a while, when boards could be procured, a more pretending domicil was erected, with generally two rooms, a board floor and brick chimney, on one side of which was a huge oven. One of the rooms was called the " square room " and only used when friends called. In the earliest days wooden plates were used, then pewter, and lastly "Queen's ware, which was displayed in the most pretending manner by the housekeeper on a contrivance called a "*dresser*," which occupied nearly one half of one side of a room.

What did they eat? One common article of food was bean porridge, which was eaten for breakfast and sometimes for supper. When milk became plenty brown bread and milk was eaten for supper. Another common article, which was used to some extent, was baked or boiled pumpkin and milk. Pumpkins were preferred to squashes. Turnips and parsnips were the vegetables mostly used, of which large quantities were raised and eaten. Potatoes were not common, it being a wonder with some how some large families could dispose of a barrel. The corn eaten in the green state was that grown in the common field,—sweet corn was unknown. Wheat, although raised in large quantities, was not much used in every day life, but company was usually treated with wheaten bread. Barley cakes were made and eaten, but buckwheat was not relished. Indian puddings were almost an every day diet, and it is said some families had them three hundred and sixty-five times a year. They were considered more palatable, by some, when there was an admixture of sweet apple. Meats of all kinds were consumed more freely one hundred years ago than now. Wild game, such as bears, deer, turkeys and smaller game was plenty, so that it required but little effort to supply a small family. Later, beef and pork, for which there was no remunerative ready sale, were eaten unsparingly.

What did they wear? As soon as a sufficient area of land was cleared, large quantities of flax and wool were raised, which were carded, spun, woven and colored by the industrious matrons and their daughters, and afterwards manufactured into wearing apparel and bed clothing for the family. Shoes were not worn much in summer by the male members of the household and in some cases females went without. The latter were very careful of their shoes, and it is said that, in some instances, they would, in going to church on foot, carry their shoes, and at some convenient place before arriving, slip them on ; whence it is presumed originated the saying "going to church barefoot." Shoemakers were wont to go from house to house in their neighborhood with their benches and tools and manufacture a year's stock of boots and shoes for each family, which was called "whipping the cat."

What did they drink? Drinking was social, flip being the common strong drink, which was drunk from the same mug by all. Wines were used principally by the gentry on convivial occasions —every well-to-do family having a side-board. Blackstrap was not a favorite drink and was only used by those who had lean purses. Toddy and Eggnogg were freely drunk, especially the former, and cider was a common drink both of the rich and the poor.

What were their amusements? The amusements of our forefathers were few but eminently social. Among the rural population, the husking, and quilting bees were preëminent. Those occasions were quite frequent. Especially was this the case when some damsel in the neighborhood was about to be married. The married women would gather in the afternoon and do the quilting, and in the evening all the young people would assemble in season for supper, during which some old crone was always on hand to tell the fortunes of the unmarried, by the tea grounds left in their cups, which proceeding was relished by young and old. On some occasions the young men would bring along some broken-down fiddler, who, for a few coppers, would scrape his fiddle till chanticleer warned him of the rising sun. House warmings, house and barn raisings, the old fashioned muster and the fourth of July completed the list of entertainments. None of the common people had such a thing as a carpet on their floors and a cooking stove was not known. The floors most used were sanded with white sand. The utmost precaution had to be taken lest their fires should go out, which was done by burying a brand deep in the ashes,—there were no matches then. Woe to the luckless man, who had lost his fire during a cold, wintry night. Perhaps a two mile tramp on a cold, frosty morning was the penalty for the neglect. Sometimes, however, the lost fire could be restored by the use of a gunlock.

Travelling was performed on foot or on horseback.   Up to 1792 no stages had passed through our streets for the roads were not in a suitable condition for a vehicle of that kind. The " chaise " was the first pleasure carriage, which came into use about 1808. Some fifteen years later pleasure wagons were introduced into town. Aaron Holskins, Jonathan Livingston and a member of the Bellows family, it is said, owned the three first. Going to meeting horseback in those early days was sometimes attended with no little danger,—the husband mounted in his saddle on a strong horse, holding a child before him, his wife mounted behind on a pillion with one hand holding another, and with the other clinging to her husband, were sometimes unceremoniously thrown into a pile by the road-side by a restive horse, much to the chagrin of the parties.   Such was the life of the early settlers.

VOTES FOR GOVERNOR.

List of persons voted for for Presidents and Governors of the State from 1785 to 1878 *with the number of votes cast for each person.*

The first time the legal voters of the town exercised their franchise in voting for a Chief Magistrate of the State, was on the 16th day of March, A. D. 1785. The Chief Executive was then styled PRESIDENT, and the persons voted for were as follow.

		Votes.			Votes.
1785.	George Atkinson,	45	1790.	Joshua Wentworth,	68
	*John Langdon,	9	1791.	°Josiah Bartlett,	70
1786.	John Langdon,	38	1792.	°Josiah Bartlett,	57
	°John Sullivan,	14		VOTES FOR GOVERNOR.	
	George Atkinson,	4	1793.	°Josiah Bartlett,	27
1787.	°John Sullivan,	49		John T. Gilman,	26
	Benjamin Bellows,	52	1794.	°John T. Gilman,	55
	Scat.	9	1795.	°John T. Gilman,	70
1788.	John Sullivan,	22		Benjamin Bellows,	8
	°John Langdon,	46	1796.	*John T. Gilman,	61
1789.	°John Sullivan,	22	1797.	°John T. Gilman,	128
	Josiah Bartlett,	49	1798.	°John T. Gilman,	140
	Scat.,	1		Scat.	2

		Votes.			Votes.
1799.	°John T. Gilman,	109	1814.	°John T. Gilman,	240
1800.	°John T. Gilman,	121		William Plummer,	145
	Jeremiah Smith,	18	1815.	°John T. Gilman,	210
1801.	°John T. Gilman,	132		William Plummer,	125
	John Langdon,	12	1816.	James Sheafe,	234
	Scat.,	10		° William Plummer,	159
1802.	°John T. Gilman,	93		Scat.,	1
	John Langdon,	80	1817.	Jeremiah Mason,	205
1803.	°John T. Gilman,	161		°William Plummer,	145
	°John Langdon,	77		Scat.,	1
1804.	°John Langdon,	165	1818.	William Hale,	155
	John T. Gilman,	165		°William Plummer,	117
	Scat.,	1		Scat.,	6
1805.	°John Langdon,	152	1819.	°Samuel Bell,	209
	John T. Gilman,	125		William Hale,	14
1806.	°John Langdon,	157	1820.	°Samuel Bell,	251
	Timothy Farrar,	54		John T. Gilman,	1
	Scat.,	18		Scat.,	1
1807.	°John Langdon,	130	1821.	°Samuel Bell,	217
	John T. Gilman,	31		Scat.,	8
	Scat.,	20	1822.	°Samuel Bell,	193
1808.	°John Langdon,	157		Scat.	2
	Jeremiah Smith,	71	1823.	Samuel Dinsmore,	111
1809.	°John Langdon,	157		°Levi Woodbury,	125
	Jeremiah Smith,	153		Scat.,	1
	Scat.,	4	1824.	Jeremiah Smith,	122
1810.	Jeremiah Smith,	185		*David L. Morrill,	253
	°John Langdon,	162		Scat.,	20
	Scat.,	2	1825.	*David L. Morrill,	253
1811.	°John Langdon,	163		Scat..	10
	Jeremiah Smith,	168	1826.	°David L. Morrill,	240
1812.	John T. Gilman,	176		Ezekiel Webster,	19
	°William Plummer,	176		Scat.,	19
1813.	°John T. Gilman,	207	1827.	°Benjamin Pierce,	185
	William Plummer.	189		Scat.,	2
	Scat.,	2	1828.	*John Bell,	186

		Votes.			Votes.
1828.	Benjamin Pierce,	98	1841.	Enos Stevens,	213
	Scat.,	4		*John Page,	178
1829.	John Bell,	177		Scat.,	1
	*Benj. Pierce,	109	1842.	Enos Stevens,	104
1830.	Timothy Upham,	174		John H. White,	110
	*Matthew Harvey,	114		*Henry Hubbard,	171
	Scat.,	1		Scat.,	2
1831.	Ichabod Bartlett,	153	1843.	*Henry Hubbard,	148
	*Samuel Dinsmore,	143		John H. White,	130
	Scat.,	2		Anthony Colby,	22
1832.	*Samuel Dinsmore,	128		Daniel Hoit,	10
	Ichabod Bartlett,	122		Scat.,	1
	Scat.,	4	1844.	Anthony Colby,	192
1833.	*Samuel Dinsmore,	178		*John H. Steele,	142
	Arthur Livermore,	37		Daniel Hoit,	25
	Scat.,	3	1845.	Anthony Colby,	204
1834.	*William Badger,	133		*John H. Steele,	137
	Scat.,	2	1846.	*Anthony Colby,	213
1835.	*William Badger,	167		Jared W. Williams,	165
	Joseph Healy,	150		Scat.,	1
	Scat.,	2	1847.	Anthony Colby,	217
1836.	*Isaac Hill,	185		*Jared W. Williams,	188
	George Sullivan,	105		Nath'l S. Berry,	20
	Scat.	1	1848.	Nath'l S. Berry,	204
1837.	*Isaac Hill,	128		*Jared W. Williams,	173
	Scat.,	3		Scat.	1
1838.	James Wilson jr.,	258	1849.	*Samuel Dinsmore,	184
	*Isaac Hill,	198		Levi Chamberlain,	159
	Scat.	1		Nath'l S. Berry,	21
1839.	James Wilson,	227	1850.	*Samuel Dinsmore,	193
	*John Page,	195		Levi Chamberlain,	167
	Scat.,	6		Scat.,	10
1840.	Enos Stevens,	226	1851.	Thomas E. Sawyer,	190
	*John Page,	203		*Samuel Dinsmore,	178
	Scat.,	1		John Atwood.	19

Year	Candidate	Votes.	Year	Candidate	Votes.
1852.	*Noah Martin,	204		*Joseph A. Gilmore,	225
	Thomas E. Saywer,	177	1865.	*Frederick Smyth,	191
	John Atwood,	24		E. W. Harrington,	151
1853.	*Noah Martin,	178	1866.	*Frederick Smyth,	184
	James Bell,	177		John G. Sinclair,	150
	John W. White,	14	1867.	*Walter Harriman,	185
1854.	James Bell,	189		John G. Sinclair	163
	*Nath. B. Baker,	165	1868.	*Walter Harriman,	215
	Jared Perkins,	21		John G. Sinclair,	211
1855.	*Ralph Metcalf,	185	1869.	*Onslow Stearns,	181
	Nath. B. Baker,	157		John Bedell,	213
	Scat.,	18	1870.	*Onslow Stearns,	175
1856.	*Ralph Metcalf,	204		John Bedell,	213
	John S. Wells.	188	1871.	James Pike,	176
	Ichabod Goodwin,	6		*James A. Weston,	222
1857.	*William Haile,	187	1872.	*Ezekiel A. Straw,	200
	John S. Wells,	157		James A. Weston,	230
	Scat.,	1	1873.	*Ezekiel A. Straw,	200
1858.	*William Haile,	201		James A. Weston,	213
	Asa P. Cate,	167	1874.	Luther McCutchins,	194
1859.	Asa P. Cate,	202		*James A. Weston,	234
	*Ichabod Goodwin,	214	1875.	*Person C. Cheney,	208
1860.	*Ichabod Goodwin,	215		Hiram R. Roberts,	248
	Asa P. Cate,	208	1876.	*Person C. Cheney,	189
1861.	George Stark,	184		Daniel Marcy,	252
	*Nathaniel S. Berry,	204		Scat.,	1
1862.	George Stark,	162	1877.	*Benj. F. Prescott,	199
	*Nathaniel S. Berry,	197		Daniel Marcy,	241
	Scat.,	5		A. S. Kendall,	1
1863.	Ira A. Eastman,	195	1878.	*Benj. F. Prescott,	198
	*Joseph A. Gilmore,	205		Frank A. McKean,	232
	Walter Harriman,	3		A. S. Kendall,	1
1864.	E. W. Harrington,	184			

Those marked thus * were elected.

POPULATION OF WALPOLE AT DIFFERENT PERIODS.

In 1749 Walpole had 1 family—in 1759 6 families viz: John Kilburn's, Benjamin Bellows,' Asa Baldwin's, John Hasting's Fairbanks Moore's and Timothy Messer's. In 1763 about 15 families, according to tradition ; in 1767, 308 inhabitants, according to a census taken by the selectmen of the town at that time; divided thus: 24 married men from 16 to 60 ; 52 unmarried from 16 to 60 ; 104 boys under 16; 1 man over 60; 72 unmarried females; 52 married females and 3 *widows*. In 1775, 658 inhabitants; in 1790, 1245; in 1800, 1743; in 1810, 1894; in 1820, 2020; in 1830, 2034; in 1840, 1985; in 1850, 1979; in 1860, 1868; in 1870, 1830; in 1878, 1997.

In 1767, Keene contained 430 inhabitants, Swanzey, 320, Winchester, 428, Hinsdale, 158, Chesterfield, 365, Westmoreland, 391, Alstead, 130, Charlestown, 334, Claremont, 157, Newport, 29, Cornish, 133, Plainfield, 112, Lebanon, 162, Hanover, 92, Orford, 75, and Haverhill, 172.

POSTMASTERS.

The following named persons have held the appointment of Postmaster in Walpole village from 1795 to the present time. From 1795 to 1816 the information obtained was from Washington, D. C. and thereafter from Concord, N. H. and local sources. It appears thrt the first Postmaster in town was Samuel Grant, appointed Apr. 1 1795; Oct. 1 1797, David Carlisle; Jan. 1, 1799, John Hubbard; Oct. 1, 1799, Alexander Thomas; Oct. 1, 1802, Guerdon Huntington; Oct. 1. 1804, Francis Gardner; July 1, 1807, William Pierce; July 1, 1808, Oliver Allen; Aug. 1, 1816, David Stone; compensation $240.75. In 1817, Oliver Allen, compensation, $258.72; in 1820, David Stone, compensation $207.42. From 1826 to 1842, Josiah Bellows 3d. From 1842 to 1845, Geo. Allen. From 1845 to 1849, Theron Adams, Walter Mead, and Nathan G. Babbitt. From 1849 to 1853, Edward Crosby. From 1853 to 1861, Amherst K. Maynard. From 1861 to 1869, with the exception of three months or so when Philip Peck was the incumbent, William C. Sherman. From 1869 to the present time, 1879, Ransom L. Ball.

WALPOLE AS IT IS.

The area of the town at the present time is 24,331 acres, about eighty per cent. of which is under improvement, and more than one half of the improved land is arable, and of the best quality. This land, which, one hundred and twenty-five years ago, was covered with a heavy growth of timber, constituting one continuous vast wilderness—the habitation of the red man and of ferocious beasts of prey, is now the abode of 1897 civilized inhabitants, pursuing their various avocations without molestation or fear. According to the census above stated, the number of males is 980, of females, 917 ; of Irish immigrants 109, of Irish descendants, 399 ; of English immigrants, 29 ; Canadians, 14 ; Germans, 9 ; colored persons, 10 ; the latter all belonging to one family. Persons, over sixty years of age, 233 ; over seventy, 111 ; over eighty, 21 ; over ninety, 2 ; under twenty-one, 692. Insane persons, 3 ; *Non compos mentis*, 2, and demented, 1. There were also found eleven pairs of twins.

The pursuits of the inhabitants are principally agricultural, the broad acres yielding an abundance to all who are willing and ready to plant and reap in their proper season.

The valuation of the town, in real estate, is $894,900 ; value of 494 horses, $36,365 ; of 8,551 sheep, $27,302 ; stock in banks, $36,700, in trade, $11,756, money in hand, $52,650 ; valuation of mills, $3,160 : making the aggregate value of taxable property, $1,079,500.

There are five churches ; First Congregational, Fred Lyman Allen, pastor ; town Congregational, (Unitarian) William Brown ; Christian, John M. Woodward ; Episcopal, at Drewsville, E. A. Renouf, Keene, rector' ; and Roman Catholic, North Walpole. The aggregate yearly salaries paid for preaching, in all the churches, is about $3,400.

The number of school houses in town is fifteen, in which sixteen schools are kept, at an annual cost, on an average, of about $3,700.

The number of stores in town, where are kept dry goods and groceries, is four: E. K. Seabury and Geo. P. Porter, in the village; W. A. Bond, Drewsville, and Daniel Lockwood, at North Walpole. Also, one drug and variety store, C. C. Davis; one tinshop, B. P. Owen; one harness shop, Henry Allen & Son; one millinery shop, Misses Fuller; two meat markets, Holden Brothers, and Lyman Chandler & Sons; four blacksmith shops, E. W. Barker, D. W. C. Ordway, A. Beckwith, and F. Lebourvean, proprietors: one shoe store, R. L. Ball; two public houses, Wentworth house, Charles G. Maynard, and one hotel at Drewsville, Thomas Taunt proprietor; three sawmills and two gristmills; one tannery, A. F. Maynard; one sash and blind factory, Joseph Fisher; three post offices, R. L. Ball, P. M., village, W. A. Bond, Drewsville, and Daniel Lockwood at North Walpole. There are, also, one printing office and one photograph gallery in town; one tailor and hairdresser, R. Knapp; one dressmaker's shop, Mrs. M. Q. Watkins; and two or more shoemakers' shops.

W. A. & C. B. Bond of Drewsville, in 1846, commenced the manufacture of pill boxes for David Janes & Sons, Phila., Pa., and have continued the business to the present time. They manufacture 45,000 gross annually, besides manufacturing picture frames for advertising, of which they have made 300,000. Considerable job-work is also done at their shop—sometimes necessitating the employment of several workmen.

In 1877 Alvah Walker, Boston, Warren Walker, Bellows Falls, Vt., and Charles M. Blake of Bellows Falls, formed a copartnership under the style of "Walker, Blake & Co.," with a capital of $100,000, and erected suitable buildings, and commenced the manufacture of "Lager Beer," about one half mile east of Cold River R. R. station. The business is in successful operation at the present time, employing eleven hands constantly, making about 15,000 barrels of beer annually, and consuming 3,700 tons of ice and 40,000 pounds of malt. The amount of ice used annually, if piled four feet high and four feet wide, would make a continuous line nearly one and five-sixths miles in length.

Walpole can boast of a "Thief Detecting Society"; one of the oldest in the country, having been inaugurated in 1816. The society has an ample fund, sufficient to meet any exigency that may arise. The society seems to be a favorite with the town, as its long exist-tence would indicate. In several instances in its history it has been a potent help in ferreting out misdemeanors that have been committed in the community.

The present savings bank was chartered in June, 1875, and went into operation the following October. The first president was Benjamin F. Aldrich, who remained in office till June, 1877, when John W. Hayward was chosen, and is the present incumbent. Josiah G. Bellows was chosen secretary and treasurer, in 1875, and holds the office at the present time. The trustees, now in office, are John W. Hayward, Benjamin F. Aldrich, Thomas B. Buffum, Edwin K. Seabury, Alfred W. Burt, Bolivar Lovell, Geo. H. Holden, Henry C. Lane, Harrison G. Barnes, Winslow B. Porter and Henry Allen. On the first of January, 1879, the amount of deposits was $63,803.34, which sum is well invested.

There are five physicians in town, viz Hiram Wotkyns, J. William Knight, George A. Blake, Winslow B. Porter and Abel P. Richardson. For notice of Doct. Hiram Wotkyns see Alex. Watkins' family.

J. William Knight was born in Farmington, N. H., April 27, 1822. He commenced the study of his profession with Doct. Knight of Springfield, Vt., and completed his studies with Doct. J. H. Armsby, Albany, N. Y. He graduated at the Medical College at Albany, 1855, and came to this town the same year, and commenced practice, which he continued some eleven years, and then relinquished, on account of impaired health ; since which time he has spent his leisure looking after his affairs, and in the cultivation of his mind. He married Gracie J. Walker of Spring-field, Vt. He has no children.

Doct. Winslow B. Porter studied medicine with Doct. Newton of Worcester, Mass. ; graduated at Worcester Medical College in 1846, and also at Dartmouth, in 1856. He commenced practice at Alstead, N. H., in 1847, and continued there till 1875, when he removed to Walpole, where he is still in practice, (1880) See Porter family.

Doct. George Albert Blake was born in Raymond, N. H., April 4, 1828. He graduated at Williams College, Mass., in 1849; studied his profession with Doct. Burnapp of Holliston, Mass.; graduated at Harvard Medical College, and came to Walpole in 1853. He married Miss Margaret Harrington, an adopted daughter of Doct. Williams, in 1855, and has been a resident of town ever since he came, except a short time when he was in the druggist business in Burlington, Iowa, and when employed by the Sanitary Commission, during the war.

Doct. Abel Parker Richardson was born Feb. 19, 1834, in Lempster, N. H. He fitted for college at the Green Mountain Liberal Institute and at the Westminster Seminary, Vt. He was principal of the High School in Walpole four years. He graduated at the Dartmouth Medical College in 1864; practised his profession in Marlow, N. H. one year, and settled in Walpole December, 1865, where he has followed his profession to the present time. He married Silvia F. Symonds in 1866.

The town has but one practising lawyer, Josiah Grahm Bellows, who was born in Walpole, July 24, 1841. He fitted for college and entered Harvard, but did not graduate. He commenced the study of law in the office of Hon. Frederick Vose of this town; completed his studies with Foster & Sanborn, Concord, N. H., and graduated at the Law School in Cambridge, Mass., in 1865. He was admitted to the Merrimac county bar in this state in 1865, and to the Suffolk county bar in Massachusetts in 1867; commenced practice in this town in 1872. Besides a lucrative practice in his profession, he holds the office of Probate Judge, and is secretary and treasurer of the Walpole Savings Bank.

Free Masonry.

Columbian Lodge, No. 53, was established June 13, 1827, and the charter members were Christopher Lincoln, William G. Field and Jesseniah Kittredge, jr. At that time Henry Hubbard was Grand Master, Lemuel Cushman Dep. G. M., Isaac Hill Grand Senior Warden, and Thomas Beede G. Sec'ry. The charter was surrendered to the Grand Lodge during the Morgan troubles, which commenced in 1826, and was held till 1861, when it was applied for and obtained by Doct. Jesseniah Kittredge, William Mitchell, Jacob B. Burnham, Doct. Hiram Wotkyns and sixteen others. Doct. Jesseniah Kittredge was elected Master of the new lodge, and was reelected several times. The 2d master was Geo. Rust; 3d, Joshua B Clark; 4th, Samuel W. Bradford; 5th, Abel P. Richardson; 6th, George G. Barnett; 7th, Curtis R. Crowell. The number belonging to the Lodge at the present time is fifty or sixty—not all townsmen, however.

The beautiful scenery, fine drives and cultivated society, with other attractions in town, have created a desire with strangers to visit the town during the summer months, and spend a few weeks of quiet and enjoyable life here. For the purpose of accommodating that class of people, Mrs. Ann Wright annually opens a commodious boarding house, (which was built by David Stone, and more recently known as the Kittredge place), where, during the season, a large number are accommodated, much to their satisfaction and the pecuniary benefit of Mrs. Wright.

This town is also a kind of Mecca for those who were born here, to return as often as possible and greet their old comrades and friends with a heartfelt " how'd ye do ;" altogether making the summer season in town one of gaiety and pleasure.

If strangers or townspeople wish to take a drive alone or with their families, they can be accommodated with one, two or four horses, and carriages to match, at the Livery of William A. Maynard, who is always ready to accommodate his customers.

GEOLOGY. The rock composing Kilburn mountain is gneiss, sienite and mica slate; merging, in some places, into fibrolite, a very hard formation, which is almost indestructible. The rest of the town is superimposed upon micaceous and argillaceous slate. In the vicinity of Drew mountain, on Knapp's Hill, and other places, there are outcrops of argillacious slate. In the ravine east of the village, and on lands of Henry Fletcher and Levi Burt, are found fine ledges of mica slate. Quartzite is found between B. E. Webster's and the Fisher brook. Serpentine has been found in the gulch south of the Floyd place, but in small outcrops. There is a bed of graphite on the hill east of George R. Jennison's, but not of sufficient purity to pay for working the lode, as it is too

much mingled with argillaceous and mica slate.   Per-oxide of iron
is found in considerable quantities about one half mile east of
Thomas Keyes', on the Drewsville road.   An attempt was made
about 1868-9 to utilize the deposit, and a large outlay was made
in buildings and excavations by Mr. Albert G. Pease ; but the
enterprise was abandoned before a fair trial was made.   About two
and a half miles north of the village is a mineral spring which is
said to have been visited in by-gone days by the Indians, for the
cure of cutaneous diseases.   It is called " Abenakee Spring", on
account of a tribe of Indians known by that name, that used to
visit it.   Some twenty-five years ago (1854), a company living at
Bellows Falls made a heavy outlay in buildings for the accommo-
tion and recreation of invalids who might wish to avail themselves
of the medicinal properties of the waters.   The dreams of Saratoga were not realized, and the buildings ere long fell into a dilapidated condition, and the remnants were removed a few years since,
and nothing now is left but the gentle flow of disagreeable waters
from the bank, as of yore.

Erratic boulders, of any considerable magnitude, are not plenty
in town ; but there is one which is a monster, lying in a swamp
east of the residence of George B. Williams.   The exact meas-
urement has not been obtained ; but it is thought to be about
sixteen feet long by twelve in breadth, and something like ten feet
in height above the mud.   A photograph was made from it some
ten years since by Harvey Ball, who resided in town at that time.
There is no rock like it in this vicinity, and it might have come
from the region of the Esquimaux.

The soils near the river and on the table land east are fluvia-
tile, while back on the hills they are more tenacious ; being a
heavy loam, and having, in some instances, a small admixture of
clay : but most of the soil is arable, and well suited to all kinds of
farm crops.   The water-worn pebbles on the plain west of Drewsville bear evidence of the existence of a lake in that region, at
some remote time.

TEMPERANCE.   The temperance cause has had its day of prosperity and of adversity in this town, within the last forty years ;

one organization after another springing up, and as often dying out, for want of popularity, or persistency in its advocates.

GOOD TEMPLARS. On the evening of March 21, 1876, a meeting was held in the parlor of the Congregational church for the purpose of organizing a Lodge of the "Independent Order of Good Templars"; at the instance of Bennett Anderson of England. At that meeting twenty-three citizens were present and gave their names and assents to the rules and regulations of the order. From the date of the organization to the present time, (May 1st 1879,) they have never failed of holding a regular weekly or semi-weekly meeting but once. The Lodge took the name of its founder, and since its organization has had an accession of one hundred and four members. In connection with the temperance features of the order, they have a Dramatic Association, a class in Oratory, a Literary and Debating club, select readings and declamations, &c., to furnish entertainment at their regular meetings. Following are the names of the Charter members of this Lodge.—No. 25, I. O. G. T. Males, Geo. A. Blake, Geo. G. Barnett, Edwin Guild, Wm. W. Guild, Rev. T. S. Robie, Benj. H. Dwinnell, Alvin Dwinnell, Chas. H. Barnes, John P. Holmes, David Fisher, Wm. C. Mason, and R. S. Blanchard. The female members are Mrs. Geo. A. Blake, Miss H. E. Barnett, Carrie A. Barnett, Maria J. Guild, Anna A. Griswold, Emma J. Willard, Lillie L. Simonds, Lizzie M. Smith, Grace E. Scollay, S. Addie Bradford and Nancy Pierce.

MAPLE GROVE FARM.

In 1871, Mr. George B. Williams, then of Waltham, Mass., purchased the farm formerly owned by Dr. George Sparhawk, and known as the Sparhawk place. Mr. Williams was born in Petersham, Mass., Aug. 13, 1824, and worked on the land to the time of his majority, when he went to Boston, Mass., and soon engaged in the clothing trade; in which business he continued till 1879. His farm consists of about three hundred acres, for which he paid $8,500, and gave it the name of "Maple Grove Farm." It had been poorly cared for for many years;

but immediately after Mr. Williams came in possession he
commenced making improvements and has continued them till
now—1879. The appointments on his premises are of such a
novel, convenient and permanent nature, compared with those
generally seen on country farms, that it would amply repay
one to visit the place. He has two barns, one of which is
eighty-one feet in length by thirty-nine in breadth, and the
other one hundred and three feet in length by sixty-four in
breadth and forty-three feet in height. Within them, all modern improvements are found to subserve the purposes of convenience and the comfort of the animals. He annually cuts
from his farm about one hundred tons of hay, which, together
with about twelve acres of corn fodder and other crops, are
consumed by twelve horses and thirty head of Jersey cows.
The milk from these cows is daily made into ' gilt edged ' butter, at the average rate of one hundred and fifty pounds per
week, by a process partly his own, and sold at 50 cents per
pound. The dairy room is a model of neatness and purity.
The buttermilk is fed to an average keeping of one hundred
and fifteen swine, of all ages, from which he slaughters from six
to ten, per week. The lean portion of his meat is converted into
superior sausages, at the rate of two hundred and forty pounds
per week, which, in the cool part of the year, find a ready market at 15 cents per pound. The outer finish of his piggery is
better than most human dwellings, and his swine are as clean
as well groomed horses. The temperature, within his barns, is
kept so high that his animals never feel the cold of winter,
and, hence, they thrive as well then as in summer. Supple-
mentary to the above named conveniences he has root cellars,
ice house, smoke house and sugar house in which he makes,
in spring, three hundred gallons of pure syrup, which is readily sold at a high price. It requires the constant labor of six
men to do the work upon the farm and about his barns. It is
safe to say that the aggregate cost of improvements on Mr.
Williams' place the last eight years (from 1871 to 1879) has
equalled more than one half of the whole expenditure made
in town for such purposes in the same time.

FAMILY HISTORY.

Following is a history of the settlements, and a partial genealogy of about one hundred and fifty families that settled in town prior to 1820, as well as of their descendants. There is a large number of families, that once lived in town, of which a partial account might be given, but it would be so imperfect, for want of proper data, that it would be without general interest. A few other persons have been requested to furnish information relating to their families but have neglected to do so, therefore notices of such families will not appear.

Explanation Relating to the Succeeding Pages.

The name of the person, of each family, who first settled in town, is printed in Roman small capitals—his children are numbered with Roman figures, thus: I, II, III. The third generation is numbered with Arabic ordinals, thus: 1st, 2d, 3d, 4th; the fourth generation is numbered with Arabic numerals enclosed in parentheses, thus: (1) (2) (3) the fifth generation with the same enclosed in brackets, thus; [1] [2] [3] &c. Abbreviations, b. for born, d. for died, m. for married, unm. for unmarried, c. and ch. for children, w. for wife, dau. for daughter, res. for residence, and bap. for baptized.

Adams, Macey, an old resident of this town, was born in Franklin, Mass., in 1777; and his wife, whose maiden name was Clarinda Ware, was born in the same town, and, soon after their marriage in 1800, they came to Walpole, where they spent their days. He was a butcher, and followed the business many years, in company with George Watkins. He is remembered as an honest, upright, unassuming man and a good neighbor. He died Oct. 24, 1851; she survived him 19 years, and died July 8, 1870, aged 92 years, a woman greatly beloved by all who knew her. Ch. I. Albert, b. March 16, 1806; m. a

Miss Wilder; she died and he married the 2d time. He died
Oct. 13, 1853; H. Theron, b. Oct. 14, 1808; m. 1st. Sept. 6,
1836, Submit, dau. of William and Roxana, (Burt) Blanchard,
by whom he had one son, Theron, who died Aug. 1, 1861,
aged 21. She died Oct. 1, 1846, aged 31 years, and he subsequently married Louisa Stevens of Windsor, Vt., and died
Jan. 13, 1852. Mr. Adams was postmaster under the administration of James K. Polk, and was much esteemed by his
townsmen.

ALLEN, Gen. AMASA, came to this town from Pomfret,
Ct., soon after the evacuation of Boston by the British, in
1776. He was at Dorchester heights at the time of the evacuation, and was one of the number who worked through the
night of the 4th of March, 1776, in fortifying the place. When
he came to town he commenced business as a merchant, in a
store that stood a little west of E. K. Seabury's, but he subsequently built the "Britton" store, and was a merchant during
his active life. He had partners in business, from time to
time, but was himself the master spirit. Although he came
into town poor, he left, at the time of his death, which occurred
July 1, 1821, at the age of seventy, $75,000. He was twice
married, but had no children. His first wife died in 1811, and
in 1812 he married the widow Sarah S. Gordon, whose maiden
name was Dixon, and who was the mother of Mrs. William
Buffum. He represented the town in the Provincial Legislature in 1786-'7-'8-'9-'90-'1, and in 1806, after the State Constitution was adopted. He was also a State senator in 1802-3,
and a leading man in the affairs of the town, for many years.
He gave the church organ formerly used by the Unitarians to
the old town society, and was present when the old church bell
was cast, and dropped in the silver composing a portion of it.
He built the house now owned by Mrs. Philip Peck, which
was his home. He was a man of sanguine temperament, florid
complexion, with light blue eyes, and was rather stout than
otherwise. He was very popular with his townsmen, although
decided in his opinions,—public-spirited, yet grasping; jovial
at times, at other times the opposite; but on the whole a good

citizen. His funeral was one of the largest ever known in town. He was a staunch Republican of the old school.

ALLEN, AARON, was from Mansfield, Ct., and was one of the early settlers of Walpole. His wife's name was Sarah. He purchased a tract of land lying somewhere in the vicinity of the Taggard farm, according to a survey and map projected by one William Hayward, of the lands lying in the south part of the town, at an early date. It appears, by the records of the town, that he was a prominent man, if correct judgment can be formed by the number of important offices he held, in the town's early settlement. Besides multifarious town offices held, he was chosen to represent the town in the Provincial Assembly at Exeter, in the years 1788 and 1789. He had seven children, the oldest of whom was I. Levi, born March 12, 1771, who married Phebe Flint. Levi built the house where O. H. P. Watkins now resides and owned the farm. He became greatly interested in the ministrations of Elder Rollins, and was actively instrumental in building up the Christian church and society in the Hollow. A little incident occurred at the time Elder Rollins commenced his labors in town. Mr. Allen was greatly interested in his preaching and applied to Mr. Dickinson to allow Mr. Rollins to occupy his pulpit one Sunday, that the people of his congregation might hear him speak. Mr. Dickinson very blandly replied, "I should be most happy to accede to your wishes, Mr. Allen, but I can't have my pulpit *defiled* by such a man as Elder Rollins." This remark had a tendency to further the building up of Mr. Rollins' society :—it was just the food for opposition to feed upon, and the best use was made of it. Mr. Allen was a very honorable, high-minded citizen, and very popular with his townsmen, who kept him in office year after year for a long period. He also settled a large majority of the estates of deceased persons. He neglected his farm to do business for others, and his charges were so moderate, fearing unpopularity, that he pecuniarily ran behindhand, and he, with his family, went west and spent his remaining days. Ch. 1st. Ira, b. July 6, 1795. He was a Baptist preacher and editor, and died in Philadelphia. 2d.

Almira, b. April 13, 1797; m. Samuel Fifield Sept. 7, 1818.
3d. Charlotte, b. Nov. 15, 1800; m. a Fifield. 4th. Amasa, b.
March 6, 1803; m. Martha Hutchins June 20, 1824. II. John,
b. Dec. 22, 1772. III. Mary, b. Nov. 10, 1774; m. Dr. George
Sparhawk, Dec. 2, 1802. (See Sparhawk.) IV. Artemas, b.
October 2, 1776; d. 1777. V. Clarissa, b. May 29, 1788. VI.
Aaron, jr., b. April 17, 1780; m. Catherine, dan. of Samuel
Salter, Nov. 12, 1800. He built the house once the residence
of Henry P. Foster, but never occupied it, he dying at the
time, of lock-jaw, resulting from the kick of a vicious horse,
Sept. 16, 1815. He left a wife and seven children. She afterwards married Amos Phillips, and died March 11, 1837, aged
58 years. Ch. 1st. John, b. June 5, 1801; m. Jan. 13, 1827,
Mary, dan. of Jeremiah Robbins, b. in Westminster, Vt., Apr.
13, 1807. Ch. (1) Mary A., b. Sept. 9, 1827; m. March 18,
1856, in Boston, Cyrus Church, b. in Hinsdale, N. H. July 22,
1826. (2) John R., b. July 12, 1832; m. Rhoda Jane Cintts,
Jan. 22, 1855; his only child, Charles Homer, b. March 5, 1857,
was drowned June 8, 1864. (3) Hubbard A., b. Dec. 12, 1841;
m. Martha A. Newton of Hinsdale, N. H. Oct. 5, 1865: issue,
one son, Chas. A. Two children of John and Mary Allen,
named Levi and Martha A., d. in infancy. He d. Sept. 8, 1850.
2d. Catherine, b. May 30, 1803; m. April 24, 1826 Clement
White of Tunbridge, Vt: issue, 2 ch. 3d. Mary S., b. Feb.
7, 1805; m. James H. Fuller of this town, Oct. 23, 1823. Ch.
(1) William T., b. March 4, 1827. (2) Hubbard B., b. Oct,
22, 1829. (3) John H., b. Sept. 9, 1831. (4) Sarah L., b.
Dec. 2, 1835. (5) Harriet S., b. Dec. 17, 1838. (6) Mary
Adeline, b. Dec. 22, 1840. (7) Marshall R., b. March 2, 1842.
(8) Eliza P., b. March 2, 1844. (9) Levi D., b. July 25, 1846.
4th. Adeline, b. March 21, 1807; m. Oct. 31, 1832, James S.
White, a Christian preacher; he d. April 3, 1874: issue, 2 ch.
one living, George. 5th. Aaron, jr., b. April 9, 1809; he
resides at the West and has a family. 6th. Clarissa, b. March
17, 1811; m. Samuel Ladd Dec. 24, 1866; he d. April 8, 1876.
7th. George, b. April 5, 1813; m. Charlotte, dau. of William
Mitchell, Sept. 6, 1838, and has one daughter, Grace. Aaron

Allen, sen., d. April 8, 1804, aged 62; his wife Sarah d. Aug. 17, 1812, aged 73.

ALLEN, JAMES, came from Connecticut and settled on the place now owned by Henry Fletcher, very early in the town's settlement: but very little can be gathered in relation to the family. They were Baptists in religious views, and consequently very little can be gathered from the church records in town, for they had no sympathy with the church here. He was a mechanic and had a shop near by his house on the sand knoll, where he made spinning wheels for woolen and linen. He married Irene ———— and had five children. I. James, jr., m. and went to Warren, Vt. II. Royal, m. Fanny, dau. of Nathan Bundy, sen., and had four boys and two girls, who removed to Osselock, N. Y. III. Diadama, m. Simeon Lyman. (See Lyman.) IV. Lavinia. V. Cynthia, m. Hugh Dunshee. (See Dunshee.) VI. Molly, m. James Holden. Ch. 1st, Dana, m. a Pierce. 2d. Simon, was a manufacturer at Drewsville. 3d. Lucina, m. a Burton. 4th. Marion, lives in Ripton, Vt. James Allen died Nov. 28, 1813, aged 73; his wife died Feb. 2, 1812, aged 62.

ARNOLD, WILLIAM, was born in Westmoreland, N. H., Mar. 29, 1792, and learned the machinist's trade and worked at that business in his younger days. At what time he came to Walpole is not known, but at one time he worked for Thomas Moore as a hired man on his farm, and married one of his daughters, Naomi, Oct., 3rd 1822, who was born Sep. 14, 1795. After his marriage he worked at his trade a while in Pawtucket, R. I. where some of his children were born. He returned to Walpole and purchased the Robinson tavern stand and commenced keeping a public house in 1837, in which business he continued till the building of the Cheshire R. R. when tavern keeping was relinquished.

When he commenced keeping tavern there a large amount of travel was upon the road that passed his house, it being the Third N. H. Turnpike. Here he and his wife did their best to please, thereby securing a good share of customers, who were sure to be well cared for. After he relinquished tavern

keeping, he turned his attention to farming, which occupation
he followed till the infirmities of age caused him to suspend
labor. He d. Aug. 27, 1876. Ch. I. Elizabeth, b. May, 22,
1823; m. 1st, Levi Winchester of Westmoreland—issue 1 son,
Frank L.; m. 2d, Gilbert T. Stevens, issue 2 ch. one living.
II. Mary P. b. Sept. 27, 1824; m. O. H. P. Watkins, May 14,
1847; issue 3 ch. (see Ap.) III. William, b. Dec. 26, 1826;
m. Mary S. Stevens of Warwick, Mass., Sep. 7, 1852; issue
3 ch., 2 living. (See Ap.) IV. Sarah Jane, b. Aug. 29, 1829;
m. Henry D. Bacon. She is now a widow and resides at Be-
bee Plain, Canada. V. Sophia, b. July 19, 1834; m. Nelson
Johnson, Oct. 19, 1865; issue 2 ch., resides in Westminster,
Vt. VI. Frances N., b. Mar. 2d, 1836; m. George A. Sherman, June 13, 1866, residence, Keene, N. H.

BARNETT, JOHN, came to this town between 1790 and '95,
from Londonderry in this State, and settled on Derry Hill in
the neighborhood of others, that came from the same place.
He married Jane McCullom by whom he had eight children.
Feb. 25, 1822, as he was driving a team, with sled loaded with
wood, by some means he stumbled and fell under the sled, and
one runner passed over his neck and killed him. His age was
54. His wife died Jan. 19, 1841, aged 67. His children were
I. Robert, b. Nov. 17, 1799; m. Harriet, dau. of Apollos
Gilmore, by his second wife, by whom he had six children,
three of whom are now living in town, (see Ap.) He died
Feb. 21, 1861. II. William McCullom,, b. Jan. 17, 1801; d.
Feb. 27, 1826. III. Eliza, b. Aug. 1802; m. Warren S. Briggs
of Keene. IV. Martha, b. Nov. 24, 1804; d. 1814. V. Fanny, b. Jan. 24, 1808; m. Holland D. Fay and had five children.
VI. Sophronia, b. June 5, 1810, m. Jedd May, Fitchburg,
Mass. VII. Mary Jane, ———. VIII. John, b. Jan. 22, 1815;
m. Emily Perkins, of Perkinsville, Vt. He had three children,
one of whom survives. (See His. of Reb.)

BARNETT, GEORGE, brother of the foregoing, was born in
1768. He married Elizabeth Alexander of Londonderry,
N. H. by whom he had five children. He died Jan. 11, 1818;
she d. Apr. 20, 1823. Ch. I. Jane, b. Oct. 13, 1800; m. 1st,

Levi Walker, 2d a man by the name of Howe. II. Isaac Alexander, b. Aug. 6, 1802; died at the South. III. Robert, b. Sep. 9th, 1804; m. Julia, daughter of Josiah Bellows. He was for several years engaged in mercantile pursuits, in Boston, in the firm of Grant, Seaver & Co. About 18— his health failed and a year or two before he died he suffered from mental alienation. He left one child, Mary E. who died Apr. 10, 1873, aged 35. IV. Elizabeth Cochran; b. July, 19, 1806; d. unmarried. V. Sarah Ann, b. Oct. 7, 1808.

BARDWELL, OTIS. The Bardwells in New England are of English origin. The ancestor of Otis and the Bardwells of Montague, Deerfield &c. of Massachusetts, was Robert, who came to Boston about 1670. He was an apprentice to a hatter in London at the time of the plague and great fire there in 1665 and '6. When he arrived in Boston the Indians were committing savage depredations on the inhabitants in the valley of Connecticut river and he was sent, by the Gov. of Mass., to the troops stationed there, with dispatches, and ordered to return immediately if there did not come a fall of snow, but if snow came to remain with the troops. Snow came and he remained. He found his way to Old Hadley, where he apprenticed himself to learn the business of making *wool* hats, a branch of the business he had not learned in London. He married and settled in Hatfield, Mass., and died from injuries received in falling from the frame of a barn, at the raising, when comparatively a young man. He had four sons, one named Samuel settled in Montague and another named Thomas settled in Deerfield. One of Robert's sons, named Joel, who was a college graduate, caused the original spelling of the name to be changed from Bordwell to Bardwell, because it better agreed with the manner in which it was pronounced—*Bardle.* From the Heraldry office, in London, is obtained the signification of the name Bardwell: "*Bard* a poet and *well* good, —meaning a good Poet." It is claimed that the English Bardwells have a "Coat of Arms," the device of which is: "three scallops (shell fish) guarded by a lion *rampant*, with the following motto in English: "We fear no danger."

Otis Bardwell was born in Deerfield, Mass., Oct. 17, 1792, and was the son of Thomas and Catharine (Belding) Bardwell, who had a family of twelve children, eight of whom lived to maturity, four of the number having been our town's people. He married first, Dec. 23, 1818, Abigail, daughter of Abijah and Artemesia (Blake) Foster, of Keene, N. H., b. Aug. 14, 1799, ch. I. Abigail Foster, b. July 11, 1824. II. Catharine Artemesia, b. July 12, 1826, both of whom d. in infancy, III. Mary Ann, b. Jan. 6, 1827, m. Edmund Foster Cook, Feb. 23, 1847 and had 9 ch. 4 of whom are living. 1st Mary F., 2d Mabel, 3d Otis Bardwell, 4th Helen Temple. IV. Harriet Otis, b. July 26, 1829. V. Sarah Bellows, b. Jan. 14, 1832; m. Horace W. Eaton, May 1, 1856; d. Feb. 21, 1876. Abigail, wife of Otis Bardwell, d., Oct. 14, 1832. He m. a second time Mary, b. Sep. 2, 1800, a sister of his first wife who d. Dec. 13, 1875; he d. Mar. 27, 1871.

Mr. Bardwell began life as a stage driver, but being a man of energy and good calculation he soon became a proprietor, and in a short time was one of the owners of all the mail lines of staging in the vicinity. (See Geo. Huntington.) In the month of January 1819, about three weeks after his first marriage, in driving over Carpenter's Hill, he discovered an apple tree in full bloom, from which he picked blossoms for the lady passengers, and brought home a bouquet for his bride. Soon after 1820 he purchased of Thomas Redington the house where Henry Allen now lives, and resided there some twenty five years. In 1849 when the Cheshire Railroad was completed, he bought a plot of land in Rutland, Vt. and built the well known "Bardwell House," where, in conjunction with his son-in-law, E. Foster Cook, he kept a public house for a number of years. He was the first president of the first Walpole Savings Bank and was the custodian of considerable property left in trust by others. His second wife was a model woman and a consistent member of the Congregational church in this town for many years, and one of the leading spirits. She carried out her profession in her daily walk, being always the first of her neighbors at the house of those who were sick and in affliction. Her hand always went with her generous nature in bestowing little comforts on those that were poor and needy as well as those that were sick.

BELLOWS, BENJAMIN.   In the narrative of the preceding pages a general history of Col. Benjamin Bellows is given from the time he came to Walpole till his death. It now remains to give some further notice of him and a history of his ten children and some of their descendants separately considered.   The Bellows family is thought, and perhaps claim to have descended from a Norman family which came to England with William the Conqueror, by the name of *Belle Eau*, which, pluralized has the identical sound of the name of Bellows. If such is the case it is a remarkable coincidence that the name should afterwards become associated with the beautiful fall of water on Connecticut river.

Much labor, expense and interest have been given by different members of the Bellows family to trace their genealogy satisfactorily.   It is thought that the names, found in different parts of Great Britain, of Bellews, Bellis, Bellas, Bellos, Bellasis and Beloes, are all corruptions from the same root of which Bellows is a corruption.   The coat of arms of all those families is essentially the same.   It is described in the following manner; "The field or ground of the escutcheon is black, the bars interlaced are of a gold color, the chevron is blue, and bears three lions' heads in gold. The crest is an arm embossed, habited, the hand proper grasping a chalice pouring water, (*belle eau*) in allusion to the name, into a basin, also, proper, Motto; "*Tout d'en haut*,"—All from on high.

The grandfather of Col. Benjamin, (John Bellows,) is supposed to have come to this country in 1635, and married Mary Wood of Concord, Mass., by whom he had ten children, the youngest being Benjamin, who, it is said, was adopted by one Benjamin Moore. Benjamin married a widow Willard, in 1704, whose maiden name was Dorcas Cutter. She had four children by Mr. Bellows, three daughters and one son, Benjamin, the founder of the town of Walpole, who was born May 26th, 1712. He married Abigail Stearns of Lunenburg, Mass., the daughter of the first settled minister of the town. When he came to this town, he had five children of whom mention has been made in the foregoing pages. By his second marriage, to the widow Jennison, he had five more; many of whom, at their majority, settled in town, and they in turn had a numerous progeny. Owning a very large share of the landed estate in town, and by reason of their wealth, being better able to give their children educational opportunities, and in consequence possessing a higher social standing than their townsmen, their local influence was almost unlimited, and for the first fifty years after the town was settled they shaped and shared most of the public business in town.

Down as late as 1820, and after, the political sentiments of the Bellows family were potently felt in town. As an instance illustrating the foregoing statement, one of the voters in town, meeting his neighbor on the morning of March meeting day, inquired of him for whom he was going to vote. "O," said he, "I do n't know: I have n't asked Squire Bellows yet."

The influence of the Bellows family in town was the natural outgrowth of their wealth and higher attainments, and was in perfect harmony with the principles of human nature. No instance is known where an abuse of the family's influence was felt; on the contrary, in some instances they were more generous than wise.

Benjamin Bellows' children were I. Abigail, b. Dec. 21, 1736, d. at Northfield, Mass. while on a visit, in 1756. II. Peter, the oldest son of Col. Benjamin, was born in Lunenburg, Mass., Jan. 6, 1739. He came to Walpole with his father the year he was fourteen. At the age of twenty-one he was appointed constable of the town. He married Mary Chase, of Cornish, N. H., and settled in Charlestown, N. H. He died April 5, 1825; his widow d. April 18, 1830. He is represented to have been a person of diminutive size, witty in conversation, fond of a good time, impetuous and brave in action, and indifferent to mental or physical exertion. His descendants are scattered far and wide, and many of them are said to be highly respectable. None of his family is known

ever to have resided in town. His children were 1st. Samuel,
b. 1776; m. Martha ———; he d. April 5, 1820; she d. Mar.
8, 1843, aged 77. 2d. Benjamin, m. Polly, dau. of Elijah
Parker, July 24, 1791. 3d. Peter, m. Mehitable Jacobs. 4th.
Solomon, b. Sept. 9, 1776, m. Polly Hoyt. 5th. John, b. 1778.
6th. Polly, b. 1782, m. Stephen Parker. 7th. Betsey, b. 1785,
m. Dr. Child. III. Bellows, Benjamin, the second son of the
founder, familiarly known as the General, seems to have been
the only son of the Colonel's family who ever gained a state
reputation, although the family, as such, was widely known.
Commencing when but nineteen years old with the office of
town clerk, which he held for thirty-two years, he held almost
every office in town and county at a very early period of his
life. He was State Senator and Councilor from his districts,
was chosen a member of the Constitutional Congress in 1781,
but declined serving. He was a member of the Convention
of February, 1788, that ratified the Federal Constitution. He
was president of the electoral college in this State in 1789,
and again elector in 1797. In the State militia he rose from a
corporal to the command of a brigade. He was Colonel of a
regiment during the Revolutionary struggle, and was actively
engaged in raising troops for the same. He is described as
being a dark complexioned man, fully six feet in stature, very
courtly in manners, and firm in his decisions. He hated catch-
penny showmen, and would order them out of town on his
own responsibility. From what can be gleaned from his public
life, and what information is gained by tradition at this remote
time, the conclusion is drawn that he had a well-balanced
mind, was dignified in character, courteous in manners, persuasive in language, generous in public and private deeds, and
ever kind to his kinsmen and neighbors. His education was
mostly gained from intercourse with men, and not from books.
He built and lived in the house where Mrs. Prentiss Foster
now resides. In the latter part of his life he did not lose his
desire for appearing comely and tasteful in his dress,—still
clinging to the old Continental style. He had late in life but
little ambition and few cares; spending many hours with his

brother John discussing the news of the day over a clay pipe, of which both were very fond, or having a pleasant chat with the townspeople. In that way he descended the other side of the hill, the foot of which he reached June 4, 1802, aged 62; his wife died Jan. 15, 1817, aged 77. His death was universally lamented, not only in town, but wherever he was known. His funeral was attended by the largest number of people that ever assembled in town on a similar occasion,—the funeral procession reaching from his house to the cemetery. He married Phebe Strong of Northampton and had five children. Two, of whom not much is known, probably died young.

His children were 1st. Caleb, who m. Maria Hartwell of New Ipswich, an only daughter, who was reputed rich and well educated. Caleb's father built the house now the residence of Moses J. Hale for his son. Both families being rich the parents vied with each other in giving their children a good start in the world. The wedding is said to have been one of more than ordinary occurrence. The couple, after their marriage, made their advent into town with a retinue of friends, the bride and groom being mounted, each on a gay and spirited horse. The impression that the event made on the townsfolk at the time was of such a novel nature that tradition holds it in store to-day. It is said that her " setting out " far surpassed anything of the kind that had ever before been seen in town. Twenty - six feather beds and thirteen brass kettles, all new, were among the articles enumerated. Mr. Bellows was engaged in various enterprises through life, but did not succeed financially; on the other hand, before he died he became comparatively poor. He died April 17, 1822, aged 54. She died July 11, 1846, aged 75. Ch. (1) Ephraim Hartwell, b. Jan. 29, 1792. (2) Caleb Strong, b. August 22, 1793. (3) Benjamin Franklin, b. Oct. 22, 1795. (4) George Lyman, b. Feb. 4, 1798. (5) Mary Brown, b. Jan. 6, 1800. (6) Phebe Strong, b. June 7, 1802. (7) Laura Livermore, b. Sept. 17, 1804. (8) Caleb Strong, b. Sept. 1, 1806. (9) Moses Brown, b. Aug. 11, 1808. (10) Elizabeth Rowe, b. July 22, 1810. (11 &

12) Caroline Pinkney and Charles Cotesworth, b. May 6, 1813. 2d. Phebe. m. Samuel Grant. (See Grant.) 3d. Polly.

IV. John, better known as Col. John, was born Nov. 3, 1742, m. Rebecca Hubbard. He d. Aug. 19, 1812, aged 70; she d. Dec. 26, 1810, aged 60. He built the house and lived on the place now owned and occupied by Rev. Henry W. Bellows D. D. as a summer residence, which constituted only a small part of his immense landed estate. He had a large family of children, twelve in number, one of whom, Hubbard, lived there till he died, it being his patrimony. His family was the best educated, the most dressy and dashy of any in town at that time. John was, in disposition and general character, quite the opposite of his older brother Ben. His immense landed estate brought him a good return yearly, even in those days. He was ambitious of gain, and he succeeded before the close of his life in making a handsome addition to his patrimony, although he was an extravagant liver and had an expensive family to care for. He yearly raised a large quantity of wool, which he employed the farmers's wives and daughters, in the vicinity, to spin for him. Their visits to procure wool and return yarn, with their horses hitched about his yard, made his home wear the appearance of a public house on a festive day. The records of the town, abundantly show, although he is said to have been parsimonious, that he was no niggard, being only second to his brother Ben, in public munificence. Ch. 1st Rebecca, m. Roger Vose, Jan. 4, 1801. (See Vose.) 2d John. 3d Josiah, known as Josiah 2d, was a man who possessed in an unusual degree the power of memory and the use of language. He could talk by the hour and never hesitate for the want of the proper word to use at the proper time; and in telling a story, if there was any thing wanting to make it smooth and complete, the material was always at hand to supply all deficiences, whence he obtained the *sobriquet* of "Slick Si." He matured very early in life, and his father built the public house that once stood on the site of the residence of Thomas N. Keys and established him in the business of tavern-keeping there, at the age of eighteen. He was what they termed in those days a "roistering blade";

and his social qualities gathered round him those of the same
kith, and, probably, if the ashes of the old house could speak,
strange scenes of hilarity and festivity would be revealed.   In
1812, he built the brick mansion, now owned by F. B. Knapp,
and lived there till about 1820, when he sold out to Jacob N.
Knapp.   In the season of 1824, he removed, with his family,
consisting of his wife, five children—three sons and two daughters, and a colored woman named Rachael—to Lancaster, N. H.
He married Lydia, daughter of Dr. John Preston of New Ipswich,
N. H., about 1799, and had the following named children, all
born in Walpole: (1) Eliza, b. Feb. 27, 1800; d. Nov. 26, 1812.
(2) Charles, b. 1802; m. Eliza Willson in 1826 and had two sons
and three daughters.   (3) George, b. 1805, m. M. M. Holton of
Lancaster. (4) John, b. Nov. 29, 1807; m. 1st Mary B. Shaw;
2d m. Helen E. Stiles of Gorham.   (5) Rebecca Eliza, m. John S.
Wells and had two sons and one daughter.   She died in 1860.
(6) Fanny Stone, m. Walter Sherman, and died in Boston in
1860 without issue.   4th Roswell, m. Miss Lovell of Rockingham, Vt. 5th Hannah, died early. 6th Frances, m. David Stone;
she died in 1803 and her two daughters at about the same time,
leaving Mr. Stone without any family. 7th Sophia. 8th Hannah, m. David Stone Apr. 22, 1805, a sister of his first wife.
9th Hubbard, m. Louisa Morgan and lived and died on the
homestead.   Ch. (1) Sophia, m. J. H. Tracy a civil Engineer.
(2) Harriet. (3) John. (4) Laura. (5) Hannah.   None of Hubbard's children are now living.   10th Maria, m. Asa H. Center, May 24, 1824.   Ch. (1) Maria, m. a Hitchcock. (2) Harriet.
The 11th and 12th ch. of Col. John *probably* died in infancy.
Of Col. John's numerous descendants, not one is known to
be living in town at this time—the Vose family being the last.

   V.   Joseph, at the age of eighteen, was put in charge of
his father's large landed estate in Lunenburg, Mass., which he
afterwards inherited—a heavy responsibility for one so young.
He was an active business man and had the confidence of his
townsmen in Lunenburg, as evinced by the large number of
responsible offices he held there.   He was Lieut. Colonel in
his brother Ben's regiment when he went to Saratoga.   Through

his generous disposition to help others he became their bondsman, and was pecuniarily involved in consequence to such an extent that his entire property was seized and sold, leaving him penniless. This happened in 1784, and being in poor health at the time, this disaster wrought upon his proud and sensitive nature to such an extent that an aberration of mind, in a mild form, soon followed. His entire family consisting of himself, wife, and fourteen children were immediately brought to Walpole and tenderly cared for by his generous and hospitable brothers and kindred. His children, mostly, made highly respectable citizens, quite a number of whom lived and died in town.

He married Lois Whitney, who, it is said, was a woman of highly estimable character. He died in 1817, at the age of 73. Ch., 1st. Salmon, m. Lydia Cox, Sep. 25, 1791. Ch. (1.) Matilda, m. Samuel A. Wightman. (2.) Mary, d. unmarried; was a school teacher in Ashtabula, Ohio. 2d. John, m. 1st, Betsey Eams, and 2d, Annie H. Langdon. He, at the age of 17, went to Boston, and there from a mere shopkeeper rose to the head of a large importing house, Bellows, Corlis & Co., and retired from business at 50, with an ample fortune. The next ten years he was an officer in the city government. During this time his fortune became somewhat impaired, on account of his interests in manufacturing enterprises which were in an unhealthy state at the time; however, he saved enough from the wreck to spend his remaining days in Walpole with no fears of the wolf at the door. He died Feb. 10, 1840, aged 72. His children were (1.) Mary A. d. early. (2.) Eliza E. m. Joseph G. Dorr and had 5 children. (3) John Nelson, born in Boston, Mass., 1806; fitted for and entered Harvard University in 1820; married Mary Nichols of Cooperstown, N. Y., May 11, 1833, and had six children, all living, viz., [1] Mary Eliza, b. April 14, 1836. [2] Edward St. John, b. April 28, 1840; m. Susan Jones, of San Francisco, Cal., 1873. [3] Henry Nichols, b. May 29, 1842; m. Georgianna Lundie, of New York, 1872; had three children; one living, Stewart, b. in California, 1875. [4] Catherine Nichols,

b. July 8, 1846; m. Henry Robeson, U. S. N., 1872. [5] John,
b. Feb. 3, 1849. [6] Clifford Eams, b. March 31, 1852. Through
a portion of Mr. John N.'s life he was engaged in teaching,
but subsequently became a Unitarian clergyman, and was
settled first in Framingham, Mass., and then in Wilton, N. H.
His health at length became impaired, and he died Feb. 29,
1857. (4) Alexander Hamilton, m. Roxana Foster. He is remembered as an accomplished reader, a rare accomplishment
which seems to belong to the Bellows family in an unusual
degree. (5) and (6), twins, Henry Whitney and Edward Stearns,
b. in Boston, Mass., June 14, 1814. Henry Whitney m. first
Eliza Townsend, and had five children, two of whom survive,
—one daughter and one son, Russell N., who is a graduate and
a Unitarian clergyman. He is at the present time editor of
the Christian Inquirer, N. Y. Henry W. m., 2d, Anna, dau.
of Rev. Ephraim Peabody of Boston, Mass., with whom he
is now living.

Mr. Bellows was educated at Harvard University, graduated
in 1832, and completed his course of study in divinity at the
same place in 1837. On January 2, 1838, he was ordained
pastor of the First Congregational Church in New York,
afterwards called All Souls' Church, which relation he contin-
ues to hold (1879). He was the originator of the Christian
Inquirer in 1846, and published, in 1857, a spirited defense of
the drama, and has also been a constant contributor to numerous reviews and other publications. In 1857 he delivered a
course of lectures before the Lowell Institute in Boston on the
Treatment of Social Diseases. In 1860 he published a volume
of sermons on Christian Doctrine, and in 1868–9 "The Old
World in its New Face," 2 vols., 12mo. This is one of the best
works of the kind extant. One feels in reading it that he is
the traveler himself, so vivid are the descriptions. The work
is in our town library. During the Civil War he was President of the United States Sanitary Commission, where he
was successful in carrying through measures of vast importance to the needy soldier.

(6) Edward Stearns studied the profession of law, and was

at Adrian, Mich., in practice, when his death occurred about
the 30th of March, 1837, at the age of twenty-three. He is said
to have been a young man of superior natural ability and
mental attainments. A notice of his death appeared in the
Boston Courier of May 26, 1837 : " Mr. Bellows, in the pursuit
of his professional duties, which he had just entered upon at
Adrian, was obliged to go some distance into the thinly-settled
country north of his residence. Having reached a point
where there was no stage conveyance, he attempted to reach
his destination on foot, through a forest, and alone, for no guide
could be procured. After eleven days his friends became
alarmed at his absence, and went in search of him. He was
found dead in the woods, with no marks of violence upon his
person ; and there are sufficient grounds for believing that,
having lost his way, and after some search discovered it, he
had seated himself to rest before pursuing his journey, and,
overcome with fatigue, want of food, and cold, he had given
way to sleep and was soon chilled to death." John, by the second wife, Anna H. Langdon, had five children. (7) Mary
Ann, died aged thirteen. (8) Francis W. G. (9) Harriet A.,
m. William Allen, and had four children, viz., William L., Annie L., George H., and Mary Louisa. (10) Percival, died at
26. (11) George G.

3d. Benjamin 2d, m. Lucy Cox of Harvard, Mass., Sept. 1,
1791, and spent his days in Canada. His children were (1)
George, m. Fidetta Lovell, of Washington, N. H., and had 7
ch., of whom three d. in infancy; those that survived
were [1] Frederick, who was a livery keeper in New York,
and died worth $100,000. [2] and [3], Harriet and Mary, m.
brothers by the name of Stebbins, and reside in Boston. [4]
Charles L , b. Feb. 22, 1834; resides in Drewsville. (2) John,
m. in Canada. (3) Louisa, m. first Cooledge Butterfield; second a Richards, in Canada. (4) Lucy, m. a Tole. (5) Noble, d.
young. (6) Benjamin, d. young. (7) Frederick, m. in Massachusetts. (8) Dexter, went to Massachusetts and died there. 4th.
Joseph, b. 1771, m., first, Deborah Wright, and, second, Mary
Adams. Ch. (1) George, b. April 24, 1799. He was a physi-

cian. (2) Eliza, b. Sept. 13, 1801; m. a Mr. Ainsworth. (3), by
second wife, Henry Adams, b. Oct. 25, 1803; m. Catherine
Walley, daughter of Josiah and Mary (Sparhawk) Bellows,
June 16, 1836, and had six children; viz., Josiah, Sarah, Stella,
Fanny, Catherine, and John A., the last of whom is a clergy-
man. Two of his daughters married Charles Sanborn, Esq.,
of Concord, N. H. He, while a lad, attended the Academy at
Windsor, Vt., which in those days afforded no better educational facilities than those now had at our best common schools.
After remaining there a few months he entered the law office
of Hon. William C. Bradley, Westminster, Vt., and on completing his law studies, was admitted to the bar at Newfane,
Vt., in 1826. He commenced the practice of his profession in
Walpole, having been admitted to the bar in New Hampshire
the same year that he was in Vermont.

In 1828 he removed to Littleton N. H. where he practised
his profession 22 years, when he removed to Concord in this
state. Mr. Bellows had now gained a high reputation as a
lawyer throughout the state. Sep. 23, 1859, on the resignation of Judge Perley, he was appointed an Associate Justice of
the Supreme Judicial Court, and held the position till Oct. 1,
1869, at which time he was appointed Chief Justice. The er-
mine descended unsullied upon his shoulders and was left un-
tarnished at the time of his death, which occurred a short
time before his office would expire by limitation. He was not
a politician, but was elected a representative from Littleton
as far back as 1839, and, also, from Concord in 1856-7. At
the Law term, Dec. 1869, he rendered a decision in the case
of Townshend, admr., vs. Riley, where several hundred dollars were involved by the different modes of computing annual interest, which was sustained, and is now the law of the
State for computing annual interest where irregular indorse-
ments are made.

He was a punctual attendant on Divine service, on the Sabbath, and manifested a lively interest in the promotion of liberal Christianity. He was not an eloquent speaker in the popular sense; but possessed that kind of eloquence which was

Hon Henry A. Bellows

always well calculated to arrest the attention of the bar and
jury when he was Judge, by the clearness and honesty of purpose with which he delivered his opinions. He died very suddenly at his home in Concord, with but little premonition,
March 11, 1873, of disease of the heart. His remains were
brought to Walpole and found their last resting place with his
kindred. Without superior educational advantages he rose to
a high point of honor and trust; for his honesty of purpose,
he was esteemed, for being just he was honored, and for his
urbanity of character he was beloved. He had a deep reverence
for his Maker, and died trusting in His mercy and goodness.
(4.) Fanny Annie. (5.) Mary Stearns, b. Oct. 26, 1808. (6.)
William, m. Caroline Bullard. (7.) Harry, d. Feb. 21, 1803,
aged 9 years. 5th. Levi, never married, d. Apr. 29, 1852,
aged 79. 6th. Oliver. 7th. Abel, born in Lunenburg, Mass.,
in 1776, was one of the fourteen children of Col. Joseph
Bellows (the son of Col. Benjamin) who was brought to
this town with his father and mother in 1784, at the time his
father lost his property in Lunenburg, Mass., and became insane. Abel was cared for by the family of Gen'l Benjamin
Bellows till the time of his majority. At the time Gen'l Bellows died, in 1802, there was a vacancy in the office of county
register, an office worth then $1,000 per annum. In honor of
the memory of Gen'l Bellows, who had been register, the
judges of the court left the nomination of a candidate to fill
the vacancy to Mrs. Gen'l Bellows. Her son Caleb wanted
the office, so did her nephew Abel. It lay in her power to
give it to Abel or to her son. She quickly decided it. "Caleb"
said she, "is well off and has enough for his good. Abel
needs it, and I recommend him to the appointment." The
Judges gave it to Abel. When the time came for the people
to elect a new man, politics interposed its potent sway and
Mr. Bellows was defeated, he being a Federalist. He was often heard to say that the $1,000 received for that year's labor
was the foundation of his future fortune.

He went soon after to Canada, and formed a copartnership
in mercantile business with one Horatio Gates. He contin-

ned with Mr. Gates till about 1817 or '18, when, on account of
impaired health, he dissolved partnership and came back to
Walpole with about $40,000. He then married Miss Harriet
Houghton, of Northfield, Mass., and took a trip to Europe.
During his absence, his son Abel Herbert was born, in London. Soon after Mr. Bellows returned to Walpole he purchased the house where his son Abel H. now resides, where he
spent the rest of his life in ease and comfort, employing
his time in looking after his accumulating estate, and enjoying social intercourse with his many friends and townsmen.
He had two children besides A. Herbert, one of whom, Charlotte, died in 1824, aged five years; the other, a daughter,
Harriet Louisa, who was suddenly cut off while at school
at Lenox Mass. in the beauty and loveliness of budding
womanhood. Mr. Bellows was esteemed by his townsmen as
an unobtrusive, benevolent, kind-hearted, peace-loving citizen, always ready to do his share for the public weal and
to lend a helping hand to those in distress. He died April
7th, 1857 aged 81 years. She died Jan. 28th, 1864, aged 72.
Ch. (1). Abel Herbert, b. in London, Eng., May, 28, 1821,
graduated at Harvard University in 1842, read law in the office of the late Frederick Vose, completed his studies at the
law school in Cambridge, Mass. in 1745, and commenced the
practice of his profession in Concord, N. H. in company with
his cousin Hon. Henry Adams Bellows. He is now a resident
of Walpole. He married May, 27th 1861, at Concord, N. H.,
Julia Antoinette Warren of Boston Mass., and has ch. as
follows. [1]. Blanche Harriet. [2.] Herbert Gardner. [3.]
Arthur Benjamin.

8th. Maj. Thomas, m. Sarah S. Dana. Ch. (1.) Isabella,
d. Aug. 30, 1819, aged 6 years. (2.) Sarah J., m. Geo. W.
Grant, Jan. 31, 1844: she d. Dec. 30, 1866, aged 46. He has
two surviving children. (1.) Helen and (2.) Herbert. 9th.
Susan, m. Capt. Jonas Robeson of Fitzwilliam. Ch. (1.)
Abel Bellows, m. Susan Taylor, of New Haven. He was a
physician, d. 1843. Ch. [1.] Henry; [2.] William; [3.]
Herbert; [4.] Maria. 10th. Sarah, m. Calvin Ripley, Feb.

27, 1800. Ch. (1.) Emily, b. Dec. 23., 1799, m. Calvin
Barnes, Dec. 1, 1825. (2.) Louis, b. 1801. (3.) Thomas, b.
1803, m. Salome Dickinson, and had six ch., of whom Sarah
is one, who m. Joshua B. Clark and has grand-children who
are of the 7th generation of the Bellows blood in Walpole.
(4.) Louisa, b. 1805 ; d. July 8, 1863. (5.) Susan, b. 1810;
m. Alvin P. Haskins of Greenfield, Mass., Nov., 21, 1850.
(6.) Sarah, b. 1812. (7.) Joseph, b. 1814. Mrs. Ripley, d.
Mar. 11, 1878, aged 95. 11th. Louisa, m. Jacob X. Knapp.
(See Knapp.)

VI. Abigail, b. Jan. 13, 1759 and married for her first husband, Col. Seth Hunt, of Northampton, Mass., Mar. 28, 1779,
and 2d, Cap. Josiah Richardson of Keene, Apr. 17, 1782.
By her first husband she had one son, Seth, who was born in
1779. He was never married ; although he was not indifferent to the personal and intellectual charms of the fair sex.
It is said that he at one time had a slight attack of heart burning for Miss Patterson of New Jersey, who afterwards became
the wife of Jerome Bonaparte. He was eminently a man of
the world. Having travelled much and acquired, by so doing,
a large fund of general information, he took great pleasure in
imparting it to any one who would listen. He was one of the
finest readers that ever lived in town, and nothing would af-
fect him more unpleasantly than to hear one read indifferently.
He had an irascible temper and the whistling of a boy would
drive him almost to a state of phrensy. He was, at one time,
governor of one of the territories, after which he was addressed as such. (Gov.) The latter part of his life he lived with
his mother, in the Gen'l Allen house; but when she died he
took quarters at the tavern, where he died suddenly, Apr. 7,
1846, probably from disease of the heart.

Mrs. Richardson had one child by her second husband, who
was accidentally killed by being thrown, with herself, from a
wagon. She was full of fun and innocent pranks, from girlhood
to old age. She was independent in character, and not over-
frugal in her manner of living, which caused Mr. Richardson
to keep an eye on the larder, which greatly annoyed her, and

one day "she threatened him that when he died she would bury him in the ash-hole with his head out, that he might continue to know that was going on in the kitchen."

In her girlhood she was caught one day at church service making up faces at the minister, and the reprimand she received was sufficient to cool her fun-loving habit in that direction. She was fond of young company in her old age, when the buoyancy of youth would seem to have returned. Her countenance wore the freshness of her mind till near the close of life. She never was so happy as when recounting some funny incident to young listeners. She used to say at last, referring to her want of heirs, and as an apology for giving away her substance freely, that she did not care to leave so much as a door latch. She died May 5, 1844.

VII. Theodore. He was the oldest son of the second set of children, and was born in the fort. When he was first married he lived in a house that stood on the Knapp place one hundred rods or so south of the present brick mansion. He is said to have been a very powerful man in physical strength, and to have emulated his father in size,—tipping the beam at three hundred pounds. He was out a few months in the service of his country in 1780. Being of an easy nature he was content to let each day bring forth its favors or its frowns. He being without ambition or enterprise, either through misfortune or neglect, his once substantial patrimony wasted away and left him in advanced life without those luxuries that he was wont to have in his younger days; but his necessary wants were generously supplied by his brother Thomas. He considered it a virtue to receive, as well as to give. He died in consequence of injuries received by a barn door's swinging against him. He married Sarah, daughter of Capt. Phineas and Abigail Hutchins of this town, and settled in Charlestown, N. H. Ch. 1st. Sarah, b. April 8, 1782; m. Walter Powers. d. George, b. June 31, 1784; m. Clarissa Bellows. 3d. Polly, b. Oct. 29, 1785. 4th. Theodore, b. Oct. 10, 1787; m. Elizabeth Davis. 5th. Thomas, b. Dec. 12, 1789. 6th. Charles Henry, b. April 23, 1791; d. Aug. 16, 1802. 7th. Orlando, b.

June 30, 1793; m. Maria Bleannett. 8th. Eleanor, m. J. P. Baker. 9th. James, b. Dec. 12, 1796; d. Sept. 17, 1802. 10th. Abigail, m. Charles Watkins.

VIII. Mary, m. Maj. Martin Kinsley, October 18, 1803. Rev. Henry W. Bellows says of her that "She was cast in that mold of female nature which would have fitted her to be the wife of some resolute old Puritan in the days when wives buckled on their husbands' swords and bade them die, but not dishonor their name and faith. Tall and commanding in person, firm and original in opinions, of native dignity and elevation, free from frivolous or feminine weaknesses, she carried her self-respect with her all her days, and secured the veneration even more than the love of others. * * Possessing unusual business capacity and large experience, she managed her affairs with discretion, and was a helpmeet indeed to her husband, whose Congressional life carried him much away from home." "Mrs. Kinsley, after the death of her husband, resided chiefly in the family of her only child, Mrs. Gardner; but after her grandchildren, early bereft of a mother, ceased to need her care, she followed the family instinct of her race and repaired to Walpole to end her days. Here she lived in the family of her brother Thomas until she died.

Her religious creed and belief were those of one hundred years ago, while, on the other hand, her brother's were of a more liberal kind. This disparity of views led to many animated discussions between the Squire and herself; but neither party succeeded in convincing the other of the fallacy of views each was supposed to entertain. She had one daughter, who married Samuel J. Gardner.

IX. Thomas was born the same year his father built his new house, (1762) which is still standing, the property and residence of Rev. Thomas Bellows, the grandson of the founder. Probably this is the oldest dwelling in town. The old homestead of the founder has never passed out of the possession of the family, being highly prized by both his son and grandson.

Referring to the town records, the name of Thomas Bellows occurs frequently as a town officer, and in 1792 he was chosen

the first representative to the General Court from this town
after the adoption of the State Constitution the same year.
In 1794 he was appointed Councillor for five years; and in
1799 Sheriff of the County of Cheshire; an office which he
held for more than thirty years, discharging his duties as an
officer with fidelity, honor to himself, and to the entire satisfaction of the public.

The "Squire," as he was sometimes called, was noticeably
peculiar in his ways, in some respects. He had an infirmity of
speech, which sometimes produced a ludicrous smile on the
face of a stranger; but to an acquaintance it was of little moment. At one time a stranger inquired the distance to
Charlestown, when his peculiar nervous utterance prevented a
distinct and ready answer: and in his impatience he blurted
out: "Go 'long, go 'long, you'll get there 'fore I can tell ye."
He had a wonderful memory of dates and of personal history.
He could remember every public house he ever stopped at,
where it was, and the landlord's name. If a stranger entered
the church where he habitually attended, he was impatient
till he knew his name and from whence he came. So, too, if
a person moved into town. He had a habit of counting the
numbers of those that were at church on the Sabbath, and in
so doing he would move his fore finger slightly as he counted,
and at the same time gently move his lips, and if any family
or any member of it was absent, he knew it. An absence
from church by any person or family whose attendance was
usually constant, was followed by the inquiry whether they
were sick or well. Left with a handsome fortune, he was content to enjoy its income in part, and leave it to his children
unimpaired, with a moderate addition. In his dealings with the
world he was proverbially honest; sometimes, it was thought,
overstepping the Golden Rule by doing *better* by others than
he wished others to do by him. He lived a long and blameless life, being in his eighty-sixth year when he died. His
epitaph was the work of his life, with which his townsmen
were familiar long before his death; although not chiseled in

granite, it will endure as long as the name of Thomas Bellows is spoken ;—*An honest man.*

Thomas Bellows was born in 1762; d. April 18, 1848. He m. Eleanor Foster. She was born in 1768 ; d. Aug. 29, 1840. Ch. 1st. Isaac Foster, b. March 4, 1806 ; m. Eleanor Huntington, and had three children. 2d. Mary H., b. March 5, 1806 ; m. David Buffum. (See Buffum.) 3d. Thomas, b. Sept. 23, 1807 : fitted for college at Exeter, N. H., 1822 : entered Harvard, but graduated at Dartmouth College in 1827. He pursued theological studies at Andover, Mass. and New Haven, Conn., and was settled over a Congregational church and society in Greenfield, Mass., March, 1833, and was dismissed September, 1834, when he returned to the Bellows homestead, where he is now living (1879). 4th. Martha Eleanor, b April, 1 1811 ; m. Philip Peck. (See Peck.) 5th. Ann Foster, d. young.

X. Josiah, the youngest son of the old family, was born in 1767, and died in June, 1846. The immediate cause of his death was injuries received by being thrown from a wagon. It is said that in his youthful days he was in the habit of sowing "wild oats," but one knowing him only in advanced life would hardly ever have suspected anything of the kind.

His father was desirous of giving him a liberal education, and sent him to Yale College for that purpose, with his nephew Caleb, General Benjamin's son. But with their sanguine temperaments and impulsive natures, they could not brook the confinement incident to college life, and in a few days they returned home; choosing rather to face the frowns of indignant parents than the study of Latin accidence; thus verifying the common saying that "If you shut up a Bellows in a school room with books, if there is no other way of escape he'll go through the window."

Mr. Bellows pursued the vocation of a farmer through life. For many years he was one of the strong pillars of the town, representing it in the General Court in 1809–10, and in 1819 ; and of the Unitarian society, of which church he was a constant attendant. In person he was large, inclining to obesity ; rather taciturn in his social intercourse, his sentences being always short, approaching bluntness at times. In conversation he invariably made use of the strongest Saxon words, in laconic sentences. He was a highly respected citizen of the town, a kind neighbor and benevolent friend, but he always preferred doing things in his own way. Of all his kindred and descendants no one resembles him so much, in size, looks, and general appearance, as his grandson, Waldo F. Hayward.

He was married twice, 1st to Rebecca, Apr. 13, 1788, dau. of Hon. Thomas Sparhawk; she died in Oct. 1793; he m. 2d, his deceased wife's sister, Mary.

By his first wife he had two children. 1st Josiah 3d, b. Nov. 25, 1788; d. Jan. 13, 1842. He was twice m. 1st to Stella C., the dau. of Stephen Rowe Bradley. Ch. (1) Stella Louisa, b. Oct. 7, 1814. (2) Sarah Adeline, b. Apr. 13, 1818. (3) Gratia Rebecca, b. Jan. 1, 1821. (4) Stephen Rowe, b. Oct. 17, 1822. He married for his second wife the widow of Dr. Alfred Hosmer and had one son, Josiah Grahm, b. July 24, 1841; m. 1st Anne E., dau. of Dr. Alpheus Morrill of Concord, N. H.; she d. and he m. 2d, Katharine H. W. dau. of Aaron P. and Huldah (Burke) Howland. He is now living in town practising the profession of law, in the confidence and esteem of his fellow townsmen. Josiah 3d, better known as the Col., was an active business man in town for more than thirty years, being principally engaged in mercantile pursuits. He represented the town in the General Court in 1823-4-5, was Capt. of the artillery company that went from this town to Portsmouth in 1814. He was Town Clerk from 1831 to 1838, and Post Master from 1826 till the time of his death, besides holding many other offices of trust and honor, in town and county.

In person he was fine looking, and in address very courteous, and in nature obliging. It is said that he was the most popular Bellows that ever lived in town—knowing no one that he could call his enemy. Mrs. Bellows was a beautiful woman, and she, together with her three daughters and son, all of whom possessed a grace and loveliness of person and character seldom witnessed in one family, formed a group which would have made a charming tableau for the pencil of the artist. But that fell destroyer, consumption, blanched the cheek of the mother first, then the daughters, one by one, till the green turf hid them all from worldly vision. The Col. and his son Rowe survived but a few years, they both being victims of the destroyer of that lovely family.

2d Louisa, b. July 16, 1792; m. John W. Hayward and died in 1878. Ch. (1) Louisa, m. Rev. Chas. T. Canfield. (2) John W., b. in Wayland, Mass., July 5, 1828; m. Esther C. dau. of Dr. Ebenezer and Esther (Crafts) Morse. (See Ap.) (3) Waldo Flint, b. Dec. 26, 1831. Josiah Bellows had by his second wife, Mary Sparhawk, 3d Thomas Sparhawk. 4th Mary Bellows. (See Grant.) 5th Polly, b. Jan. 20, 1798. 6th Ellen, m. 1st Gill Wheelock, by whom she had 3 ch., (1) Ellen, m. Nathan Chandler. (2) Henry G., m. Harriet S., dau. of Joseph and Eliza Bellows Dorr. (3) George G. Mr. Wheelock died and his widow m. Jonathan Howe. 7th Edward, b. Oct. 31, 1806; died young. 8th William, b. June 29, 1808; d. May 8, 1862; m. Sarah H., dau. of Nehemiah Giles, June 16, 1836, and had two sons, William and Edward. 9th Julia R.; m. Robert Barnett, June 16, 1816; issue, one daughter, Mary, who died Apr. 10, 1873, aged 35. 10th Catherine Walley, b. in 1815, m. Hon. Henry A. Bellows. (See H. A. B.) She d. June 24, 1848. 11th Annie Foster, m. Rev. Thomas Hill; she died leaving six children, Henry, Mary, Elizabeth, Catherine Joy, Ann and Thomas Roby. It will be perceived that William, Julia and Catherine were all married at the *same time*.

BLANCHARD, JONATHAN. The Blanchards in this town, Westmoreland and Acworth, are descendants of one Nathaniel Blanchard, who lived in Shutesbury, Mass., and had six children, three of whom, Nathaniel, Isaac and Lemuel settled in Westmoreland about 1770. Nathaniel, the oldest son, settled on some land at the extreme north part of the town, now owned by Barton C. Aldrich. His wife was a DeBell of Boston, Mass. He is remembered as a famous fiddler of by-gone days. His oldest son was William, who lived for many years on the old homestead and married Roxana, daughter of Moses Burt of this town. By her he had three sons, Moses, Wil-

liam jr. and one who died young, and five daughters, one of
whom, Sally died when about 20 years old, between 1825 and
1830, the mother dying about the same time. Roxana, the
2d one married George McNeil, for his first wife, and Martha
the 3d one, for his second ; Sophronia, the 4th one, m. Hiram,
Britton, Apr. 5, 1843. Submit, m. Theron Adams. (See Adams.) Nancy, m. Hiram Hall and had several ch. The foregoing children of William Blanchard all died of consumption,
inherited from the Burt family. William B. m. again and had
5 children—two daughters. He died in this town in about 1855.
Heber, the 2d son of Nath'l, went to northern Vt. Willard,
an odd character, d. in Chesterfield, N. H. Nath'l jr., a famous clarionett player, d. in Washington D. C , when there
with a circus. Isaac, the 3d son of Nathaniel sen., was born
in Shutesbury, Mass , about 1750, and m. Miriam, dau. of Dr.
Lord, of Athol, Mass., and had six children, among whom was
Jonathan the 3d son, who was born in Westmoreland, Mar. 15,
1781, and m. Polly, dau. of Roswell Pierce of Putney, Vt., a
famous singer of patriotic songs. He (Blanchard) came to
Walpole, in 1815 and had a family of 10 ch. He was a man
of strict honesty of purpose and unobtrusive in character.
His wife, who survived him many years, possessed in a high degree Christian fortitude in affliction, and gentleness of character in demeanor. He d. July 20, 1847; she d. Sep. 19, 1872,
aged, 84. Ch. I. Adeline, b. Jan 4, 1813; d. in 1823. II. Louisa Lord, b. May 18, 1815. She has been confined to her bed
upwards of forty years, with a disease of the spine, and during
this long period she has been a model of patience and submission.
She has, from reading and conversation with visitors, acquired
a large fund of information which those who have seen more
of the world might envy. Occasionally she receives some benefactions from charitable people, one of which, worthy of note,
was from Levi Lyman in 1872, of $500, about ten days be-
fore he died. It came to her very opportunely and was received with tears of gratitude and joy. III. and IV. William
Durant and Willard Tyler, b Oct. 11, 1818. William was a
merchant in Nashua, N. H.; d. Sep 9, 1841. Willard T. lives

on the old homestead, unmarried, tenderly supplying the wants of his unfortunate sister, Louisa. V. John Pierce, b. Sep. 1, 1821; m. Annira Redeaut, Oct. 19, 1849,—resides in Putney, Vt. Ch. William Henry, Charles Pierce, George Edwin, Edward John, Hattie Ann, d. young, and Hattie Melvina. VI. Roswell Sawyer, b. Sep. 29, 1829; m. Maria Staples, of Williamstown, Vt. Ch. 1st Louisa Maria, b. Mar. 29, 1850; m. James Nash and has 3 ch. 2d Frank Russell, b. Oct. 1857; d. 1866. 3d Albert Ellsworth. 4th Ella Frances. (See Ap.) VII. Albert Isaac, d. in infancy. VIII. Albert Isaac, b. Mar. 11, 1828; m. Ann R. Russell and settled in Nashua, where he d. leaving 2 ch. IX. Charles Dinsmore, d. in infancy. X. Joseph Norton, b. June 18, 1832; m. Jane Wait of Chester, Vt. and lives in Peterborough, N. H., and has one ch. Effie, b. in 1869.

Bisco, Daniel W., was a resident of this town as early as the last decade in the last century. He was a tanner by trade, and his tannery stood about ten rods south of the residence of Henry J. Watkins, and his dwelling was located on the site of Levi H. Foster's garden. Where he hailed from has not been ascertained, nor has his wife's family name. The Biscos were considered a family of respectability in town, according to the testimony of the old citizens, now living, who knew them. He was born in 1766, and died in 1828; and his wife, Esther, died in 1826, aged 55. He held some town office for several years being considered an efficient man. In 1806 he was town clerk and represented the town in the Legislature in 1821–2. His children were, I. Sophia, born Aug. 19, 1797, and died two years later. II. Leonard, b. June 9, 1800. He carried on the business of his father for several years, and built the house where Henry J. Watkins now resides, but through some outside manufacturing speculations lost a portion of his property and afterwards relinquished his tanning business. He lived in town till about 1843, when he removed to Keene, where he was clerk of the County court and Register of Probate. During his life in Walpole he was for several years one of the selectmen and was elected Representative for the years

1831-2-5, and '6.   Mr. Bisco was, in person, noticeably good
looking, and the regularity of his features seemed to be consonant with his hand-writing, which was very legible and beautiful, and wherever seen in public records should serve as a
stimulus to those who make records for posterity to follow
his example.   He married Mellicent, the youngest daughter of
Dr. Jesseniah Kittredge sen., by whom he had two children,
1st. Henry L., born. 1833, and died May 14, 1839.   He was
a precocious and loveable child, emulating the dignity and
grace of manners of a cultivated gentleman of mature years.
2d. Josiah L., b. in 1839 and died in 1844.   He buried his
first wife in 1851.   He d. Aug. 10, 1869.   III. Elmira, b. July
17, 1802, and lived one year.

BRADLEY, GEN'L STEPHEN ROW, came to Walpole in 1818 and
lived in town till the time of his death, which occurred Dec.
9th, 1830.   He was born in Wallingford, Conn., Feb. 20, 1754,
and was the son of Moses Bradley of Cheshire, Conn., and
Mary, daughter and heiress of Daniel Row of Hamden, Conn.,
He was a descendant of Stephen Bradley, one of seven brothers
who came to America from England in 1650 and settled in
North Haven, Conn.   Stephen Row graduated at Yale College
in the class of 1775 and during his senior year he prepared and
published an almanac for that year and at this time he spelt
his middle name *Row* instead of *Rowe*.   In 1776 he joined the
Revolutionary forces as Captain, and soon rose to the rank of
Colonel, but was principally engaged in the commissary
department.   In 1778 he was engaged in teaching school and
at the same time pursuing the study of law under the direction
of Tappan Reeve, who afterwards established the law school
at Litchfield, Conn.   He made his first appearance in Westminster, Vt. in 1779 and the same year was licensed to practise
law in that state.   From that time he rose rapidly in the estimation of the sons of Vermont, till he reached the Senate
chamber at Washington, D. C.   He was very active during the
Vermont and New Hampshire boundary troubles, and his counsels had great weight.   His papers written at the time are sufficient evidence of sound statesmanship and good judgment.

Of the offices that Mr. Bradley held, the following is but a partial list. In 1782 he was one of the selectmen and town clerk, of Westminster and also received the appointment of Register of Probate, an office he held ten years. In 1783 he was appointed County Judge, for Windham Co. In 1788 he received the appointment of side Judge in the Superior Court of that State. In 1793 he was admitted to practise in the Circuit Courts of the U. S. He represented the town of Westminster in the state Assembly seven years and was speaker of the House in 1785, and was also a member of the Council in 1798. He was one of the first Senators from Vermont in 1791, drawing the *four year* term. In 1801 he was again elected to the U. S. Senate for six years during which time he was president *pro tempore* two years. When his term expired in 1807 he was returned for six years longer. Mr. Bradley is represented to have been a lawyer of distinguished abilities, a good orator, a man of cheerful companionship, ready wit, full of anecdote, of large acquaintance with mankind, and also as possessing an extensive range of historical knowledge. When he came to Walpole he purchased the mansion built by Francis Gardner, (who was for many years a lawyer of some repute in town,) and spent his declining years. He was thrice married. 1st to Mirib Atwater, by whom he had one son, William Czar, who became one of Vermont's distinguished sons and was widely known as a ripe scholar and a talented lawyer. He married 2d Thankful —— and by her had 1st Stella Czarina, who married Josiah Bellows of this town. 2d Adeline, who married S.·G. Goodrich, (Peter Parley,) and had one child. 3d Stephen Rowe jr., who was drowned at New Haven, while at school there. His third wife was Melinda Willard, of Westminster, Vt. by whom he had one daughter, Mary, who married Henry S. Tudor, and had five sons and two daughters, all born in Walpole.

In his last years, when he had given up the cares and turmoils of public life, he was wont to amuse himself in various eccentric ways. The following anecdote of him is to the point. At one time, while living in Walpole, he chanced to meet one of his poor Westminster neighbors, when he asked him how he got along with his large family. " Poorly enough," was the reply. " Well," said Mr. B., " the next time you come over, bring a bag and get some corn." It was not long before the poor man was at Mr. B.'s with his bag. " What do you want in that bag?" said Mr. B. " I came after the corn you promised me," was the reply. " Corn! I never promised you any corn," said Mr. B. " Well," said the man, " my neighbors told me, before I started, that you would not give me any." "Go to my bin and fill your bag!' said Mr. B , " and when you get home, tell your neighbors they are all a pack of —— liars."

BUFFUM, WILLIAM.—Joseph Buffum came to Westmoreland, from Rhode Island, in 1784, and settled in the south part of the town. He married Sally Haskell, of Lancaster, Mass., and had seven sons, who all possessed the family traits of strong mind, persistent will, and good common sense. Joseph, jr., was a graduate of Dartmouth, studied law, and early in life was a member of the Cheshire bar, and Postmaster at Keene. In 1818 he was elected member of Congress from this State, for one term, but refused a re-election, it is said, on account of the distaste he had for the corruption and dishonesty seen in Congress, and in and around Washington. On his return from Washington he settled down on the paternal homestead, and spent a long life there ; a recluse in a measure, avoiding all female society but his mother's, and seldom appearing off his farm for any other than the most urgent reasons. He had his books and papers for company, and was one of the most intelligent men in town. He was a man of good abilities, and strictly honest. William, the fourth son, was born July 25, 1793, and came to Walpole in 1816, and soon after established himself in the mercantile business, in which he continued till he died, October, 1841. He married, March 1, 1820, Mary Ann D., dau. of Thomas Gordon, of Sterling, Conn., and step-dau. of Gen. Amasa Allen of this town. His ch. were I. William G., b. April 11, 1822. II. Rufus E., b. Feb. 22, 1824; graduated at Dartmouth in 1844; studied law in Cambridge, Mass., and was admitted to the bar in that state. He m. Eliza M.

Farley in 1846, and had five ch., two of whom are living: Gordon C. and Ogbourne E.; m. 2d, Clara, dau. of Jonas and Sarah (Labaree) Tufts, of this town, Jan., 1878, and lives in Humbolt, Tenn. III. Joseph H., b. Feb. 8, 1826; m. Laura S., dau. of Ashbel Wheeler of Chesterfield, N. H.—issue, one dau., Laura, b. 1856. IV. George Dixon, b. July 7, 1828; resides in California. V. Edward Wheaton, b. Oct. 11, 1830; graduated at the law school in Cambridge, Mass., and was admitted to the bar in Cheshire county at the October term of 1852, and in the following January went to California, where he has resided ever since. VI. Sarah Ann H., b. September 4, 1832.

BUFFUM, DAVID, the seventh son of Joseph, was b. April 15, 1803, and came to W. in 1820, and went into the store of his brother William, where he remained three years as clerk, and at the expiration of that time became a partner, under the style of W. & D. Buffum, and continued fourteen years, when he formed a copartnership with Thomas H. Seaver. This firm continued three years. In 1840 Henry H. Baxter was his partner six months, when he took Francis Bellows as a partner. This firm dissolved at the expiration of four years, and from 1844 to 1850 he was in business alone. In 1861 he took his son Thomas in as a partner, which partnership continued five years. In 1828 he was captain of the rifle company in this town, and was Lieutenant-Colonel of the 20th regiment in New Hampshire in 1829–30. He was a member of the General Court in 1849–50, and also of the Convention called to revise the State Constitution, in 1876.

Mr. Buffum has exercised a marked influence in the civic interests of the town the past fifty years, although he has held but few town offices. His long business life and good judgment have admirably fitted him to give counsel to his townsmen in their multifarious private dealings, which has been often sought. When the War of the Rebellion broke out, although a strong Democrat, he was one of the first to sustain the government, in furnishing men and means to suppress the Rebellion. In December, 1829, he married Mary Hubbard, daughter of Hon.

Thomas and Eleanor (Foster) Bellows, by whom he has two children, I. Thomas Bellows, b. Sept. 8, 1830; m. Ann Rebecca, daughter of Frederick and Mary Ann (Watkins) Kilburn. (See Ap.) II. Ann Reynolds, b. Aug. 29, 1834.

BUNDY, JAMES.—The Bundy family was very numerous during the early settlement of the town, but much of its history remains in obscurity, and probably ever will, as no records, so far as known, were ever kept by the family. The descendants now living in town, being of the fifth and sixth generations, know but very little about their ancestry. From several sources the fact is well established that one James Bundy came to this town as early as 1762 or '3, and purchased a tract of land, of one hundred acres, lying in a long strip, running easterly from the old Jona. Jennison place. He had five sons; viz., Isaac, Nathan, James, Elias, and Asahel, and *probably* two daughters. 1st. Ruth, was married to John W. Divorse in 1781, and 2d. Sarah, was m. to Ithiel Hoadly in 1764, by parson Leavitt. None of the family were born in town, and from whence they came is not known. James was born in 1695, and died April 12, 1772. He was one of the members of the first church, formed in 1767, and held a minor town office in 1764. What information is gathered in relation to those old families is gleaned from the records of deaths, baptisms, and marriages. As far as those records go they are presumed to be correct, but may not be full. Ch. I. Isaac, m. 1st. Sarah Johnson, 1768; she d. 1787, aged 39; m. 2d. Amitia Fowler the same year. Ch. 1st. Mary, bap. 1771, m. Timothy Holmes, 1793. 2d. Sophronia, bap. 1772. 3d. Isaac, jr., b. 1794. 4th, Eunice, b. 1776. 5th David, bap. 1779. 6th. Elisha, bap. 1782. 7th. Sarah, bap. 1785. 8th. Samuel, bap. 1787. 9th. Willard, bap. 1789. Susannah, b. not known; m. Titus O. Brown in 1794. Nothing more is known of this branch of the family,—it is said that they moved into the northern part of this State. II. James, jr. Ch. 1st. Asenath, bap. 1772. 2d. Abel, bap. 1785. 3d. Samuel, bap. 1777. III. Asahel, m. 1st. Hannah ———; 2d. Esther Eastman, in 1770, from a numerous family by that name that once lived in town. He settled on the place now owned

by David C. Thompson. Ch. 1st. Esther, m. David Mead,
May 8, 1803. 2d. Hannah, b. 1772. 3d. Joseph, bap. 1774;
m. Polly Kidder. Ch. (1) Joseph K., b. 1811. (2) Mary E.,
b. 1817. Joseph, sen., lost his life in the wheel-pit at Drewsville, March 8, 1818, aged 44. 4th. and 5th. two by the name
of Asahel, died in infancy. 6th, another Asahel, who died in
Guiana, S. A. 7th. Louisa, b. 1780. 8th, Philip Eastman, m.
Abigail Griggs, 1801. He lived on the homestead, and had
children as follows: (1) Francis H., m. and lives in Boston.
(2) Cyrus. (3) Sarepta, m. John S. March, of this town July 25,
1830. (See March.) (4) Philip Eastman, jr. (5) Asahel, bap. 1809.
(6) John C., bap. 1815. (7) Ephraim G., bap. 1812. (8) Abigail, m.
George Riley of Orford. (9) Fanny, b. 1819, m. Parker Wright.
7th, Sybil, m. Dr. Francis Kittredge, in 1804. 8th, Benjamin, bap. 1791. IV. Lieut. Elias, m. and lived in town and
had two or more children; 1st, Lydia, died in infancy. 2d,
Elias S., d. Feb. 16, 1786, aged 57 years. V. Nathan, m. Zerviah Scripture in 1767, who bore him the following children:
1st, Zerviah, bap. 1772; m. Daniel Whipple in 1803. 2d, Elijah, m. Sally Kibling, in 1802. 3d, Rhoda, bap. 1782. 4th,
Abigail, bap. in 1787. 5th, John, bap. 1788; m. Lois, dau. of
John Hall. 6th, Royal, bap. 1790; m. Polly Fletcher Nov. 12,
1816. Ch. (1) Mary A. (2) Hollis M., m. Jane Ormsby, and
had three ch. (3) George H. (4) Amasa T., m. and had three
ch.; viz., George H., Amasa T., and Mary. (5) Aldis P. 7th,
Fanny, bap. 1790; m. Ariel Allen in 1809. 8th, Daniel. 9th,
Nathan, m. Jane Moore. Ch. (1) George, b. Feb. 5, 1800; d.
Aug. 22, 1871; m. Jane, dau. of Thomas Moore, Jan. 25, 1825.
Ch. [1] Emily S., b. Sept. 14, 1826; m. George W. Whipple,
Oct. 5, 1847. [2] Frances L., b. July 25, 1828; m. Isaac Brown
May 23, 1850; three ch. [3] Mary J., b. Mar. 27, 1834; m.
Hiram Watkins, June 2, 1864. (See Ap.) (2) Sophia, m. Jared
Record, of Woodstock, Vt., April, 1834.

BURT, HOLLAND, was born in Westmoreland, N. H., Nov. 12,
1790; in a small one story house that stood on the place, once
owned by Luther Knights, about fifty rods south of the old
Knights residence. He learned the cabinet-maker's trade and

married Nancy, the only daughter of Alexander Watkins, and located in Drewsville, in its palmy days, and built the large dwelling now standing on the south east corner of the common. He spent his last days in the village doing business in the old Johnson store. He died Mar. 6, 1855; she d. June 10, 1871. Ch. I. Sarah E. D., b. Dec. 12, 1815; d. Feb. 15, 1826. II. Alfred W., b. Dec. 9, 1817; m. Caroline Burroughs, by whom he has three children now living in town. He learned the trade of a carpenter and joiner, and many of the best houses in town are samples of his thoroughness of workmanship. He has been chosen several times as one of the selectmen of the town and always discharged his duties faithfully, and has also been entrusted with other public and private business. III. Holland J., b. Mar. 6, 1819; d. Feb. 26, 1826. IV. Nancy E., b. Apr. 14, 1823; d. 1824. V. Sumner A., b. Jan. 11, 1825; m. Anna E. B. Shaw, Boston, Mass. VI. John H., b. June 6, 1827; m. Mary J. Cushing, Milton, Mass. VII. George L., b. Nov. 3, 1829; m. Ellen A. Derby of this town. Sarah, Holland and Nancy all died within a period of thirteen days, and were buried in the same grave. Sumner, John and George all learned the carpenter's trade and have become famous builders in the vicinity of Boston, where they live. The four surviving boys are all substantial, reliable citizens and have never dishonored their progenitors.

BURT, MOSES, one of the old Revolutionary patriots, was the son of Aaron Burt, of Northfield, Mass., a wholesale merchant there of whom the first settlers of Walpole used to purchase goods before a store was opened here. Moses was born in Northfield, Feb. 14, 1756 and came to Walpole in 1775, with Samuel Wiers, and purchased what was then known as the Chandler meadows. Aug. 14, 1777, when he and another man were stooking wheat they heard the reports of cannon at the battle of Bennington and they immediately left home for the scene of strife. (See narrative.) He enlisted in the army for three months and when the time expired he returned to Walpole; but was soon drafted to serve nine months longer, which term he served out. In 1783 he married Submit Ross, sup-

Luther Burt

posed to have been an inhabitant of this town, and had ten
children. I. Roxana, b. Apr. 8, 1784 ; m. William Blanchard
and had ten children. (See Blanchard family.) II. Abiathar,
b. Sep. 10, 1786 ; d. at Westmoreland, Oct. 11, 1875; m. Mehitable Turner, of Mansfield, Ct. b. 1788 ; d. 1864. Ch. 1st Livonia,
2d Philenia, 3d Mehitable, 4th Abiathar, jr., 5th Eleazer, 6th
Abiathar, 7th Eliza, 8th Mary, 9th Ursula Sophia, 10th Submit Ross, 11th Eunice Caroline, all born between 1806 and
1827. III. Ross, b. 1788 ; d. 1806. IV. Moses, jr., b. 1790 ; d.
1796. V. Luther, b. Aug. 8, 1792 ; d. Nov. 1, 1866. He was a farmer by occupation, and by industry, economy and the exercise
of good judgment accumulated a good property, besides bringing up a large family of children, and died at a ripe old age without an enemy. He married Irene, dau. of Hugh and Cynthia
(Allen) Dunshee, b. July 9, 1795 ; d. Mar. 2, 1877. Ch. 1st, Levi,
b. May 12, 1812 ; m. Mary, dau. of Benj. H. and Elizabeth (Gates)
Floyd. Ch. (1) Theron, b. June 10, 1836 ; m. Mary Collins; d.
Nov. 6, 1863. (2) Alonzo, b. June 10, 1838 ; m. Ellen, dau. of
Heber and Pruda (Walker) Cole, of Westmoreland. (3) Mary
Jane, b. May 6, 1844; m. Geo. Clark, of Keene, and has 3 ch.
2d, Mary J., b. Dec. 31, 1814 ; m. Nelson Wilbur, of Westmoreland, Feb. 14, 1833. Mr. Wilbur died very suddenly at
one of his neighbor's, while making a call, Apr. 19, 1874. At
the time of his death he was Representative elect to the General Court from that town. Ch. (1) Curtis B., b. Jan. 9, 1834;
m. Rhoda, dau. of Preston and Vashti (Wellington) Titus, and
has two ch., Ellen and Edward. (2) Rovena M., b. June 1, 1836;
m. Charles Townsend—issue 3 daughters. (3) Emily, b. Nov.
23, 1837 ; m. Timo. Moriarty, 1861 and has 1 ch. Bessie. (4)
Warren N. b. Oct. 5, 1843 ; m. Nellie M. Hendricks and has 2
ch. (5) Frank S. b. Nov. 29, 1851 : m. Ida, dau. of Charles
Knights of Westmoreland, 1879. (6) Laura E., b. June 16,
1854; m. Herbert Hall 1876; issue, 2 ch. (7)Jennie A., d.
young. (8) Fred L., b. Apr. 20, 1859. 3d, Curtis D., d. young.
4th, Laura M., b. Mar. 31, 1821. (See Porter family.) 5th,
Amasa, b. Dec. 28, 1822; m. Elizabeth Streeter, of Chesterfield, N. H., 1845—issue 3 ch. (1) Munroe S. (2) Willis. (3)

Lizzie—all m. 6th, George, b. Mar. 6, 1825. After he became of age he followed the business of peddling dry goods, and being a good salesman he accumulated an amount sufficient to give him a start in the world, when he went to Kansas sometime before 1860, where he, in a short time, accumulated a handsome property.

Aug. 21, 1863, a band of brigands from the Southern States, calling themselves bush-whackers, made a raid into Kansas, and he, with many others, fell a victim to their bloody hands. He was first robbed of his watch and what money he had about him, and when he supposed they had all left he stepped out of his dwelling upon the side walk, when a straggling, drunken outlaw rode up and deliberately shot him through his lungs. He lived long enough to tell a friend where he had buried a large sum of money. The miscreant who did the bloody work soon bit the dust by the unerring aim of trusty rifles in the hands of the outraged citizens. 7th, Henry, b. July 22, 1827, lives on the old homestead—one of the town's trust-worthy citizens. 8th, Andrew Jackson, b. Sep. 17, 1830; d. 1854; m. Charlotte, dau. of Levi and Charlotte (Burt) Reed and had 2 ch., Waldo and Edna. VI. Submit, b. Mar. 14, 1794; d. July 19, 1873; m. James Wier. (See Wier family.) VII. Hannah, b. June 24, 1797; d. Dec. 15, 1849; unm. VIII. Sophronia, b. Aug. 8, 1799; d. Sep. 29, 1841; unm. IX. Charlotte, b. Oct. 11, 1801; d. Feb. 1833: m. Levi Reed; issue, 4 ch. 1st, Charlotte E., b. Jan. 22, 1825. 2d, Levi J., b. May 27, 1827. 3d, Benj. Burt, b. May 26, 1829. 4th, Lucy, b. Apr. 24, 1831; m. H. N. Shaw. X. Sophia, b. 1804; d. 1829.

CAMPBELL. JAMES, was a lineal descendant of John Campbell, Duke of Argyle, who was born in Argyleshire in 1660, and was an officer in the army of William the Third, at the battle of " Boyne waters." At the close of the war the Campbells settled in the north of Ireland. One of the Campbells, named Henry, was born in 1697, and married Martha Black, who sailed with his wife and five sons for America in 1733. James Campbell was the youngest of the five sons and was born in Londonderry the same year that his father arrived

Henry Beat

in America, and died at Cambridge, Vt., Apr. 11, 1816. He was a soldier in the Revolutionary army for three years, and was wounded at the battle of Stillwater. After the close of the war he settled in Acworth, having purchased a farm there in 1781. He was often in office during his sojourn in Acworth, and the accuracy with which he kept the town records and the legibility of his penmanship were remarkable for those days. He was a surveyor and conveyancer, and taught school winters from 1783 to '91. He was elected Register of Deeds for the county of Cheshire in 1803, and held the office by re-election until his death in 1825, without opposition. Precisely at what time James Campbell came to Walpole has not been ascertained, but probably about 1800. He lived in a house that formerly stood where Isaac M. Graves now lives, and the Register's office is now Mr. Graves' wood-shed. During his life in Walpole he was for many years Justice of the Peace. Before coming to Walpole he married Desire Slader by whom he had ten children. I. Henry, b. 1793; d. 1855; m. Sarah Cummins and had four children. II. Emily, b. 1794; m. Lewis Gilmore and had six children. III. James Harvey, b. 1795; d. at Mason, N. H., 1851. IV. Mason, b. 1799; m. Mary L. Chaddick and had seven children, and is the only surviving member of James Campbell's family. V. Solon, b. in 1801; d. in 1827. VI. Lewis, b. in 1802, Aug. 17; d. Apr. 23, 1877. He was, after his father's death, from 1825, till 1836, the courteous Register of Deeds for Cheshire county. His legible hand-writing and the care and pains he bestowed on the County records will ever be brought to mind on opening the folios of the office. VII. Sarah Slader, b. October 1, 1804; m. John S. Walker. VIII. Jane Chandler, b. November 4, 1807; m. Cyrrel Carpenter and had three children. IX. Mary Wilder, b. June 13, 1810; m. Elbridge Keyes, of Keene. X. Edna Augusta, b. Aug. 2, 1814; m. William Whitaker—issue, one child. The Campbells used to claim a relationship to the Scottish clan of that name. The family was one of highest respectability in this town and some of the descendants of those five sons who first came to America have occupied high positions of trust and honor in various parts of the United States. James Campbell's wife, Desire, was a woman of many virtues and highly esteemed by her neighbors and acquaintances. She was very large and obese, and consequently not active. In 1823, her son Solon, a young man, went to the yard to milk the cow, but returned with an empty pail, saying to his mother, "The cow wont allow me to milk her," whereupon she took the pail, saying "I guess I can milk her." No sooner had she entered the yard, than the cow plunged at her with all the fury of a maddened bison, tearing her abdomen in a most shocking and dangerous manner. It was thought that her injuries would prove fatal immediately; but she lingered and suffered, for two long years, the most intense agony, which she bore with patience and Christian fortitude; but at length she had to yield. She died May 22, 1825, aged 53. He died the following Oct., at the age of 65, from no other cause than grief at the loss of his wife. He was a mason, and at his death the funeral was conducted by the craft, and was large and imposing—the procession reaching, it is said, from his house to the village.

CARLISLE. The history of the family that once lived in this town bearing the name of Carlisle, is involved somewhat in obscurity; although patient research and inquiry have been made for more than a year. The following imperfect history of the family has been gathered from many and various sources. It appears from what information is gathered, that one David Carlisle came to this town, early in its settlement, from Lunenburg Mass., but originally from Ireland, and that he was a man somewhat advanced in life appears from the fact that his wife, Lattice, was born in 1704, and died in 1791. He settled on the place now owned by Edwin Guild, or in that immediate vicinity. He brought with him an under bed filled with charlock, a pernicious weed, which he emptied on to his land. Some of the seeds of the weed were in the bed, and took root, and have since spread over considerable territory in town, giving the farmers much trouble when it mingled with their crops. How many children Mr. Carlisle had is not known. One, however, David, remained on the place after his father's death and was known as Captain David. He had a family of nine children, by his wife Sarah, who outlived him *forty-one years*, and died in Dec. 1838, aged 99. He died in 1797, aged 57. It is impossible to give the names and times of birth of his children in regular order, as no record has been found. Ch. 1st, John, b. in 1768; m. Rebecca, dau. of Eliphas Graves, in 1794. He d. Feb. 10 1833; she died Aug. 21, 1848, aged 80. Ch. (1) Rebecca, b. July, 14, 1794; m. Ruel H. Keith of Newport. (2.) Fanny, b. Oct. 24, 1795; m. Calvin Graves of Cooperstown N. Y. (3) George, b. Oct. 27, 1797. George's father was a shoemaker, by trade, and carried on the business for many years in the building now standing at the south end of the village and occupied as a dwelling by Mrs. Levi Hooper. He lived in the house now owned by the daughters of the late Jared Miller. When George was a small lad, in digging in his father's garden, one day, he chanced to turn up a Spanish real, the value of twelve and one half cents. That real was the nest egg of his future wealth. He laid it by and added to it till the sum amounted to one dollar, when he bought a sheep, which he leased to a farmer for a certain time for one half the increase. When the increase of his sheep was sufficient he purchased a cow, which was leased in a similar way. He said in a letter to his son ; "I never felt so rich before nor after as I did the day I found that Spanish real. At the age of sixteen he entered the store of Stone & Bellows, then in trade in town, as clerk, and at the age of twenty he was entrusted with a large inventory of goods to dispose of in the western wilds. Westport, Ky. was his first stopping place ; and not finding a ready market for his goods there, in about six months he removed to Cincinnati, O., then a comparatively small place, where he found a quick, and remunerative sale. The next year, by order of the firm, he went to St. Louis to purchase buffalo robes, many of which were sent here. On returning to Cincinnati, he went into the store of Daniel Brooks & Co., Stone & Bellows being the Co. In 1822, he assumed the business of the house alone, and subsequently went into the

firm of Carlisle, Mason & Co. During the rest of his business
career he was a partner in four different firms and for many
years President of the La Fayette bank. With a keen eye he
foresaw the prospective growth of the "Queen City" and invest-
ed his surplus gains accordingly. He built extensively in order to enhance the value of his adjacent lands, which proved
a very wise undertaking, for much of his wealth was the result of the appreciation of real estate.

He made money every year during his business life in Cincinnati, except one, and that was in 1828, the year he was married, when he was absent from the firm six months, and
entrusted his business to his partners, which fact brings to
mind Poor Richard's maxim, "If you do n't keep your shop,
your shop wont keep you." From letters of advice written by
him to his sons the idea is gathered that his *beau ideal* of a *man*
was to be a successful merchant. It is also inferred by the same
that he was a far-seeing, honorable, and punctual man. He
generously remembered his connections in his native town in
his will, besides bestowing many generous gifts on them while
living. He died in 1863, leaving a large property, estimated
to amount to more than one million dollars, all of which he
accumulated by energy, honesty, and a close application to
business, in a little more than forty years.

2d, David. This David is supposed to be the printer who
has heretofore been noticed as David Carlisle, jr. His wife's
name was Abigail. Ch. (1) Mary, b. Dec. 26, 1795. (2) Julius
Quartus, b. July 4, 1798. 3d, Daniel, b. 1773; m. Phebe Fenton Oct. 7, 1793, and d. March 14, 1813, of spotted fever. She
afterwerd married a man by the name of Farnsworth, and d.
Jan. 28, 1828, aged 53. Ch. (1) Adeline, b. Feb. 13, 1800, m.
John Black Sparhawk. She was a woman who was much
esteemed by her neighbors and acquaintances; she died Sept.
4, 1869. (2) David, b. Jan. 6, 1803. (3) Frederick, b. Oct. 5,
1806; m. Emeline Livingston and moved to Ashtabula, Ohio,
where he now resides. Mr. Carlisle has by his industry accumulated a competency, and is esteemed a generous, peaceable,
and highly respectable citizen of the town. (4) Daniel Webber,

b. June 17, 1812. 4th, Levi. 5th, Thomas. 6th, Sarah, m. David Boynton, in 1786. 7th, Lattice, m. Samuel Joslyn; she died; he then married her sister Mary, who was the widow of John C. Dana. 8th, Nancy, m. Amherst Stewart in 1795. 9th, Betsey, m. Abner Powers 1800.

CARPENTER, ZACHARIAH, was from Rhode Island, and was born in 1766. He m. Lydia, daughter of Samuel and Amy Wightman, and settled in this town early in the present century. He was for many years a tavern-keeper near the railroad station at the mouth of Cold river. He had a family of eight children, as follow: I. Albert, b. June 10, 1814; d. Oct., 1879; m. first, Mary Wilder of Keene, N. H., and had seven children, four of whom are living; viz., 1st, Edward, lives in South Royalston, Mass. 2d, Emily, lives in Rutland, Vt. 3d, Henry, lives in Rutland, Vt. 4th, Thomas, lives in the city of New York. m. second, a widow Gage of Westminster, Vt. II. Amanda, m. Capt. Elijah Holbrook, of Surry, N. H. III. Caroline, m. Warren Daniels of Keene, and lived for a while in this town; but subsequently removed to Rutland, Vt. IV. Amy, m. a Gaskell of Clarendon, Vt. V. Frances, m. a Pettis, and settled at Bellows Falls, Vt. VI. Elmira, m. Thomas Heaton of Drewsville, Oct. 30, 1821, and d. June 6, 1823, aged 24. VII. Thomas K., d. young. VIII. Samuel, of whom nothing is known. Zachariah Carpenter died Feb. 22, 1837; his wife died July 28, 1847, aged 73.

CARPENTER, DAVIS. There were two families by the name of Carpenter living in town about the year 1800. The one of which the following account is given lived on the elevation of land in the south-east part of the town known as "Carpenter's hill." He purchased the place once owned by Josiah Goldsmith. The mainly-traveled road through Walpole to Boston passed by his door. He kept a public house there for a score or more of years, and brought up a numerous family, many of whom were persons of respectability. The date of birth of three of his children is not known, two of whom are supposed to be the oldest members of the family. Abigail, his mother, died in town, Nov. 30, 1816, aged 94. Ch. I. Amasa, d. March

13, 1838; m. Rebecca Mason, March 21, 1798. Ch. 1st, Calvin,
b. May 14, 1798; m. Laura, dau. of Levi Fay. 2d, Sally, b.
June 10, 1800; m. Joseph L. Fay. 3d, Althea, b. April 7, 1802;
never married. 4th, Elsie, m. W. H. Scovil. II. Sylvester, m.
Lydia Bowker, second wife, Aug. 23, 1826. Ch. 1st, Walter, b.
June 12, 1808; studied medicine and went west. III. Walter,
m. Abigail Bowker, Oct. 18, 1812. IV. Ruth, m. William
Kingsbury March 3, 1820. V. Sally, b. June 26, 1796, and d.
the next year. VI. Lucy, b. Oct. 1, 1797; m. Charles Bugbee,
in 1822. VII. Davis, jr., b. Dec. 25, 1799; became a physician
and went north. VIII. Cyril, b. Oct. 29, 1801; went north.
Miriam, Davis Carpenter's wife, died June 11, 1803, aged 43.
He m., the same year, the widow Lucy Bowker of Westmoreland, who had the following children: Cushing, Lucy, Sally,
and, it is said, two others. IX. Miriam, b. Oct. 8, 1804; m.
Charles E. Chase of this town, Nov. 17, 1825. X. Nancy Cushing, b. Sept. 6, 1806; m. Dr. Foster Hooper of Fall River,
Mass.; d. July 22, 1834. XI. Sophia, b. Dec. 16, 1808; m.
Luther Proctor; d. Oct. 12, 1836. XII. Louisa, b. Aug. 10,
1810; had bad luck in her marital relations. She went north
among her friends. XIII. Eliza, b. Dec. 29, 1812; m. William
Barron, and lives at Bellows Falls.

CHAFFIN, JOEL, was a resident of this town as early as 1795.
He was born in Holden, Mass. He was a carpenter by trade,
and was the principal workman at that business in town for
more than a quarter of a century. He used to frame his
buildings by what was then called the *scribe* rule, where every
part was fitted and *scribed*, or marked, for a certain place, before
raising. In those days a gouge was used for starting the place
of boring holes, after which the old *pod auger* was used, a tool
without a screw, and was forced into the wood by much physical exertion. Many of the old buildings in town are silent
witnesses of his toil and handiwork. He married Olive Stickney, of Holden, Mass., and lived in a house that once stood on
the east side of the road, opposite the residence of George
Watkins. He died April 2, 1829, aged 65; she died Nov. 21,
1833, aged 78. Ch. I. Royal, b. Aug. 2, 1793; m. Betsey Rice,

and is now living in Holden, Mass. II. Phebe Smith, b. June 3, 1796; m. Albert Locke, and went to Saratoga after living in town a few years. III. Polly, b. Oct. 30, 1797; m. Thomas Wilder, and had several children. She died in Worcester, Mass., where the Wilders moved about 1843. IV. Willard Stickney, was a physician, b. Mar. 24, 1799; m. Sophia Doolittle and practised his profession in Winchester, N. H. He died in this town April 12, 1831, of lumbar abscess. V. Charles Chandler, b. Jan. 12, 1807; m. first, Charlotte Bailey; second, Harriet, a triplet daughter of Caleb Farnham, of this town. He was a resident of this town for several years, and lived in the Hooper neighborhood and carried on the shoemaking business. He left town about 1842 or '3 and went to London, Ohio, and is still living.

CHASE, JONATHAN H., was born in Sutton, Mass., and was left, at a tender age, by his father, who went into the Revolutionary service, which was the last he knew of him. He married Martha, dau. of Aaron Kimball of Grafton, Mass., and came to Walpole in 1804, and purchased what is now known as "Lane's Mills," where he remained a few years, when he removed to the south part of the town, and established the business of tanning, which has been described in the narrative portion of this work. Mr. Chase was a very industrious citizen, utilizing every means to turn an honest penny. One peculiar trait of his character was never to sacrifice utility to ornament. He had a strong inclination for invention, and was easy only when getting up some novel improvement. He was a strong Universalist in sentiment, and nothing delighted him more than an argument with an opponent on the subject of religion. He was an obliging neighbor and a peace-loving, good citizen. He survived his wife seven years, and died Feb. 24, 1865, aged 87 years. Ch. 1. Charles E., b. in Grafton, Mass., Nov. 6, 1802, and came to Walpole with his parents. He m. Miriam, dau. of Davis Carpenter, of this town, Nov. 17, 1825. Mr. Chase has lived in four different states: first in Massachusetts, 28 years in New Hampshire, 47 in Westminster, Vt., and 54 in the state of affinity with one wife,—a circumstance which seldom occurs. He and his wife early became connected with the Methodist church, and have ever lived a spotless life. He has basked in the sunshine of prosperity and drunk from the bitter cup of adversity; but his cheerfulness and integrity never have been shaken. Ch. 1st, Martha K., b. in 1826; d. in 1863, unm. 2d, Frances L., b. in 1829; m. Addison P. Brown, and lives in Brooklyn, N.Y. 3d, Charles E., jr., b. in 1832; m. Rhoda Wetherell, of Westminster, Vt., and lives in Charlestown, Mass. 4th, Nancy C., b. in 1833; m. Charles N. Harris, and resides in Schuylerville, N. Y. 5th, Mary E., b. Dec. 22, 1844; m. first, Charles Harrington; second, J. F. Pease, and resides in Syracuse, N. Y. II. Aaron Kimball, b. July 8, 1806; m. first, Adeline, dau. of Danforth Clark of this town, Dec. 3, 1828; she d. 1840; m. second, Angeline Ranney, of Westminster, Vt., April 26, 1841; his third wife's maiden name, with whom he is now living, was Louisa Holton; m. Nov. 9, 1859. By his first wife he had two children: 1st, Mary Adeline, b. Aug. 4, 1833; m. Thomas C. Ball; issue, one ch., Ida. 2d, Clark, b. Dec. 12, 1837; m. Ellen Fisher, of Westminster, Vt., and resides at Bellows Falls. III. Mary Kimball, b. Sept. 12, 1812; m. Henry W. Hooper, of this town, and lives in Charlestown, N. H. (See Hooper.) IV. Sarah S., b. April 30, 1818; m. Seth B. Cragin, and had three ch., only one of whom is living, Louisa, who m. Nathaniel Nutting, of Westminster, Vt. Mrs. Cragin d. Dec. 9, 1849, and her oldest dau. Frances, d. in 1861, aged 21 years.

CLARK, DANFORTH, came to this town, about 1800, or perhaps a few years before, (the exact date cannot be ascertained) from Sturbridge, Mass. The maiden name of his wife was Mercy Alton. Mr. Clark first located on Boggy meadow, but did not remain there many years; for, having purchased of one Wier the farm on which Henry Houghton now resides, he removed there and spent the most of a long life. In 1838–9 he sold his farm and purchased a home in Chesterfield, but remained there only a few years, when he removed to Bethel, Vt., where he lived till he died, at an advanced age. He was a shoemaker by trade, and when not engaged on his farm he utilized his time in making boots and shoes for his neighbors. He did but very little at shoemaking when pegged work became the fashion. His children were I. David who m. Mrs. Juliet, widow of Abel Dickinson, whose maiden name was Willard, from Winchester, N. H., by whom he had four children, viz., Ellen, Mary, Dickinson and David Parker; the last named is the only one now living and at this time, (1879) resides in Winchester, N. H. Mr. Clark lived for many years on the place now owned by Mrs. Lyman Houghton, after which he removed to Westminister, Vt., and from thence to Bethel, Vt., where he died. II. Benjamin, went to Mohawk, N. Y., early in life; married there and had a family of several children. III. Griffin, m. Julia Abbott, and settled in Tunbridge, Vt., where he lived during life, and died there. By his wife he had several children. IV. Betsey m. Elisha C. Coolidge and settled in Woodstock, Vt. V. Maria never married; she died July 25, 1836, aged 40. VI. Mary Ann, m. Danforth Davis, settled in Bethel, Vt. VII. Adeline, m. Aaron K. Chase, (See Chase). VIII. Loren W., m. Tirzah, dau. of Capt. Joseph Fay, by whom he had three ch., two sons and one daughter, who all lived to maturity. He m. 2d, Mrs. Milly, widow of Caleb Livingston; she died and he married a third time. IX. Thomas Jefferson, died unm. Jan. 19, 1835, aged 29. X. Curtis Cullen, studied the medical profession, attended medical lectures at Woodstock, Vt., and, after obtaining his diploma, commenced practice in Chesterfield, N. H. in company with Dr. Harvey Carpenter, about 1838-9. His education was superior to that of the other members of his father's family, which made him more communicative and social: although, like the rest of the family, he was somewhat odd in general demeanor. He was fond of fun and a good story teller, always perceiving the ludicrous in life readily, and making the most of it in his narrations. He d. Dec. 21, 1840, aged 30 years.

COCHRAN, GEORGE, was the son of Robert Cochran of Londonderry, N. H. and was born Oct., 1764, at the same place. He m. Mary Anderson, of Newcastle, Me., in 1801. He came to this town in 1790, and purchased one hundred acres of wild

land of David Humphrey of Portsmouth, N. H., some ten
years before he married. The family were Scotch-Irish like
most of the settlers on Derry Hill. This family, it is said,
brought the old Irish white potatoes with them, which have
been planted on that soil till a recent date. Ch. I. Robert, b.
Mar. 26, 1802, and d. unm. at the age of 27. II. Jane, b. 1805,
Feb. 18, m. Mason Fay and has five children. III. Samuel, b.
Dec. 10, 1812, m. Relief, daughter of Levi, and Charlotte (Watkins) Leonard, June 21, 1849. Ch. 1st, Mary b. May 1, 1850,
m. James Cochran of Pembroke, N. H., and resides there;
2d, George, d. in infancy; 3d, Ada Isabella, b. Feb. 4, 1854;
4th, Lucy Jane, b. Feb. 23, 1856; 5th, James Buchanan, b.
July 17, 1858; 6th, Sarah Frances, b. July 30, 1860; 7th,
Robert, b. Nov. 13, 1862.

COCHRAN, JONATHAN. A man bearing the name of Jonathan
Cochran, a distant relative of the foregoing, was the first settler on the farm now owned by Edward A. Watkins. After a
few years he sold out to one Amos Cross, and left town, and
nothing more is known of him.

CREHORE, EBENEZER, came to Walpole as early as 1780. A
deed in the possession of his grandson, John D., of Cleveland,
Ohio, discloses the fact that he purchased of one of the Bellows
family a plot of fifty acres of land embracing the site where
Mrs. William Buffum now resides, and the tradition in the
Crehore family is that he built the house. He was a mechanic
by occupation and did all the turning, by a foot lathe, for the
pews of the old meeting-house, which was built in 1789. The
old lathe is in the possession of Henry S. Allen, of this town,
and does good service yet. It is inferred from old deeds in the
possession of his grandson above mentioned that he was a
large landholder on Carpenter's hill at one time, where he lived
and died. He d. Sept. 23, 1819, aged 54; his wife, Hannah, d.
Oct. 5, 1805, aged 71. Ch. I. Hannah, b. Aug. 1, 1794; m.
Samuel Johnson, Aug. 1, 1821. II. Charles, b. Apr. 6, 1798,
m. Lucy Bowker, Apr. 9, 1826. He d. Oct. 21, 1831; she m.
Luther Proctor subsequently and had children. Ch. of Charles,
1st, John Davenport, b. Nov. 22, 1826; graduated at Dart-

mouth, and became a civil engineer; m. and located in Cleveland, Ohio, where he now resides. He is at this time writing a work on the subject of his profession, and is a man of more than common ability. 2d, George, b. Dec. 18, 1827, is an enginer in the western States. 3d, Eleanor, b. Feb. 26, 1830— graduated at one of the New England seminaries and was considered a lady of fine attainments. It is not known whether she married or not; 4th, Charles Ebenezer, b. Dec. 25, 1831, never married. III. George, b. Apr. 12, 1802, m. and moved to Surry and became a substantial farmer there. How many children he had is not known Only the births of three have been found. Ch. of George and Mary Crehore: 1st, Robert b. Mar. 26, 1802; 2d, Jane, b. Feb. 18, 1805; 3d, Samuel, b. Dec. 10, 1812.

DENISON, DANIEL. The history of the Denison family in Walpole is somewhat imperfect. It appears from a letter in possession of the author, written by one W. Cleft, of Mystic Bridge, Ct., that Daniel Denison, who married Mehitable Foster of Saybrook, Ct., removed from that place to this town about 1762, and a son of his, by the name of Jo n, came with him. The father died here, aged 92. The Denison homestead was located on the opposite side of the road from the old Titus homestead, fifty rods north of the residence of Caleb Foster.

Daniel Denison had a daughter named Diadamie who was baptized by Thomas Fessenden, June 27, 1773. There were three other men by the name of Denison. Whether they were the sons of Daniel or his grandsons, it is not easy to determine—probably the former. One, named Daniel jr., m. Chloe Watkins, in 1781, and another, Jedediah, m. Lydia Griswold, Feb. 26, 1782, and the third, Eber. m. Hannah Hall in 1788. There was another, *supposed* to be a daughter of Daniel, who m. Edward Watkins. The children of John were 1st, Lucy, b. Sept. 25, 1777; m. Benjamin Marsh, and had five sons and five daughters; 2d, John, b. June 25, 1780—died in infancy; 3d, Paul, b. Feb. 9, 1782; 4th, John, b. June 27, 1784; moved to Ohio in 1824, and had one son and six daughters; 5th, Elijah, m. Sally Fay, Jan. 29, 1812, and went to Rochester, N.Y., and

died there in 1850.   He had three sons and one daughter; 6th,
Ziba, baptized Apr. 27, 1787, and m. Parnell Graves and moved
to Herkimer Co., N. Y.   He had four children.   One, Luther
Denison, m. Nancy Rice, Sept. 22, 1811; but to what family
he belonged has not been ascertained.

DENNIE, JOSEPH, familiarly called Joe Dennie, when he resided in Walpole, was not a native of this town, but was born
in Boston, Mass., Aug. 30, 1768.   He was educated at Harvard
college graduated in 1790, and studied law as a profession.
He practised his profession for a short time; but the practice
was very distasteful to him, and having been roughly repri-
manded by the judge, when trying a case, for the unprofes-
sional course he pursued, he left his profession with disgust
and turned his attention to literary pursuits.   At one time he
thought of preparing for the Episcopal ministry but relinquished it for some cause unknown.   In 1795, having acquired some
reputation by literary contributions to various newspapers his
services were secured on a weekly journal published in Boston,
called the "Tablet," but he remained there but a short time.
In the summer of 1795, Dennie came to Walpole, he being
then twenty seven years of age, and became the editor of the
Farmer's Museum, then in the third year of its existence.   The
Museum soon attained a wide popularity under his management.   His style of writing was of that degree of elegance
that he was often mentioned as the "American Addison."
His most notable contributions to the Museum were a series
of essays entitled the Lay Preacher, although he wrote many
others equally good.   Those essays were widely copied by the
press of the whole country and gave their author a general reputation as a graceful and humorous essayist.   The publishers
of the Museum (Thomas & Carlisle) failed in 1798, and in 1799
Dennie was a candidate for Representative to Congress, but failed of being elected, he being at the time a Federalist.   Poor
Dennie was now adrift upon the world seeking office and employment in various places, but in 1801 in conjunction with a
partner, by the name of Dickens, commenced the publication
of a literary monthly called the "Portfolio," in Philadel-

phia, Pa. He continued its editor till the time of his death, which occurred June 7, 1812. Tradition says he was very fond of dress and had a weakness for large shoe-buckles and white stockings. He is represented to have been a slender, undersized man, with restless, sparkling eyes, pale face, and always ready for fun and frolic. When he was engaged in writing he dashed off line after line apparently not considering what he was about. Like many persons of genius, when preparing matter for the press he had always to be driven for copy.

Royal Tyler, of Brattleboro, who afterwards was Chief Justice of Vermont, was one of Dennie's boon companions and used to come to Walpole often to spend a day with him. Dennie, it is said, wrote one of his best Lay Sermons in a room in the old Crafts tavern, (now Charles G. Maynard's) where a company were playing whist. It was delivered to the printer's "Devil," in fragments and he had to go for it no less than a dozen times. When he called the last time Dennie was engaged in a rubber of whist. "Here," said Dennie to his friend Tyler who was present, "Play my hand while I give the Devil his due." He is said to have indulged too much in wine and late suppers while in Walpole, and after he went to Philadelphia he became associated with the "Tuesday Club," which was composed of many of the most talented writers and wits in the country. Here, no doubt, he indulged in his convivial habits to excess, being surrounded by a larger number of men of the same tastes of himself than when in Walpole. The "Portfolio", during the time that Dennie was its editor, (about eleven years) was considered the best literary publication in the United States. Although always needy in purse, Dennie ever found some friend to supply his immediate wants at all social gatherings, of which he was generally the life and the soul. He died at the age of forty two. No doubt the festive bowl, working on a frail constitution, was the cause of his early death. In his day no one in the country excelled him as an essayist. He possessed splendid talents and ready wit, and was ever genial in company.

DICKEY, MATTHEW, John Dickey m. Margaret Reed in

county of Antrim, Ireland, and immigrated to Londonderry, N. H. in the year 1733, with six children; Adam, Matthew, John, Ellen, Isabel and Barbara.

Adam Dickey, of the second generation, married Jane Strahan and settled in Londonderry, N. H. and had thirteen children, four of whom settled in Acworth, namely John, James Adam and Benjamin, and were the progenitors of the numerour Dickey families who have lived in that town. Matthew was the twelfth child and was born April 29, 1772; came to Walpole in 1794, and married Betsey Murch, Nov. 8, 1795, and took up wild land of the Atkinson allotment, on Derry Hill, where he spent a long life of industry, economy and thrift. He had a family of eleven children, eight of whom survived to adult age. I. Sophia, b. Jan. 23, 1797, m. Calvin Fay, in 1815, and settled in Prattstown, N. Y. He died leaving two children, Calvin, and Lucy. She afterwards m. Henry Goodenow of Keene, and had three children: viz. Henry, George, residence Chicago, Ill., and Horace, residence, Keene. She died June, 1872. II. Betsey, b. Jan. 20, 1800; m. Jacob B. Burnham and lived in Walpole, during life, died July 18, 1863. Ch. 1st, Nancy, m. David A. Russell. (See Russell.) 2d, Antoinette, m. Edward Wellington and removed to Saginaw, Mich. 3d. Laforest. III. John, b. Aug. 3, 1801, and died very suddenly, while chopping underbrush on the farm now owned by J. M. Comstock, Dec. 22, 1722. IV. George M., b. Feb. 3, 1803, went to Mentor, Ohio, and m. Rachel Corning in 1833. Ch. 1st, Warren. 2d, Viola. 3d, George. 4th, Matthew. V. Cyrus, b. Oct. 14, 1804; d. Aug. 8, 1841, unm. VI. Clement S., b. Mar. 12, 1806; m. Betsey P., dau. of Thomas and Eunice (Alexander) Russell, Nov. 14, 1839. Ch. 1st, Josie H., b. July, 26, 1842, d. Feb. 3, 1877. 2d. Albert C., b. Dec. 11, 1843, lives with his father in town, unm. VII. James, b. Oct. 31, 1807, removed to Ohio in 1831; m. Harriet Corning in 1834, d. at Walpole, Sept. 1855. Ch. Helen, Wallace C., residence, Cleveland, O., and Edward J., residence, Mentor, O. VIII. Lewis, b. Nov. 1, 1820, and lives on the old homestead unm. Matthew's wife d. Dec. 15, 1860, aged 88.

DICKINSON, PLINY. Of Pliny Dickinson some account has
already been given under the head of Church history, in this
work, and it is regretted that a *full* detail of his family cannot
be given, for want of data, which have been sought for but
not obtained. Mr. Dickinson was born in Granby, Mass.,
in 1777, and was settled over the old church and society in
Walpole, in 1805, as colleague, at first, of Thomas Fessenden.
He commenced boarding with Col. Caleb Bellows, when his
future wife, Mary Brown, daughter of Col. Caleb and Mary
(Hartwell) Bellows, was but five years old, she being born
Jan. 7, 1800. He was married about 1819; but where, and
by whom is not known by the author. His ch. were I. George,
m. Lucy Evans now dead; his residence is Minneapolis, Min.
II. William, is a physician, residence, St. Louis, Mo. III. Eli
Horton, d. June 26, 1844, aged 20 years, a young man of much
promise. IV. Edward C., bap. Dec. 1827. V. Samuel P. bap.
1829. VI. Mary, d. aged 4 yrs. VII. Joseph. VIII Phebe
C., d. June 6, 1839, aged 4 yrs. Mr. Dickinson d. Aug.
27, 1834. His widow subsequently m, James Crawford, of
Putney, Vt., Apr. 27, 1838, and had 2 ch., when he died and
she married the third time a Mr. Smith, and is now living, a
widow, in Maquoketa, Iowa. Mr. Dickinson held his pastorate
twenty-six years. He was a man of more than ordinary ability, proud in his demeanor, punctilious in his habits, persistent in his views, and had a morbid foreboding of future wants,
which may be inferred from his letter of acceptance and the
accumulation of a handsome property, on a salary of $500 per
annum. He, it is said, was very able in prayer and wrote
fine, scholarly sermons, which strongly partook of the old
school model, being doctrinal rather than practical. His pastorate glided smoothly along, not many events occuring out of
the usual routine to disturb him. But on one Sunday a little
event turned up which greatly annoyed him, and happened on
communion day, when two coarse Amazonian girls attended
his church, a place where they had gone for the first time in
their lives. When the ordinance of the supper was about to
be administered, in their ignorance, they took seats with the

communicants, and partook of the sacrament with them. Their uncouth demeanor aroused the curiosity of the congregation, and, on inquiry they were found to be the daughters of one Thomas Darby, a Welch weaver, who lived just over Walpole line, in the woods, in Westmoreland. Mr. Dickinson feeling that the Lord's table had been defiled did not rest easy till he went to their home, early in the following week to rebuke them for sacriligious conduct, and, on arriving there, found no one at home but the old Welchman, their father, in his log cabin, busy plying his shuttle. Mr. Dickinson, in his bland manner, related to uncle Tom, the way his daughters had conducted themselves, intensifying the enormity of such sacrilegious conduct. The old man listened with due reverence and attention till the parson got through, when he replied; "Weel, weel, I'm soory. I'm burned soory, for I've allus told my gals to keep out of bad company." It is said the parson did not prolong his visit.

DREW. The subject of this sketch Thomas Collins Drew, was, in some respects, one of the most remarkable men who ever lived in town. With a keen eye to perceive, an active brain to analyze, energy to pursue and firmness of will to hold, he never had an equal during his active life. Of his parentage and childhood nothing is known, except that he was born, in 1762, in Chester, a small town near Londonderry, in this State, from whence a small colony early came to this town, in 1793-5. A man living in Londonderry, by the name of McNeal, wanting a boy to bring up, sought one in the almshouse at Portsmouth, and, from the large number found there, he selected Tom, he being the most sprightly looking lad, according to his notions. The customary documents were drawn up, binding the services of young Drew to McNeal to the time of his majority. Young Drew immediately set out with his future guardian for Londonderry, and, in due time arrived, and remained for a while, not feeling perfectly contented to remain in a dull, lonely town, while away was excitement incident to the Revolutionary war, which was then pending and was better suited to his ardent nature. Accordingly, at the first opportunity he left his quiet home, *sans ceremonie*, and did not return till the Revolutionary struggle was over. He had about eighteen months longer, then, to serve McNeal, but he had no use for him. Wm. T. Ramsay, being in Londonderry at that time, and in want of help on his purchase in Walpole, bought the remainder of young Drew's time for a pair of old stags, when soon after Drew made his advent in Walpole, and served out his time on Derry Hill with Ramsey. During his stay he was full of all kinds of harmless mischief. Occasionally his master would send him to a grist mill that stood near where Geo. W. Graves now lives, and after his leaving, the miller would always find some parts of his mill out of gear, and would exclaim, "I would as soon see the d——l coming to my mill as Tom Drew!" When he became free he employed his time in doing any odd jobs that might by chance turn up, where he could gain an honest penny.

About this time he attended a dancing school at the Craft's tavern (now Chas. G. Maynard's) where he met his future wife, who was a sister of one Joshua Quinton, (Quintaine) a clothier, doing business in a mill that once stood on what is called, at this time, Blanchard's brook. Mr. Quinton was a proud man and had a laudable pride for his sister, who was his housekeeper, whom he used to bring to the dancing school Drew and his future wife were mutually smitten, and Mr. Quinton too soon learned that his sister was clandestinely married to Thomas C. Drew—Mr. Quinton thereby losing his housekeeper. Nor was this all, he felt disgusted and grieved at the course his sister had taken in marrying a town pauper, so much so that he sold out his business and left town never to return to live. Drew and his wife spent their honey-moon in a little house that once stood just in front of the residence of Mrs. Ephraim Holland and was known as the Parson Mead house. Drew is next heard from in Rockingham, Vt., speculating in "Grant Lands," then in Canada, buying and selling wild lands there, and speculating in anything that might chance to turn up. When he was married, he could neither read nor write; both of which were taught him by his wife. In 1800, he espoused the political doctrines of Thomas Jefferson, who was that year elected president of the United States, and was one of five who established and maintained the "Political Observatory" here, which has heretofore been mentioned.

At one time he was Col. of the 2?th Reg. of N. H. militia. In 1802, he was elected a member of the General Court, and again in 1804, '5 '7, '8, and '9, he was elected Councilor from this district two years and was nominated for the State senate, but was defeated. In middle life he held many offices of honor and trust, being at one time the most popular man in town. Mr. Drew had a tall, commanding figure, square face, high forehead and a large, straight cut mouth. He was a great talker and at town meeting he always made it a point to ' air his eloquence.' It was a rare treat to hear Col. Drew and Henry Foster discuss the momentous questions that arose town meeting days. Drew generally threw down the gauntlet which was immediately picked up by Foster, and no greater incentive was needed to call the voters out than the set-to's of Drew and Foster. Foster was a hard speaker, but he was logical and persistent beyond measure, while Drew was eloquent and persuasive. That a boy who could neither read nor write at the age of twenty-one could made his advent in the then cultivated town of Walpole, and by his own energy and perseverance secure the suffrages of the people for so many offices over those " to the manor born," and perpetuate his name in the name of the village where he resided, (Drewsville) argues that Thomas Collins Drew was more than an ordinary man. Ch. I. Charles Collins, b. July 13, 1807, d. unm. II. Francis Gardner, b. Feb. 22, 1809; m. —— Hartwell of Langdon; d. without issue, Feb. 27, 1872. III. Sarah Eliza, b. 1796; d. Sept. 14, 1870; m. first Dr. Joseph Bond, and had two sons, 1st, Josiah, born at Drewsville, N. H., graduated at Trinity College, Hartford, Conn., read law and commenced practice at Kenosha, Wis., where he now resides; 2d, Thomas D., b. at Drewsville, married and resides at the same place with his brother. Dr. Bond died at Drewsville, July 7th, 1832, aged 43. His widow married Hope Lathrop (See Lathrop.) Mrs. Lathrop, when a child, was noticed as one possessing more than ordinary grace, intelligence and sprightliness of character. In mature years she manifested many of the qualities peculiar to her father,— a strong will and resolute mind. She was a devoted Episcopalian in sentiment, and for many years a " mother in Israel " to St. Peter's Church at Drewsville.

DRURY.

The name of Manoah Drury is found in the town records as early as 1776; and, almost yearly, for many years afterwards, his name occurs as one of the subordinate town officers. He first settled on Derry Hill on a place lying west of the residence of Stansbury Dinsmore. By the old inhabitants he is represented to have been fashioned purposely for pioneer life, being rough and daring in early life. In his mature years he was converted, and joined Mr. Fessenden's church, and when the old meeting house was built he signified his readiness to support the gospel by purchasing five pews. Nothing is known of his wife excepting that her name was Martha. In the latter part of his life he lived in a house that once stood a few rods west of the residence of Oliver Hall. The personal appearance of his children, it is said, was anything but prepossessing, nature having made a striking contrast between symmetry and angularity of person. They were all very tall and large, and of dark complexion, their height varying from six feet to six feet seven inches, the females in the family not being an exception. Although forbidding in appearance they were harmless in disposition and fond of fun and jokes, never sparing their own want of personal charms, as a subject for jokes. Ch. I. Sampson, b. Nov. 12, 1774; d. young. II. Martha, b. Sept. 14, 1776; m. Allen Watkins, Sept. 1797. III. Sampson, b. Nov. 23, 1778; m. Ruth Sherman, Jan. 14, 1812. Ch. 1st, Lucien. b. May 19, 1812; 2d, Thomas, b. Aug. 21, 1814; 3d, Nancy, b. Feb. 17, 1817; 4th, Amanda, b. Dec. 5, 1819; 5th, Sarah, b. June 21, 1820; 6th, David, b. May 17, 1822; 7th, Andrew Jackson, b. Aug. 21, 1824; 8th, Persis Annie, b. March 5, 1828.

Many anecdotes have been related of Sampson Drury. Among the great number are the following. At one time a family of strangers moved into the neighborhood where he resided and at the same time an Indian doctor was known to be in town. The stranger woman having a sick child, and Sampson passing the house, she mistook him for the Indian doctor and called him in to treat her child. Sampson gravely responded to her call, and, seeing that the child was most likely troubled with worms, recommended some common medicine, by which it obtained immediate relief. The reputation of the Indian, for skill in treating infants immediately spread throughout the neighborhood, and it was many weeks before she found out that her fancied Indian doctor was no other than one of her neighbors. At another time he and his sister Persis, who was plain looking, like himself, were riding in a wagon through the village, and perceiving several people standing about, he nagged up his horse to his best speed requesting her at the same time to be sure and cover her face so that no one could see it. IV. Elijah, b. Nov. 14, 1773. His children by his wife Grace, were 1st, Luke, b. Feb. 18, 1804; 2d, Nathan Nichols, b. Aug. 30, 1805; 3d, Thomas Madison, b. May 21, 1808; 4th, Addison, bap. 1808. Perhaps there were more, but the above names are all that are found in the record of births. Elijah worshipped his bottle and at times its contents overcame his sobriety, when the wags in the village would embrace the opportunity of playing off some joke upon him. One day he came into the village mounted on his faithful Rosinante and stopped at the public house kept by Maj. Grant, where John Jennison now resides. It was very evident about sundown that he had worshipped too long at the shrine of Bacchus, and he was urged by the wags to speedily make for home, they stating at the same time that they would help him to mount his horse. He finally consented to start and found his horse at the door ready to mount. Some of the wags during their parley with him had procured a rope and made one end of it fast to the hitching post, while the other end was tied to the crupper of the saddle. When he was safely astride his horse one of the party slyly unbuckled the girth and at the same time gave the old horse a sudden start by applying a switch. Matters soon came to a crisis; the tug between Elijah's hands and the old horse's mouth was sharp and spirited; but Rosinante was the winner. Elijah, dropping the reins and grabbing the old horse by the tail, broke his fall, which otherwise might have proved serious. The rope magically went out of sight, and the cause of the sudden mishap long remained to Elijah a profound mystery. At one time when he chanced to be on Boston Common where an itinerant speaker was holding forth on some subject in which he was interested, he took a seat immediately in front of the speaker. When the speaker had closed his remarks he wanted some one to "pass round the hat" for his benefit. Elijah, appearing to him to be the right sort of a man for the purpose, was invited, and he accepted without reluctance. He collected about fourteen dollars and was soon seen making off with his collection, when he was hailed and requested to return it. His reply to the summons was, "Let every dog do his own begging" and went on unmolested. He invited his friends to a drinking bout in the evening and spent the fourteen dollars with his comrades. He is said to have been a voracious eater, and the following story, in substance, is related of him. At one time he went to Keene to market some farm produce, and among other things he had a quarter of lamb, which he sold to Davis Carpenter, who then kept the old Goldsmith tavern on Carpenter's hill, for two shillings. On his return, late in the day, having gone without his dinner, he called for a meal at Carpenter's. The quarter of lamb had just been roasted and was, with other things, placed on the table before him. When he had completed his dinner it was found that not only the quarter of lamb had wholly disappeared; but other toothsome etceteras in proportion, for all of which he had paid *twenty-five cents.* V. David, b. Nov. 23, 1780. VI. Molly, b. Dec. 29, 1782. VII. Persis, b. Mar. 1. 1789, never married. VIII. Austin, birth not known. He was living in Boston not many years since, engaged as a truckman. He partook of the size and physical strength of his brothers and sisters.

DUNSHEE, HUGH, was born in Londonderry, this state, in 1753. He was a descendant of the Scotch Presbyterians that settled in the north of Ireland nearly two hundred years ago. In his younger days he went into the wilds of Maine and spent several seasons there in hunting and trapping. About 1784 he came to Walpole with Dr. Abraham Holland, and worked for him as a hired man about three years, when, in 1787, he married Cynthia, daughter of James Allen of this town, and located on land lying north of Henry Burt's, a portion of which is still held by his descendants. He died Dec. 1, 1829, from cancer in the face, after having suffered many years. His wife died Nov 12, 1816, aged 45 years. Ch. I. Betsey, b. 1789; m. Alpheus Paul, and had two sons, 1st, Nelson, d. in Maria, N. Y. 2d, Albert, m. and went to Utica, N. Y., and was killed in the war of the Rebellion. II. John, b. 1790; m. first, Annette, dau. of Montgomery Wires, of this town, by whom he had one son, Lewis, b. in 1822; 2d, m. Caroline M., dau. of Preston and Vashti Titus, by whom he had three ch. (See Ap.) Lewis d. April 3, 1864. John Dunshee m. Olive Abbott, of Springfield, Vt., for his second wife, and died Oct. 28, 1848; his wife died about 1850. III. William, b. 1792; d. 1873. He was a miller and mechanic, and in the latter part of his life lived in the Valley. He married Melinda, dau. of Jonathan Fletcher, of this town, and had five children that lived to maturity. 1st, Osborn, m. in Maine, and has a family. 2d, Loren, lives in Massachusetts. 3d, Carlos E., m. Sarah, dau. of Gardner and Fanny (Graves) Dodge, of this town, and lives in the Valley. 4th, Henry, killed in California. 5th, Louisa, m. first, a Lane; m. second, George Hoadley. IV. Laurinda, b. April 2, 1800; m. Carlton Wiers, in 1826, and had two ch., Lewis and Diana. He resided in Stockholm, N. Y., and died there in 1849; his first wife died in 1846. V. Diantha, also m. Carlton Wiers, and died in 1871, aged 72 years. VI. Irene, b. 1796; m. Luther Burt. (See Burt.) VII. Fanny, b. 1803; m. Jonathan Emery and removed to Stockholm, N. Y., and has seven children.

VIII. Allen, b. June 10, 1814; m. Martha, dau. of Samuel
Pierce of Westmoreland, April 4, 1839; she d. Dec. 30, 1877.
Ch. 1st, Herbert A., b. Feb. 3, 1846. 2d, William L., b. Sept.
9, 1854. He follows the sea. 3d, Allen L., d. in infancy.
Allen Dunshee is now (1879) living with his second wife, who
was the widow Fisk, and dau. of John Curtin of Westmoreland; m. June 24, 1878.

EMERSON, MOSES, Dr., came to this town sometime between
1775 and 1780, and settled on the Dea. Moses Fisher place. He
m. Comfort Eastman and had one son, Jonathan, when he
suddenly disappeared from town, and nothing more is known
of him. Jonathan was born in 1781; m. Lydia Crosby, of
Dummerston, Vt., b. 1793. He d. March 26, 1861; she d.
June 5, 1875. Ch. 1st, Caroline F., m. Silas Angier, Nov. 8,
1838;—issue, eight ch., five living. 2d, Mary Jane, b. Feb. 3,
1822; m. William B. Mason, June 2, 1841;—issue, two ch.,
none living. 3d, John Crosby, b. Oct. 12, 1823; m. Oct. 23,
1855, Urana C., dau. of Holland and Susan (Veasey) Mason;—
issue, three ch. (See Ap.) 4th, George Eastman, b. Sept. 11,
1825; d. Sept. 3, 1853. 5th, Sarah Abigail, b. Feb. 21, 1827;
m. William B. Mason;—issue, five ch. (See Ap.) 6th, Harriet
Maria, b. Sept. 25, 1830; m. Charles W. Wyman;—issue, six
ch., four living.

EMORY, JOSHUA. He lived in the Valley, and m. Ruth Nott,
Jan. 21, 1781, and had the following ch.: I. Abigail, b. Jan.
15, 1782; m. John Mather, of Rockingham. II. Polly, b. May
6, 1784; m. Jonathan Royce, jr., of this town. III. Hannah,
b. May 29, 1790; m. Joshua Shepard, Dec. 7, 1815. IV. Phebe,
b. March 23, 1788; m. Bela Frink, of this town, Feb. 10, 1825.
V. Samuel, b. July 14, 1792; m. Catherine Shepard. VI. Moses,
b. June 17, 1794. VII. Cynthia, b. July 22, 1795; m. Samuel
Hall. There was a Hannah, b. April 16, 1786, supposed to
have died early, as there was a subsequent Hannah.

ELDRIDGE, ELISHA, lived in town as a farmer, some fifty or
more years, on the place now known as the Lemuel Starkweather place. He had, by his wife, whose maiden name was
Cynthia Hanks, as many as eight, and perhaps more, children.

I. Sally, b. Jan. 2, 1787; m. Samuel Grant, of Alstead. II. Silas H., b. Feb. 18, 1789. III. Almira, b. March 24, 1794; m. Lemuel Starkweather. (See Starkweather.) IV. Percis, b. Aug. 5, 1796; m. Archibald Starkweather. (See Starkweather.) V. Cynthia, b. Nov. 13, 1799; m. ———. VI. Elisha, jr., b. Jan. 7, 1803. VII. Horatio, b. June 10, 1805; he was a sailor. VIII. Sophronia, b. 1810, and d. Sept. 28, 1816.

ELDRIDGE, JOHN, with his wife Jerusha, lived in town contemporaneously with the foregoing Elisha; but where he lived and to whom he was related is not known: he may have been a brother of Elisha. Ch. I. Jerusha, b. Jan. 8, 1797. II. & III. Harry and Harriet, b. Sept. 26, 1798. IV. Fanny, b. Aug. 6, 1800.

FARNHAM. The name of Farnham first occurs in the church records as early as 1769, when one Benoni Farnham was admitted to Parson Fessenden's church as a member. The descendants of Roger Farnham know nothing of their ancestors beyond their grandfather. There was one Ebenezer Farnham who married Lydia Graves, in 1775. He lived contemporaneously with Roger, and the old church record discloses the fact that they had children alternately every other year for seventeen years, who were presented, one yearly, at the baptismal font of parson Fessenden. In the absence of any knowledge to the contrary, there is a strong belief that Ebenezer and Roger were brothers, and that Benoni was their father. Nothing is known of the Farnhams before their advent into this town. Roger Farnham, the progenitor of the Farnham blood now remaining, was born in 1746, and his wife, Priscilla Hall, was born in 1752. They were married April 23, 1788. To what Hall family his wife belonged is not known, but it is quite certain that she did not belong to Jonathan Hall's family. It is asserted that she belonged to one of the numerous Hall families in Vermont. The only cue that has been obtained is the following: Caleb Farnham, the son of Roger, was full of practical jokes and witticisms, and one of the old citizens says that when Caleb was playing his jokes, his father would say, "There is a good deal of old Roll Hall in Kale;" but she could not have been his (Roll's) daughter, for he was married about the same time as Roger Farnham. Priscilla *probably* was a sister of Roland Hall. Ebenezer Farnham and his family left town, and their whereabouts is unknown. Roger Farnham lived on the place now owned by Henry P. Hall, his grandson. He was for many years deacon of the old church, and lived an exemplary life. He died Oct. 1, 1830; she died May 2, 1837. Ch. I. William, (Billy) b. July 21, 1779; m. Eliza, dau. of Samuel Salter, Feb. 24, 1803. Ch. 1st, Eliza, m. Josiah Williston, of Saxton's River. 2d, Calista, m. Oscar Butterfield of Townsend, Vt. 3d, Lucinda, m. Ira Ranney of Westminster, Vt. 4th, Catherine, m. Bradford Hall, of Westminster, Vt. 5th, William, b. Feb. 7, 1816, m. Martha, dau. of Oren and Nancy Closson, of Westminster, Vt., June 6, 1839; d. April 8, 1869;—issue, one dau., Mary, who married Oscar W. Rogers. 6th, George Salter, m. Caroline VanMater;—issue, four children. 7th, John Allen, m. Fanny W. Closson, a sister of William's wife, and lives in Hornellsville, N. Y. II. Lucinda, b. April 30, 1781, and d. Nov. 22, 1792. III. Caleb, b. July 9, 1783; m. Hannah Capron of Chesterfield, N. H., b. March 29, 1786. He was a carpenter by trade, and is remembered as a man full of fun and good nature. Ch. 1st, Priscilla, b. Feb. 22, 1807; m. Lewis Davis, of Bradford, Me. 2d, Ebenezer Hall, b. May 22, 1809, and went to Maine. 3d, Caleb, b. May 5, 1812; m. a woman in Worcester, Mass., who still survives him. 4th, John Capron, b. May 29, 1814; m. Emeline Wilbur, of Westmoreland, where he now resides. 5th, Emeline Gale, b. Nov. 11, 1816; m. Dexter Knight, of Sullivan, N. H. 6th, 7th, and 8th, triplets: Harriet, Maria, and Louisa, b. Feb. 25, 1820; Harriet m. Charles Chaffin as his second wife; Maria m. Emerson K. Rice, Sept. 6, 1841; and Louisa d. Dec. 8, 1828. IV. Mary Davenport, b. Aug. 26, 1785; m. Moses Sherman, Aug. 15, 1803. V. Lucretia, b. Sept. 29, 1789; m. Recompense Hall, March 31, 1806. (See Hall.) VI. Priscilla, b. Oct. 26, 1787; m. Ambrose Arnold, of Westminster, Vt., and had two sons, Ambrose and Fenelon; he died, and she m. again, a Ranney, of Westminster, by whom she had other children. VII. Lydia, b. Feb. 14, 1792; d. Mar. 25, 1793. VIII. Charlotte, b. April 28, 1795; m. John Griggs, Sept. 2, 1816.

FARNHAM, EBENEZER.—Following is the record of the family of Ebenezer Farnham, who is *supposed* to have been the brother of Dea. Roger Farnham. There is no record of the birth of his children to be found; but each child received the ordinance of baptism from the font of parson Fessenden, it is *presumed*, about the time the children were born, as was then the custom. Ch. I. Phebe, bap. 1780; m. Daniel Calkins, in 1800. II. Hannah, bap. 1780. I I. Ebenezer, jr., bap. 1781. IV. Jesse, bap. 1783. V. Becca, bap. 1786. VI. Rhoda, bap. 1788. VII. Asher, bap. 1791. VIII. Edward, bap. 1795; and IX. Lydia, bap. 1797. This family suddenly disappeared from the town records; but where they went is unknown.

FAY, JOSEPH, the progenitor of the Fay families in Walpole, came from Mystic, Mass., during, or before the Revolutionary war, and settled on some land opposite the residence of John C. Emerson. When the men of this town were called upon to serve their country in the great struggle for Liberty and Independence, he was among the number who was willing to fight and die for the liberty of coming generations. He was wounded at some of the engagements near Saratoga; of which wounds he afterwards died, leaving a wife and four or more children. At this remote time it is impossible to gather much information in relation to the family, as there are but few of his descendants now living in town. Lucy, his wife, died Dec. 10, 1834, aged 92. Ch. I. Capt. Joseph, b. 1763; m. Sarah Graves of this town, and settled on a farm east of John W. Taggard's, where he lived during life. He died Sep. 13, 1831, aged 68; she d. Apr. 25, 1847, aged 84. Ch. 1st, Calvin, d. young. 2d, Artemas, went to Ithica, N. Y. and was a lawyer there. 3d, Luther, m. a Kibling and went to Strafford, Vt. 4th, Sarah, went to Rochester, N. Y. 5th, Fanny, m. Willard Griswold, of this town. 6th, Rebecca, m. a Gilbert and went to New York. 7th, Robert, m. Annie Cummings of Marlboro, N. H.; d. July 22, 1826, aged 31. 8th, Betsey, m. William

Howard, of Rockingham, Vt., and at one time resided in this town. 9th Joseph Lewis, m. Sally, dau. of Amasa Carpenter, of this town, occupation farming. 10th, Tirzah, m. Loren W. Clark. (See Clark.) 11th, Allen, m. a Kingsbury, of Alstead; she died and he married her niece by the same name. He went to Milford, Mass., and established himself there as a physician, had an extensive practice and rose to eminence in his profession. II. Holland, m. Lucy Stevens and settled on the elevation of land in the eastern part of the town, known as "Fay Hill," and spent his days there. He was deacon of the old church for many years and was familiarly known as Deacon Fay. He lived a life of purity and uprightness of character, and died Sep. 30, 1844, aged 75. Ch. 1st, Calvin, m. Sophia, dau. of Matthew Dickey, of this town, and went to New York. 2d Luther, m. Betsey Morrison, settled in town, d. Dec. 24, 1830, aged 35. 3d, Lucy, m. Thomas Howe, of Rindge. 4th, Charlotte, m. Eliphaz Allen, of Rindge. 5th, Calista, m. Gilman Powers, of Rindge. 6th, Holland Dana, m. Fanny Barnett and settled in town. 7th, Oliver Stevens, m. Deborah Perkins, of Perkinsville, Vt., both died the past winter, (1879). 8th, Caroline, m. Rev. Josiah Knights, and went to Randolph, Vt. 9th, Sophia Maria, m. John Wetherbee, of Rindge. There were three other children in Deacon Fay's family all of whom died in infancy. III. Levi, married Mary Prentiss, and lived on a farm now owned by William Arnold, lying east of the residence of Eli Graves. His children were. 1st, Orlando P. who went off early to Plattsburg, N. Y. 2d, Levi. He studied medicine with Dr. Bond and went West. 3d, Mary, m. Levi Waldo and moved into the western country. 4th, Willard, m. 1st, Phebe Downs, 2d, Laura Williams, and went west. 5th, Harriet, m. Harry Jennison and lived and died in town. 6th, Ruth Prentiss, b. July 7, 1799; m. Henry S. Allen, now living (1879) in town. 7th, Laura, m. Calvin Carpenter—lived in town. 8th, Pauline, m. Simeon Ballou and lived and died in Keene. 9th, Mason, m. Jane Cochran of this town and had three children, George, Mary and Robert, he now lives in Hanover, N. H. 10th Stephen, m. Amanda, dau. of Elisha Angier,

lived, and died in town Jan. 19, 1862, aged 53. 11th, Clarissa,
m. George Hooper and is now living in Putney, Vt. IV. Reuben, b. Apr. 3, 1776; m. Hepsibeth, dau. of Nehemiah Kidder and went to Windham, Vt. Of the three above-named Fay
families, consisting of 34 ch., only one is living in town to-day,
and but few of the descendants.

FESSENDEN, THOMAS, the second settled minister of the town,
was born in Cambridge, Mass., in 1739, graduated at Harvard,
in 1758, settled in Walpole as the minister of the town in 1767
and died May 9, 1813, aged 74. He was minister of the town
forty six years, eight years, however, with a colleague, (Rev.
Pliny Dickinson) leaving his sole and active pastorate thirty
eight years. During that long period he must have written
nearly four thousand sermons. It is said that he was a man
of fine scholarship for those days. He was active with his pen
when not engaged in parochial duties, and wrote several
pamphlets on points of religious doctrines. In 1804, he wrote
and published a work entitled "The Science of Sanctity," of
308 octavo pages. It has been remarked, that the above mentioned work, is one of the most lucid works extant on that
subject. Although Mr. Fessenden was considered sound in
the Orthodox creed in those days; still that work discloses
thoughts not consonant with the views held by that denomination at the present day. From what is gathered from his writings, and what little information is gleaned from the old citizens of the town, it is infered that he was a man of more than
common natural and acquired abilities—liberal in his views and
popular as a preacher. He was fond of amusements, and at
the social gatherings of the young, he frequently honored them
by his presence. He was jolly in his nature, fond of a good
joke, and good at repartee. He liked a good dinner with his
parishoners and never seriously objected to sipping a mug of
flip with them on account of its being derogatory to the *cloth*
to do so. On one occasion he preached a sermon to which
some of his parishoners took umbrage, and urged him to re-
tract the next Sabbath, which he promised to do. In his sermon the next Sunday, he made allusion to the offence he had

given and said : "*If he had said any thing in his last Sabbath's discourse that he did not mean to say he was very sorry for it*," and he "hoped his apology would be satisfactory."

Whether he was married when first settled is not known, but he was soon after, for his oldest child was born in 1771. His children by his wife Elizabeth were I. Thomas Green, born April 12, 1771, graduated at Dartmouth college in 1796, studied law in the office of Stephen R. Bradley, in Westminster, Vt., and died in Boston, Nov. 11, 1837. He was a person of robust constitution, tall in stature, of dark complexion, rather forbidding in aspect, but full of fun. When pursuing his law studies, he was wont to amuse himself in writing humorous poems for the "Farmer's Museum," edited by Jo. Dennie. In 1801 he went to England as an agent for one Perkins, for a newly invented machine called "metallic tractors," which involved him in pecuniary embarrassment. The English physicians were violently opposed to the introduction of the "tractors," which brought forth from the ready pen of Fessenden a long poem in retaliation. It was entitled, "Dr. Caustic; or, Terrible Tractoration;" and had an immense sale in London, after which it was published in this country, in three editions, in as many years. The work is a strange compound of erudition, doggerel verse, and nonsense. The design of it was to satirize the English Medical Faculty and at the same time bring the tractors before the public. He returned to America in 1804, and was engaged in various avocations till 1822, when he commenced the publication of the "New England Farmer," with which he was connected during the remainder of his life. He edited the "Horticultural Register" and the "Silk Manual." His other works were "Original Poems," "Democracy Unveiled," 1806, "American Clerk's Companion," 1815, "Ladies' Monitor," 1818, and "Laws of Patents for New Inventions," 1822. For versatility of genius, ready wit, biting sarcasm, and as a popular journalist, no native townsman has been his equal. II. Elizabeth, b. in New Salem Jan. 21, 1773; m. Royal Crafts, a brother of John Crafts, formerly of this town, April 5, 1795. III. Martha, b. Jan. 11, 1775; d. unm.

at Brattleboro, Vt. IV. Joseph, b. Jan. 7, 1777. V. William,
b. Jan. 15, 1779. He was a printer in Brattleboro in 1804. VI.
Samuel, b. Dec. 18, 1780; d. April 25, 1802. VII. Catherine,
b. Nov. 3, 1783; m. Artemas Ainsworth, of Bethel, Vt., Sept. 27,
1810. VIII. John, b. Oct. 5, 1785. IX. Anne, b. July 18, 1788.

FLOYD, BENJAMIN, the progenitor of one of the old families
in town, was born in Boston, Mass., Feb. 22, 1738. When
the Revolutionary war broke out he entered the service of his
country as a soldier, and continued three or four years. At
the age of about twenty-three he married Lydia Bond, of
Sturbridge, Mass., b. March 30, 1742, and commenced married
life in the same town, where their first child was born. He
then lived about six years in Weston, Mass., and then removed
to Townshend, Vt., and from thence to Walpole about 1772.
He took up his abode near where his grand-daughter, Eliza,
now resides, and spent his days there. He was a blacksmith,
and followed the business through life. He and his son Holloway made all the nails, hinges, and door-latches for the old
hill meeting-house. He belonged to parson Fessenden's church,
and was a constant attendant on his ministrations. He d.
April 22, 1812. Ch. I. Polly, b. March, 1772; m. Abraham
Hall, and had seven children. (See Hall.) II. James, b. Sept.
4, 1764; m. Phebe, dau. of Joel and Hannah (Thompson)
Aldrich, of Westmoreland, and had one daughter, Sally, who
m. Noah Moulton. He d. Nov. 11, 1793. III. Lydia, b. at
Weston, June 1, 1768; m. Jonas Temple, of Westmoreland,
and had six ch., one of whom, Pruda, d., aged about 20 years.
She was buried in the cemetery at Westmoreland, and was
disinterred by one Noble Orr, a medical student in town, for
anatomical purposes, immediately after the burial. Orr had an
accomplice, a brother student, it is said, who was a native of
this town, whose name is withheld for considerate purposes.
The first knowledge gained of this nefarious transaction was
that a portion of her grave clothes was found on the fence
enclosing the cemetery. When this discovery was made the
greatest excitement prevailed throughout the town, and continued for a long time. Orr did not live many years after;

but before he died he wrote a letter to the bereaved parents, stating that the body was not dissected, but buried behind the college buildings at Hanover, N. H. The letter came too late to assuage the mother's grief, for she was already dead and buried. IV. Benjamin Holloway, b. in Townshend, Vt., Jan. 23, 1771; m. Elizabeth Gates, May 13. 1796. Ch. 1st and 2d, Laura and Sophia, b. Sept. 12, 1797. The former d. young. Sophia m. Roswell Pierce of Putney, Vt., and had six children. She resides in Lyndon, Vt. 3d, Holloway, b. 1799; m. Orpha Pierce, of Putney, Vt., and had one child. 4th, Eliza, b. March 6, 1801, and lives on the old homestead, unm. 5th, Harry, b. July 15, 1803; m. Anna Closson, of Westminster, Vt., and had three children, only one of whom survives, Emily, who m. Samuel Cobb, of Westminster, Vt. Harry Floyd has lived to see three generations of his own family, who are living at this time (1879) under the same roof with himself in Westminster, 6th, Benjamin, b. May 1, 1805; d. in Mexico, unm. 7th, Almina. b. July 28, 1807; m. Joel Aldrich, and had two children: a daughter, who died in infancy, and a son, Benjamin Floyd, m. Ellen, dau. of Dr. Safford, of Westminster, Vt., and resides in Springfield, Vt., and is cashier of the Bank there. 8th, Lydia, b. March 3, 1810; d. young. 9th, Mary H., b. Aug. 27, 1812; m. Levi Burt, and had three ch., two living, Alonzo and Mary. 10th, Laura, b. 1815; d. young. Benjamin H. Floyd d. Sept. 27, 1815, and his widow afterwards married David Aldrich; the issue of this marriage was one son, David Bond, who died aged eleven years. V. Hannah, b. Feb., 1773; m. John Watkins, March 15, 1797, and had two ch. He d. and she m. second, Ebenezer Ash, by whom she had six ch., one of whom, George, became a Congregational preacher. VI. Horace, b. March 1, 1775; m. Chloe, dau. of Nathan Watkins, and had three ch. VII. Ira, b. 1777; m. in New York, and had five ch. VIII. Hepsibah, b. Sept. 3, 1779; m. Eli Russell; issue, seven ch. (See Russell.) Elizabeth Aldrich died Sept. 2, 1863, aged 87 years.

FLETCHER, JONATHAN, the centenarian, was born in Leominster, Mass., Aug. 29, 1753. He came to Walpole in 1780, when

he was twenty-seven years of age and purchased fifty acres of
land of Gen. Benjamin Bellows (to which his son afterwards
made additional purchases) built himself a cabin in the wilderness and lived on the same place seventy-three years, where he
died having attained to the unusual age of one hundred years
five months and four days.

The census of 1840, disclosed the fact that there were but
twelve persons living in the State, who were one hundred
years old and upwards, therefore Mr. Fletcher, at his death,
was not only "one in a thousand," but one in *twenty-four thousand.* He is the Methuselah of our town, as no other person
is known to have lived to that extraordinary age, although
quite a number have approximated to it. He was in build a
slender man, rather undersized, with a thin chest and somewhat stooping in carriage towards the close of his life. He
was out a short time in the Revolutionary struggle but never
in any engagement. He was industrious when it was day,
frugal in expenditure, temperate in habits, unobtrusive in demeanor, kind in his family and cheerful in disposition.

He voted at every presidential election, and was punctual at
town meetings, and in later years was honored with a seat in
the desk, near the town officials, on account of impaired hearing. He was fond of reading and read much, having read the
Bible through twenty-nine times in twenty-seven years, as he
told his son. Watts' hymns were frequently read and from some
of them he derived much consolation. When the Cheshire
railroad was being constructed he felt afraid that he might not
live to the time of its completion ; but he did and stood in his
doorway with dimmed eyes and streaming locks which had been
silvered by the frosts of ninety-six winters and witnessed the
fiery steed with a long train pass over the ground where sixty-
nine years before he felled the trees to build his first cabin.
What must have been his musings, imagination only can paint.
He retained his faculties, with the exception of hearing, to
the last, and was as well as usual the day before he died. In
the evening, while the family were unconscious of any special
change, he calmly peacefully and without a struggle passed away.

He married Abigail Goodenow, June 11, 1781, b. Nov. 1,. 1759; d. Sept. 28, 1825, they having lived together forty-four years. He died Feb. 2, 1854. They had a family of eight children, viz.: I. Joanna, b. Feb. 15, 1782; m. Elias Burbank, Oct. 11, 1801, and removed to Gaines, N. Y., died there leaving eight children. II. Miriam, b. Feb. 1st, 1784; m. Daniel Plumley, Dec. 31, 1811, issue three children. III. Polly, b. Sep. 17, 1785, m. Royal Bundy, Nov. 13, 1816, and had six ch. IV. Levi, b. Oct. 10, 1788, d. in infancy. V. Alvan, b. July 11, 1790, m. Elizabeth Holden, Jan. 2, 1812; and lived in town some time; but subsequently removed to Ripton, Vt., where he died—issue, 7 ch. VI. Israel, b. May 26, 1792; d. July 23, 1859; m. Abigail Fuller of Athens, Vt., Apr. 4, 1826; she d. June 9, 1859. Ch. 1st. Henry H., b. July 28, 1827; m. Mary E. Barnes, of Jamaica, Vt., Sep. 1854, (for ages of ch. see Ap.) 2d. Jonathan Curtis, b. Apr. 29, 1835; m. Diantha Emery, of Stockholm, N. Y., Feb. 10. 1860. (See Ap.) VII. Melinda, b. July, 21, 1794; m. Wm. Dunshee, Aug. 30, 1821. (See Dunshee.) VIII. Salome b. May 29, 1796, d. Jan. 1868 unm.

FISHER, MOSES, was born in Franklin Mass., Oct. 13, 1763; his wife, whose maiden name was Mary Hixon, was born in the same town, Jan. 31, 1770. He d. Oct. 23, 1854; she d. May 7, 1861, aged 91. Mr. Fisher came to Walpole about 1800 and settled on the place now owned by his son Moses. He was an industrious, peaceable citizen of the town and was for several years deacon of Rev. Pliny Dickinson's church. At one time he had a mill on the brook that ran past his house, where cotton yarn was manufactured, and his son David peddled it about the country. The mill was washed away by a freshet in 1826. Ch. I. David, b. in Franklin, Mass., Aug. 11, 1789; m. Mindwell Parks. He was a surveyor, miller, and farmer by occupation. He was one of the selectmen of the town for several years and represented it in the Legislature, in 1852. He was a staunch supporter of Universalism and lived a blameless life. He died Dec. 5, 1867, she d. Dec. 23, 1871, aged 72. Ch. 1st. Joseph, m. Adeline Whitney, lives

'in town, and has had four children. (See Ap. for ages.) 2d.
Metcalf, d. young. 3d. Caroline, d. young. 4th. Charles, m.
Emma J., dau. of Oliver Martin. 5th. David, d. unm., at sea.
II. Julia, b. July 1, 1791; m. Ira Emory. III. Nancy, b.
Mar. 11, 1793; m. Abel Hill and lived and died in Cavendish,
Vt.; she had thirteen children. IV. Isaac, b. May, 22, 1796,
m. Julia Ann Richardson of Westmoreland; d. Dec. 21, 1870;
she d. Jan. 27, 1870, aged 68. Ch. 1st. Judson, b. Nov. 13,
1824; m. Louisa Hanes. He is a Unitarian minister of ability and is now settled in Illinois and has two sons. 2d. Ellen,
b. 1826; m. Rufus E. Smith of Alstead; and had two daughters. 3d. Andrew J., b. Aug. 25. 1830; m. Clarissa, dau. of
the late Henry Mellish, and had seven children, only three of
whom are now living. (See Ap.) V. Eunice, b. June 18,
1799; m. Enoch Gale, and removed to Ohio, and had three
children. VI. Mary, b. July 6th, 1807, the first of the family born in Walpole; m. Orin Bunker, and had four children,
none of whom are now living. VII. Moses, b. May 16, 1815;
m. Dec. 22, 1842, dau. of Richard Starkweather, and has three
children. (See Ap.)

FOSTER, HENRY, was the sixth child of Rev. Jacob Foster
and of the sixth generation from Reginald, who came to this
country from Essex, county of Devon, England, in a ship em-
bargoed by King Charles the first, and settled in Ipswich, Mass.,
about the year 1638. He possessed Plum and Hog islands,
which remained in the family for several generations. Rev.
Jacob Foster was born in Holliston Mass., March 10, 1732;
graduated at Harvard University in 1754 in the class with
Gov. John Hancock. He was ordained pastor of the church
in Berwick, Me., in 1756, At his own request he was dismissed from his charge and entered the Continental Army as chap-
lain in 1777. Subsequently he was installed pastor of a church
in Packersfield, N. H., (afterwards Nelson) in 1781, where he
remained ten years: when he took a dismission, and died
there in 1798. He married Hepzibah, daughter of Dea. Henry Prentiss, of Cambridge, Mass, who was a cousin of Hon.
John Prentiss of Keene, N. H. many years editor of the New

Hampshire Sentinel. Henry Foster was born at Berwick, Me., Sep. 17, 1766. He attended the Academy at Exeter, N. H. for a season, after which he came from Nelson to this town, about 1790, to engage in teaching school. Susannah, daughter of Capt. Levi Hooper, was one of his pupils, of whom he became enamored, and afterwards married, May 24, 1792. His marriage induced him to buy a farm in the neighborhood of his father-in-law, where he remained during life. He taught school several winters after his marriage. Although bred in the severe orthodoxy of his day, in his mature years he took a wide departure from the teachings of his father, and nothing delighted him more than a discussion on religious topics with his townsmen, he always taking the most extreme opposite views from the religious conventionalities of the day. He preferred Blackstone to theology, and acquired a better knowledge of the law than many of his contemporary practitioners. He was also a diligent student in science, and, being far in advance of his neighbors in knowledge, and of decided opinions of his own, he was not so popular as he might otherwise have been with many of his townsmen; still his weight of character had a potent sway, and everybody feared his criticisms. He held the office of deputy sheriff many years, was selectman one year, and for some time justice of the peace. Ch, I. Sally, b. June 1, 1792; m. Dr. Ebenezer Crain, of Springfield, Vt., and had thirteen children; d. Aug. 19, 1839. Ch. 1st, Henry Foster, a physician, m. Helen, dau, of Judge Porter, of Springfield, Vt., and had eight ch., six living, one of whom, Richard, is a physician. 2d, Joshua. 3d, Susan. 4th, Mary Ann; m. Joseph Merrick, of Pennsylvania: they have two ch. living. 5th, Louisa Maria. 6th, Pauline. 7th, Frank Eleazer. 8th, Noble, m. Kate Snyder, of Pennsylvania, niece of Gov. Snyder; they have two children living. 9th, Frederick, m. Martha Williams, of Springfield, Vt., and had six ch. 10th, Sarah. 11th, Francis. 12th, Franklin E., m. Fanny Whitney, of Cambridge, Mass.; they have five ch.; residence, Chicago, Ill. 13th, Charles S., m. first, Lina Matterson, of New York City; issue, one ch.; m. second, Laura B. Merriam, of Greenfield, Mass.,

and had four ch. He has been a successful wholesale merchant
in Boston, Mass. II. Susan, b. Aug. 24, 1794; m. Levi Hall,
and had six ch.; d. Nov. 27, 1838. (See Hall.) III. Henry
Prentiss, b. Oct. 10, 1796; m. first, Philena, dau. of Thomas
and Eunice (Alexander) Russell, of this town; d. April 27, 1839.
Ch. 1st, Caleb, b. March 22, 1825; m. Isabel Eliza, dau. of
Edmund E. and Isabella (Hosmer) Marsh, they have four
ch. (See Ap.) 2d, Henry Thomas, b. Oct. 15, 1826; m. Hannah M. Fuller, of Westmoreland, April 29, 1855; d. April 17,
1879,—issue, six ch. (See Ap.) 3d, Elizabeth Philena, b. Nov.
1, 18—; m. Dr. Andrew J. Huntoon, of Langdon, N. H.,—
issue, four ch., one living,—residence, Topeka, Kan. Henry
Prentiss Foster m. second time, Eliza, dau. of Daniel Marsh,
Nov. 11, 1840. ch. 4th, Charles Marsh, b. Oct. 17, 1841; graduated at Harvard University in 1863, and at the Law School,
Cambridge, in 1865; removed to Topeka, Kan., in 1868, and
is now in practice there. IV. Levi Hooper, b. Feb. 1, 1799;
m. first, Fanny M., dau. of Henry and Fanny (Gage) Fitch,
May 8, 1822; she d. June 2, 1868; m. second, widow Harriet
Temple, Jan. 18, 1872; she d. Aug. 12, 1876; m. third, widow
Mary S. Crossett, Dec. 5, 1876. Ch. 1st, Geo. H., b. April 2,
1825; m. Lydia Ham,—issue, four ch., two living. 2d, Helen
M., b. June 17, 1830; m. Edward F. Hooper, Dec. 16, 1857,—
issue, one ch., d. in infancy; resides in Putney, Vt. 3d, Fanny
Sophia, b. Dec. 25, 1834; m. Edward Kenard Reynolds, of
Maryland, April 1, 1858,—issue, two daughters. 4th, Isabella
H., b. Aug. 24, 1840; m. Henry M. Elwell, of Langdon, May
18, 1863,—issue, three ch.; she d. Oct. 26, 1869. V. Sophia,
b. June 25, 1800; d. Aug. 9, 1802. VI. Sophia, b. Feb. 28,
1803; m. Dexter Anderson, June 25, 1826. Ch. 1st, Helen S.,
m. Dr. Orison H. Smith, Sept. 10, 1850; resides in Brooklyn,
N. Y., has three ch. 2d, Charles Dexter, m. Ada A., only dau.
of Dr. Thomas Powers, of Woodstock, Vt.; m. second, Helen
H. Holmes, 1864. 3d, Lucy Merrill, m. Dr. Blanchard, and has
one ch. 4th, Henry Foster, graduated at Dartmouth, studied
law, and is now in practice in New York. He m. Belle Fitz
Randolph, of New York; residence, Rockaway, N. J. 5th,

Caroline L., m. Robert S. Southgate, 1865,—issue, three ch. 6th, Belle S., m. Dr. Herman J. Smith, 1865; resides in Lowell, Mass.,—issue, three ch. 7th, Lizzie T., m. Rev. Mr. Southgate in 1865, pastor of the Congregational church in Dedham, Mass. Mr. Anderson's children were all born between 1827 and 1847; the two oldest are not living. VII. Caleb, b. 1803; d. 1820. VIII. Jacob, b. 1807; d. 1809.

GAGE, ASA.—Asa Gage was from Haverhill, Mass., and his name is found on the town records as early as 1777. Where he first located is unknown; but the last of his residence in town was in the Valley, on what is called at the present time the Abraham Nichols place. He was a farmer and carpenter by occupation, and was the father of the largest number of children of any man that ever lived in town, there being twenty-one in all; fourteen of whom were born in town, and seven after he moved to St. Johnsbury, Vt., which was early in the present century. It is said his daughters were very gay and attractive. Ch. I. William, b. 1779; m. Sarah, only dau. of Capt. Levi Hooper. He never had any children that survived. He was familiarly known as Captain Gage, and was, in his middle life, a very good looking, social, and neighborly person. For many years before he died he was totally blind, and, to gain a livelihood, he manufactured and sold a kind of cathartic pills, which at one time were quite famous. In his last days he was an object for commiseration, as he was dying daily from the effects of a cancer in his neck, which finally terminated his existence, May 13, 1849. He owned the house where Rev. N. G. Allen now resides. II. Hannah, b. Oct. 21, 1778; m. John Burt, of Rockingham, Vt. III. Sally, b. Mar. 19, 1781; m. a man by the name of Damon, who was a harness-maker in town. IV. John, b. Dec. 8, 1782; m. Betsey Merriam, Aug. 1, 1803. Ch. 1st, John Taylor, b. Nov. 14, 1803. 2d, Laura, b. July 22, 1805. 3d, William, b. Feb. 12, 1807. 4th, Maria, b. May 18, 1809; m. John Kilburn, son of Elijah, of this town, and is now living at Fall River, Mass. V. Fanny, b. April 15, 1784; m. Henry Fitch, of Rockingham, Vt., Nov. 16, 1800. She was the grandmother of the children of Levi

H. Foster. VI. Josiah, b. Dec. 15, 1785; moved to the state of Vermont. VII. Samuel, b. Oct. 24, 1787. The foregoing children were born of his wife Dolly, who d. Aug. 25, 1788, aged 36 years. VIII. Royal, the first child of his second wife, Elizabeth, was born Feb. 15, 1791. He lived in Westminster, Vt., and was a preacher of the Methodist denomination, though probably never licensed as such. In his last years he manufactured and sold a preparation called "Canker Balsam," a kind of *cure-all* for all human maladies. He wrote and published a pamphlet, about 1845, on the principles of *non-resistance*, and took the conduct of strange cows in approaching each other to illustrate it. He said, in substance, that two strange cows were often seen approaching each other, when one would be seen to drop her head and brace herself in a belligerent attitude, with eyes flashing vengeance, while the other would seemingly approach with indifference, and manifest no resistance; when, in a few minutes, the belligerent cow would gradually raise her head, and both would commence grazing peaceably. "Now," he said, "*if* human beings would only take lessons from the cow, we should have no more quarrels and wars between nations." IX. Betsey, b. Jan. 13, 1793. X. Burah *alias* Becca, b. March 20, 1795. XI. Polly, birth not known; m. John Jennison, in 1794. XII. Dolly, bap. May 3, 1778; m. William Hews, in 1795. XIII. Sophy, bap. May 20, 1799. XIV. Olive, bap. Sept. 24, 1801. The descendants of Asa Gage are numerous, and are scattered all over New England and the far West, many of whom are highly respected citizens.

GILBERT, EBENEZER, was born in Norton, Mass., in 1760, and after a while he found his way to Surry, N. H., and married Joanna Howard of that place. He removed from Surry to Walpole in the spring of 1797, and purchased his place of one Nathaniel Cross. His children were most of them born in Surry. Soon after he settled in town he planted a butternut tree in his yard, which is still thrifty, and is a monarch of its kind. It has afforded an ample shade in summer, and borne nuts in profusion for three generations to crack. He died Nov.

29, 1829; she died March 28, 1836, aged 71 years. They were buried on "Carpenter's Hill," where were also three of his children, one of whom, Sally, who married Asahel Robbins, was forty-five years of age; the other two were infants. There was also a son by the name of Cyrus, b. Sept. 5, 1797, and a dau., Huldah, who m. Thomas Wyman. (See Wyman.) Nothing more is known of the son. Asa, b. Dec. 21, 1792, is still living (1879) on the old homestead, who m. Frinday Howard, of Winchester, N. H., June 11, 1820, and had the following ch.: 1st, Thankful Hawkins, b. June 19, 1821; m. Harding Ball, July 4, 1841, and has four ch. (See Ap.), and resides on the Gilbert homestead. 2d, Harriet Sophia, b. May 6, 1822; m. Charles A. Kendall, April 11, 1843, and lives in Gardiner, Mass., and has ch.: (1) Charles A. (2) Warren H. (3) Henry W. (4) Hattie L. (5) Emma E. 3d, George Howard, b. June 26, 1823; m. Mary Jane, dau. of Mason and Jane (Cochran) Fay, May 5, 1852, and has ch.: (1) Ella J. T. (2) Elmon H. (3) Mary I. (4) George H. He went south after his majority, and was for several years a teacher there. He served as chairman on the board of selectmen in this town at the opening of the Rebellion, and did efficient service. He now resides in Keene, N. H., cultivating a taste for science and literature, for which he has a strong *penchant*. 4th, Arad, b. Oct. 25, 1824; m. Hepzibeth Forbush, and resides in Hinsdale, N. H. Ch. (1) Fred M. (2) Alice Amanda S. 5th, Daniel Henry, b. July 3, 1827; m. Sophia, dau. of Charles and Amy (Sherman) Watkins. 6th, Lorinda, b. Oct. 30, 1828; m. Geo. F. Conant, and is a widow, with four children, residing in Gardner, Mass. Ch. (1) Ella I. (2) Fred H. (3) Frank. (4) Erwin C. 7th, Charles, b. May 7, 1830; m. Jane Davis. He was wounded in the battle of the Wilderness, and died of his wounds, in the hospital at Washington, D. C. They had two ch. 8th, Dexter Wright, b. July 19, 1832; m. Eliza Jane Cooley, and has ch.: (1) Ethan A. (2) Charles F. He resides in Keene, N. H.

GILMORE, APOLLOS, was born in Wrentham, Mass., May 24, 1768, and died in Walpole, April 15, 1854. He came to Walpole soon after his majority, and lived where his daughter, Mrs.

Robert Barnett, now lives. He was a cooper by trade, and many families living in town to-day can show specimens of his honest, thorough handiwork. For more than fifty years he rang the old town bell on the hill, and such was his punctuality in the discharge of his duty that people used to remark that "Gilmore's clock regulated the sun." He rang the bell at noon and at nine o'clock at night; and the duration, number of strokes, and intervals in ringing did not vary from the beginning to the end of the year, so methodical was he. Mr. Gilmore married three times. His first wife was Julia Heaton, and by her he had one son, Lewis, b. June 17, 1792, in Bellingham, Mass.; m. Emily, dau. of James Campbell. His second wife was Susannah Reed. Ch. II. Harriet G., b. Jan. 27, 1800; m. Robert Barnett. (See Barnett.) III. George Shepard, b. Oct. 22, 1812; d. Oct. 25, 1815.

GRANT, SAMUEL, known familiarly as Major Grant, was born in Watertown, Mass., in 1770, and came to this town about the time of his majority. He was lame and learned the trade of saddle and harness-maker, and carried on the business several years after he came to Walpole. He married Phebe Strong, the daughter of General Benjamin Bellows, Nov. 13, 1791, and built the house now occupied by John Jennison, where he kept for some time a public house. Gen. Bellows dying in 1802 he came in possession of the patrimony of his wife, which consisted in part of a large farm in the southeast corner of the town, known as the "Seven Barns." Here, during a quarter of a century, he was engaged in sheep husbandry, keeping as many as a thousand at a time on the farm, and employing considerable help to care for them. With his help he was honorable, but very exacting, carrying his points of nicety to the extreme, it is said; not allowing, for instance, his men to step upon his grass while curing. He was a model farmer for orderly arrangement, but the income from his farm was not commensurate with the nicety of its appearance. In his day and generation, he was one of the leading men in town, which he represented in the General Court in 1797, '99, 1817, and in 1838; besides holding many offices of trust. Ch. I.

Phebe Strong, b. Sep. 25, 1792; m. Leonard Stone of Watertown, Mass. II. Samuel Salisbury, b. Feb. 16, 1794, of whom but little is known. III. Benj. Bellows, b. Apr. 23, 1796; m. Mary, the dau. of Josiah Bellows. He, early in life, went to Boston, and, for many years was engaged in mercantile business, in the importing trade, under the the firm of Grant, Seaver & Co. During the financial depression of 1837 to 1840, this firm suffered with the whole country, and was forced to succumb after paying $30,000 extra interest to save themselves from sinking. Through shrewd management, and the help of friends, he managed to save a competency from the wreck, and returned to Walpole about 1842, where he spent his declining years. He possessed many of the traits of character, for industry and nicety, peculiar to his father, and was one of those men who hated to see any one idle. He d. Jan. 17, 1870. Ch. 1st, Edward Bellows, b. Jan. 3d, 1822; m. Maria L. W. Mead, of Watertown, Mass. 2d, Benjamin Bellows, b. Oct. 8, 1824; m. Emily Goodall, of New York city, where he now resides and is occupied as a bank clerk. IV. Geo. Gordon, b. June 19, 1800, and died the same year. V. Sarah Watson, b. Oct. 2, 1802; m. Dr. Hiram Hosmer, of this town. (See Hosmer.) VI. Charles Christopher, b. Nov. 7, 1805; m. Lucy, dau. of Daniel Brooks, and went to the state of Maine. VII. Mary Bellows, b. Aug. 20, 1808, and was drowned when a child, in 1810. VIII. George W., b. Apr. 16, 1812; m. Sarah Isabella, dau. of Maj. Thomas Bellows. He is a fur dealer in New York, and spends his summers in his native town. His wife died Dec. 30, 1866.

Samuel Grant died Apr. 12, 1844, aged 79. His wife died Aug. 27, 1847, aged 77.

GRAVES. The Graves family is one of the oldest that settled permanently in town. Aaron Graves and his wife, Phebe, from Saybrook, Conn., were in town before 1750, and it is thought, brought a number of their children with them; and it is said a brother by the name of Nathan came with him; but of Nathan very little is known; except that he had two sons, Azel and Joel, the latter of whom settled just in the border of Westmoreland, on a plot of land known as the Graves pasture and now owned by Henry Burt. Joel was a clockmaker and went by the *sobriquet* of Jinglefoot Graves. Where Aaron settled it is difficult to ascertain. He died Aug. 8, 1814, aged 92 years; she d. Mar. 20, 1813, aged 85. Ch. I. Tryphena, m. Aaron Royce, Dec. 13, 1775. II. Recompense, b. Jan. 20, 1756; m. Hannah Little, May, 20, 1781. Ch. 1st. Salina, m. Ebenezer Hall. 2d. Jesse, bap. 1784. 3d. Charity, bap. 1786. 4th. Hannah, bap. 1788. 5th. Daniel, who had ch. (1.) Lena. (2.) John Lyman, and perhaps others. III. Jesse, b. Apr. 11, 1758; d. 1775. IV. Aaron jr., b. Feb. 11, 1760; d. Oct. 3, 1816; m. 1st, Rhoda Wheeler and had one son, Anson, who married Asenath Slade, of Alstead. He was b. Feb. 19, 1784; she was b. Apr. 6, 1787. Ch. (1.) Newcomb, b. Sep. 1, 1807; m. Lucy Loveless, of Ohio. (2.) Fanny, b. Aug. 19, 1809; m. Gardner Dodge of this town, (See Ap.) (3.) Rhoda Ann, b. Oct. 2, 1811; m. Lyman Stearns, (son of Jesse,) Sep. 8, 1834. (4.) William G., b. Sep. 11, 1814; m. Rebecca Netherton, of Kentucky. (5.) Pamelia, b. Mar. 26, 1818; m. David Martin of Ohio. (6.) Henry, b. Dec. 9, 1820; m. Harriet Chaffin of Ohio. (7.) Sarah, b. May 27, 1823; m. Stephen Bartlett of New Hampshire. (8.) Eliza b. Feb. 18, 1827, m. George Atchison. (9.) Ellen, b. July 25, 1830, m. Moses Tuttle. This family removed to Illinois and not much is known about them. Their father is remembered as a famous fox hunter. Aaron Graves jr., m., for his second wife, Fanny, dau. of Levi Aldrich of Westmoreland, Dec. 7, 1815, by whom he had, (1.) George, who was a printer at Bellows Falls. (2.) Emily, who m. a Hitchcock. There was an incompatibility of disposition between Aaron Graves jr., and his 2d wife and they did not live together long. V. Hannah, b. Nov. 8, 1761, m. Simon Buel, Nov. 15, 1786, and had a large family of children in town. VI. Samuel, b. Feb. 20, 1763; m. Elizabeth ——, and lived on the place now owned by Caleb Foster. He d. June 4, 1846; she d. June 13, 1858, aged 83 yrs. Ch. 1st. Rebecca, b. Feb. 5, 1796, d. July 4, 1821. 2d. Laura, b. Nov. 29, 1797; d. Mar. 2, 1869. 3d. Alvah, d.

in infancy. 4th. Lucinda, b. Aug. 31, 1801, d. Apr. 19, 1814, 5th. Jesse, b. July, 23, 1803; m. Almira, dau. of Ebenezer Wellington. He lived in town and had a family of 12 children, 7 of whom are now living, and d. Feb. 28, 1864: she d. March 4, 1869. 6th. Ambrose, b. Dec. 16, 1807, m. Persis Wheeler of Westmoreland, and had several children, one of whom, (Andrew) resides in town (See Ap.). 7th. Aaron M., b. Mar. 24, 1813, m., 1st, Abigail Sanderson, 2d, Marancy Hunt, and had children by both, and is now living in Westmoreland with his fourth wife. VII. Abner, b. Feb. 5. 1766; m. Mary, dau. of Eliphas Graves, and went to Cooperstown, N. Y. He was once post rider, before the establishment of post offices. How many children he had has not been ascertained; but he had one son, by the name of Calvin, now living, who m. Fanny, dau. of John Carlisle. VIII. Roxana, b. Dec. 4, 1772. IX. Lydia, m. Ebenezer Farnham, Sep. 29, 1795. (See Farnham.)

GRAVES, JOHN.—Members of the Graves family assert that John Graves was induced to come to Walpole by Aaron, sen. above named. Whether John was a brother of Aaron is not positively known, but *probably* he was; at any rate the two were closely related. John Graves's name first appears on the town records, as "fence viewer," in 1762, and again in 1764 as one of the Selectmen, and also in 1778, when he is styled Deacon. He was one of the twenty-five members of the old church, under Thomas Fessenden, in 1767. When he came to town he purchased a large tract of land, which is still held by the Graves family, extending east from "Lane's Mills" to, and including, the place now owned by William Graves. It is said that his sons Eliad and Eliphas, came to town before his son John, jr., who was familiarly known as "Squire," and "Lieut." John. He (John, jr.) was the Graves who represented the town in the Vermont Assembly. (See historical part.) There are no records of the births of his children, therefore they cannot be arranged in their proper order. Children of John, jr., who lived on the place now owned by Charles H. Graves. 1st. Samuel, b. 1768; m. Sarah Clark; d. Dec. 3, 1798. Ch. (1) Elizabeth, m. 1st an Ellis, 2nd a Warn. (2) Amasa. (3) Wil-

liam Wayne, m. Margarett Fishback. (4) Samuel, jr., m. Sarah Palmer. 2d. John, 3d; m. Hannah Wyman, Apr. 2, 1787;
d. Oct. 28, 1792, aged 29 years. 3d. Lydia, m. David Hall,
Dec. 3, 1778. (See Hall.) 4th. Nancy, m. John Gould, Sept.
28, 1783. 5th. Rebecca, m. Asa Titus. (See Titus.) 6th. Margarett, d. young. 7th. Parnell, m. Ziba Dennison, Jan. 1,
1811. 8th. Darius, m. Zerviah Hovey, Feb. 10, 1780. 9th. and
10th. Amos and Allen, twins, Amos m. Hannah Russell, Oct.
20, 1800. II. Eliphas, m. 1st. a Webb; m. 2nd. Hannah Kel-
sey, of Newport, N. H., Nov.3, 1793, and settled on the farm
now owned by Geo. W. Graves. Ch. 1st. Rebecca, m. John
Carlisle, Mar. 19, 1794. 2nd. Isaac, b. in 1767; m. Roxana,
dau. of Eliad Graves, (cousin). He d. Feb. 20, 1813; she d.
June 18, 1868, aged 92 years. Ch. (1) Rebecca, d. unm at an advanced age. (2) Caleb Paschal, b. 1798; d. 1844, He m. Re-
becca, dau. of Ebenezer Wellington, Dec. 20, 1823. Ch. [1]
Maria, m. Dr. Lockhart B. Farrar, and moved to Ohio. [2]
Harriet Augusta, m. Shubael Bennett, of Westmoreland, N. H.
[3] Sarah Elizabeth, m. Rufus Leonard, Mar. 23, 1852. [4]
Isaac M., m. Esther, dau. of Asahel B. Hodskins. [5] Eli, m.
Edna Hall. [6] William. [7] Geo H. [8] Ira, m. Wealthy
Murray, of Potsdam, N. Y. (3) Sophronia. (4) Calvin, m.
Margarett Titus. (5) Abigail, d. unm. (6) Hannah, m. ——
Pond, of Keene, N. H. (7) Adeline, d. unm. Two others died
in infancy. For ages see Ap. 3d. Eliphas, jr., m. Lucy Gates
of Lyndon, Vt., Oct. 3, 1793. 4th. Lydia, m. John Maynard,
Apr. 28, 1811. (See Maynard.) 5th. Sterling, m. Jemima, dau.
of Josiah Griswold, Apr. 18, 1805. Ch. (1) Calvin W., b. Jan.
24, 1806; m. first, Martha Ingalls, Apr. 9, 1826; m. second,
name unknown. Ch. [1] Josiah G., studied medicine and is
now a practising physician in Nashua, N. H. [2] Frederick,
d. in 1843, aged 15 years. (2) Caroline M., b. Sept. 4, 1808; m.
Nahum Stone, at one time editor of the "Museum", Aug. 31.
1830. (3) Josiah G., b. July 13, 1811; m. Mary Boardman of
Nashua, N. H. He is remembered by many citizens of the
town as a famous school teacher. He studied the medical profession and after completing his studies commenced practice in

Nashua, N. H., where he has resided ever since, a period of more than 40 years, in the practice of his profession. He has not only risen to eminence in his profession there; but met with pecuniary success in life. (4) and (5) two that died young. (6) Joseph Hubbard, b. Oct. 8, 1820; he also studied medicine, but died of consumption early in life. (7) Charles Henry, b. Sept. 13, 1824; m. Lucinda M. Thatcher of Newport, N. H. (See Ap.) 6th. Mary, m. Abner Graves, and went to Cooperstown, N. Y. 7th. Abigail, b. 1782: m. George Farrar, May 26, 1819; she died May 13, 1861. 8th. John, m. Lucy, dau. of Jeduthan Russell of this town, and settled on the homestead of his father. He died Jan. 31, 1860, aged 85 years. Ch. (1) Harriet, b. June 24, 1804; m. Levi Hooper. (2) Martha, b. July 5, 1806. (3) John Hubbard, b. Dec. 19, 1808; m. Lydia A. Smith of Rochester, N. Y. (4) George W., b. Apr. 5, 1812; m. Stella, dau. of Ruggles Watkins. (See Ap.) (5) William, b. Aug. 15, 1813; m. Hannah L. Pierce of Nashua, N. H. (6) Mary, b. July 14, 1820. III. Eliad m. Abigail Clark, and located on the place now owned by William Graves, and spent a long life there. He is remembered by the old citizens of the town as a very diminutive man, in size, and bent almost double, in advanced life, which has been a physical peculiarity of several members of the Graves family. Ch. 1st. Roxana, m. Isaac Graves, (cousin.) 2d. Sarah, m. Capt. Joseph Fay, (see Fay,) d. Apr. 25, 1847, aged 84 years. 3d. Barnabas, m. a widow Whitney. 4th. Eliad, jr., m. Mary Taggart. What became of him is not known. Eliad Graves sen. d. Apr. 13, 1828.

GRAVES, EZEKIEL. There was a man by the name of Ezekiel Graves, who once lived in town, said to have been a relative of the foregoing families. He was killed by some accident in the month of June, 1813, aged sixty-five years. He had five children baptized at one time (1794) whose names were as follows: Sylvanus, Abner, Orange, Hannah and Pamelia. Hannah was the wife of Thomas Cunningham. Nothing more has been ascertained concerning the family.

GRISWOLD, ASAHEL, had the following family of children, born in town. I. Ethan. II. Maria. III. Carlos. IV. and

V. John and Sarah. The latter m. a Pierce of Boston. VI. Caroline. VII. Gardner. All removed to the West.

GRISWOLD, ELISHA. Elisha and Lucinda Griswold had the following family of children born in this town, but where they lived is not known. I. Harry Willard, b. Nov. 2, 1795. II. Willis, b. July 6, 1797. III. Ethan, b. Nov. 6, 1799. IV. Polly, b. Aug. 24, 1801.

GRISWOLD, GILBERT, was from Connecticut and belonged to one of the numerous families by that name that settled early there and were of great respectability. He came to this town between 1780-90, and was for many years a farmer and tavern-keeper, on the place now owned by Gardiner Dodge. Every thing about his farm was kept in perfect order, and at every entrance to his various lots he had a *gate, even* into his woodlands. He was a jolly, good natured man, and his society was sought for his social qualities. He was born June 6, 1761, and married Rebecca Nichols, who was born Mar. 2, 1768. He d. June 2, 1827; his wife d. Mar. 15, 1837. Ch. I. Gilbert, jr., b. Apr. 16, 1788; m. Louisa Wells of Keene, and went to Illinois in the early settlement of that state and founded a town there which took the name of Griswold. II. Calvin Webb, b. Oct. 15, 1791; m. Sally C. Goodnow of Westmoreland, and lived and died in this town, Ch. 1st. Calvin, b. Jan. 20, 1818; m. Alma A. Green, and had three children; Emma E., Frank G., and John C. 2d. Louisa, b. Oct. 30, 1819; m. Rev. T. C. Pierce of Boston. She has one child, Louisa. 3d. Nichols, b Dec. 5, 1820; d. young. 4th. Sarah, b. Aug. 22, 1822; m. Moses J. Hale. Ch. (1) S. Louisa, m. Charles Gilbert; she d. 1879. (2) Isabella, d. young. (3) Charles B. (4) Abbie E., m. Waldo F. Whitney, a dentist, of Boston. (5) Lillia R. (6) Gilbert G. (7) Perly W., d. young. (8) John E. (See Ap.) 5th. Gilbert, b. June 27, 1824. He never m; lives in Nevada. 6th. John Milton, m. Mary Stearns of Boston; he had two ch. by his first wife, and three by his second. 7th. Charles Webb, b. May 11, 1829; m. Addie W. Homer, of Belmont, Mass. He keeps a hotel in New York city and his life, so far, has been a pecuniary success. III. Rebecca, b. Sept. 4,

1794; m. Orrick Look. She had two ch. (1) Rebecca, m.
Charles Darby, and lives in Chester, Vt. (2) Orrick, m. Eliza
Goodell; lived and died in Boston. IV. George Stanley; m.
Harriet Lovel, of Rockingham, Vt., and is still living. He is
remembered by many as the one who taught them to "trip the
light fantastic toe." He has three ch. all living in Rockingham.

GRISWOLD, JOSIAH, married ——, and lived on the place
where George Watkins now resides, and d. Jan. 1, 1821, aged
71. His ch. were I. Josiah, jr., m. ——. II. Jemima, m.
Sterling Graves, Apr. 18, 1805. (See Graves.) III. Phebe, m.
Asa Hurd, Feb. 7. 1797. IV. Lovisa. V. Susan, m. Joseph
Cobb, Apr. 17, 1811. He was a shoemaker in town for several
years. VI. Siba, m. William Pierce, of Westmoreland, Oct.
14, 1811. VII. Daniel, m. Lettice Stickney. VIII. Willard,
m. Fannie Fay. IX. Hubbard, m. Ruth Sylvester and went
to Dansville, N. Y. Besides the foregoing children, there
were two named Cara: one or both of whom died young.

GRISWOLD, STEPHEN, lived in this town about the year 1800;
he married Elizabeth Poor, Apr. 2, 1798, and had two children,
but subsequently removed to Westmoreland and had the care
of the toll bridge on Connecticut river there. Ch. I. Elizabeth
Stevens, b. Jan. 28, 1799. II. Stephen Andrew, b. Jan. 18,
1805, and died soon after his majority.

GUILD, WILLIAM, came to this town in 1808, from Franklin,
Mass. He bought the Col. Webber farm, now owned by George
Jennings. He sold a part of the Webber place and purchased the farm owned by Capt. Ware, his first wife's brother;
here he lived till 1838, when he moved into the village, where
he spent the remainder of his days. He died Oct. 16, 1858, aged
83. He was married twice, the first time in 1798, to Waitstill
Ware; she died July 1, 1812, and, the following December, he
married Lydia Field. By his first wife he had two children;
I. Julia, born in 1798, and married, in 1820, John L. Wellington, of this town, and moved into western New York. The
fruits of this marriage were twelve children, two of whom lost
their lives in the Rebellion. Eight of the remainder died with
their friends at home, and two are now living; the oldest and

the youngest. She died in 1854, and he in 1879. II. Increase
Sumner, born Jan. 17, 1800; married Esther Wolcott, Feb. 8,
1824 and moved to Bethel, Vt. Children 1st, Esther Aurora, b.
June 21, 1825; m. 1st, Issachar Williams, who lived but a few
weeks. m., 2d, Charles J. Kenrick, and has three children, and
now lives in Tunbridge, Vt. 2d, Wm. Wolcott, b. Aug. 23,
1827; m. Eliza Jane Alexander, of Fitzwilliam, and has had
seven ch., of whom five are now living. (See Ap.) 3d, Edwin
Jennison, b. Oct. 24, 1829; m., first, Oct. 12, 1858, Esther L.
Knights, who died in 1864, July 26, leaving two sons, Arthur
E. and Elmer, the latter of whom has since died. He subsequently m. Sophia Chase, of Concord, Vt., and has three
children by the second marriage. (See Ap.) 4th, Helen Augusta, b. Feb. 11, 1832; m., Mar. 11, 1855, Oscar Mellish and
lives in Newton, Mass. 5th, Harriet Eliza, b. July 21, 1834;
d. July 30. 6th, Mary Ann, b. Sep. 10, 1836; m. 1857 Wm.
Mellish, who fell through the R. R. Bridge at Cold river station, and died from injuries received, Jan. 1868, leaving a widow and three young children. 7th, Julietta, b. Feb. 8, 1840:
m. Frederick J. Hubbard. (See Ap.) 8th, Josephine Annette,
b. Sep. 30, 1847; m. E. P. Hall, May 16, 1872 and went to
Victor, Iowa; she d. Dec. 1876. By his second wife, who died
in June, 1859, he had three children. III. William jr., b. Aug.
16, 1813; d. Nov. 1840. He was a young man of fine abilities
and highly respected by all who knew him. IV. Mary Jane, b.
Jan. 17, 1815: m. George Aldrich—two children. V. Ebenezer, b. Dec. 22, 1816; m. Sarah M. Brown, in 1842. He died in
Dec., 1844, leaving one daughter, an only child, who m. Richard W. Musgrove, of Bristol, N. H.

HALL, JONATHAN. All the Hall families now living in town
are the descendants of Jonathan Hall, who made his advent
here soon after 1760, but precisely at what time is not known.
There was a Mrs. Philippi Hall who came to town about the
same time *supposed* to be the mother of Jonathan, who was
born in 1684; and died 1774. There was also a Peletiah Hall,
who *may have been* a brother of Jonathan, who came at the time
of the fore-named, and lived and died in town. He married

Lydia Hunt in 1778, *supposed* to be his second wife. He died Jan. 11, 1784, aged 82. He had a son Peletiah who married Lydia Dexter in 1782. There was a Roland Hall in town who lived contemporaneously with Peletiah, who married Elizabeth Willard, in 1777.

Jonathan Hall settled on some land lying north of William Hooper's residence; the remains of the old cellar still indicating the site of the dwelling, where he lived. His son John lived there after the father died. The premises subsequently came into the possession of Levi H. Foster, through his father, Henry, who is still the owner.

The ages of Jonathan Hall's children cannot be ascertained except by conjecture from comparing baptisms, deaths and marriages. Ch. I. Sarah, born 1741, seems to have been the oldest. She married Capt. Levi Hooper, in 1770. (See Hooper). II. Elisha, b. 1746; m. Philippi Smith, 1770; d. May 24, 1818. He lived in the house where Mrs. Geo. Joslin now resides, which was built by his brother Abraham. He died without issue. His brother, Recompense, occasionally visited him and would address some one in his presence thus; "Her's Lisher and Philippi Smith haint a child in the world but I've got sons and *darters*." III. Abraham, birth unknown; he m. Polly, dau. of Benjamin Floyd, in 1783. Ch. 1st, Isaac, died, Oct. 4, 1795, aged 11 years. 2d, Electa, d. July 24, 1797, aged 5 years. He left Walpole about the year 1800 and settled in Bath, N. H., where he spent his days. Five children were born to him in Bath, making seven in all. He was the largest and most physically powerful man ever born in town. At the age of sixty his weight was 425 pounds, and when he went from place to place an ox cart was the vehicle. IV. Recompense, m. Phebe Gary, in 1775, and lived in Westminster, Vt. Ch. 1st, Phebe, m. Mr. Hockadene. 2d, Recompense jr., b. 1787; m. Lucretia, dau. of Dea. Roger Farnham, Mar. 31, 1806. He was a carpenter by trade and lived on the Dea. Farnham homestead, and died Mar. 22, 1860; she d. Aug. 18, 1863, aged 76. He had a set of double front teeth which were unimpaired up to the time of his death, and, being

an inveterate smoker, using a clay pipe, he wore a semicircle
in both upper and lower teeth, which just fitted the stem of
his pipe. Ch. (1.) Emily, b. Sep. 10, 1808, m. John N. Hodskins. (See Hodskins.) (2.) George, b. Apr. 30, 1811;
d. Nov. 11, 1830. 3d, Joseph Mason, b. Sep. 2d, 1818; m.
1st, Jane Chapin and had one dau. 2d, m. Deborah the sister
of his first wife, who survives him. (4.) Henry P., b. Oct. 19,
1827; m. Caroline, dau. of Geo. Watkins. (5.) Sophia, m.
Jonas Gassett. 3d, Lucy, m. Josiah White. 4th, Josiah, m.
first, Roxana Streeter, and second, Lucy Reed. Ch. (1.) Charles,
m. Morial L. Rice ; she d. Mar. 23, 1864, aged 53. (2.) Lucia,
m. Fessenden Parker. (3.) Cynthia, m. William Ellis. (4.)
Adeline, never married. 5th, Ebenezer, b. 1788; m. Selina,
dau. of Recompense Graves; d. Apr. 9, 1862. Ch. (1.) Edwin, b. Mar. 29, 1811; m. Sabrina Burbank and lives in Michigan. (2.) Susan, b. Oct. 25, 1813; d. unmarried. (3.) Hiram
b. April 3, 1816; m. Nancy, daughter of William Blanchard. (4.) Lucinda, living unmarried. 6th, Susan, m. Calvin
Chaffee. 7th, Betsey, m. Burk Chaffee. 8th, Ruth, m.
Timothy Bishop. 9th, Thankful, m. Joseph Budson. 10th,
Samuel, m. Maria Atherton. V. Jonathan jr., (Old Munn,)
who has heretofore been mentioned in the general narrative. Where he lived in town is not known ; but the
names of his children, or a portion of them, have been found
in the various town and church records. viz., (1.) Samuel, (2.)
Eunice. (3.) Rebecca. (4.) Jonathan, 3d. m. Phebe Britton,
Apr. 10, 1806, and went to Surry and was the father of thirteen children, and the grandfather, through his son Henry
of Westmoreland, of Charles B. Hall, of this town. (5.) Elisha,
m. Lucinda Badger in 1805. VI. John, m. Submit ——— and
lived on the homestead of his father and had the following
children : (1.) Silas. (2.) John, m. Betsey Warren, in 1813.
(3.) Luther ; (4.) Calvin; (5.) Sally ; (6.) Submit; (7.) Benjamin ; (8.) Lois, who m. John Bundy, in 1818. VII. Dav-
d, b. 1750 ; m. Lydia, dau. of John Graves jr., in 1778, and
lived opposite the residence of Preston Titus. Ch. 1st, Rebecca, m. Samuel Martin, Dec. 26, 1805. (See Martin.) 2d,

David jr., b. 1784; m. Lucinda D. Burbank, d. Oct. 26, 1839; she d. Aug. 8, 1840, aged 51. Ch. (2) David jr., m. first, Jane, daughter of John Turner, March 8, 1838, second wife's name unknown. He is a stage proprietor and driver. (2.) Prudy, m. Joseph Norton, (3.) Louisa, m. Eward Shattuck, (4.) Levi H. went to Georgia. 3d. Rhoda, m. Jonathan Russell jr., July 23, 1807, and lived at Saxtons River, Vt. 4th, Lydia, m. Jonathan A. P. Bates, Jan 2d. 1806. 5th, Tirzah, m. Richard Russell and went to Nunda, N. Y. 6th, Ezra b. 1786, m. Priscilla, dau. of Jeduthan Russell. He lived on the homestead of his wife's father, and at one time kept a public house there. He d. Aug. 20, 1863. Ch, (1.) Gardner E., b. Sep. 12, 1809, m. first, Emily, dau. of Hugh Dunshee, by whom he had 3 sons; Henry, Warren, and George. His 2d wife was Arabella A. Simonds, whose maiden name was Shattuck. He was for many years passenger conductor on the Cheshire & Fitchburg railroads. He d. 1878, June 28. (2.) Orin, b. June 27, 1813; m. Maria H. Wakefield, of Newport, N. H. (3.) Martin G., b. Apr. 22, 1818; m. Maria, dau. of Thomas Nichols of this town, June 3, 1840. (4.) Armstrong S., b. July 19, 1821, m. Emma A., dau. also of Thomas Nichols and went to California, where he now lives. (5.) Almira, b. May, 27, 1823, m. Josiah W. Batchelder, and lives in town. 7th, Levi, b. 1792, m., 1st, Susannah, dau. of Henry Foster. She d. Nov. 27, 1838, when he m. Mary Britton, of Surry, who survives him. Ch. (1.) Isabella, b. Dec. 25, 1814, m. Dan Gray, Sep. 1831, by whom she had one son and one dau. (2.) Oliver, b. Dec. 4, 1816, m. 1st, Marietta, dau. of Charles Watkins, and had 3 ch. He m. second, Ellen A., dau. of Luther Knowlton, (See Ap.). (3.) Jacob Foster, b. in 1819; d. Sep. 8. 1874, unm. (4.) William, b. June 4, 1826, m. 1st, Percy I., dau. of Stephen Tiffany, of this town; she d. Jan. 24, 1866; when he m. Louisa P., widow of Alfred Seward and dau. of Levi Ball. (5.) Mary, b. 1830; m. Stephen J. Tiffany, d. May 29, 1868. (6.) Edna A., b. Aug. 5, 1835; m. Eli W. Graves of this town. (7.) (by 2d wife,) Levi A. b. Sep. 24, 1842; m. Estelle M., dau. of John Hooper. 8th. Isaac, m. Ann Brooks,

of Westminister, Mass. He was extensively engaged in the
staging business many years ago. He left town early in life.
VIII. Elizabeth, m. a Gould of Westminster. She was an
iveterate smoker and is remembered by the oldest inhabitants
as an occasional visitor to her family conections in Walpole.

HIXON, EZRA, came to this town from Franklin, Mass., and
bought the place now known as the Bunker farm, in 1805 or
1807. He was born in Franklin, Feb. 16, 1781, and married
Eunice Ware, born in Needham, Mass., Jan. 18, 1782. He died
in Brookfield, Vt., to which place the family had removed in
1835, Dec. 11, 1872; she died at the same place, July 6, 1861.
Ch. I. Clarissa, b. in Alstead, N. H., Jan. 16, 1805; m. William
Fisher, and d. in Everett, Mass., Nov. 28, 1875. II. Olive Ware,
b. in Alstead, Oct. 30, 1806; m. Ephraim Prentiss, of this town,
and had two ch., Maria and Nancy; both married, and live in
Hyde Park, Mass. III. Timothy Ware, b. at Walpole, May 15,
1809; m. and lived in Boston; d. at Hyde Park, Mass., Nov.
28, 1878. He is remembered by the old citizens as the chubby,
red-faced boy that began life going from house to house with
a small tin trunk in his hand, selling small wares and cleaning
old watches. At length he turned up in Boston, as a keeper
of livery, and by borrowing small sums of money and always
being punctual in payment, he was soon enabled to command
any amount of credit he desired, which put him in the way of
enlarging his business, so that he, by good judgment and
shrewdness, accumulated money very fast. After accumulating
a sufficient sum, he turned private banker, and, it was said at
one time, was worth $500,000. How much property he had at
the time of his death is not known. IV. Albert, b. at Walpole,
July 30, 1812; m. a Goodenough, of Brookfield, and is still
living at that place. V. Avery, b. at W., Feb. 2, 1816; m. an
Allen, of Brookfield, Vt. VI. George Lawrence, b. at W.,
Aug. 23, 1818, and lives in Medford, Mass. VII. Ezra Lewis,
b. at Walpole, Aug. 14, 1824; d. at Brookfield, Vt., Sept. 10, 1866.

HODSKINS, AARON, came here very early in the settlement of
the town and located soon after on the place now owned by
the George D. Kingsbury heirs. It would seem that his father

(Aaron) came with him, as, at one time, Aaron jr. (the Squire) is spoken of in the town records as Aaron 3d. He is styled Lieut. Aaron; but it is not positively known whether he was in his country's service or not. He was born in 1741 and died Apr. 17, 1813; his wife, Eunice, was born in 1742; died Mar. 20. 1829. For many long years he toiled, cleared up his farm and fed and clothed a family of twelve children, eight of whom became adults. It would appear that sheep husbandry was commenced early on the farm, for tradition says that the wolves made sad havoc with his flocks. (See narrative.) His children were, I. Nabby, b. June 29, 1776; d. unm. Apr. 28, 1838. II. Eunice, b. Oct. 8, 1867; m. Jonathan Bixby III. Aaron jr., b. Aug. 17, 1769; m. Rhoda, dau. of Nathan and Esther, (Lions) Watkins, June 16, 1796. He was for many years known as the "Squire," as he was at one time a justice of the peace. He, early in the present century, commenced sheep husbandry and was one of the best, if not *the* best farmer in town, and accumulated a competency by his vocation. He was intellectually a strong man and exercised a commanding influence in town. He was one of three who first introduced pleasure wagons in town, as has been previously noticed. He was a man whose counsel was much sought by his neighbors and townsmen and his influence many times gave direction to the civic measures of the town. In religious sentiment, he was a firm believer in Universalism, and was the leading spirit in building the second meeting-house on the hill. In person he was tall and his weight was rising of 200 pounds, with dark complexion and shaggy brows, and his whole aspect was such as to inspire deference and confidence. Ch. 1st, Esther, b. Oct. 7, 1791; m. Ira White, Oct. 23, 1822, and went to Ohio, where he soon died, leaving two boys. 2d, Willard, b. Feb. 21, 1795; m. Laura White, Mar. 31, 1819. Ch. (1) Harriet, b. Apr. 7, 1820; m. Joseph Burt, June 8, 1845, neither of whom are living. (2d) Maria Isabella, died young. 3d, Asahel Bundy, b. June 31, 1800; m. Cynthia, dau. of David and Martha (March) Hodskins, Sep. 8, 1822. Asahel lived on the old homestead most of the time during life and followed the vocation of his father.

At one time he had the best flock of fine wool sheep in town, from the fleeces of which he had manufactured a suit of blue cloth, which he wore on special occasions as a kind of advertisement. He was a man of positive views and an ardent Whig in the time of the tariff excitement, although he had been just as vehement a Republican of the old school before. He was a good farmer, and any one wishing to purchase good sheep, fine wool, or good neat stock, knew where to find them. He died July 5, 1864. Ch. (1) Ellen A., b. Aug. 16, 1825; m. Geo. D. Kingsbury, Dec. 24, 1846, and has two sons; he d. Sep. 28, 1876. (2) Mary Ann, b. Aug. 11, 1827; m. Asa Spaulding, Apr. 8, 1847, one child. He was a Universalist preacher. They both died two years after their marriage. (3) Esther A., b. Apr. 28, 1835; m. Isaac M. Graves, July 26, 1855, and has three ch. (4) Cornelia A., b. May 18, 1842; m. John M. Bixby, Sep. 10, 1865; resides at Grand Rapids, Mich., and has two ch. living. (5) Sarah M., b. Aug. 19, 1844; m. Franklin S. Lane, Jan. 7, 1869, and resides in Charlestown, Mass., and has one ch. (6) (7) (8) d. in infancy. 4th, Almira, b. 1807; m. Ebenezer Stowell—issue three ch. who died in infancy; she d. Dec. 3, 1875. IV. Hannah, b. Mar. 25, 1773 and married a Watkins. V. Judith, b. July 19, 1775; m. Joshua March, June 6, 1799. (See March.) VI. David, b. Mar. 25, 1777; m. Patty, dau. of John March, June 23, 1799; d. in 1825, age 57. Ch. 1st, Cynthia, b. Aug. 23, 1799; m. Asahel B. Hodskins. 2d, Hannah, went to Osselock, N. Y. 3d, Martha, m. Amasa Allen. 4th, Ira, m. Susan Brown, of Surry and had five ch. 5th, John Nelson, b. June 20, 1808; m. Emily, dau. of Recompense and Lucretia (Farnham) Hall, and had four sons. (See Ap.) 6th, Hiram, m. Charlotte Adams, of Ashby, Mass. and had one ch. 7th, Abigail N. 8th, George M. 9th, Rebecca G. 10th, John M., d. young. VII. Luther, b. Oct. 11, 1779; m. Patience Turner, Mar. 14, 1805. VIII. Tabitha, b. May, 28, 1788; m. Elijah Turner, Feb. 10, 1808. IX. Ebenezer. X. Daniel. XI. Betsey. XII. Asa,—all died young. XIII. Eunice, m. Samuel Shipman, July 29, 1788.

HODSKINS, HENRY. A family of children of Henry Hodskins and wife were baptised as follows : 1st, Henry, 1773. 2d, and 3d, Hepsibah and Thomas, 1779. 4th, Phinehas, 1781, and Martha, 1788. No person is found in town who has any knowedge of this family.

HOLLAND, ABRAHAM, Dr., was born in Barre, Mass., in 1751, graduated at Dartmouth, studied the medical profession, came to this town immediately after completing his studies, and commenced practice about 1780, or perhaps a year or two later. He was the third physician that settled in town, it is said. He married Abigail Baldwin, from Shrewsbury, Mass., and when he first brought his wife to town he boarded with Col. John Bellows. He soon after purchased the farm now owned by Maj. Britton, and built that house. He was twice married: his second wife was a widow Fisher. He went to Newfane, Vt., and lived several years; but returned in his old age, and lived with his son Nathaniel, and died at the advanced age of 96, on Feb. 18, 1847; his wife Abigail died June 13, 1822, aged 73. Ch. I. Polly, m. William Salisbury, of Derby, Vt., March 9, 1814. Her children were Mary, Harriet, Stella, William, and Annie. II. Nathaniel, b. 1788; m. Keziah Richardson, of Alstead, N. H., May 26, 1819. For several years he kept a public house in Boston, after which he returned to Walpole, and kept the house now owned by Charles G. Maynard till his declining health caused him to relinquish it. He died April 25, 1835, aged 47; his wife died in 1878. Ch. 1st, Henry Baldwin, m. Anna Brigham, of St. Louis, and they had two ch., Charles and a daughter. 2d, Isabella, m. Hudson E. Bridge, of St. Louis, formerly of this town, and had three ch.; she d., and Mr. Bridge m. his first wife's sister, Helen Augusta, and had by her five ch. 3d, Maria, m. Harrison Parker Bridge, also of St. Louis, and formerly of Walpole, and had one child. 4th, Charles, never m., and d. young. 5th, Emma, never m., d. in her teens. 6th, Ephraim Richardson, is a roving character, and is now in California, unm. 7th, Julia Rebecca, m. John W. Beach, of St. Louis; no ch. 8th, Leonard Bisco, m. Elnora, dau. of William Mitchell, of this town, and has ten ch. (See Ap.) III. Ephraim, b. in 1790; m. Nancy, dau. of Rev. Samuel Mead. He went to Keene and kept the Phœnix Hotel there when first married, and subsequently removed to Boston and kept a hotel on Howard Street known as "Holland's Coffee House." He at length returned to his native town and built the house where his widow now resides, and lived there till his death, which occurred April 30, 1859. Ch. 1st, Henry E., b. July 6, 1823. He studied the medical profession, graduated at the Medical College in Boston, Mass., and commenced practice in Northfield, Mass. When the rebellion broke out he went into the service of the Union as a surgeon, where he d., unm., March 28, 1865, aged 41. 2d, Harriet, b. March 18, 1826; m. Thomas N. Hastings, of Boston, by whom she had two sons, Edward H. and Thomas N. 3d, Edward Morse, b. Feb. 28, 1828; he d. unm. at the age of 51, Dec. 27, 1878. 4th, Daniel Denny, b. Oct. 20, 1829; m. Eliza Hardy, and had two ch. He early went to California, where he now resides. 5th, Orlando Sartwell, b. Oct. 13, 1831; m. Bertha Held and had one daughter; he d. in 1878. 6th, Frederick Henderson, b. Jan. 7, 1834; m. Annie, the widow of his cousin, Henry Holland, of St. Louis, where he now resides; no ch. 7th, George B., b. March 17, 1838; lives with his mother, unm. 8th, William Ward, went out as a sutler in the army of the rebellion, and died there Nov. 12, 1863, aged 23 years.

HOOPER, LEVI, the progenitor of the Hooper family in Walpole, was born in Bridgewater, Mass., in 1742. When quite young he went on a whaling voyage to Hudson's Bay, and on his return enlisted as a soldier in the last French war, which ended in 1763. He enlisted for nine months, and when the time of enlistment had expired he was unable to get his pay unless he would stay three months longer. At the expiration of the next three months he found himself no better off, when he and two other soldiers deserted and made for home, guided by blazed trees, till they arrived at Charlestown, No. 4, where they stopped for the night. The next day they reached Walpole, and stopped in a log hut that stood on the site of the present cider-mill which stands on the Hooper premises. The soil and the heavy growth of timber pleased him so much that

Foster Hooper M.D.

he was induced to return, after visiting his friends, and locate in town. He returned to Walpole in 1771, and soon after buried his wife, whose maiden name was Susanna Leach, and, the same year, married Sarah, the daughter of Jonathan Hall, by whom he had six children. He paid £160, lawful money, to Samuel Chase for his farm, in 1775, and located on the southern part. In 1781 he had built and moved into the Mansion, so called, now the residence of George D. Hooper, where he lived till he died, in 1806; she died Feb. 9, 1823, aged 81. He was second lieutenant in a company of General Bellows' regiment, in Revolutionary times, and afterward captain. He was a man of resolute character, held many town offices, and accumulated a competency for old age. Ch. I. Susannah, b. 1772; m. Henry Foster, May 24, 1792. (See Foster.) II. Salmon, b. Aug. 7, 1774; m. Rebecca Foster, Nov. 8, 1795. Ch. 1st, Rebecca, b. March 31, 1797; m. George Flint, July 26, 1830; three ch. 2d, Mary, b. May 4, 1799; m. Alfred Flint, April 14, 1819, and had four ch., three daughters and one son, Col. Franklin Flint, U. S. Army. She m. the second time, Asa P. French, May 1, 1843, and had one son, Frederick F. 3d, Levi, b. April 7, 1801; m. Harriet, dau. of John Graves, Jan. 19, 1826, and had nine ch., born in town; viz., (1) William Foster, b. Jan. 12, 1827; d. Dec. 13, 1867. (2) Frances Maria, b. Oct. 5, 1828; d. in infancy. (3) Frederick Hubbard, b. June 12, 1830; studied medicine, and is a practising physician. (4) Martha Ellen, b. July 30, 1832; m. Josiah W. Knight, and had one son; d. Nov. 22, 1864. (5) Ira H., b. April 7, 1835; m. Ellen, dau. of Abner Wheeler,—issue, two ch. (6) Sarah Louisa, b. Sept. 5, 1837; d. March 30, 1839. (7) Henry H., b. Sept. 9, 1840; d. Dec. 31, 1864. (8) Mary E., b. Apr. 5, 1843; m. Henry Weymouth. (See Ap.) (9) George L., b. May 14, 1846; residence, Boston, Mass. 4th, Sally, b. Apr. 22, 1803; m., first, Artemas Adams, Jan. 26, 1823; ch., three sons; m., second, Daniel T. Potter, of Troy, N.Y., May 12, 1833; m. third, Silas M. Bates, of Watertown, Mass., April, 1839. 5th, Foster, b. April 2, 1805; m. first, Nancy C., dau. of Davis Carpenter, Nov. 6, 1832; m., second, Nancy L. Wood, of Meriden, Mass., in 1836; ch., three sons and three daughters. Dr. Foster Hooper was a man of more than ordinary natural ability. In his younger days he taught school, and is remembered by the author of these pages as his first male teacher. He studied medicine, obtaining his professional education at Burlington, Vt. He went to Fall River in 1826, where he enjoyed, for more than a generation, an extensive practice, and was held in high estimation by the medical fraternity. He was one of the prominent men in Fall River during his residence there, and in all the civic transactions in the city he took a leading part. He was elected to the Legislature in 1831; was county treasurer three years, and in 1846 and 1848 he was in nomination for member of Congress, but was defeated each time by a small majority. In the cause of education he always took great interest, and was at one time chairman of the Board of Education. In 1853 he was a member of the State Convention to revise the Constitution. Up to 1856 he was an ardent Democrat in politics, when he went into the Republican ranks, and was, if anything, more active than he had previously been in the Democratic party. In short, Dr. Hooper was the leading spirit in Fall River for more than forty years. He went to New York in October, 1870, to attend a Unitarian convention, which was to be held there, and when on the boat on his way thither he was taken ill; but arrived at the Fifth Avenue Hotel, where he was taken worse, and physicians were summoned; but he died in about an hour, from disease of the heart. 6th, Laura, b. June 3, 1807; m. George Kilburn, Dec. 18, 1825, and had ten ch., nine living, six daughters and three sons. 7th, Hepsibeth, b. April 14, 1809; m. first, Jonathan Griffin, April 6, 1830, and had one child, Elizabeth R.; m. second, Azariah Shove, of Fall River, and had seven ch. 8th and 9th, Emily and Salmon, b. in 1811 and 1813, d. in infancy. 10th, Emeline, b. Feb. 23, 1820; m. Jonathan Slade, of Somerset, Mass., May 29, 1851, and has one child, a son, now in college. 11th, Salmon, b. Dec. 3, 1822; m. Selina Stone, of Paris, Me., July 5, 1846, and had three ch. II. James Winslow, b. 1776; died young. III. James, b. 1778; m. Eleanor, dau. of Ebenezer Wellington,

Jan. 18, 1802, and settled on the old homestead of his father. He had some aspirations in the military line, and was at one time captain of a company, and was ever after called Captain Hooper. He was a member of the Legislature in 1830, and one of the selectmen of the town several years. He d. May 30, 1867; she d. Feb. 26, 1858. Ch. 1st, James, jr., b. Aug. 31, 1803; d. Dec. 31, 1877. He m. Mary, dau. of Ephraim Lane, Jan. 19, 1826. He was an honest, industrious, and thriving farmer in town, for more than forty years, and accumulated a competency for old age. The fruits of their marriage were two daughters, and one son, Warren, who is a successful merchant in Boston. 2d, Henry W., b. Nov. 28, 1807; m. Mary K., dau. of the late Jonathan H. Chase, April 10, 1832, and had seven ch. He removed to Charlestown, N. H., in 1853, where he now resides, a thrifty farmer. 3d, Charles, b. Dec. 16, 1809; m. Almira, dau. of Ephraim Lane, May 23, 1839. He has been for a quarter of a century extensively engaged in general farming, sheep husbandry, and tobacco culture, in town, and has had his days of sunshine and shadow,—accumulating large gains and meeting with heavy losses. He has no children. 4th, William, b. Feb. 21, 1812; m. Elvira Pulsifer, of Rockingham, Vt., and settled on the homestead of his father and grandfather. He has two ch., George Dana and Frank W., the latter of whom received a classical education, and is a ripe scholar. He is now a successful teacher of the High School in Keene. 5th, Ellen, b. Dec. 10, 1816; m. Charles L. Jones, Aug. 13, 1839, and lives in Boston,—no ch. 6th, Frances R., b. Nov. 11, 1819; m. Lucius A. Jones, Aug. 3, 1842, and lives in Boston, Mass.; she has two sons. 7th, Harriet, b. Oct. 12, 1824, and lives with her brother Charles. It is safe to say that no four sons belonging to one family, born in town, have been more pecuniarily successful, as farmers, than the four sons of Capt. James Hooper. IV. Elisha, b. 1781; m. Jemima, dau. of Stephen Ormsby, May 29, 1803, and settled on the farm now owned by John L. Houghton. Mr. Hooper was a farmer, and was deacon of the Christian church in the Hollow for many years, lived an exemplary life, and died May 11, 1851; she d.

Nov. 9, 1870, aged 86. Ch. 1st, George, b. July 7, 1805; m. Clarissa W., dau. of Levi Fay, March 30, 1830; they had two ch., one living, Edward. Mr. H. and wife are now living in Putney, Vt. 2d, Caroline, b. Feb. 27, 1807; m. Levi Ball, and has three ch. living. 3d, Phebe L., b. Sept. 13, 1809; m. Lyman Houghton, July 4, 1837. (See Ap. for ch.) 4th, Lewis, b. April 6, 1812; m. Mary Metcalf, and had ch. (See Rebellion.) 5th, John, b. June 22, 1818; m. first, Abigail Ball, May 26, 1840; m. second, Agnes L. Flanders, Dec. 21, 1870; had six ch., by first wife, five living. 6th, Lucy, b. Sept. 19, 1820; m. John B. Russell, and had one daughter and three sons, one of whom, Edward, is a clergyman. 7th, Sarah, m. Samuel W. Bradford, and lives in Keene. V. Sarah, b. 1783; m. William Gage, Aug. 9, 1801; no ch. He d. May 13, 1847.

HOSMER, JONAS, was born Oct. 24, 1758, and was in the Revolutionary war, and was wounded in General Sullivan's retreat from Rhode Island. He was brother of Abner Hosmer, who was killed at the same time with Capt. Davis, at the battle of Concord, April 19, 1775. He came to this town, a single man, from Acton, Mass., in 1783, and worked here, at the trade of a mason, for Eliphalet Fox, who lived on Carpenter's Hill. He purchased the farm now owned by his son Edwin, of Jonathan Jennison, in 1785, and lived upon it till his death, which occurred Feb. 1, 1840, age 81. Mr. Hosmer was for many years deacon of the old town church, and was considered a man of spotless character and a good citizen. He married Betsey Willard, of Harvard, Mass., Dec. 15, 1785, by whom he had twelve children, four of whom died in infancy, and no further account will be given of them. Those who survived were as follow: I. Olive, b. July 14, 1792; d. Aug. 5, 1833. II. Eli, b. Sept. 13, 1794; m., twice, Olive and Lucy Robbins, cousins, and had two ch. He followed the vocation of a teacher, and was favorably known as such. III. Harriet, b. July 3, 1796; m. Stephen Stearns, of this town, and had one child, Josiah W.; she d. Dec. 20, 1827. (See Stearns.) She possessed all the womanly virtues, and was highly respected wherever she was known. IV. Hiram, b. Sept. 14, 1798. He learned

the trade of a cabinet-maker, and was a very ingenious workman. Some of his work may be seen in town at this time.
Subsequently he studied medicine, and after completing his
studies went to Watertown, Mass., where he had an extensive
practice, and became eminent in his profession. He married
Sarah, the daughter of Samuel and Phœbe (Bellows) Grant, of
this town, by whom he had four children, two of whom died
in infancy, and the third, a daughter, died in her teens, of
consumption; and about the same time the mother died, also,
of the same disease, leaving the father and husband with an
only daughter, Harriet Grant, who was born Oct. 9, 1830, and
inherited the frail and feeble constitution of her mother and
sister. Her father, in his imaginations by day, and in his
dreams by night, saw his only daughter and earthly solace
wasting away by that insidious disease that had heretofore visited his family, and he determined, if possible, to ward off the
hand that was seemingly reaching forth for another victim.
He knew very well, as a physician, that it would not do to keep
her within doors as children are usually kept; therefore he
gave free rein to any whim or caprice that might enter her
head, provided that physical development might result from it.
He used to say "There are many years for the mind to develop,
but only a few months for the development of the body;" and
he was anxious that nothing should interfere with its healthy
growth, if freedom would give it. Dr. Hosmer's house was
but a short distance from the quiet flow of Charles River, and
here her wild nature was wont to disport itself during her early
years. She was furnished with boat and skates, and here she
learned to swim like a duck, dive like a loon, skate with the
wind, and row like a trained *athlete*. Her father supplied her
with a gun and pistol, and a pony to ride was at her command;
with the first she was considered the "best shot" in the region,
and with the latter she became a bold, graceful, and daring
equestrienne. A clay pit was in the vicinity of her home, which
afforded her an opportunity to gratify her innate qualities of
mind by moulding cats, dogs, horses, and any and every thing
that she fancied, bedaubing herself like a child in making mud

cakes. She was very fond of hunting, and when she went forth on an occasion of the kind she used to dress in a kind of hybrid costume, somewhat resembling a boy, which greatly facilitated her movements. A favorite dog always accompanied her on her hunting excursions, which she took much pains to bedeck fantastically with brilliant colored ribbons, and with a tiny bell attached to his collar.

Her father fitted up a room for her own special use, and the stuffed skins of the fur and feather tribes of the forest, which she brought down with her gun, were made to contribute to its furnishing. She used for an ink-stand a sea-gull's egg, placed in the head of a stuffed kingfisher, and in a conspicuous place in her room was a crow's nest, which she climbed a lofty pine to procure, when at school at Lenox, Mass., as an evidence of her daring and agility. According to an eye-witness, her room wore the appearance of a miniature museum. Up to the age of sixteen she had scattered *wild oats* in profusion, and their growth had become so rank that her father was anxious that she should do something for her intellectual improvement. She had been sent to school occasionally, but she cared nothing for books, and her untamed nature gave her teachers much care and perplexity; and on one occasion it is said she was expelled from school. Her father at length placed her in charge of Mrs. Sedgwick at her school in Lenox, Mass., where she remained three years, her father stipulating that her physical training should not be abridged during the time. At the end of the prescribed term her physical strength and powers of endurance were truly remarkable. When she returned home she commenced taking drawing and modeling lessons of Mr. Stephenson, of Boston, Mass., frequently walking there and back daily, a distance of fourteen miles, besides giving close attention to her lessons. About this time she completed the bust of a child, and the head of Lord Byron, which were evidences of developing genius. She could not obtain from books and the instructions of her father the anatomical knowledge she wanted, and she was driven to the alternative of seeking the desired information at the Medical College in St.

Louis, it being then the only institution of the kind in the country where females could be admitted as students. When firmly installed in her new quarters she set aside the prudish conventionalities of society, and bid defiance to the tongue of animadversion. She carried a pistol in her pocket for protection from insults, but never had an occasion to use it; for her bold, defiant manner was a sure safeguard against rude insults. She received a diploma for her attainments while at St. Louis, and no stigma rested upon her character when she left. Before she returned to Watertown she made several extended excursions about that broad field, and among others she ascended the "Father of Waters" as far as the falls of St. Anthony, on a steamer. The captain of the boat became interested in her peculiarities, and spoke of a cliff which had been considered insurmountable, and gave her to understand that no woman could surmount it. But what was his astonishment when he saw her scale the height with the agility and grace of the mountain chamois, and perch herself on the topmost pinnacle. The height is now known as "Hosmer's Cliff." When she returned to Watertown, she wrought a small copy of Canova's bust of Napoleon for her father, in a studio fitted up for her by him; her own small and delicate hands doing all the chipping, etc.

Her first original undertaking was "Hesper," which was much admired. At this time she hinted to her father that Rome was a better place for her to pursue her studies; and he responded to the gentle hint, and due preparations were soon made, when she set out and reached the far-famed city by way of England, Nov. 12, 1852. She had been in Rome but forty-eight hours when she secured the instructions of Mr. Gibson, the first artist in the place and was soon installed in his studio, and for some time was engaged in copying. In 1855 she produced a full length figure in marble called "Œnone." Her father at this time having become somewhat pecuniarily embarrassed, could not support her expensive living in Rome, and she was therefore thrown upon her own resources, in a measure, for support; and in order to "raise the wind" or do something that might yield an immediate return, she produced "Puck," one of Shakespeare's fairies, which met with a ready sale. A companion piece, called "Will O' the Wisp" soon made its appearance and by the sale of both she was enabled to pursue her studies without anxiety. In 1857 she returned to her native shores bringing with her a well-earned reputation, to which she added on her return to Rome, by the production of "Zenobia" the Queen of Palmyra, which settled her reputation as an artist. Miss Hosmer received large offers for this work on the other side of the Atlantic, but all were refused, as she was determined it should have a place among her own countrymen. In 1860 she revisited her native land, on account of the illness of her father; and while here she received an order for a colossal statue of Thomas Hart Benton, for the city of St. Louis, which was completed in 1868. A further sketch of the career of Miss Hosmer would not be in accordance with the plan of this book. It will be sufficient to say that she is now (1879) forty nine years old; and for the last twenty seven years she has resided in Rome, diligently at work producing in marble the wonderful and beautiful conceptions of her versatile mind. Within the last fifteen years a large number of enviable works have been the offspring of her genius, equal, if not superior to those already enumerated; every one of which, adds new lustre to her wide-spread fame. Wherever art is known on either side of the Atlantic, Miss Hosmer's name stands preëminent, and she will be known to posterity as one of the most remarkable women of the nineteenth century. V. Isabella, b. Feb. 6, 1801; m. Edmund A. Marsh, of this town, and had ten children, six of whom lived to maturity. (See Marsh.) VI. Alfred, b. May 7, 1802, and learned the shoemaker's trade of John Carlisle. He soon relinquished his trade, studied medicine and became a skilfull physician. He m. Mary Ann Grahm by whom he had three children, two of whom arrived at manhood; 1st. Alfred, now a practising physician in Watertown, Mass. 2d. Elbridge, m. Ellen Makepeace, and d. Dec. 4, 1868, aged 34, leaving one child, Ethel. VII. Edwin, born Mar. 7, 1805; m. Maria, the dau. of Adams Whipple. Ch. 1st.

George Edwin, b. Dec. 12, 1836. At his majority he went to Illinois, a mere boy, and bravely faced the ordeal incident to a new settlement; but now it is said he is the owner of 11,800 acres of land in Texas, besides several hundreds in Indiana and Illinois. 2d. Helen M., b. Jan. 14, 1841; m. E. K. Seabury of this town. (See Ap.) Edwin is the only surviving member of the family, and has always resided in town; by occupation a farmer. He represented the town in the Legislature in 1843. VIII. Elbridge, b. Sept. 28, 1807; m. Faith C. Sabin and had one child. He graduated at Dartmouth College and followed teaching as a vocation. He died in Cleveland, Ohio, Sep. 14, 1852. Jonas Hosmer's first wife died in 1813, and he subsequently married Mrs. Abigail Cook, whose maiden name was Sparhawk. She died Feb. 13, 1843, aged 77. It is a singular occurrence, that in a family so large, no wrong doing has ever been imputed to one of its members.

HOWLAND, AARON PRENTISS, was a direct descendant in the sixth generation, from John Howland, who came over in the Mayflower and landed at Plymouth in 1620; whose name is the thirteenth to the compact signed on board the vessel, at which time he was 28 years old. John Howland was Lieutenant in Miles Standish's troops. He married Elizabeth, daughter of Governor John Carver, and died, Feb. 23, 1672. One of his great-great-grandchildren, John Howland, who was born Feb. 13, 1720, graduated at Harvard College, in 1741, and was ordained Sep. 24. 1746, a minister of the second church in Carver, Mass., and continued in his ministry there *fifty eight years*, until his death, which occurred Nov. 17, 1804. From an obituary notice of him, published in the newspapers at the time, it is inferred that he was a man of great force of character, distinguished for learning and piety, and well known throughout the State of Massachusetts. He left a family of eleven children: six sons and five daughters, two of whom, James and Charles, came to Walpole and settled, between 1790 and 1800; the former on a farm now owned by William W. Guild, and had two sons: James, b. Feb. 9, 1799, who died unmarried, and John, b. Dec. 19, 1795, who married

Sophia Snow, and moved to Woodstock, Vt., and had a large
family. He is still living, (1878.) John, sen. was a soldier in
the Revolutionary war and was at the surrender of Burgoyne's
army. Rev. John Howland's salary was inadequate to support and educate so large a family, hence they had to learn
trades or become farmers. Charles Howland, the father of
Aaron P., was an ingenious mechanic, a cabinet-maker by
trade; and settled in the Valley, where he lived, and died
Nov. 28, 1826, aged 62, soon after the majority of his son
Aaron P. He married Elizabeth Crease, of Boston, by whom
he had one or two children that died in infancy, and Aaron
Prentiss, who was born in 1801. His wife, Elizabeth, died May
28, 1830, aged 67. Aaron P. married Huldah Burke of Westminster, Vt., whose mother was a cousin of Silas Wright, of
New York, and who is a second cousin of Hon. Edmund
Burke of Newport, N. H. Mr. Howland was early in life
thrown upon his own resources for a livelihood, and learned
the trade of a carpenter, to which he applied himself with diligence, never letting an opportunity slip where he could turn
his labor or a penny to his advantage. Possessed of more than
ordinary natural abilities, he early commenced doing business
by contract, rather than laboring by the day for others. In
his multifarious undertakings his sound judgment was seldom
at fault. He exercised for many years a marked influence in
the affairs of the town, and was entrusted with much of its
business.   One peculiar trait in his character was that he
would work for others with as much diligence as he would for
himself. He represented the town in the General Court in
1853-4; and was United States District Assistant Assessor
during and after the war till his death, which occurred July
9, 1867. Mr. Howland's education was limited, it being only
what was obtained at our common schools, in the rural districts, seventy years ago; a matter which he keenly felt during life, and which prompted him to give his children a good
education, which was a matter of concern to him paramount
to all others during their nonage. With the Puritan religious
views of his ancestors, he was a firm pillar of support to the

Congregational church and society in town. Under different circumstances, with his native comprehensive ability, he might have achieved a name and fortune with the more highly favored of the land. But as it was, with his practical mind, by industry and economy, he left at his death a handsome property. Ch. 1st. Elizabeth, d. June 10, 1832, aged 4 years. 2d. Charles P., d. Oct. 5, 1832, aged 1 year and 11 mo. 3d. Fred I., d. June 30, 1836, aged 3 years. 4th. Henry E., b. June 30, 1845; graduated at Yale College, July 26, 1854, and studied the profession of law: m. Louise Miller, of N. Y. city, Oct. 5, 1865, and is now doing a prosperous business at 49 Nassau St., New York, under the firm name of Anderson & Howland. 5th. Alfred C., b. Feb. 12, 1838; m. Clara Ward, of N. Y. city, Jan. 26, 1871. He is a landscape painter; his headquarters are New York city. He received his professional instructions in various schools on the continent of Europe, during the American Rebellion. 6th. Katherine H. W., b. Jan. 29, 1841; m. Josiah Grahm Bellows, Esq.

HUBBARD, LEVI, came to Walpole, from Holden, Mass., in 1791, and purchased the John Kilburn farm, and was the first of the name that settled in town. He was born Feb. 24, 1764. He married Abigail Jones, who was born in Acton, Mass., Dec. 17, 1765, in 1792, when they came to Walpole to live. The old farm is still in the possession of the Hubbard family. He had nine children. I. Daniel, b. Sep. 9, 1793; m. Catharine Griffin, of Alstead, N. H., Aug. 24, 1817; d. at Walpole, Nov. 1, 1839, and left a widow, nine sons and one daughter. Ch. 1st, Leonard Clark, b. Aug. 7, 1818; m. first, Caroline, dau. of John P. Maynard, and had 4 ch.; m. second, Marion Kimball, of Saxtons River, Vt.—no issue. 2d and 3d, William and Willard, b. Sep. 21, 1821; William m. Maria Bennett, of Surry, and had one ch.; Willard, m. Elvira B. Cooke, of Rockingham, Vt.—no issue. 4th, Daniel Woodward, b. May 10, 1823; m. Lizzie Chaffin, of Acton, Mass. 5th, Catherine Elizabeth, b. July 30, 1825; m. Lewis Chaffin, of Acton, Mass.—issue 2 ch. 6th, George, b. Nov. 18, 1827; m. Maria Wright, of Weathersfield, Vt. and has 4 ch. He was the only soldier that went from

Walpole into the Mexican war. 7th, Albert, b. May 29, 1829; m. Hannah Catherine Livermore, of Alstead, and lives in Gilsum—issue 4 ch. 8th, Levi Flagg, b. Sep. 10, 1832; m. first, Hannah Maria Howe, of Brookfield, Vt., 2d, Mary Fenn, of Ludlow, Vt.—issue 2 ch. 9th, Henry Jonathan, b. Oct. 1, 1834; m. Mary Jones, of Rockingham, Vt.—no issue. 10th, Frederick James, b. Aug. 23, 1838; m. Juliette, dau. of Increase S. Guild, Jan. 10, 1859, 2 ch. (See Ap.) II. Susan, b. June 1, 1795; m. Ezra Perkins and lived in Rindge, N. H.; she d. leaving no ch. III. Matilda, b. May 22, 1797; m. George Coffin, of Acton, Mass., where they lived for some time after marriage, but subsequently removed to Chester, Vt., where they both died, leaving no issue. IV. Samuel Jones, b. Apr. 30, 1799; m. Clarissa Ann McAllister, of Lempster, N. H., and died suddenly, from injuries received by an accidental fall, on the morning of July 20, 1874. Ch. 1st, Celissa E. b. Feb. 7, 1837; m. Ashbel Stoddard, of Chesterfield, N. H. 2d, John L., b. Dec. 13, 1838; m. Frances A., dau. of David C. and Mary P. (Moore) Thompson. 3d, Oliver J., b. Mar. 17, 1843; m. Serena I. Stoddard. 4th, Mary A., b. Oct. 31, 1845, m. Leroy N. Colburn. 5th, Samuel E., b. Jan. 25, 1849; m. Jennie M. Sanders: resides in Westminster, Vt. V. Eliza, b. June 27, 1801; m. twice, and died in Ludlow, Vt., without issue. VI. Lydia, b. July 6, 1803; m. Peter Hall, of Westminster, Vt., by whom she had four ch. She is now living, a widow, in Missouri. VII. Abigail, b. Aug. 17, 1805; m. Phinehas Underwood, of Putney, Vt., and lived there till her husband died, when she married again and moved to Chester, Vt., where she died leaving no issue. VIII. Levi F., b. March 13, 1808; removed to Michigan and d. there unm. IX. Nathan W., b. Sep. 4, 1810; d. in town unm.

The Hubbard family have been characterized for industry, sobriety and frugality; seeking rather to gain an honest livelihood by industry upon the soil than to enter the whirlpool of anxiety and speculation; and, as one of the descendants writes: "So far as I have any knowledge of the Hubbards, no one of the descendants of Levi Hubbard has ever been imprisoned for any *crime* or even for *debt*, which I think speaks well for the race."

HUNTINGTON. There appear to have been two families by the name of Huntington in town, about the year 1800. The Christian name of the head of one family was Guerdon, who was postmaster here in 1802–3, and died, of consumption, July 24, 1804. His wife's Christian name was Temperance, and at her husband's death she was left with six children, who were baptized Sep. 6, 1804. Their names were as follows; I. Mary Buckingham, who m. Ephraim Brown of Westmoreland, Nov. 9th, 1806; II. Ralph Ripley; III. Elizabeth Mason; IV. Nancy Amanda; V. Joseph Morgan, and VI. Guerdon Williams. They did not remain long in town after Mr. Huntington's death. The Christian name of the head of the other family was Gamaliel, who was a brother of the foregoing and his wife's name was Katurah, they came from Windham, Conn. to Walpole, about 1780. He was b. 1761, and d. Feb. 2, 1813; she d. July 5, 1831, aged 68. The family lived, late in life, in the neighborhood of the residence of Wm. Shipman, in indigent circumstances. Ch. I. Abigail, b. 1784; d. 1848. She never married, but was long favorably known as the efficient housekeeper of her brother George, when he kept the village tavern. II. Emeline, b. 1786; d. in 1808. III. William b. 1789; m. ———. Ch. whole number not known. When the family resided in town there were two daughters and one son, George, who married Rebecca, the daughter of William Mitchell, and went west. IV. Lydia, b. 1791; d. in 1813, of spotted fever. V. Oliver, b. 1795; d. 1857. For several years he was connected in business with his brother George. In 1835, Mar. 30, he married Sophia, daughter of Ephraim Lane, when he purchased the farm on which Geo. H. Angier now resides, and lived there till he died. His children were one son, who died in youth, and three daughters, two of whom are mutes and have married mutes. VI. Laura, b. 1797, d. in 1800. VII. Levi, b. 1799; d. in infancy. VIII. George, b. 1801; d. 1876. He m. late in life, Harriet, only child of Zephaniah Kidder, by whom he had one daughter, Mary.

George commenced life at the bottom round of the ladder. His parents being poor, his early life was spent with Josiah Bellows 3d. At his majority, he had $75 which he could call his own. Soon after becoming of age he was employed as clerk, by Nathaniel Holland, in the village tavern. Mr. Holland's health failing he was obliged to sell his establishment, and Mr. Huntington was the purchaser, and in a few years was able to pay the last cent due for it. At that time the business of the house was remarkably good, it being the place where stage passengers either supped, or stopped over night. The charge for a meal at the house was thirty-three cents and was considered an *extortionary* price. He, in company with Otis Bardwell and Peletiah Armstrong, controlled all the stage routes through the place, and some others, and they were enabled to secure the transporting of the mails, nominally at their own figures. In 1837 he leased the public house to Reuben Brown, and gave his attention wholly to the staging business in which he continued till 1849–50 when the rail road was completed, and on some lateral routes, some time longer.

In middle life he was one of the most comely looking and best dressed men in town; standing six feet and more in stature, and straight as an arrow. He was early honored by his townsmen by being chosen to represent them in the State Legislature and in offices of the town. He was at one time Sheriff of the County, and later one of the directors of the Cheshire rail road, and also of one of the Keene banks. At one time his friends urged his fitness as a candidate for the National Legislature. Within a few years he was considered one of the wealthiest men in town, at which time he paid the highest tax. Late in life, when surrounded by all the comforts and conveniences, and many of the luxuries of life, and still retaining a robust constitution, he, with many others in town, went heavily into tobacco culture. Holding his crops for higher prices, and, in the meantime, purchasing of others and paying high prices, in a short time, he found himself in such pecuniary embarrassment that he was unable to extricate himself, and at his death his estate was found heavily insolvent.

Mr. Huntington was genial in nature, a kind neighbor, and a much respected citizen. IX. Elnora, baptised in 1813; m. Isaac F. Bellows, and lives in Lancaster, Mass. She has three children, George, Grace and Anna.

JENNINGS, ISAAC, was born at Holliston, Mass., Mar. 15, 1777; m. Thankful Moore, and came to Walpole, Feb. 8, 1808, and settled on the place now owned by Joseph Kidder, where he lived till his death, which occurred Oct. 18, 1851. His wife was born July 10, 1780; d. Aug. 21, 1861. Mrs. Jennings possessed a very amiable disposition, which endeared her to her immediate friends and neighbors, and which won the esteem of all her acquaintances. Ch. I. William, b. Apr. 7, 1803; d. Feb. 13, 1877. II. Mary Ann, b. Apr. 17, 1806; m. Capt. Stephen H. Darby. III. Isaac, jr., b. Mar. 17, 1808; d. Nov. 2, 1862. IV. Susan E., b. Jan. 13, 1812; m. George Watkins. (See Watkins.) V. Alonzo, b. Aug. 2, 1813; m. first, Adeliza, dau. of Alexander Watkins, jr.; second, Clarissa, dau of Charles Watkins,—issue 4 ch. VI. George, b. March 17, 1819; m. Lydia Williams—issue, 6 ch. VII. Sumner, b. Feb. 28, 1821; m. Patience Clark; d. Dec. 15, 1866.

JENNISON, ROBERT, came to this country with his brother William, and settled in Watertown, Mass., at an early date: William subsequently returned to England from whence he came; but Robert remained, and from him have descended all the numerous Jennison families in this country. John Jennison was the fourth son of Samuel, and Mary (Stearns) Jennison, and was born in Watertown, Feb. 19, 1710. He married Mary Hubbard, of Groton, Mass., born Apr. 12, 1725. She was the daughter of Maj. Jonathan and Rebecca (Brown) Hubbard. He, (Jona.) died in Lunenburg in 1751, and his widow, (Mary,) married Col. Benjamin Bellows, of Walpole. She had six children that came to Walpole with her, viz. 1st. Mary, b. Nov. 12, 1741; m. Josiah Willard, of Keene. 2d. JOHN, b. June 15, 1744, known as Capt. John; married 1st Keziah, dau. of Josiah and Catharine Spring, of Ashford, Conn; b. Oct. 21, 1745; d. April 10, 1771. His children were, I. Josiah, b. Nov. 1, 1767; married in Savannah, Ga., Apr. 22, 1792, Ann

Chamberlain.   II. Samuel, b. Aug. 29, 1769 ; m. Ruth Porter
Steele.   Capt. John married for his second wife, Sybil Bishop,
of Woodstock, Conn.; ch. III. John, jr., b. Feb. 7, 1773, and
m. Polly, dau. of Asa Gage, in 1794.   IV. Rebecca, b. Aug.
13, 1774 ; m. Elijah Kilburn. (See Kilburn.)   V.   Mary, b.
Dec. 7, 1777 ; m. Solomon Godfrey, Sep. 20, 1801, and bore
him several children. VI. William, b. Dec. 29, 1798 ; m. Phebe
Fields, an estimable woman, Dec. 14, 1804, one of twenty one
children by the same father. Ch. 1st. Edwin, b. Aug. 26, 1805 ;
m. Mary B. Shannon, by whom he had four children, two of
whom survived; (1) Edwin Shannon, who is deputy collector
of customs in Charleston, S. C.   (2) Helen, who m. ——
Adams, a cotton manufacturer, and lives in Conway, Mass.
Edwin Jennison graduated at Dartmouth, and became a Congregational clergyman; but his health became impaired and
he had to relinquish his profession, and resort to a farm in
Winchester, N. H., where he now lives. (See history of ch.)
2d, Orville, b. Mar. 17, 1808 ; m. Lucy M. Field, of Danville,
Vt., who bore him three daughters,   He now lives in Iowa, a
widower. 3d, Eliza Emma, b. Apr. 11, 1814 ; m. Charles G.
Livermore, and had four ch.—three sons and one daughter.
She now lives in Worcester, Mass. 4th, Phebe Augusta, b.
July, 1820 ; lives in Worcester, unm.   William Jennison had
two children, who died in infancy.   VII. Lucinda, b. Sep. 3,
1780 ; m. Prosper Booth, Nov. 3, 1809.   VIII. Levi, b. Dec.
13, 1781 ; m. first, Prudence, dau. of James Fuller, Sep. 27,
1813 : and second, Eliza A. Howard, of Alstead ; he lived and
died in Alstead. The number of his children is not obtained.
Capt. John Jennison, the progenitor of the foregoing race
died Oct. 16, 1804, aged 61 ; his wife, Sybil, d. Mar. 16, 1819,
aged 75.   He was the recipient of Col. Bellows' bounty to the
extent of fifty acres of land, comprising a portion of the farm
now owned by William T. Ramsey.   Previous to the time
John Jennison occupied the farm, it had been leased to Timothy Messer, who had cleared a considerable portion of it. Col.
Bellows wanted it for his step-son John, and Messer was
forced, reluctantly, to leave.   Mr. Jennison spent his days

there, when it was occupied by his son William, where he
spent the greater portion of his life in sheep husbandry.
There are none of the foregoing family remaining in town.
William Jennison died July 2, 1855; his wife May 13, 1860,
aged 77.

The third child of Mary (Jennison) Bellows died in infancy.
The fourth, Rebecca, b. 1748, d. Feb. 5, 1771. The fifth d. in
infancy, and the sixth, JONATHAN, b. Dec. 25, 1751, m. Rhoda
Ashley of Hartland, Vt. Col. Bellows gave Jonathan fifty
acres of land which was the nucleus of the farm now owned
by Edwin Hosmer, our townsman; there he settled, and remained till 1784-5 when he sold it to Deacon Jonas Hosmer,
and removed farther south, on to the farm now owned by
Chas. A. Watkins, where he lived till he died, when it was occupied by his son Thomas, and then by Thomas's son John,
and lastly by John jr. Jonathan was the progenitor of all persons bearing the name of Jennison remaining in town to-day
(1879.) Jonathan's children were, I, and II, girls by the name
of Nabby. III. Jonathan jr., b. 1775, m. Danae Danham. Ch.
1st, Harry, b. Nov. 28, 1800; m. Harriet Fay, of this town,
and had children, one of whom, Josiah, is living in town, (See
Ap.) 2d, Levi Durham, b. Aug. 11, 1802. 3d, Luraney, b. Apr.
27, 1807; m., late in life, David C. Thompson. 4th, Rhoda, b.
Dec. 23, 1808. 5th, Horace Allen, b. Jan. 11, 1801. IV.
Thomas b. 1776, m. Martha Moore. Ch. 1st, Thomas Moore,
b. Nov. 18, 1805; m. Fanny A. Hixon, Feb. 21, 1839. 2d,
John, b. June 14, 1807; m. Elvira, dau. of Thomas Russell.
Ch. (1) Geo. R., b. Jan. 13, 1834, m. Emily, twin dau. of Geo.
Sparhawk, and resides in town. (2) Wm. White, b. Aug. 31,
1835, died early. (3) John jr., b. Oct. 4, 1837; m. Mary E.
Grout of Westminster, Vt.; died Nov. 29, 1875. (4) David A.,
b. Jan. 28, 1838; m. Laura Brockway, of Rockingham, Vt.
(5) Charles H., b. Aug. 28, 1839. He was in the war of the
Rebellion, lives at the West. (6) Mary E., b. Mar. 3d, 1842;
m. Frank George, of Bellows Falls. (7) Warren H., b. Mar.
28, 1848. (8) Frank R., b. Dec. 31, 1847; m. Lydia Mills and
lives at the West. V Nabby, b. Mar. 22, 1778; she lived in

town, unmarried, to old age, and d. Jan. 28, 1870. VI. Martin, b. June 30, 1799; went south. VII. Rhoda, b. Sep. 3, 1780, m. Pliny Bliss, June 4, 1812, and moved west. VIII. Daniel, b. Nov. 3, 1782; he was a physician and settled in Hartland, Vt. IX. Charles, b. a year or two later, what became of him is not known. 3d, Daniel Ashley, b. Sep. 3, 1808; went to the state of New York. 4th, Mary Holland, b. June 5, 1813, m. Oct. 21, 1838, John W. Lovejoy, of Littleton, N. H., and is still living. 5th, George Charles, b. Oct. 4, 1818; still living in Philadelphia, Penn. There was a Mary that died July 28, 1811, aged 1 year. Jonathan Jennison sen., d. Sep. 11, 1835, aged 84.

JOHNSON, ISAAC. There was a man, who lived, and owned a large farm, in the early settlement of the town, somewhere in district No. 5 or 9, by the name of Isaac Johnson, whose wife's name was Mary. He was an early member of parson Fessenden's church, and was in the habit of taking too much "*overjoyful.*" (See ch. his.) He had a large family who were baptized by the parson and among the number was one whose name was *Stephen*, who was baptized in 1773; five years after the birth of Dr. Stephen Johnson; he, also, had a grandson, Stephen, who was baptized in 1788. The Johnsons suddenly disappear from the various records belonging to the town, and it is supposed they went away. It is claimed by the descendants of the Johnson family that the Doctor, whose history follows, came from Connecticut, which might be the case, and still the Stephen baptized in 1773 might be one and the same person. It is, however, a matter wholly hypothetical. He might have been born in town and left when the Johnson family did, to return to his native town as Dr. Stephen Johnson.

DR. STEPHEN JOHNSON came to town about 1790, a full-fledged physician, from Connecticut. No knowledge has been gained of the place where he was educated, nor with whom he studied. He commenced practice with Drs. George Sparhawk, Jesseniah Kittredge, sen., and Abraham Holland as competitors. He was married, Dec. 31, 1793, to Persis,—or Percy,— the oldest child of Col. Christopher Webber by his wife Han-

nah. He spent the remainder of his life in town, and d. Jan.
29, 1836, aged 68. She d. April 6, 1846, aged 78. His farm
and home were in dist. No. 5, a few rods north of the residence
of David C. Thompson. His practice could not have been
large, although the services of a physician were more frequently
required in those days than at present. From accounts given
of him by those who knew him personally his character was a
strange compound of gentleness and the opposite—winning at
one time with smiles, and repulsing at another with frowns.
His wife was highly esteemed by her friends and neighbors for
gentleness of character and good sense; but her patience was
sorely tried at times, by the unreasonable demands of her husband, whom she had done her best to please. He would, at
times, when his services were required at a distant part of the
town, in unpleasant weather, severely berate the messenger, and
declare he would not go; but no sooner would the words escape
his mouth than he would order his horse brought to the door.
It is related of him that he kept a large number of geese, which,
together with their goslings, in summer, made his door yard
their head-quarters, and sorely annoyed him. One day he told
his hired man that he would pay him twenty-five cents for every
gosling's head he would chop off, not thinking he would do it;
but, hearing an unusual clamor among his geese, he stepped to
the door, and found his man making brisk work at decapitation,
when he immediately broke his engagement, and paid the man
for four heads he had already severed. His family consisted of
only five children : I. Maria, b. Apr. 13, 1795; m. Capt. Stephen
Tiffany, Oct. 18, 1818; d. Mar. 1, 1872. II. Sally A., b. Jan. 18,
1797; d. unm., Dec. 14, 1845. III. Stephen Sumner, b. Apr. 18,
1801; m. Content B., dau. of Israel Wightman, of this town, Apr.
23, 1823. Ch. 1st, Frederick, d. in infancy. 2d, Eliza Ann,
b. 1828; m. Elijah Holbrook, of Surry, and removed to Wis-
consin. 3d, William Herman, lawyer in N. Y. city, b. July 12,
1833; m. first, Sarah, dau. of Benjamin Gates, of this town;
ch., Grace E., Edward S., Wm. G.; m. second, S. Jennie, dau.
of Wait Chatterton, Rutland; ch. Wait C. and Stanley M.
4th, Percy W., b. 1830; d. March 4, 1849. 5th, Stephen, was a

merchant at Keene, b. 1836 ; m. dau. of John Draper, in 1863 ; d. May, 1869. 6th, Fanny, b. 1834 ; m. George H. Babbitt, and lives at Bellows Falls. 7th and 8th, George, d. in infancy, and Henry, m. Ella Uptegraph, Mt. Vernon, Ill., and res. there. 9th, John, b. Aug. 9, 1841 ; m. Augusta, dau. of Erastus Hines, Rochester, N. Y., is a physician in N. Y. city. IV. Frederick, b. July 16, 1804 ; d. July 16, 1825 ; He was a physician. V. Percy, b. Oct. 25, 1808 ; m. Alpheus Clark, had one son, Frederick and died Jan. 9, 1829.

KIDDER NEHEMIAH.—The Kidders are an old family in this country, and many of them have been highly honorable and distinguished in the walks of civil live. The branch of the family of which the following account is given came from England to this country at an early date, at the same time the Kittredge family came. The first that is known of them is that a Mr. and Mrs. Kidder (Christian names not given,) and their children,—two sons, Nehemiah and Lemuel, and a daughter,—lived in Tewksbury, Mass. Nehemiah, m. Abigail, dau. of Dr. Francis Kittredge, and first settled in Tewksbury, but subsequently came to this town, in 1788, soon after the Kittredge family came. She died at the time of the birth of her ninth child, Amy, who was born Dec. 18, 1789, and was cared for by her uncle, Dr. Jesseniah Kittredge. (See David Mead.) Nehemiah and Abigail's other children were I. Hepsibeth, m. Reuben Fay, of this town, and settled in Windham, Vt., where they lived and died. II. Abigail, m. Asa Stowell, of Rockingham, Vt. III. Ducy, m. John Hardy, of Tewksbury, Mass. IV. Polly, m. Joseph Bundy, of this town. V. Joseph, went to Pottstown, Me. VI. Nehemiah, went to Nashua, N. H. VII. Susanna, m. David Searles, of Maine. VII. Zephaniah, m. Mary, dau. of Ephraim Stearns, and had one dau., Harriet W., who m. George Huntington, Sept. 5, 1854. IX. Abiah, b. Sept. 14, 1786 ; m. Achsah Winchester, b. Aug. 1, 1787 ; m. June 10, 1808. Ch. 1st, Abiah jr., b. Oct. 10, 1808 ; m. Emily Fuller, and settled first in Walpole, but subsequently removed to Belmont. His first wife died, and he married Mary A. Sleeper, of Belmont, Mass. He was one of the ministers,

it is said the third, who preached in the Hollow. 2d, Achsah,
b. Dec. 5, 1809; m William Wellington, of this town. (See
Wellington.) 3d, Jesseniah K., b. June 26, 1811; m. first,
Mellicent Pratt, of this town; second, Harriet L. Howard, of
East Andover, N. H. 4th, Mary W., b. July 11, 1822; m.
Clark Hubbard, of this town. Her husband came to a melan-
choly end. About 1845 he was dangerously sick of typhoid
fever, and was in a state of delirium at a house that stands, or
did stand, some three-fourths of a mile east of the Valley
school house. The attending physician had recently given
him a large dose of calomel. A man by the name of Prouty
had the care of him, but he eluded the vigilance of Mr. Prouty,
in an unguarded moment, and ran from the house in a westerly
direction, being immediately pursued by Mr. Prouty, who was
unable to overtake him, so that he soon found his way into a
large body of woodland lying west of the Starkweather place,
and was soon out of sight. Mr. Prouty immediately notified
the neighbors, who at once turned out *en masse* in pursuit of
him. The day passed, and no tidings of his whereabouts were
obtained. The next day a large proportion of the male population of the north part of the town went in search, but their
humane efforts came to naught. The pursuit was kept up for
several days by squads in different sections of the town till,
finally, as no trace of him was discovered, the pursuit was
abandoned. A year or two afterwards Mr. I. F. Bellows, in
looking after some stray sheep near the little brook at the head
of Newton's pond, discovered a *skull* near the path he was
traveling, and on turning it over it seemed to be that of a
human being. His feelings were greatly excited on such a
discovery, and, on looking about, the entire skeleton of an adult
person was seen on the bank a few feet distant, *minus* the head.
The proper authorities were soon notified, and suspicion was
entertained by them that the remains were those of Hubbard.
When he escaped he had on his pantaloons, vest, and stockings,
which his wife recognized as those worn by her husband;
when his bones were removed and decently buried. The position in which the bones were found indicated that he died in a

sitting posture with his left arm thrown around two sapling hemlocks. 4th, Elvira, b. April 23, 1816; d. young. 5th, Moses, b. Nov. 14, 1817; m. Laura W. Haven, and is a preacher of considerable celebrity in Woodstock, Vt. 6th, Elvira, 2d, b. Mar. 6, 1821; m. Seth Ross, of Walpole. 7th, Julia A., b. Oct. 29, 1823; m. George Sabin, formerly of Westmoreland. 8th, Joseph, b. July 26, 1825; m. first, Caroline Tuttle, of this town, and second, her sister Susan, with whom he now lives in town. 9th, Emily J., b. Oct. 30, 1829; d. in infancy.

KILBURN, JOHN.—The name of Kilburn is found among the names of English nobility back as far as the time of Chaucer, and the line of descent can be directly traced from that time to the present. The name is spelt in different ways by the old English families, as well as in this country, but the sound is the same. Kilburn, Kilborn, Kylburne, Kilberne, Kilborne, are some of the various ways the name is found spelled. The origin of the name is the same. The name is made up from two words, *Keele* and *Bourn*, which signify, the former, cold, and the latter, water,—*cold water.* The coincidence of the names of the first settlers of this town meaning about the same thing is very singular; *Belle Eau*, pluralized, meaning beautiful waters, and *Keele Bourn*, meaning cold water or cold stream.

Thomas Kilburn, the ancestor of all the Kilburns in this country, came over from England in 1635, bringing with him his wife and five children. John, therefore, belonged to the fifth generation of Kilburns in this country. He was born in Glastonbury, Conn., in 1704; was residing in Springfield, Mass., in 1725. On the 26th of October, 1732, he was married in Middletown, Conn., to Mehitable, daughter of Andrew and Mehitable Bacon. Ch. I. Mary, b. in Middletown, Nov. 12, 1733. II. Mehitable, b. Feb. 16, 1734,5. III. John, jr., b April 1, 1736. IV. Mary, m. 1756, to Noah Smith, of Hadley, afterwards of Brattleboro, Vt. The first wife of John Kilburn d. in Glastonbury, Conn., in 1737. His second wife was Hannah Fox, of Glastonbury, Conn.; she d. Jan. 1, 1807, aged 84.

Mr. Kilburn became the first settler in Walpole in 1749. He

removed to Springfield, Vt., but subsequently returned to Walpole and died here. Capt. John came to Walpole with his father, and married Miss Content Carpenter, the daughter of Rev. Ezra Carpenter, of Swanzey, N. H., March 10, 1762. He resided in Walpole till the winter of 1793, when he removed to Shrewsbury, Vt., at which place he died July 20, 1819, aged 83. His wife died Oct. 22, 1813, aged 73. Ch. 1st, Theodosia, b. May 10, 1763; d. Jan. 23, 1766. 2d, John, Esq., b. Aug. 30, 1765; m. Anna Ashby, of Shrewsbury, Vt., where he settled. He removed to Canton, N. Y., and died there in 1847, aged 82. He had five children. 3d, Theodosia, 2d, b. Dec. 23, 1768; m. Martin Ashley, of Shrewsbury, Vt., Aug. 15, 1787. 4th, Ezra C., b. Sept. 30, 1772; m. Sarah, the widow of Samuel Graves, whose maiden name was Clark, and had a daughter, Esther, in 1807. He d. in Keene, N. H., in 1853. 5th, Elijah, b. Sept. 30, 1772; m. Rebecca Jennison, dau. of John and Sybil Jennison, in 1798. He d. in town in 1847; she d. in 1849. Ch. (1) Harriet, b. in 1799, in Walpole, where all of his nine children were born. She d. in 1830, unm. (2) Mary H., b. in 1801; m. Noah Smith, July 15, 1825; resided, at last accounts, in the town of Russell, N. Y. (3) Josiah, b. in town; m. Emily Bonney, of Littleton, N. H., where he settled and still resides. He was elected a member of the New Hampshire legislature in 1842-3. He had three children, viz., Benjamin West, Emily, and Edward. (4) George, b. in 1803; m. Laura, dau. of Salmon and Rebecca (Foster) Hooper, Dec. 18, 1825. He commenced business in this town as a carpenter and master builder, and carried on a considerable business, employing a large number of workmen. From some cause he was unable to proceed with his business so as to leave a margin of profits to himself, and a suspension of business became necessary about 1840. He left town owing many people a considerable amount of money, being willing but unable to pay his creditors. He removed to Fall River, Mass., where he obtained employment and remunerative pay. He remained at Fall River several years, but subsequently removed to Lonsdale, R. I., where he was for a number of years superintendent of the Lonsdale Cotton

Manufactory and Bleaching Co. He is now well advanced in years, and has retired from active participation in business. Within a few years he has paid a portion of his old debts in Walpole, being under no other than a moral obligation to do so. Such acts are highly creditable. His income has been very large in Lonsdale, and it is supposed he has an ample competency of this world's goods laid by for all his future wants. (5) John, b. in 1808; m. Maria E. Gage and settled in Fall River, Mass., where he died Dec. 4, 1846. His children are Louisa R., Edward J., Maria, Charles, and Helen. (6) Frederick, b. April 4, 1809; m. Mary Ann, dau. of Alexander and Mary (Sherman) Watkins, June 29, 1825. She was b. Dec. 3, 1813. They lived for several years in Littleton, N. H., where he was at one time one of the selectmen. He removed back to his native town several years since, and was honored by representing the town in the General Court in 1858-9. He is a carpenter by trade, although a portion of his life has been spent in farming. He was engaged for several years in setting "turbine" water wheels in various mills and factories about the country. He has four children living. (7) Elijah C., b. in 1811; m. Hannah S. Carter, of Wayland, Mass. He at one time owned the Major Jennison farm in this town. He sold out and removed to Fall River in 1847. During his stay in Walpole he was highly esteemed as a citizen, and his removal was much regretted. He represented the town in the legislature in 1846. He is a machinist, doing business under the style of E. C. Kilburn & Co. It is understood that prosperity has smiled on his efforts in Fall River till within a short period. (8) Rebecca, b. in 1815; m. Rodney Smith, Oct. 20, 1841. (9) William J., b. Sep. 21, 1818, settled in Augusta, Me,, where he was for many years engaged as a wholesale merchant, in dry goods, in the house of William J. Kilburn & Co. He was a member of the Common Council of the city of Augusta, in 1851-2. He subsequently removed to Keene, N. H., and established himself in trade there. 6th, Elizabeth, b. Feb. 3, 1776, m. Willard Colby, of Shrewsbury, Vt. They both died many years ago. 7th, Esther, b. Oct. 12, 1788; m. Daniel Robinson, of Massena, N. Y., Feb. 21, 1864.

KITTREDGE, FRANCIS, DR. It is curious to note how some incident, seemingly trivial at the time, and wholly disconnected with what follows, changes the whole aspect and condition of an individual's future life. Following is a case in point. More than a hundred years ago, (the precise time not known,) one of the Bellows family of this town broke his leg, and as surgeons were not plenty in the vicinity, his friends were forced to the alternative of sending to Tewksbury, Mass., to procure one. There they found Dr. Francis Kittredge, who came to Walpole, set the bone, and stayed till his patient was out of danger. During his stay, he was persuaded to take up a lot of land and remove to Walpole. He selected the farm now owned by Charles E. Watkins, which was then an unbroken forest. He had by his wife, Abigail, sixteen children, several of them dying in infancy. Dr. Frank, as he was called, was a celebrated " bone setter," which in those days was a *special* gift. In connection with his son Jesseniah, the celebrated salve, known at the time as " Kittridge grease, " was prepared, which was highly valued for its supposed healing properties. He was famous, as was also his son, Jesseniah, in treatment of old sores and chronic complaints in general. How many of Dr. Frank's children were born in town has not been ascertained nor how many lived to maturity. Their ages are not known, and consequently cannot be methodically arranged. He died April 17, 1808, aged 80 years and she died Feb. 15, 1812, aged 82. Ch. I. Stephen, b. 1765; m. Elizabeth Eaton, May 16, 1791; d. July 25, 1800. He was a physician, probably studied with his father. His ch. were 1st, Stephen jr., b. Oct. 3, 1791: became a doctor and went to Cincinnati and died early. 2d, Roswell, b. May 8, 1793; who also was a physician, and went West, and died young. 3d, Betsey, b. Dec. 24, 1794. 4th, Sukey, b. Dec. 5, 1795. 5th, Ebenezer Eaton, b. Feb. 3, 1799. He studied medicine and went to Louisiana and became owner of a large sugar plantation, and accumulated a colossal fortune. He was alive at the commencement of the Rebellion, but has since died. II. Paul, was a physician, m. Rebecca Martin in 1809, and settled in Chelmsford, Mass. He had one child, Paul Crosby, who was b. here April 7, 1809. III. Francis, a physician, who m. Sybil Bundy in 1806, and settled in Woburn, Mass. IV. Rhoda, m. Amaziah Porter in 1789, and lived in Langdon. V. Achsah, m. Job Giddings in 1794 lived in town and had four or more children. VI. Molly, m. Robert Earl in 1796. VII. name unknown, m. a Crosby and died in town. VIII. Elizabeth, m. Amos Godfrey, of Westminster, Mar. 13, 1803. IX. Abigail, m. Nehemiah Kidder, the progenitor of the Kidders in this town. X. Mrs. Beckwith; XI. Jesseniah, b. 1764; m. Lydia, dau. of Thomas Bond, of Brookfield, Mass. This is the Dr. Jesseniah who built the house now standing on the old Kittredge homestead and was the father of a large family belonging to the generation preceding the one now on the stage. He seemed to have a prophetic vision of the future wants of coming generations, when he made architectural beauty subordinate to magnitude of proportions, which has since been realized in the shelter of two large families since the Kittredge family left it.

The Dr. was a lame man, and he used to ride in an old-fashioned two wheel carriage, in the summer, to make professional visits, which the inhabitants called a *quill wheel*. The old carriage was recently in possession of Elias W. Knowlton. His old bells that he used in winter, which could be distinctly heard a mile, were recently in the possession of some of our townsmen. He had an extensive practice although he lived contemporaneously with doctors Sparhawk, Holland and Johnson.

His children were 1st. Sally, b. April 27, 1794; she never married. 2d, Lydia, b. April 29, 1796; m. Francis Fisher, a commission merchant of Boston. 3d, Jesseniah, b. Feb. 24, 1800. He studied medicine with his father, and, after completing his professional studies, commenced practice in his native town, which he continued uninterruptedly for more than forty years, when the infirmities of age and other reasons caused him to relinquish it. He moved first to Keene, and subsequently to Belmont, Mass., where he lived with his daughter

Helen, till he died, in 1877. He was conscious of his coming dissolution and watched the ebbing tide with interest and calmness. From time to time, as the sand in the glass told the passing hour, he would feel of his pulse and remark the probable time he could live, and continued to do so until he became unconscious. The Dr. was for a long time a mason, attaining to a high position in the craft, on account of his historic knowledge in masonry and his social standing. In the temperance cause he was an exemplary pattern, never having drunk a glass of intoxicating liquor, as a beverage, in his life-time. In 1851 he represented the town in the legislature and for a score or more of years was town treasurer. In his daily intercourse with his neighbors, he was genial and talkative; as a physician he was careful and attentive, and his exemplary life made him honored by his peers and respected by the young. He married Mary B., daughter of Leonard Stone, of Watertown, Mass., by whom he had five children. (1) Thomas, who died in China. (2) Helen, who m. David A. Russell. (3) Sarah, who m. Lewis J. Colony, and (4) Samuel, who m. Harriet, dau. of Milan Harris. 4th, Thomas Bond, b. Feb. 17, 1802; m. Caroline A., dau. of Moses Smith, Hartford, Conn. He graduated at Harvard, studied medicine with his father and Dr. Moses Hale, of Troy, N. Y. He attended lectures in Boston and took his diploma in 1826, and commenced practice in Claremont, N. H., but for the last twenty nine years has resided in Keene, and has been a pension examining surgeon since 1863. He has three children, two sons, Asahel S. and Henry G.; his daughter's name is Jessie. 5th, Eli Bond, b. Aug. 2, 1804; d. in 1825. He was a promising medical student at the time of his death. 6th, Millicent, b. Sep. 16, 1806; m. Leonard Bisco. (See Bisco.)

KNAPP, JACOB NEWMAN, one of our most highly esteemed, adopted townsmen, was born in Newburyport, Mass., Nov. 7, 1773, and died at his home in this town, July 27, 1868, being at the time of his death in his ninety-fifth year. He was the second of nine children, of poor,' but respectable parents, who were unwearied in their efforts to advance the educational in-

terests of their children. Their whole library consisted of the
Bible, Josephus, Shakspeare, and a few pamphlet sermons.
Early in life Jacob attended the town schools, where for ten
years he studied the spelling-book, the Psalter, and the Bible,
and received instruction in writing and ciphering. Of the incidents in connection with his early school life he had to the last a
most vivid recollection, a rehearsal of which would fill pages.
In his seventeenth year he commenced teaching, a business
which he followed through his active life. The wages of teaching in those days, were six dollars a month in addition to board.
His first school was in Loudon, N. H., and consisted of forty
pupils of both sexes, and all ages. The urchins under ten, wore
long leather aprons, which shone with the smearing of bean porridge, and the little girls took snuff because it was the fashion.
The next summer he started in pursuit of another school, with
all his worldly goods tied up in a handkerchief, and after travelling four days, found a situation in Sanbornton, N. H., where
he continued four years, the idol of the place. He next entered Philips Academy, Andover. He did not think at first,
of fitting for college, but was persuaded to begin Latin, and,
being appointed writing master in the Academy, was enabled
to remain. Just at the time of completing his preparation for
college, a schoolmate of his, Cassius Lee, of Va., died, who
bequeathed him fifty guineas, by the aid of which he entered
Harvard; and by transcribing college documents, teaching
winters, and a loan of two hundred dollars, managed to pass
through his four years course, and honorably graduate in 1802.
After graduating, he immediately resumed teaching in the
town school of Charlestown, Mass., and at the same time commenced to study theology with Dr. Jedediah Morse. Having
studied three years, he then preached a while in Salem and
Boston, but never with a view to settlement. In 1803 he took
charge of a private, boys' school, in Salem, and continued
there ten years, being highly respected. His health being impaired, he thought to regain it by making a trip west on horseback, and on his return, with health renewed, he opened a home
school for boys, in Brighton, and four years later removed it to

Jamaica Plains, where he taught, fitting young men for college, till 1824, when he removed to this, the native town of his wife, where he ever afterwards lived. His teaching must have been lucrative, for, during his life as a teacher, he not only helped his parents to needed comforts and two of his brothers to a liberal education, but saved a competency for himself. Mr. Knapp, although educated in the severe religious doctrines of a century ago, did not cling to them in mature life. After coming to Walpole, it is said, he sowed the seeds of Unitarianism, which ere long ripened into a church, on the ministration of which he was a constant attendant and an ever ready supporter. He never sought, or held any public office, but his natural and acquired ability would have honored any position within the gift of the people. In stature Mr. Knapp was above the medium, with no flesh to spare. He always dressed in a neat and comely fashion, usually wearing a white necktie, believing that cleanliness was next to Godliness. His language was always pure, consise, and strictly grammatical. Occasionally he would make some remarks in public meetings, and at such times the eyes and ears of all were attentive. In his last years, when it would seem the fountain of life was well nigh dry, he seemed to manifest a lively interest in the world's progress. He was like a sturdy old oak, its leaves remaining green when all others had faded and gone, reluctant to yield its foliage to winter's stormy blast. He retained his faculties to the last, not even losing his Latin, as the following instance will show. On the occasion of his son's offering him a little light wine, a few hours before he died, he asked, "What is it?" "Hock," was the reply. "*Hic, hæc, hoc*," said he, slowly moving his hand as if waving off the glass, "I thus decline it." Taking him for all in all the town will not soon look upon his like again. In his death the town lost a valued citizen, and the church to which he belonged a strong pillar of support. He married June 3, 1819, Louisa, daughter of Joseph Bellows, sen., by whom he had two sons; I. Francis Bellows, born in Roxbury, Mass., May 29, 1820; graduated at Harvard in 1843, and studied for the ministry ; but chose subsequently to relinquish the profes-

sion, and pursue the occupations of farmer and teacher.
Recently he has been engaged in translating an Icelandic work
from Latin into English. He lives, unmarried, at the family
homestead much of the time. II. Frederick Newman, b. Nov.
19, 1821; graduated at Harvard College the same year as his
brother, and also studied for the Unitarian ministry. He married Lucia Alden, dau. of Rev. Claudius and Maria Bradford,
of Montague, Mass., May 9, 1855. He has four ch., one dau.
and three sons. He was first settled as colleague of Dr. Pierce,
of Brookline, Mass. During the late war he early and enthu-
siastically rendered efficient service in the U. S. Sanitary Commission, being the superintendent of the Special Relief Department, and associate secretary of the Eastern Department.
After the close of the war, he was settled over the first church
in Plymouth, Mass., which pastorate he held for several years.
He now has charge of a Home School for boys, in Plymouth,
which has been established for several years.

KNOWLTON, LUTHER, came to Walpole from Framingham,
Mass., in 1800, and purchased, of one James Knapp, the place
on which his son Elias Ward now lives, where he spent his
days. He married Prudence Dadman and had five children.
I. Paulina, b. Nov. 1, 1801; d. Aug, 30, 1831, unm. II. Eu-
nice, b. Mar. 8, 1803, m. Mark Webster, Jan. 3, 1832; Ch. 1st,
Eliza, m. Franklin O. Pierce, who died a few years after. 2d,
Ezra, m. Victoria Willson, of Gilsum. 3d, Edwin E., m. Emily Upham of Westminster, Vt. 4th, Augusta, m. Ira Blake, of
Surry. 5th, Henry. 6th, Franklin P., m. Augusta Ziminer of
Norwich, Conn. III. Luther D., b. Apr. 6, 1806; m. Mary
Ann Derby, of Dublin, N. H., Feb. 14, 1832, who was b. May,
17, 1808, and died Dec. 1866. Ch. 1st, Ellen, m. Oliver Hall,
(see Hall.) 2d, Clinton. 3d, Albertine, both of whom d. early.
IV. Charles, b. Mar. 8, 1809. V. Elias Ward, b. Oct. 8th,
1811, m. Margaret Cannon, Sep. 3d, 1844. Ch. 1st, Francis E.,
d. young. 2d, Mary J.; 3d, Lucy E.; 4th, Chauncy E., m. Susan G., daughter of Andrew Roy, Apr. 3, 1878; 5th, Henry
W. Elias Ward's wife died and he married, the second time,

June 28, 1859, Emeline W. Foster, by whom he has two ch., 1st, Edward A., 2d, Warren D. (For ages see Ap.)

LANE, EPHRAIM, was born in Bedford, Mass., Mar. 22, 1767. Soon after his majority he wended his way to this town, on foot, with a pack strapped to his back and stopped over night at the tavern of Alexander Watkins. Here he made inquiry for mill property, for sale, and was told of the property afterwards known as "Lane's Mills" which he purchased in about 1790, of one Graves. Soon after he returned to Massachusetts, and married Elizabeth Danforth, of Dracut, and came back to Walpole and commenced married life in a little house that once stood just north of the residence of Mrs. George Joslin. For a few years he lived in various places till at length he purchased the little farm where Chas. B. Hall now lives and there he remained till his death, which occurred Aug. 15, 1837. For several years he followed milling for a business, till he had accumulated by industry and frugality the nucleus of his subsequent gains. His education was necessarily limited; but he early learned that one hundred cents make one dollar, which many of our college educated young men learn too late, if at all. He was for many years the monied man in town and loaned it at a high rate of interest, and in this way, and by tilling his small farm, and practising rigid economy, he brought up a family of nine children, and left a handsome sum at his death. His wife was a highly estimable woman, posssessing all the womanly virtues, and although schooled to prudence and economy in her younger days, she was ever ready to help the needy and destitute. In her girlhood she passed through the fiery ordeal of poverty and want. She worked out as a servant girl for *twenty-five* cents per week, and was paid in flax which she spun into fine thread and sold to the gentry to work into lawns. In that way she procured money to purchase her scanty wardrobe. Think of this, you damsels, who complain of $10 per week wages. He had seven girls who all made model housewives and six of them good mothers. They have all lamented the want of sufficient educational advantages in their youth; but their father, thinking their advantages supe-

rior to his, could not be made to see the propriety of a better
education than was obtained at our common schools in those
early days. Ch. I. Rebecca, b. Apr. 7, 1798; m. David Pulsipher, of Rockingham, Vt., Mar. 15, 1815, and had nine children, one of whom, Mrs. William Hooper, is the only one of
the family now living. II. Susan, b, Oct. 1st, 1796; m. Elias
Pulsipher of Rockingham, Jan. 30, 1720, and had 4 ch. III.
Betsey, b. Jan. 25, 1799; m. Horace Reynolds, of Putney Vt.,
and had two children, one son and one dau. IV. Mary, b. Sep.
3, 1801; m. James Hooper jr., Jan. 19, 1826. (See Hooper.)
V. George, b. Nov. 25. 1802; m. first, Sarah, dau. of Hugh
Dunshee, Apr. 4, 1831; m., second, a Miss Houghton, of Coventry, Vt., and had children by both wives. He died 1878.
VI. Phebe, b. Jan. 22, 1806: m. Chester Wier, of this town,
Mar. 3, 1829. He died Jan. 22, 1837, aged 33; she still sur-
vives him in widowhood. They had four children, two died
young, the others, Julia and Henry lived to adult age. Julia
m. Thomas Seaver who died a few years after their marriage;
she died in 1878. VII. Sophia, b. July, 10, 1808; m. Oliver
Huntington, Mar. 30, 1835. (See Huntington.) VIII. Almira, b.
Jan. 8, 1811; m. Charles Hooper. (See Hooper.) IX. Lewis, b.
Apr. 22, 1813; m. Mary P., dau. of Elisha and Sally (Russell)
Angier, Oct. 27, 1841; issue, two sons. They reside in Keene.

LATHROP, HOPE, was born in Tolland, Conn., about 1799.
In his youth he learned the plater's trade, in Westminster, Vt.,
and removed to Drewsville, N. H., in 1819, where he followed
that business a few years. He was appointed deputy sheriff,
soon after he came to Drewsville, and held the office for some
time, while he also kept a hotel at the same place. He was one
of the directors of the Connecticut River Bank at Charlestown
for a long period, and was president of that institution at the
time of his death. For a number of years he was postmaster
at Drewsville, and a merchant at the same time. He was a man
of more than ordinary intellectual ability, to which were added
indomitable energy and persistency of character; he was cau-
tious and sagacious in his business transactions, and, making
the accumulation of wealth a paramount object of attainment,

he succeeded in amassing a large property from a humble beginning. He married, first, Fanny, dau. of John Cooper, of Alstead, by whom he had three daughters : I. Sarah E. B., m. Bolivar Lovell. (See Lovell.) II. Lucia A., m. Norman Farr, of Bellows Falls, Vt., and resides there. III. Fanny, d. in infancy. Mr. Lathrop's wife died June 4, 1837, and he married, second, Sarah E., widow of Joseph Bond, M. D., and daughter of Thomas C. Drew, of Drewsville. (See Drew.) Mr. Lathrop died Dec. 31, 1878, under the following lamentable circumstances. As he was going to Charlestown on business, driving his own team, in crossing the Vermont Central railroad track, or being upon it, near the Peter Evans house, he came in collision with the engine of the mixed downward train, and received such injuries as to cause his death in about five hours, in the mean time lying in an unconscious state. His kindred were immediately summoned and were present at his death.

LAWRENCE, OZIAS, came to Walpole in 1813, from Franklin, Mass., where he was born, and settled on the place where Clement Dickey now resides. He married Mary Fisher, of Medway, Mass., and had children as follow : I. Polly, m. Calvin Messenger, of Grafton, Vt. II. Anson, b. in Franklin, Feb. 14, 1799; m. Sally, dau. of Ebenezer and Sally (Sheldon) Ash, and had ch. as follow: 1st, Mary S., b. Nov. 28, 1822; m. Lorenzo Dow Pressy, 1844, and has one son, Eugene E., m. Maria Mason, of Keene, and lives in town. 2d, Sarah L., b. June 30, 1826; d. young. 3d, George F., b. Dec. 5, 1827; m. Lydia Warren, of Lawrence, Mass., and resides in Worcester, Mass. 4th, William A., b. Oct. 18, 1829; m. Emma Wells, of Portland, Me.; lives in Newtonville, Mass. 5th, Solon C., b. April 9, 1831; d. in Illinois, 1856. 6th, Lowell A., b. Feb. 16, 1834; d. 1850. 7th, Henry F., b. Sept. 16, 1837 ; m Amy E., dau. of Charles and Amy (Sherman) Watkins, Nov. 9, 1859. (See Ap.) 8th, Leonard W., b. Sept. 30, 1840; d. in the U. S. service at the hospital in Philadelphia, March 23, 1862. III. Fisher, b. 1806; m. at Claremont, N. H. He was a musician in the service of the United States when he died. Ozias Law-

rence d. Aug. 21, 1826; his wife d. March 29, 1852.   Anson
Lawrence d. March 25, 1864.

LINCOLN, CHRISTOPHER, was born in Hingham, Mass., Nov.
8, 1779; came to this town about 1820, and established himself
in the tailoring business here.   He was a descendant of Daniel
Lincoln, who came from Hingham, Eng., in 1643, and settled
in Hingham, Mass., in the following line of descent: 1st,
Daniel, jr., 2d, Joshua, 3d, Joshua, jr., 4th, Christopher.   He
lived in town about ten years, and came to his death when
returning from Keene, with others, where he had been as a
juryman in a capital case, by being thrown from a wagon, on
the hill east of William Arnold's, Oct. 11, 1830, when he
received such injuries that he died the 18th of the same month.
He married Eliza, dau. of John Williston, of Boston, Mass.,b.
Dec. 10, 1785, by whom he had eleven children: 1. Christopher
C., d. young. II. Samuel W., b. June 12, 1808; resides in
Quincy, Mass., unm. III. Eliza A., b. June 16, 1810; d. Dec.
30, 1866. IV. Christopher, 2d, d. young. V. Eleanor, d. young.
VI. Mary J., b. June 15, 1815; m. James N. White, of Boston,
—issue, two ch. VII. Harriet N., b. Jan. 14, 1818. VIII.
George C., b. July 9, 1821; m. first, Miranda Evans, Windsor,
Vt.; m. second, Anna Leach, and has six ch. IX. Sarah M.,
b. April 5, 1823; m. Griffin C. Reynolds, res., Abbington,
Mass.,—issue, two ch. X. Charles Sprague, b. April 20, 1826;
m. Louisa E. Plimpton, and has five ch. He fitted for college,
it is said, after his majority, in nine months, under the instruction of Rev. Ezekiel H. Barstow, and graduated at Harvard
College in 1850.   He was a teacher before he entered college,
and taught awhile after graduating. In the mean time he
studied law, and for a period was in the law school at Cambridge.   In 1855 he established himself as a lawyer in Boston,
where he has been doing a successful business up to the present
time (1879). XI. John Bradford, b. Dec. 8, 1828; m. Anna
——; d. Oct. 30, 1864, leaving one son, Frank.

LIVINGSTON, JOHN.   The Livingston families that have resided in this town, were children of John Livingston, who
came from Londonderry, Ireland, some time in the last part of

the eighteenth century, and settled, or at one time lived, in a
house that stood in Westmoreland, on land once owned by
Luther Knights, about fifty rods south of the Knights dwelling
house, on the old road to Westmoreland village. The family
claim to be Scotch-Irish. John Livingston was born in 1734,
and died in 1807. There are no direct means of ascertaining
the order of succession in which his children were born, nor
the births of but few of them. Following is an imperfect account of them. Ch. I. Eleanor, b. in 1762, and died in 1842.
II. John, jr., b. in 1768, and died in 1816. He was a black-
smith and gun-smith by occupation. He lived in the house
now owned by John C. Brown, and his shop stood a few rods
east. It would appear, from statements made by descendants
of the Livingston families now living, that the gun-making
establishment was of considerable importance. Guerdon
Huntington, an uncle of the late George Huntington, was a
partner of John Livingston in the gun establishment, and tradition says that from one hundred to one hundred and fifty
men were employed in the years from 1793 to 1802. It is also
stated, that when the establishment was broken up in Walpole, the tools and machinery were bought by parties in
Springfield, Mass., and removed thither, and formed the nucleus of the present armory there. *If* the foregoing statements
are *true*, it is certainly remarkable that the history of such an
extensive business is not more generally *known*. From what is
known of John Livingston he appears to have been a man of
great force of character, and one who snapped his finger at the
common observances of society, and made laws unto himself.
Following is his marriage, copied from the town records ;
"This may certify that, on the 25th of August, 1793, John
Livingston, jr., and Sally Little came before me : and the said
John declared he took the said Sally to be his lawful wedded
wife, and the said Sally declared she took the said John to be
her lawful wedded husband." "Attest—Andrew French, Justice of the Peace." His wife was a hired girl of General Amasa Allen, at the date of the marriage. His children were, 1st,
Polly, born *probably* in 1794. 2d, Eliza, m. a German by the

name of Emde, and went west.   3d, Harriet, m. Ralph Farnsworth, and lived and died in town.   Her children were Sarah,
John S., and Mary.   4th, Sally, m. Samuel Hunt, and lives in
Lowell, Mass.   5th, John, jr., d. Sep. 29, 1813, aged 3 years.
6th, Henry, d. in infancy,—the two last died of *"Spotted Fever."*
7th, Robert, d. young.   8th, David, d. Oct. 15, 1815, of *hydrophobia*, mention of which has been made in the annals of this
work.   III. and IV. David and Samuel, were twins.   David was
a sailor, and died in foreign lands.   V. Robert, went to Canada
and was a Colonel in the English service.   VI. Polly, m. ——
Burt, and went to Canada.   VII. Rebecca, m. John Wier, and
lived in town. (See Wier.)   VIII. William, settled in New
Boston, this state.   IX. James.   X. Jonathan, b. 1776; m.
Catherine, daughter of Moses and Abigail (Foster) Dorr, of
Westmoreland, N. H.   He first lived on the place now owned
by Levi Ball, in a house that once stood in the orchard east of
Ball's residence.   In a few years he removed to the village, and
occupied the house where Amherst K. Maynard now lives,
and worked at the trade of a black-smith ; and where he commenced making steel traps for Bellows & Stone, in about 1816.
After remaining in the village four years, he returned to his
former place of residence, and for several years continued in
the service of his employers, Bellows & Stone.   In about 1827
or 8, he purchased the Gen. Aldrich place in Westmoreland,
where he lived till his death, which occurred July 2, 1850.   He
was a man of much individuality of character, and many of his
quaint sayings are remembered and repeated.   His wife was endowed with superior qualities of mind and heart, and possessed
great force of character.   She died very suddenly of disease of
the heart, July 1, 1839, aged 56.   Ch. 1st, David, b. July 14,
1805 ; m. Sophia W., dau. of Levi and Martha (Earl) Green,
of Westmoreland, and had 5 ch., 4 living.   2d, Abby Foster,
b. Feb. 27, 1807 ; m. Lyman Watkins. (See Watkins.)   3d,
Emeline, m. Frederick Carlisle. (See Carlisle.)   4th, Catherine,
b. Apr. 27, 1811, lives in Westmoreland, unm.   5th, Eleanor,
b. in 1813.   6th, Robert Warren, b. Feb. 1817. 7th, Cornelius
Dorr, b. in 1823.   The three last named died in the fall of 1824,

of the then prevailing epidemic,—dysentery. 8th, Helen, b. Feb. 7, 1826; m. Alexander S. Watkins, and died in 1856. She possessed an amiable and gentle disposition and was beloved by all who knew her virtues. XI. Caleb, was also a black-smith and had a shop at the south part of the town, near his brother Jonathan's. He m. Milly, dau. of Thomas Dinsmore, of Alstead, by whom he had five children, 3 sons and 2 daughters, 1st, John, died at the South. 2d, Henry D.: m. Orothy Ann Upham, of Weathersfield, Vt., and had three ch., two daughters and one son; the latter, William, died in the U. S. service, during the Rebellion. One daughter, Georgianna, is still living. Henry Livingstone's first wife died, and he married Emeline Shelly, o Westmoreland, where he soon after died. 3d, William, (son of Caleb) died in 1838. He was a youth of much promise. 4th. Eleanor. 5th, Martha. The two last married and removed to Vt. Caleb Livingston died in 1835, aged 51. His widow m. Loren W. Clark, and died about 1868.

LOVELL, ALDIS, was the third son of Elijah and Abigail G. Lovell, and was born in Rockingham, Vt., Aug. 2, 1789. He worked on his father's farm there until he was twenty two or twenty three years of age, when, becoming weary of farm life and labor, he commenced attending school, at Chester Academy, where, he remained awhile, and from there he went to New Market, N. H. and fitted for college in 1818. He then entered the law office of Hon. Daniel Kellogg, of Saxtons River, Vt., and remained two years reading law, when he was admitted to the bar at Newfane, Vt. He commenced the practice of his profession in his native town; but soon removed to Drewsville, N. H., where, and in Alstead, he continued practice till the time of his death, which occurred Mar. 12, 1866. He held but few public offices: the most important being County Solicitor, from 1840 to 1850. Mr. Lovell possessed very tender and generous feelings, was eminently social in his intercourse with mankind, enjoyed the rehearsal of a good story and could tell one well himself. He was a close observer of human nature, and was fond of making a travesty of the weak side of it. As a lawyer he was honest, and in the pursuit of justice, he was untiring. Nothing would make him more impatient than to see wrong-doing go unpunished. He married Martha, dau. of Paul and Martha (Haskell) Willard, of Lancaster, Mass., and grand-daughter of Col. Henry Haskell, of Revolutionary memory. She was born at Lancaster, May 26, 1799, and died at Drewsville, Aug. 12, 1851. Ch. I. Aldis, d. in infancy. II. Maria, d. at Drewsville, in 1836, aged 12 years. III. Bolivar, b. at Drewsville, Aug. 30, 1826; m. June 28, 1848, Sarah E. B., dau. of Hope and Fanny (Cooper) Lathrop, of Drewsville, b. Mar. 1829, and resided at Alstead, N. H. Ch. 1st, Martha Ellen, b. ——— m. S. T. Smith, M. D., of Alstead—issue 2 ch. 2d, Hope Lathrop, b. July 8, 1851. 3d, Aldis, b. July 14, 1859. Bolivar Lovell received no education, except what he acquired at Drewsville, up to the age of sixteen, when he went into the employ of Cragin & Hartwell, merchants, Providence, R. I. Here he remained three years, when he returned to Drewsville, and commenced the study of law, in the office of his father, at Alstead, about 1845. In 1847 he was appointed Deputy Sheriff, and acted in that capacity, still pursuing his law studies in the office of Lowell and Wait, at Alstead, till 1855, when he was appointed sheriff for the County of Cheshire, which office he held for ten years. In 1862 he received the appointment of U. S. Assessor of Internal Revenue for the third New Hampshire district and acceptably discharged its duties about eight years. In 1869 he was admitted to the Sullivan County Bar, at Newport, N. H., and has since practised his profession at Alstead. In 1873-4 he was elected a member of the Governor's Council. IV. Henry A., b. Feb. 12, 1837; m. Georgie B., dau. of Ignatius Fellows, of Hopkinton, N. H., and resides in Alstead, engaged in mercantile business. V. Willard A., b. Apr. 9, 1840; m. Julia A., dau. of Lyman Chandler, of Alstead, N. H.; d. July 26, 1872. (See Drewsville.)—issue, 1st, Henry W., d. in 1869. 2d, Willard H., b. at Alstead, Dec. 23, 1872. Willard A. Lovell, at his death, was a farmer and deputy sheriff.

LYMAN, SIMEON, was a poor boy who was brought up by

Robine Lowell.

Samuel Wiers, of this town, and when he became of age his foster father furnished him with tools to commence life at the trade of a blacksmith, in a shop that once stood on land near the Lyman homestead, on the east side of the highway. He married Diadama, dau. of James Allen, sen., and lived in a house near his shop till April 4, 1846, when he d., aged 81. His ch. were I. Levi, m. Lovisa, dau. of Samuel Wiers. Mr. Levi Lyman lived, during a long life, on the spot where he was born, and probably no man who ever lived in town has done so many hard days' work, or ever made longer days than he did; although it would seem he had no one to work for, as he lived and died without issue! He always had more or less hired help about him, and when in the field at work he was sure to lead them, which state of things continued to advanced life. His nervous sensations were not acute, as the following anecdotes will show. At one time, when preparing to start for Dublin, with a flock of sheep to be pastured there, his horse stepped upon the toes of one foot; but he did not stop to ascertain the injury done. A portion of the distance going thither he walked, in order to keep his sheep in the road. On returning, late at night, he said, "I thought my great toe did not feel quite natural, and on pulling off my boot I found it crushed and the nail off, besides other severe bruises on my foot." At another time he broke his arm, which for a long time necessitated the use of a sling. One of his townsmen, thinking it an opportune time to find him in the house, he wishing to make some settlement with him, was surprised to find him in his meadow, *ditching*, in a cold November blast. His sense of taste also partook of the same obtuseness. One day he was in his neighbor Burt's garden, with others, and Mr. Burt, knowing his insensibility to taste, invited him to taste of a plant that was growing in his garden, the leaves of which were exceedingly bitter and stringent, and to tell him whether it was bitter or sweet. Mr. Lyman plucked two or three leaves and chewed them a moment, when he said, "I can't tell exactly, but I should think, of the two, they were slightly *bitter!*" Mr. Lyman indulged in none of the luxuries of life, and was seldom from home, except when business called him. He was sparing to himself, but liberal to others, when he chose to be. On one occasion he held a note of $1500 against a man in Northfield, Mass., who had been his hired man for several years. After his debtor had paid him the interest then due, Mr. Lyman remarked, "I think we had better square up, you've been a pretty good boy," at the same time presenting him with his note.

He accumulated, by industry, frugality, temperance, and honesty, a landed estate, the most valuable of any in town. The amount of his entire property has not been publicly known, but was thought to have been from $75,000 to $80,000. When the infirmities of age and the loss of sight compelled him to remain in-doors, well knowing that the tide of life was fast ebbing, he was anxious about the disposal of his property. In his lonely meditations he sought out several poor but deserving people, who received from him liberal benefactions, and the balance went to his relatives. He died June 1, 1872, aged 78, bequeathing to posterity the example of a blameless life. II. Allen, m. a Bicknell, and settled in the state of New York. III. Jesse, was killed by the falling of a tree, in New York. IV. Lavinia, also m. a Bicknell, of New York. V. Diana, m. Daniel Ross, and had one son, Levi, who is living in town, and one daughter, who d., aged 16.

MARCH, JOSHUA, the grandson of Joshua, and the oldest of ten children of John March, was born Feb. 12, 1762. The other children were Samuel, Sarah, Daniel, Abigail, Hannah, Elizabeth, Molly, Martha, George, and Susannah, all born between 1763 and 1792. Joshua married Judith, the daughter of Lieut. Aaron Hodskins, jr., born in 1799. He lived, it is said, in the Hollow, west of the residence of Esdras Smith, and was a shoemaker and miller, which is inferred from charges made in an old account book of his. The steep pitch in the highway west of the brook is called "March Hill," from his mill and residence being in the vicinity. His children were I. Rebecca Garrish, b. Sept. 14, 1799, who is still living. II. John Smith, b. Nov. 26, 1803; m. first, Serepta, dau. of Philip

E. Bundy, July 25, 1830; m. second, Abigail Griggs. Ch. by
first wife, 1st and 2d, d. in infancy. 3d, George B., b. Aug. 3,
1836; m. Maria Minard, of St. Charles, Ill., in 1859. 4th,
William, b. April 14, 1836; m. Frances E., dau. of Jared and
Sophia (Bundy) Rickard, May 12, 1859; resides in town. 5th,
Jane, b. April 7, 1838; m. Thomas R. Marston, and has four
ch.; resides at Charlestown, N. H., in the hotel there. 6th,
Mary, b. April 13, 1843; d. Oct. 23, 1866. 7th, Sarah Ann, b.
Jan. 24, 1845; m. Ai A. Jacobs, lives at Cedar Rapids, Mich.,
and has one child. 8th, Abby, b. April 28, 1849, unm. III.
Aaron Hodskins, b. July 22, 1806. IV. Hannah Nelson, b.
April 2, 1815; lives in town, unm. Joshua March d. June 11,
1841, aged 79. Judith, his wife, died Oct. 13, 1852, aged 77.

MARSH, DANIEL, son of Ebenezer and Sarah (Farnham) Marsh,
was born in Haverhill, Mass., June 3, 1765. At the age of sixteen he enlisted in the Revolutionary army, but, being below
the regulation size and weight, he was rejected as a soldier;
but the spirit of patriotism or adventure was stronger than parental authority or army regulations, and he was finally admitted into the ranks as officer's assistant, in which capacity he served during the remainder of the war, under Gen'l McDougal. One
winter he was steward in Gen'l Washington's family, where he
delighted to assist Mrs. Washington in her domestic affairs in the
kitchen. One anecdote related by him was, that when Martha
was baking *flapjacks* it was stipulated that every one that
broke in turning should be his, and he sometimes thought
the good woman broke them purposely. After the war was
over his parents removed to Derry, N. H., whence, he, with
others, came to Walpole, in 1781, and pitched his future home
on Derry Hill, purchasing the wild land of Theodore Atkinson. Three years later, after making a clearing and building
a habitation, he returned to Derry, and married Jane, daughter
of Dea. Edmund and Hannah (Thurston) Adams, of Newburyport, Mass., who was born Feb. 13, 1773. Her father was
cousin of President John Quincy Adams and it is said that
there was a striking family resemblance between them. His
family were known for their scholarly attainments. Jacob, a

son, accumulated $20,000, as a teacher, which he left, at his death, at the age of thirty-six, to found the "Adams Academy" in Derry, N. H., which still bears his name. Daniel Marsh had a family of eleven children and died at the age of 86; his wife at the age of 92. Ch. I. Edmund A., b. May 19, 1779; m. Isabella, dau. of Dea. Jonas Hosmer, Oct. 9. 1823. Ch. 1st, Hiram H., b. July 22, 1824: and, at his majority, went to Chicago, Ill., established himself in the mercantile business and retired from active life at the age of fifty—a rich man. He now lives in California. 2d, Isabella Eliza, b. Sep. 11, 1826; m. Caleb Foster. (See Foster.) 3d, Harriet M., b. Sep. 4, 1828, m. Willard Albee, of Charlestown, N. H.—issue 3 ch. 4th, Sarah J., b. June 22, 1831; m. Chas. C. Fuller, and lives in Terre Haute, Ind. Two ch., 5th, and 6th died in infancy. 7th, Emily A., b. Feb. 25, 1837; m. Fenelon Arnold, of Westminster, Vt. one ch. 8th, 9th, and 10th, died young. II. Hannah, b. Feb. 10, 1799; d. June 13. 1831. III. Eliza, b. July 5th, 1801, m. Henry P. Foster, Nov. 11, 1840. (See Foster.) IV. Sarah, b. Oct. 6th, 1803; d. June 4, 1868. V. Jane, b. Dec. 4, 1805, m. Edmund Adams, Oct. 16, 1828, and had three children, 1st, Lucien Harper, m. first, a Miss Adams; m. second, Miss Dora Francis, of Hartford, Conn., and is a missionary in Turkey—they have 3 ch. The third child, Daniel, b. in Derry, N. H., Jan. 22, 1833; m. Olive Thomas of Topeka, Kansas. Daniel Adams went to Kansas in 1847 and grew up with the state and accumulated a handsome fortune. He was one of the most active and enterprising men in the state, and, besides holding many public offices under the General Government, Leavenworth and Topeka are indebted to him for many of the finest public buildings in those cities. He died June 13, 1879, leaving three children. VI. Daniel, b. Aug. 26, 1808, d. July 21, 1872. VII. Amos, d. young. VIII. Benj. also d. young. IX. Farnham, b. May 21, 1816; m. Judith B. Moultrop and has four children. (See Ap.) X. Katherine, b. Sep. 9, 1817; m. George Joslin, Oct. 15, 1848. Ch. 1st, William Thayer, b, July 11, 1849; d. Dec. 22, 1863. 2d, Katie Isabel, b, July 29, 1851; m. Geo. W. Field, of Surry, N. H., Sep. 1871.

3 ch. 3d, Frank M. 4th, Lizzie C., 5th, Jessie Fremont. (See Ap.) XI. Amos d. young.

MARTIN, JOHN, was born in Portsmouth, N. H., in 1759, and, when a lad, went to Londonderry in this state to live with a man till his majority. At the age of seventeen he enlisted into the service of his country in the Revolutionary struggle, in which he remained three years. He was in the engagements around Saratoga, and at the surrender of Burgoyne and his army. Immediately after, about one hundred years ago, he married Rebecca Adams, and came to this town, and located on the Wier brook, so called, on a plot of land about four rods wide and fifty rods long, in a lone and desolate place, south of the residence of Edward A. Watkins, which is known to this day as " Martin's vineyard." Not many years since a hop vine might have been seen growing from the *débris* of the cellar, blooming and bearing annually and " wasting its fragrance on the desert air." He did not remain there long, but purchased of Col. Caleb Bellows, the sand bank now owned by Loring Ganzer, in the south part of the town, where he spent most of his days, and was the father of fourteen children, by one wife, who all lived to mature age. He died in 1849. His children were, I. Samuel, m. Rebecca Hall, and had eight children. 1st, Harvey, d. at the age of 15. 2d, William, m. ———, dau. of Joseph Russell. 3d, Rebecca, m. Kendall Crossfield, of Keene, N. H. 4th, Lydia, m. Sylvanus Titus. 5th, Rhoda, m. Loring V. Ballou and went to Cleveland, Ohio. 6th, Almira, m. Jos. Carpenter, of Keene. 7th, Emily, m. a Hutchins, of Boston. 8th, Ezra, d. at sea. II. Polly, m. Asahel Streeter, of Chesterfield, and had six children. III. John, went west. IV. Rebecca, m. Paul Kittredge. V. William, had 6 ch. and lived till he was 84. VI. James, m. Susan Fairbanks. VII. Betsey, m. James Hall, of Littleton, Mass., and had eight children, five girls and three boys. VIII. Jonathan, never married. IX. Washington, never married. X. Adams, never married. XI. Nancy, m. James Stearns and had five children. XII. Susan, m. Aaron Emory and had 8 ch. XIII. Stephen, is a physician and lives in Janesville, Wis. XIV. Oliver, b. Feb. 25, 1807 ;

m. Lois Derby, of Dublin, March 19, 1834. Oliver was the youngest child and began life with nothing but his hands and a determination to be something. At the age of eleven years, he worked for John H. Wiers, for his board, and a year or two later he was paid $4.00 per month. At the age of fifteen he went to live with Capt. John Dunshee, of this town, where he remained till his majority and received for the six years service $100, which was the nest egg for his subsequent accumulations. He worked for various persons, by the month, saving his earnings, till the age of twenty seven, when he married and commenced life independently. He soon after purchased the farm now owned by Allen Dunshee, where he remained for several years, making various improvements on the buildings—making the old one story house what it now is, as one of them. He subsequently sold out, and purchased the Thomas Seaver place, now owned by C. R. Crowel, and raised the house to two stories, with other improvements; and lastly purchased the Macy Adams place and built the house where he now resides, with his second wife, whose maiden name was Louisa Stevens, whose first husband was Theron Adams, and whose second was Walter Mead Esq.

Mr. Martin has for forty years had the superintendence of the Boggy meadow farms. He was a member of the legislature in 1860—61 and has been one of the selectmen of the town several years. He has always been ready to do his part in public matters pertaining to the town, and for many years has been a pillar of strength in the Congregational Society. In his business transactions he has always exercised good judgment for himself, by which, and by persevering industry, he has accumulated more than a competency. He has in many cases lent aid to the deserving, and of the poor no one ever went from his door empty handed. Ch. 1st, Emily J., b, Feb. 24, 1835; m. Charles Fisher. (See Ap.) 2d, Isabella, b. Aug. 29, 1842; m. Chas. L. Mead, of Brattleboro, Vt., May 12, 1864— issue 4 ch., 3 living. 3d, Elenora L. d. in infancy.

MASON, JOSEPH, was the great-great-grandson of Hugh Mason, who came from England to this country early in the sev-

Oliver Morton

enteenth century, with his brother John, and settled in Watertown, Mass. John settled in Dorchester, and was one of the
first settlers. He removed, in 1635, to Windsor, Ct., and was
an officer in the Pequot war, of which he wrote a history. He
was made Maj. Gen. of all the forces in the colony, which
office he retained till his death. He was also Deputy Governor,
and held the office till the infirmities of age disqualified him.
He died in 1673, aged 72. Joseph Mason of this town, was the
4th of 12 children, of Joseph, III, in America whose average
age at the time of their deaths was *eighty-three years*. Such an instance of longevity in one family, at this time, is without a parallel. He was born in Concord, Mass., Mar. 17, 1751, and was
a soldier in the Revolutionary war. He m. Lucy Flint, of Carlisle, Mass., Apr. 1786, who was born May 10, 1765. He d.
Feb. 18, 1834; she d. June 6, 1833. He came to Walpole about
1787, and first settled on the place known as the Scovill farm.
He had a brother by the name of Elijah, who came to town,
and who once owned the Capt. John Flint farm. Joseph
Mason buffeted the storms in that inhospitable place many
cold and piercing winters, far removed from neighbors, and
almost from civilization, and had a family of *fourteen children*,
of whom Joseph, jr., was the oldest, who was born in Carlisle,
Mass., Dec. 14, 1786, and came to Walpole, when a child, with
his parents. He married Harriet, dau. of Stephen and Phebe
(Calkins) Ormsby, of this town, Nov. 29, 1817, when he was
thirty years old, and they had ten ch. 1st, George Ormsby, b.
Sep. 25, 1818; resides in San Francisco, Cal. 2d, William
Henry, b. Oct. 7, 1820; m. Harriet E. Dow, and resides in
Salem, Ill.,—issue 5 ch. 3d, Charles Holland, b. Aug. 9, 1822,
m. Rachel S. Wright, of Cannilton, Ind., where he resides, and
is a lawyer by profession. 4th, Harriet Irene, b. Aug. 29, 1824,
m. Dauphin W. Buckminster, of Roxbury, N. H., and resides
in Keene. 5th, Edward, b. Mar. 26, 1826; d. young. 6th,
Frances Emeline, b. Aug. 16, 1827. 7th, Joseph Everett, b.
Aug. 18, 1829; m. Mattie B. Plummer, of New Albany, Ind.,
and resides in Evansville, same state. 8th, Ellen Corinna, b.
July 31, 1831. 9th, Andrew Robinson, b. Nov. 30, 1833; m.

Lucy Lawrence, of Keene, and has two ch. 10th, Leonard
Bisco, b. June 29, 1836; m. Ella A. Davenport, of Beloit,
Wis., and has 2 ch. Joseph Mason jr. was schooled in adversity,
but notwithstanding, he managed, by dint of energy and perseverance, to acquire an English education sufficient to enable
him to utilize his time, winters, in teaching common schools;
while in summer he labored on the land, till in time he was in
a pecuniary condition to purchase the Capt. John Flint farm,
of his uncle Elijah. Soon after this his parents became infirm,
and he had to lend a filial, helping hand for their support, nor
was this all ; he became a foster father to all his brothers and
sisters. He gained an enviable reputation as a teacher, some
sixty years ago, and many are now living in town, who well
remember that good behavior was one of the cardinal virtues
in the school-room, when under his care. He had a great desire to have his children acquire a good education, and, to, that
end, always manifested a lively interest in our common schools.
As a farmer, he stood among the first in the orderly manner
in which he conducted his business and the neatness about his
premises. No drones were allowed to occupy his hive—he
had a place for everything and everything was in its place. His
religious sentiments were deep and strong, and held out to
the last, in the belief of a glorious immortality. He died Oct.
14, 1874 ; she died Jan. 25, 1864, aged 69. II. Mary, b. Sep.
28, 1788; m. first, John Blake, and had 8 ch ; m. second
Abram Ballou, and had three ch.: d. 1867. III. Lucy, b. July
7, 1790; m. John Chamberlain, and had 10 ch.; lived in Johnson, Vt., d. in 1845. IV. Irena. V. Ruth. VI. Catherine; the
preceding three died young. VII. Martin, b. July 16, 1797;
m. in 1828, first, Mary S. Barker, issue, 4 ch.; m. second, Betsey A. Hobart : d. 1870. He was a physician. VIII. Irena,
b. July 16, 1799 ; m. Leonard Everett, who was a merchant of
Canton, Mass., and had 3 ch.; d. Feb. 5, 1834.   IX. Holland,
b. July 31, 1801; m. Susan Veasie, May 15, 1827, and had 8
ch., 4 of whom are living : 3 d. young, and one, Emma, d.
July 21, 1864, aged 25 years. Of those living, 1st, Urana, m.
John C. Emerson. (See Emerson.) 2d, Rufus. 3d, Carrie,

m. George Scoville, and lives in Charlestown, Mass. 4th, Hattie O., unm. Holland Mason, like his brother Joseph, was a school-teacher, during the winter season, in his youth. He died Jan. 11, 1879. X. Josiah Flint, b. May 22, 1803 ; m. Maria Tyler in 1839, and had three ch. He is a clergyman, and resides at Council Bluffs, Iowa. XI. Ruth Wheeler, b. July 14, 1805. XII. Emeline, b. July 13, 1808 ; m. in 1834 to Leonard Everett, of Canton, Mass., and had 4 ch.; d. June 11, 1857. XIII. William Bond, b. Sep. 10, 1810 ; m. first, in 1841, Mary Jane, dau. of Jonathan Emerson, of this town, and had 3 ch. She died in 1846, and her children about the same time. He m. second, in 1849, Sarah A., a sister of his first wife, by whom he has five children. (See Ap.) XIV. Rufus Putnam, b. Oct. 25, 1813 ; m. in 1840, Caroline Otis, and has 5 ch.; lives in Chesening, Michigan.

MAYNARD, JOHN. Of the early life of John Maynard very little is known, as his father died when he was but three years old, and, being deprived of a parental home, he could learn but little of his ancestry, to impart to his children. He was born in Chesterfield, N. H., Mar. 28, 1785, and was brought up in one of the Blake families, in Keene, N. H. He learned the saddler's trade, in Chester, Vt., and came to this town early in the present century and worked for Maj. Grant, as a journey-man, for a while, and then commenced business for himself. He at one time owned a line of staging from this town to Chester, Vt., and built the original house afterwards owned by Dr. Morse. He married Lydia, dau. of Eliphas Graves, Apr. 28, 1811, by whom he had ten children, two of whom died in infancy. Those that survived were the following; I. Lorinda Hart, b. Feb. 2d, 1812 ; m. William C. Sherman, Mar. 28, 1837. II. Fanny R., b. Apr. 2, 1813; died Feb. 8, 1834, a form-er wife of William C. Sherman. III. Amherst Kingsbury, b. Dec. 19, 1814 ; m. Maria Geer, of Charlestown, N. H., June 13, 1844. Ch. 1st, William A., b. Mar. 27, 1845 ; m. Frances Perry, June 10, 1868. 2d, Charles G., b. Sep. 28, 1846 ; m. Mary G., dau. of Thomas Dinsmore, of Alstead, Oct. 25, 1877. 2d, Lizzie M., b. May 17, 1852. 4th, Mary E., b. Jan. 25, 1858.

Mr. A. K. Maynard carried on the manufacture of boots and shoes from about the time he was married till 1870, when physical infirmities compelled him to relinquish business. He was postmaster from 1853 to 1861. IV. Mary Augusta, b. Nov. 22, 1816; m. Augustus Faulkner, Sep. 7, 1864, issue one son, George M. V. George Carlisle, b. Dec. 2, 1819; left Walpole, Aug. 26, 1833, for Cincinnati O., and went into the shoe store of Stedman, Shaw & Co.; George Carlisle, his cousin, being a silent partner. The style of the firm was afterwards changed to Stedman, Maynard & Co. Here he remained in business till 1864, having, during the time, accumulated a handsome fortune. He d. July 18, 1865, in Walpole, unm. VI. Susan Amanda, b. Mar. 15, 1822. VII. Lydia Ann, b. Sep. 17, 1824. VIII. Sarah Jane, b. Mar. 24, 1827. John Maynard d. Mar. 25, 1868; his wife d. Apr. 28, 1863.

MEAD, MOSES, was born in Waltham, Mass., in 1755, and married Lezee Viles, who was born in 1759. He was a soldier in the Revolutionary war, and came to this town in the last decade of the eighteenth century, and located first on the Stephen Johnson place, which he subsequently sold, and took his pay in notes of the Gloucester bank, which proved worthless, and reduced his pecuniary means to such an extent that it came well nigh ruining him. Fifty dollars of the notes are now in the possession of Mrs. Oliver Martin, of this town. He subsequently purchased a plot of land—now owned by the Mead heirs—a little north of the village, and built a grist-mill, where grain was ground for many years for the towns-people. In connection with his milling business he manufactured rakes, which business was subsequently carried on by his son David. His rakes were of a superior manufacture and were in demand wherever known. He died Feb. 26, 1818; his wife, Oct. 11, 1841. They had twelve children, most of whom were born before he came to town. Ch. I. Moses, b. March 7, 1778; d. in this town, suddenly, June 16, 1818. II. David, b. Oct. 23, 1779; m. first, Esther, dau. of Asahel Bundy, May 8, 1803; m. second, Amy, dau. of Nehemiah Kidder, and widow of Joseph Frink, March 11, 1831; she d. April 23, 1879, aged 90. He d.

Aug., 1848, aged 69. His first wife d. in 1818, aged 35. Ch. by first wife: 1st, Fidelia, b. Aug. 6, 1803. 2d, Mary, b. May 21, 1805. 3d, Joseph Bundy, b. Dec. 5, 1807; m. Alice Rust, of Alstead. He d. March 17, 1865; she d. Aug. 11, 1859, aged 50. Ch. (1) Sumner Rust, b. Sept. 21, 1835; he is married, lives in Boston, and is a successful merchant. (2) George, b. May 22, 1838; lives in Boston also. 4th, Esther, b. April 10, 1810 5th, Sophia, b. Oct. 13, 1812. 6th, Francis Kittredge, b. May 20, 1816. 7th, Walton Viles, b. July 19, 1817. The two last live in Hingham, Mass. III. Susannah, b. March 22, 1781. IV. Elizabeth, b. Feb. 20, 1783. V. Jacob, b. Jan. 20, 1795; was drowned at the age of 11 years. VI. Abner, b. March 19, 1787. VII. Nathan. VIII. Sophia, b. Feb. 20, 1792. IX. Walton, b. March 14, 1794. He was a much-respected citizen of the town, and was for many years Justice of the Peace and town clerk, and was appointed postmaster under Prest. Polk's administration. He married, in advanced life, Elizabeth Parker, of Charlestown, N. H.; she died, and he subsequently married Louisa, the widow of the late Theron Adams, Jan. 2, 1854. He d. Nov. 25, 1866, aged 72. X. Fidelia, d. young. XI. Clarissa, b. Aug. 27, 1796; d. Nov. 3, 1878. She had a daughter, Maria L., who, when young, was a successful schoolteacher. She married Noah R. Cook, of Keene, where she now resides, a widow. Mrs. Cook has a highly cultivated mind, and possesses some poetic genius. When living in Walpole she was highly esteemed for her gentleness of disposition and goodness of heart.

MEAD, SAMUEL, Rev., commonly known as parson Mead, was born at Harvard, Mass., in 1762, and graduated at Harvard in the class of 1787, and prepared for the ministry; after which he went to Alstead, N. H., and was settled over the Congregational church and society there, Jan. 15, 1791. He preached there till April 28, 1797, and, during that time, he discovered that he was preaching to his people a doctrine he did not believe, which was the cause of his resignation. He embraced the tenets of Unitarianism, and was the first to promulgate that doctrine in this region. He preached occasionally afterwards, but was never again settled. Mr. John Crafts, of this town, a wealthy man for those days, died in 1791, aged 34, leaving two children and a widow. The parson (Mead), thinking that preaching was good for nothing without practice, made a very laudable endeavor to fulfill the injunction of Scripture, to "visit the widow and the fatherless," etc., and the consequence was that Mrs. Crafts doffed her weeds and became Mrs. Samuel Mead, July 19, 1792. Mrs. Mead's maiden name was Esther Sartwell, a descendant of Ensign Obadiah Sartwell, one of the first settlers of Charlestown, N. H. At the time of the marriage there was considerable talk about town in relation to the parson's good luck in capturing the "rich widow." Mr. Mead took upon himself the guardianship of the children and the settlement of the estate, and in attempting to sell the "Crafts Tavern", without due legal proceedings, one David Stevens assailed him through the columns of the "Farmer's Museum," which had just commenced being published. Mr. Mead replied through the same columns with so much vituperation that Stevens' batteries were forever silenced. He lived in a house that once stood near the residence of Mrs. Ephraim Holland. Ch. I. Caroline, b. 1793; never married. II. Hannah W., b. 1795; m. Phinehas Handerson, Esq., of Keene, March 25, 1818. She had eight ch., seven daughters and one son. III. Nancy, b. in Alstead, March 15, 1798; m. Ephraim Holland, July 23, 1820. (See Holland.) IV. Orlando, b. 1800; m. Maria Dix Wellington. He was a broker, in Boston. Ch. 1st, William, m. Abby Nichols. 2d, Maria, m. Edward B. Grant. 3d, Esther, m. William Underwood. 4th, Orlando, m. widow of Elbridge Hosmer. 5th, Henry, d. in Cuba. 6th, Isabella, m. Henry Milliken, of Boston. 7th, Harriet, m. Lora B. Bacon, of Boston. Mr. Mead's step-son, John, went to Chicago in its early days, and lived and died there. Esther m. Dr. Ebenezer Morse. (See Morse.)

MELLISH, STEPHEN, the son of John Mellish, an old resident of Dorchester, Mass., was born Oct. 22 1772. He married Roxalana, dau. of Nathaniel and Sarah Eaton, of Mansfield, Conn., who was one of a family of thirteen children; and a

brother of hers was Gen. Wm. Eaton, U. S. Army, Consul to
Tripoli, and commander of the American forces during the
war with Algiers. Stephen was married in Greenwich, Conn.,
May 10, 1796, and started for New Hampshire the same day,
on horseback—one horse bearing the burden of both. He was
a cabinet-maker by trade and a very ingenious workman, his
ingenuity being transmitted to several of his posterity. He
lived in various places in town, at one time on the place now
owned by John Selkirk, where he built the house that once
stood on the site of the present dwelling. He was a fine looking man and very gentlemanly in his intercourse. He had a
family of twelve ch. I. Roxana, b. in Walpole, Feb. 24, 1797;
m. Henry Slade, Jan. 22, 1822. Ch. 1st, George Henry, b.
Dec. 22, 1822; m. first, Frances Dana; m. second, Julia A.
Huntress—issue, by first wife, 1 ch. 3d, John Walker, b. June
13, 1826; m. Lizzie A., dau. of Thomas and Caroline O.
(Reed) Gould—issue 2 ch. 4th, Leonard. 5th, Charles. 6th,
Calvin E. The 2d, and the two mentioned last d. young. II.
Clarissa, b. Mar. 13, 1798; m. Feb. 12, 1821, Harry Gilbert.
Ch. 1st, Harriet M., b. Jan. 3, 1822; m. John Pope, of Bos-
ton, Mass.—issue 5 ch. 2d, Sarah E., b. Jan. 26, 1825; m.
Oscar F. Gilbert—1 ch. 3d, Esther R., b. May 25, 1827; m.
John M. Perley, and had 10 ch, 4th, Clarissa E., b. May 21,
1829; m. David I. Dutton, and had 5 ch, 5th, Stephen S., b.
1835; m. first, Eliza A. Tibbitts, of Brooksville, Me.; second,
Emma F. Dow, of Coventry—issue 3 ch. 6th, William H., b.
Aug. 1, 1840; d. young. III. William Eaton, b. June 16, 1799;
m. Hannah, dau. of Frederick and Molly (Pierce) Pope, of
Dorchester, Mass. Ch. 1st, Oscar, b. Nov. 24, 1831: m. Helen
A., dau. of Increase S. and Esther, (Wolcott) Guild, of this
town. 2d, Oriana, b. Oct. 29, 1833: m. Charles H. Smith, of
So. Boston, Mass.—1 ch. 3d, Olivia, b. Oct. 18, 1857; m. John
H. Bird—1 ch. 4th, Walter E., b. June 15, 1843, m. Lizzie E.
Ball—issue 2 ch. IV. Eliza, b. Oct. 17, 1800; m. first, Solo-
mon Gilbert; m. second, Rufus Pierce, of Putney, Vt. Ch. 1st,
Mary A., b. Mar. 23, 1835; m. Wm. H. Lyman—1 ch. 2d,
James M., b. Nov. 21, 1837; m. Helen F., dau. of Silas and

Caroline F. (Emerson) Angier, of Alstead, N. H.—issue 6 ch.
3d, George M.,, b. Nov. 21, 1837. 4th, Charles H., b. July 19,
1841; m. Sarah Louisa, dau. of Moses J. and Sarah (Griswold)
Hale, of this town—issue 4 ch. V. Samuel, b. July 3, 1802;
m. Huldah, dau. of Justus and Huldah (Veasey) Lane. Ch. 1st,
Mary F., b. Nov. 19, 1831, m. Asa H. Burge, of Langdon,
N. H. 2d, Emily A., b. June 14, 1836. 3d, Huldah A., b. Aug.
10, 1839. VI. Stephen J., b. May 23, 1805; m. first, Mary A.,
dau. of Bill Blake; m. second, Mary Closson, of Westmoreland, N. H. Ch. 1st, Algernon S., b. Aug. 21, 1831; m. Julia
Tracy—issue 2 ch., issue by first wife 3 ch. 2d, Leonard B.,
b. Nov. 17, 1832; m. Mary A. Hatch, of Springfield, Pa., and
had 2 ch. 3d, Mary A., b. Feb. 23, 1836. VII. Henry, b. Mar.
30, 1804; m. Sarah Blackman, of Dorchester, Mass. Ch. 1st,
Clarissa, b. in Dorchester, Mass., Apr. 29, 1829; m. Andrew J.
Fisher, of this town—issue 7 ch., 3 living. (See Ap.) 2d, James
W. B., b. Nov. 1830; m. Mary Ann, dau. of Increase S. and
Esther (Wolcott) Guild, of this town—issue 5 ch., 3 living.
(See Guild.) 3d, Emeline, d. young. 4th, Julia A., b. Nov. 10,
1836; m. Chas. A. Pope and had 3 ch. 5th, George H., b.
Sep. 10, 1837; m. Sarah Holden, of B. Falls—issue 3 ch., 2
living. 6th, Caroline, b. Mar. 2, 1839; m. Edward A. Darby,
(poet) who d. Nov. 9, 1867—issue 3 ch. (See Ap.) 7th, Mary,
d. young. 8th, Chas. B., b. July 30, 1845; m. first, Catherine
Gates; m. second, Elvira Thompson—1 ch. Henry Mellish,
was a man who possessed more than ordinary intellectual powers and was a natural mechanic, which is proved by the number of his inventions and patents obtained for them. He represented the town in the General Court in 1856-7, and was at
one time a practising physician in town. He was a great
reader, and took a lively interest in the world's progress. In the
last years of his life he was engaged in horticulture. He lived
a blameless life, and died, much respected by his townsmen,
Oct. 20, 1878. VIII. Sarah S., b. Apr. 4, 1807; m. Samuel
Pope, of Woodstock, Vt.—issue 4 ch., the youngest, Eugene
A., m. Ella M. Brown, and has 1 ch. IX. John, b. Mar. 30,
1809; d. 1827. X. George, b. Apr. 20, 1811; m. Angela, dau.

of Rev. Russell Streeter—residence, Woodstock, Vt. XI. Emma, b. July 22, 1815; m. James R. Hyde. Ch. 1st, William E. d. in infancy. 2d, George Mellish, b. in Antrim, N. H., Feb. 19, 1845; m. Sarah V., dau. of Horace P. and Mary A. (Seaman) Mitchell, of Watertown, N. Y.—residence, Worcester, Mass. XII. Emily, b. in 1816: d. in infancy. Stephen Mellish, d. July 21, 1849; his wife d. in Woodstock, Vt., Mar. 5, 1869, aged 96 years. There are but two of the old family living in 1879.

MERRIAM, JOHN, came to Walpole in the month of November 1782, from Littleton Mass, and bought fifty acres of land in the south east corner of the town, on which he built a substantial habitation, cleared six acres of the land and sowed it to winter wheat the same season. This fifty acres was the nucleus of a farm of 300 acres, which he afterwards possessed. This old farm has been in the possession of the Merriam family one hundred and seven years. At the time of the battle of Bennington, a *courier* was dispatched to inform him that soldier's would pass his house on their way to the scene of conflict and he must prepare to furnish them with water, the next day. Accordingly every available vessel that would hold water was filled from his well and ready for use. The following day 3,000 soldiers drank and filled their canteens from his well, and passed on to Col. Josiah Goldsmith's tavern, where they were again refreshed by devouring a whole ox, which he had been ordered to prepare for them. He was born Oct. 1726, and m. Fanny, dau. of Josiah Goldsmith, who was born, 1729. He d. 1814; she d. 1824. Ch. I. John jr., m. Susan Brockway, of Surry, and moved to Barton, Vt. He was in the Revolutionary service and was wounded seven times in his *trousers*, so tradition says, i. e. seven bullet holes were made in his *pants* without any injury to himself. II. Richard, m. Susan Skinner and went to Hartland, Vt. III. Hannah, m. Dyer Wilcox, of Surry; she d. and he afterwards m. a Howard, of Acworth, N. H. IV. Lydia, m. Thomas Messer, (see Messer.) V. Daniel b. Aug. 2, 1769, m. Sally, dau. of Rev. Ebenezer Bailey, of Westmoreland, N. H. Ch. 1st, Clarissa, b. Feb. 28, 1797; d.

Sep. 17, 1865, unmarried. She had a memory strikingly remarkable, being able to repeat all of Watts' hymns and also
much of the Bible. 2d, Sarah, b. June 2, 1800, m. Josiah
Emerson of Alstead, and had six ch. one of whom is the wife
of Samuel H. Porter of this town. 3d, Rhoda, b. May, 28, 1802;
m. Daniel Emerson of Alstead, and had five sons and one
daughter. 4th, Almira, b. Oct. 20, 1805. m., first, William
Goodenow, of Keene, m. second, Joseph Paige, of Boston ; d.
Jan. 29, 1879. 5th, Eliza, b. Sep. 22, 1807. 6th, Daniel jr., b.
Feb. 28, 1810 ; m. Sep. 17, 1840, Emily E. Robinson, of Surry,
b. Mar. 17, 1818 ; Daniel jr. was moderator, tax collector and
one of the board of selectmen in this town for several years,
and represented the town in the General Court in 1842. More
recently he has taken but little interest in town affairs. Ch. (1)
Ellery R., b. Apr. 23, 1841 and resides in Boston, Mass. (2) and
(3) Elmore E. and Emily, (twins,) b. Apr. 23, 1844. Emily m.
Milton Blake of Keene and has 3 ch. (4) Hattie L., b. Aug 15,
1846 ; m. Luke J. Paige, of Boston, Mass., and has 1 ch. (5)
Jennie M., b. Mar. 22, 1850. (6) Susan Jane, b. Apr. 29, 1853.

MESSER, TIMOTHY, one of the earliest settlers of this town,
was born in Methuen, Mass., and his wife, Hannah Marble,
was a native of Haverhill, Mass. Soon after marriage they
moved to Connecticut, expecting to find a *wilderness* there;
but, being disappointed, came to Walpole some time before
1760, and took up land where William T. Ramsay now lives,
of Col. Benjamin Bellows. The family and their effects were
poled up Connecticut river in a double *dug-out*, while he drove
his cow upon the bank. On the above named place he toiled
till a clearing was effected sufficiently large to raise 300 bushels of wheat in one year, (before mentioned,) when he was
obliged to vacate the land to make a home for John Jennison,
one of Col. Bellows's step-sons. During his stay on the place
he and his family underwent many privations. At one time
he left his family almost destitute of food and went to Northfield, Mass., and worked for a man long enough to pay for a
bushel of corn, which he got ground, and brought to Walpole,
on his back, a distance of forty miles, guided by marked trees.

On another ocsasion Mr. Messer was driven to the alternative of killing his pig, which he wished to fatten more, to supply his large family with meat, or let them suffer the pinching privations of hunger. He concluded he must kill his pig, and in returning home from a distant neighbor's where he had been to procure a knife to slaughter it, he started a sleeping buck deer, which, in his precipitation to escape, became entangled by his horns in a fallen tree top. Mr. Messer seeing the entangled condition of the animal, sprang upon it with the agility of a catamount, and killed it on the spot. The meat afforded a temporary relief to the hunger of the family, and the skin was sufficiently large to make two pairs of breeches for the boys. He was thus enabled to keep his pig a while longer. Mr. Messer ever afterwards considered this circumstance one of Divine interposition. The births of his children cannot be given in their order of succession, as there are no data. Ch. I. Mary, m. Isaac Johnson, jr., Dec. 21, 1771, supposed to be the oldest. II. Hannah, m. Samuel Parker, Apr. 15, 1779. III. Thomas, b. July 15, 1756; m. Lydia Merriam, b. at Lexington, Mass., Dec. 26, 1758, who came to Walpole with her father, when but fourteen years old. He had a large family of children, all born in town. In 1801 he removed to Westminster, Vt., and died Jan. 27, 1811; she d. Jan. 21, 1841. Ch. 1st, Hannah, b. Dec. 9, 1783; m. Ellery Albee, of Westminster, Feb. 1814, at which place he and his wife resided during life. He d. Sep. 17, 1852; she d. Oct. 2, 1851. Ch. (1) Almeda V., resides in Westminster, unm. (2) Albert Merriam is a lawyer in Springfield, Vt. 2d, Lydia, b. Mar. 11, 1789; m. Isaac Cobb, then of Walpole, May, 1813, who was a wheel-wright by trade, and the original part of C. B. Lucke's house was his shop. He d. 1831; she d. May 19, 1876. Ch. (1) Calista A., m. William K. Church, now lives with her brother, Stephen K. Cobb, Westminster. (2) Stephen K., m. Harriet, dau. of Leonard Cragin. 3d and 4th, Calista and Verrilla, (twins,) b. 1794; both d. young. 5th, Nancy, b. Aug. 18, 1796; m. Sumner Albee, of Chesterfield, N. H. 6th, Verranda, b. June, 1801; m. Jehiel Fletcher, he d. in Keeseville,

N. Y. 1872; 2 ch. IV. Oliver, b. Feb. 4, 1761. He had some infirmity which impaired his usefulness. V. Timothy, b. Nov. 9, 1763. VI. Abigail, never married. VII. and VIII. Daniel and Samuel, went to Shrewsbury, Vt., of whom but little is known. IX. Nathaniel, m. Betsey Mason, and for a time lived in Walpole, in the Valley, but subsequently removed to Marlow, where he spent his days and had a family. Among his children was Nathaniel, jr., who m. Betsey Town, and was the father of William Hopkins Messer, of Marlow, who m. Lucy Ann Pierce, and is the father of Jennette, the wife of Charles M. Russell, of this town. X. Phebe, m. Joel Burroughs, of Alstead, and had 12 children, all born between 1774 and 1802, with about two years intervening between their births. The 1st was Daniel. 2d, Joel. 3d, Thomas. 4th, Hannah. 5th, Eunice. 6th, Anna. 7th, Richard. 8th, Simon. 9th, Phebe. 10th, Polly. 11th, Annice. 12th, Cyrus. Thomas, b. in 1778; m. Lois Martin, Feb. 17, 1811, and had three children or more, of whom one, is Caroline, m. Alfred W. Burt, of this town. 2d, James Martin. 3d, George. Mr. Thomas Burroughs died, after which his widow became the wife of Stephen Stearns. A daughter of Nathaniel Messer 2d, of Marlow, m. Gordon Turner, of Alstead, N. H.

MILLER, JARED, was born in Alstead, N. H., Feb. 4, 1792, and married Irene Lewis, of Lyme, Conn., Oct. 20, 1816, who was born Jan. 24, 1794. He came to Walpole in 1820, and established himself in the shoemaking business, at the south part of the town, in district No. 9. There he remained eight years, when he removed into the village, where he lived and continued in the shoe business till nearly the close of his life. He manufactured sale boots and shoes for the western market, in connection with custom work, the latter of which was faithfully done. No customer ever complained of poor work that came from his shop. He was a man of positive views and strictly honest habits. He died May 29, 1870. Ch. I. Mary Ann, b. Aug. 25, 1817; d. July 10, 1841, unm. II. Phœbe, b. Sept. 2, 1819; m. Hartson Wight, April 2, 1839. III. and IV., two by the name of Sarah, d. in infancy. V.

Harriet, b. Jan. 30, 1827; m. Jason Hodgkin, June 5, 1856, who died soon after. VI. Charles, b. Nov. 2, 1829; m. Mary E. dau. of Foskitt Farr. For a while he was in the shoe business with his father, but subsequently became a photographer, and established himself in Burlington, Vt., where his business was very profitable during the rebellion, and he accumulated a handsome fortune. He died Aug. 12, 1866, leaving a widow and two children. VII. Clarinda, b. Jan 25, 1832; m. George Houghton, a shoe manufacturer, April 10, 1859,—issue, seven ch., four living. VIII. Ellen, b. Sept. 12, 1834.

MITCHELL, WILLIAM.—The ancestors of the Mitchell family living in town were from Scotland, and John Mitchell, the father of William, for a while after coming to this country, lived in Malden, Mass., where he married Phœbe Lynde, of the same place, b. April 6, 1761, and died in Walpole, Nov. 4, 1848. He died in Westmoreland Jan. 17, 1798. They were married June 6, 1779. William was born in Malden, April 28, 1788, and when he was quite young he removed, with his parents, to Westmoreland, and lived in the block house that once stood a few rods north of the cemetery, which was built for the protection of the people of Westmoreland against the butchery of the Indians. Most of the family of nine children were born in Westmoreland, and after the death of John, the father, his widow remained on the place a number of years.

William is the only surviving member of the family, and the oldest person living in town at the present time (1878). He married Rebecca Martin, April 15, 1812, who was born Dec. 19, 1794, and died at Walpole, Sept. 13, 1860. He came to this town early in the present century and established the business of a harness maker, in connection with which he kept a barber's shop. He followed the above-named business till he had to relinquish it on account of the infirmities of age. His children were as follow: viz., I. Charlotte, b. in Lancaster, N. H., Dec. 10, 1813; m. George Allen, of this town, Sept. 6, 1838; they have one child, Grace, b. in Walpole March 13, 1846. II. William, jr., b. in Walpole Sept. 17, 1815; d. unm.

Apr. 10, 1840. III. James Lynde, b. in W., Aug. 5, 1817; m. first, Mary J. Coburn, of Lowell, Mass., and had four ch.: 1st, William. 2d, James, d. young. 3d, Eleanor Farnham, and 4th, Submit, who d. early. He m. second, Rebecca B. Coburn. James Mitchell is favorably known in New England and the city and state of New York as a hotel-keeper—a business he has followed some thirty or more years. When his parents became old and feeble he provided for them a comfortable home for their declining years,—a laudable exhibition of his generous character. He is now the proprietor of the Hotel Brunswick, New York. IV. Phebe, b. Nov. 11, 1819; m. Ransom L. Ball, June 28, 1848, and has three ch.: 1st, Ella Rebecca, b. Aug. 28, 1849. 2d, Jennie Mitchell, b. Aug. 3, 1851. 3d, Elnora Holland, b. Aug. 1, 1859. V. Sarah Louisa, b. Nov. 9, 1821; unm. VI. Mary Abigail, b. Oct. 17, 1824; d., unm., Jan. 2, 1858. VII. Edward Courtland, b. Aug. 8, 1827; m. Emily Beals, Boston, June 25, 1854. Ch. 1st, Edward Courtland, b. May 4, 1855. 2d, James William, b. Sept. 4, 1857. 3d, Emily Louisa, b. Sept. 5, 1860. 4th, Cora, b. Feb. 6, 1861. 5th, Frank Kendall, b. June 25, 1866. 6th, Benjamin E. Bates, b. Sept. 21, 1868. VIII. John Eaton, b. Feb. 3, 1830; m. Nancy O'Brien, Dec. 26, 1857; second wife's name unknown. Ch. 1st, Mary Martin. 2d, William. 3d, Martha. (See Ap.) John enlisted into the United States service near the commencement of the late Rebellion, and served three years. (See His. of Reb.) IX. Rebecca, b. June 26, 1833; m. George Huntington, June 3, 1858, and lives at the West. X. Elnora, b. Aug. 9, 1835; m. Leonard Bisco Holland, Aug. 20, 1857, and has ten children.

MOORE. Thomas and Jehoiada Moore were among the early settlers of Derry Hill. Jehoiada married Lois Baker, Dec. 3, 1797, but did not become a permanent settler. Thomas settled on the place now known as the 'Moore farm,' about one half mile west of the residence of Lewis Dickey, where he industriously spent his days. He married Elizabeth Duncan and had six children; I Lettice Cochran, b. Oct. 2d, 1793; m. a Nourse. II. Naomi, b. Sep. 14, 1795; m. William Arnold and always lived in town. (See Arnold.) III. Jane, b. June 2, 1797,

m. George Bundy of this town; she d. the present year, 1879.
(See Bundy.) IV. Polly Pinkerton, b. Nov. 24, 1799, m. David
C. Thompson. (See Thompson.) V. Elizabeth, b. Sep. 6, 1801;
m. Daniel Whipple jr., and went to Lyndon Vt. VI. John, b.
Oct. 17, 1803; never married, but lived and died in town, Feb.
25, 1848, aged 44.

Thomas Moore died, Sep. 1, 1826 aged 63; his wife, Elizabeth, died Aug. 25, 1823, aged 63.

MORRISON, SAMUEL. Of this man and his family not much information has been gathered. He came from Londonderry,
this state, about the same time the little colony of Scotch-Irish
settled on Derry Hill, (1790), and was of the same nativity of
those that settled there. He settled on the place recently owned by the late Mark Webster where he and some of his children lived for nearly half a century. He married Jane Wier,
and had the following children. I. Robert, II. Joseph, III.
John, IV. Thomas, V. Samuel, jr., who was found dead by the
road-side, Jan. 28, 1850, with a jug pretty well filled with rum
lying by his side. His age was 58 years. VI. Polly, m. a
Christy. VII. Betsey, m. Luther Fay. VIII. Jane, m. John
Cooper. There may have been more children of this family.
It is said that some of them accumulated good fortunes. Samuel Morrison died Dec. 3d, 1833, aged 91 years, and his wife
died Dec, 25, 1815, aged 64.

MORRISON, WILLIAM, or Billy, as he was called, was a brother of the foregoing. He settled on land now owned by Elias
W. Knowlton, and lived in a house that once stood east of his
residence, near a little brook. He with his family moved from
town some forty years ago, and have made their way in the
world to their pecuniary advantage. This family consisted of
the following children as far as known. I. Priscilla, II, Mary,
III. Prudence. IV. Calvin. V. George, lives at Rockingham,
Vt, VI. Sherburne. One thing quite remarkable about this
family was the *red* hair and *black* eyes belonging to all the children.

MORSE, EBENEZER. It is said that the surrounding scenery
where people are born and brought up has a tendency, in no

small degree, to mould and modify their character. If such
is the case, the subject of this sketch is no exception. Born
in Dublin, N. H., in 1785, near its placid lake, and cradled in
view of the firm and towering old Monadnock, his character
seems to have been a strange compound of the serene and
gentle aspect of the one, and of the firm and rugged appearance of the other; at one time full of pleasant and laughable
stories, at another wearing a forbidding, unapproachable
countenance. However, his appearance was not a true index
of what was within. He was graduated at Dartmouth, 1810,
and, after studying the medical profession, came to this town
and rented an office-room in the north-east corner of the old
Johnson tavern, now the residence of Fred A. Wier. At that
time (1813) a tumble-down wall ran north from his office, near
which stood a sapling elm, "about the size," as he said, "of a
whip-stock," which has since grown to its present dimensions.
The Dr. had some taste for literature, and occasionally, in his
leisure hours, courted the muses; but it is thought the court-
ship was not very satisfactory to him. He was a very interesting prose writer, and will long be remembered as rescuing
from oblivion not a little of the early history of his adopted
town. He had an extended practice for many years, compet-
ing with Drs. Johnson, Sparhawk, Holland, and the Kittredges.
In the later years of his practice, his hobbies were good nurs-
ing and bread pills, which he thought quite as efficacious as
blue pills and jalap. When the war of the rebellion broke out,
the fire of his youth seemed to burn afresh, and his counsels
were much heeded by his townsmen, in its incipient stages.
In stature the Dr. was tall, being six feet and three inches when
erect. His head was noticably round, with a face of harmonious
features. Being frugal in his own expenditures he was always
at war with prodigality; and being conservative in his views,
he hated innovation. The foolish customs and frivolities of
the age he never failed to sarcastically rebuke. He was often
heard to say of some foolish custom, "O, that's *genteel*," in a
manner that had more meaning than the words. By many
families in town he will be long remembered as a man on

whose judgment they could rely. In 1816 he married Esther, the only daughter of John Crafts, by whom he had the following children. I. John Crafts, b. Apr. 4, 1818; m. Joanna Paige Emmons, Jan. 2, 1851: has had five children, four of whom are living. He is a merchant in Boston. II. Charles Orlando, b. Oct. 25, 1819. He went to Egypt a short time previous to his death, to try the effect of the dry climate on his health, but returned without receiving any benefit. He died of consumption, Mar. 9, 1845. III. George Mason, b. Aug. 27, 1821. He is a physician, in Clinton, Mass., where he went soon after completing his medical studies, about 1847-8. He m., first, May 6, 1846, Eleanor Carlisle, dau. of Carlton Chase, first bishop of New Hampshire, residing at Claremont, where he commenced practising his profession, and they had 7 children, of whom only one is living. His wife died, and he married Jan. 15, 1863, Mary Frances Stearns, by whom he has 2 ch. IV. Edward Everett, b. Sep. 26, 1824; d. May 9, 1827. V. Esther Crafts, b. Mar. 19, 1830; m. John White Hayward, June 2, 1851. Has 3 ch. (See Ap.) VI. Henry Lewis, b. Oct. 1, 1832; m. Mary Tarbell Homer, Sep. 24, 1867,—2 ch. He resides in Boston. VII. Frank, b. July 23, 1828; d. Sep. 4, 1840. Ebenezer Morse d. Dec. 30, 1863, his wife d. June 11, 1879, in her 88th year. Subjoined are some specimens of the Dr.'s poetic musings. They were written for the occasion of the Centennial celebration of the town of Dublin, N. H., in 1852, in response to a *toast* that was prepared for him. After making some happy preliminary remarks he introduced the following lines:

There's a 'witching enchantment in that little grove,
Where we children and lambs in the shade loved to rove,
Till "old crazy Stanford" was seen there one day,
Which spoiled all our innocent frolic and play.
The rocks in the fields, where we labored, can show
The marks of the harrow, plough, shovel and hoe.
I can see all the brooks where the trout used to play,
The meadows and ponds where we fished and made hay,
Can hear the shrill notes of the loon, which, so fond,
Is calling her mate from a neighboring pond.

That primitive church, alas! where is it now?
Where our fathers and mothers in faith used to bow.
By the side of Beech Mountain for years it had stood,
Recording the prayers of the pious and good.
I remember the pews, with their pretty turned slats,
And the posts where the men used to hang up their hats.
These last were a happy resort for the head,
And lengthened the naps when long sermons were read,
But the music every one used to admire,
When they heard Ensign Twichell lead off in the *quire!*
The christening font very seldom was dry
Where Christ, with his blessings on children, was nigh.
Here Sprague taught the truths which religion adorn,
And left all his treasures for children unborn.
That bright crystal spring never dried,
Where the boys used to eat bread and cheese by its side.
Here were spent the long noonings of which we were fond,
And picked the sweet berries that grew round the pond."

Then he made allusion to a sonnet he addressed to a lady, with whom he was enamored, but which she never received,—the lady being present on the occasion; two lines which he remembered were as follows:

"With merry heart, I saw her twist off
The magic *thread from her pine distaff*."

After some further remarks, he alluded to the old spinning-wheel, thus:

"The boys dressed the flax, the girls spun the tow,
And the music of mother's foot-wheel was not slow,
The flax on the bended pine distaff was spread,
With squash shell of water to moisten the thread.
Such were the pianos our mother's would keep,
Which they played on while *spinning* their children to sleep.
My mother's I'm sure, must have borne off the medal,
For she always was placing her foot on the pedal.
The warp and the filling were piled in the room,
Till the web was completed and fit for the loom.
Then labor was pleasure, and industry smiled,
While the wheel and the loom every trouble beguiled;
And here at the distaff, the good wives were made,
Where Solomon's precepts were fully obeyed."   .

Speaking of *pleasure* carriages, the only ones in use till 1813, he alludes to a couplet of Dr. Caustic, (Thomas Green Fessenden) who, writing more than seventy- five years ago, describing a fancy ball, says :

> "My girl, the prettiest of a million,
> Shall ride behind me on a pillion."

NICHOLS, THOMAS, was born in Shirley, Mass., in April, 1750. He married Elizabeth Boynton, of Lunenburg, Mass., and immediately after was called to serve his country in the Revolutionary war. After his discharge he moved with his family to Stoddard, N. H., in 1779, where he remained twenty years, previous to removing to Walpole in 1799. Here he purchased a farm previously owned by Col. Benjamin Bellows. He died May 22, 1839. He was the father of nine children, three of whom settled in town: the place of settlement of the other six is not given. Ch. I. Thomas, jr., b. May 10, 1780; m. Pruda Thompson, b. Aug. 21, 1782. He d. June 1, 1865; she d. Jan. 1865. Ch. 1st, Louisa, b. May 13, 1807; m. a man by the name of Perry,—issue, one dau., Frances, who m. William A. Maynard. 2d, George, b. Aug. 6, 1808; d. Feb. 8, 1842. 3d, Charles, b. June 19, 1810; went to Boston, and subsequently to New York, and has not been heard from since. 4th, Samuel, b. Oct. 25, 1812; studied medicine, and graduated at the Medical College at Harrisburg, Pa.; m. Saphira Smith, of Unity, N. H., and is now a practising physician at Bellows Falls, Vt. 5th, Maria, b. June 20, 1815; m. Martin G. Hall, and lives in town. (See Ap.) 6th, Edward, b. June 28, 1816; m. ——, and lives in Alexandria, N. Y. 7th, Mary Ann, b. Feb. 7, 1818; m. Sumner Gove, and lives in Acworth. 8th, Edna Augusta, b. Nov. 20, 1819, and lives with her sister in Acworth, unm. 9th, Amy Ann, b. Dec. 5, 1822; m. Armstrong S. Hall, and lives in California. 10th, Elmira, b. Aug. 1, 1823; went south. 11th, Sophia, b. Sept. 26, 1826; not living. II. Sarah. (See Watkins.) III. Samuel, b. in Stoddard, N. H., Dec. 10, 1787. When ten years of age he came with his parents on their removal to Walpole, and, with the exception of two or three years, resided in town during life. He obtained a good education, for those days, and early cultivated a taste for reading, which he always retained. He was brought up a farmer, but was engaged in teaching, a portion of his time, for sixteen years. During the war of 1812 he enlisted in Col. Bellows' company and went to Portsmouth, and was secretary to the colonel of the regiment to which he belonged during the campaign. In 1816 he m. Mary, dau. of John Rice, of Walpole. She possessed all the virtues belonging to womanly character, and was tenderly loved by husband and children. In 1821 they settled in Drewsville, where he engaged in mercantile and manufacturing business during active life; and, although his gains were moderate, he managed, by strict integrity and close attention to business, to bring up a family of six girls and give them advantages of such culture as to make them ornaments of the society in which they move. He took an active and prominent part in the political and civic interests of the town, and was many times elected to fill various town offices. He was twice elected a member of the State Legislature,—in 1847 and 1848, —receiving the full strength of the old Whig party, to which he was a staunch adherent. He was a man of positive views, but strictly honest, and a good neighbor. He was a Baptist in religious sentiment, and labored hard to establish a permanent society in Drewsville. (See narrative.) His first wife d. April 22, 1834, after which he was twice married. He d. Sept. 20, 1858. Ch. 1st, Caroline E., m. William Storer; lives in Cambridge, Mass., and has had four ch.: William N., Ellen M., Walter, d. 1856, and Henry J. 2d, Mary A., m. Edwd. Crosby; she d. April 3, 1844. She had two ch., (1) Mary N., m. Alfred L. Barber, Nov., 1861; d. March 31, 1871. (2) Grace. 3d, Eliza A., m. Edward Crosby, second wife, and lives in Boston. Ch. (3) Samuel N. (4) Annie E., m. Geo. M. Jeffers, Sept. 9, 1876; d. Feb. 15, 1878. (5) Edward H. 4th, Ellen Martha, m. V. A. Turpin, and lives in Chicago, Ill. 5th, Maria, m. Henry Johnson, and resides in New York. 6th, Harriet Haynes, m. Edward Frye, who d. March, 1869; she lives in Chicago, Ill. IV. Rhoda, m. Joseph Haynes, March 9, 1822.

ORMSBY, STEPHEN, was from Windham, Ct., and came to Walpole some time about 1790. He brought his wife, whose maiden name was Phœbe Calkins, with him. He was a barber

by trade, and had a shop where the Unitarian meeting-house
now stands, which was the resort of John Livingston, George
Aldrich, and a coterie of others of the same kith. His children were 1. Jemima, m. Elisha Hooper. (See Hooper.) II.
Lucy, b. 1788; d. Feb. 10, 1869. She is remembered as the
good-natured maiden lady who taught many of those now living
their A B C s, and cared for their little wants. III. George,
b. 1796; m. Martha, dau. of Nathaniel Blanchard, of Westmoreland, and had four sons; one of whom, George, is a
professor in one of the western colleges. IV. Harriet, m. Joseph
Mason. (See Mason.) V. Mary, b. 1798; m. Samuel Whiting,
of Concord, Mass., and had five ch.,—three d. young. The
surviving ones were 1st, Thomas S., m. Rhoda Mead, of Hanover, N.H., and had three ch., two of whom are living; she d.
March 15, 1863. Ch. (1) Mary, d. about 1868. (2) Clarence.
(3) Lucia. 2d, Mary H., m. George Miller, of Lowell, Mass.;
he d. 1865.

PECK, PHILIP, was a descendant of Joseph Peck, the ancestor
of most of the name in this country, who came from Hingham,
Eng., to Hingham, Mass., in 1638. Joseph subsequently removed
to Rehoboth, where the ancestors of Philip remained till his
grandfather, Solomon, removed to Royalston, Mass., in 1779,
and purchased thirty acres of land, to which he afterwards
made additions. His son, Benoni, married Eunice Rogers, and
lived on this farm till 1862, he then being in his eightieth year.
Philip was the oldest son of Benoni and Eunice (Rogers) Peck,
born Jan. 16, 1812. He worked on his father's farm till about
the age of eighteen, when he came to Walpole (1830), and
entered the store of Col. David Buffum, as clerk. After some
years he formed a copartnership with William Bellows, under
the style of Bellows & Peck. This firm was unfortunate in
business, and dissolved about 1841. Mr. Peck afterwards
resumed trade alone, but was soon burned out; after which he
relinquished active business, and spent much of his time in
reading books and the newspapers of the day. He was a great
admirer of Horace Greeley, and was a subscriber to the New
York Tribune for more than twenty years. He was one of the

first in town to cast an anti-slavery ballot, and continued yearly to do so till the Republican party was formed. He adhered to the fortunes of Andrew Johnson, and was appointed postmaster under his administration, and held the office about three months, till his appointment was overruled by Congress, and he was dismissed from office, when he became disgusted with politics and political intrigues. When the library became the property of the town, he manifested a lively interest in its success, and was one of the library committee for several years. Mr. Peck possessed a keen intellect and a sensitive nature, and at the time of his death, which occurred Sept. 15, 1875, was one of the best-informed men in town on the political and financial condition of the country.

He married, Nov. 21, 1839, Martha Eleanor, dau. of Hon. Thomas and Eleanor (Foster) Bellows, by whom he had two sons: I. Henry Philip, b. Aug. 31, 1840; d. July 13, 1852, from injuries received by a fall from a horse. II. Thomas Bellows, b. Aug. 18, 1842; fitted for college at our High School and the Latin School in Boston; graduated at Harvard College in 1863, after which he made the tour of Europe. He now resides in Melrose, Mass., with his mother, and does business in Boston. He is gratefully remembered by the citizens of Walpole for the efficient services rendered when on the town library committee.

PORTER, VINE, the progenitor of the Porter families now living in town, was born at Crown Point, N. Y., Sep. 22, 1801. He married Hannah Pike, of Morristown, Vt., who was born in Brookfield, Vt., June 27, 1801. For a while after marriage he resided in Morristown where four of his children were born, viz., I. Winslow B., b. Nov. 21, 1823, (see Physicians in Walpole.) m. Laura M., dau. of Luther and Irene (Dunshee) Burt, of this town. Ch. 1st. Warren W., 2d, Mary B., m. John G. Shedd—residence Chicago, Ill. II. Samuel H., b. Nov. 26, 1825; m. Harriet A., dau. of Josiah and Sarah (Merriam) Emerson, of Alstead, N. H. Ch. 1st. Emma A., b. in Boston, Mass., Nov. 9th, 1854; m. Spaulding S. Shedd—resides in Oneida, Ill. 2d, Frank W. 3d, John Lincoln. (See Ap.) III.

W. B. Porter, M. D.

Wm. H., b. May 10, 1830, m. Clementine R., dau, of Robert Balch, of Johnson, Vt. He is a physician, settled in Surry, N. H. Ch. 1st, Myron H., b. June 3, 1855. 2d, Ellen H., b. Dec. 22, 1861. 3d, Katie H., b. Jan. 26, 1865. IV. James H., b. June 1, 1832; m. Ellen M., dau. of Warren Wentworth, Alstead, N. H. issue 1 ch. Fred W., b. in Boston in 1864. James H. resides in Chicago, Ill., and is general western passenger ag't for the Great Western railroad. V. George P., b. in Walpole, June 23, 1834; m. Sarah J., dau. of Royal Ladd of Hoosick, N. Y. Issue 1 ch. Mabel. (See Ap.) Vine Porter removed to this town and settled on what is now known as the Corey farm, Mar. 31, 1834, and lived there till Sep. 24, 1843, when he died, leaving a widow and five boys, the oldest being 20, and the youngest 9 yrs. Although those boys were left at the lower round of the ladder they have, by dint of heroic determination and perseverance, guided by the counsels of a good mother, managed to keep the wolf from the door, and ascended one *round* after another till all have acquired a good English education and become highly respectable members of the community — two of them became physicians. Although cradled in poverty, they may ere long thank Heaven that they were not born with a gold spoon in their mouths.

REDINGTON. The Redington brothers, Thomas and Isaac, came to Walpole, prior to the year 1890, from Lunenburg, Mass. Whether their father and mother, Benjamin and Ruth, ever lived in town is uncertain; but in a record of deaths, in the town, made by the late Lewis Campbell Esq., of Keene, a former resident of Walpole, is recorded the following; Benjamin Redington died Aug. 23, 1811; aged 82; Ruth, his wife, d. Mar. 14, 1798, aged 61. Benjamin, their son, d. Feb. 25, 1790, aged 27. Sukey, a dau. of the above, d. Sep. 7, 1799. Thomas, one of the sons that lived in Walpole d. June 26, 1824, aged 58, and his wife, Mary, d. Dec. 21, 1825, aged 52. Among the marriages solemnized by Pliny Dickinson is found recorded; "John Brooks, and Nancy Redington, Mar. 8, 1807." It is *inferred* that the Nancy above named was a daughter of

Benj. and Ruth, as there was no other family by the name of Redington living in town at that time.

THOMAS and ISAAC REDINGTON were merchants in town some twenty five years, doing business principally in the old brick store, some times in company, sometimes separately and at other times in company with Josiah Bellows 3d. Both were married and had families of children. Isaac built the house where Edwin Hosmer now resides, and lived therein; and his brother Thomas lived in the Ruggles house. Both families were highly respectable. Isaac represented the town in the legislature in the years 1813–14 and 16, besides holding town offices of responsibility. Children of Isaac and Mary Redington. 1st, Isabella Brigham, b. Feb. 28, 1798; m. Phinehas Fisk. 2d, Isaac Dana, bap. Sep. 27, 1801. 3d, Caroline Stearns, b. Oct. 14, 1803; m. Oliver Holman, of Keene. 4th, Ruth Louisa, b. Aug. 13, 1805; m. Benj. F. Adams and went to Chicago, Ill., and is still living. 5th, Edward Cadwell, b. July 19, 1809. 6th, Henry P., bap. July 18, 1814; m. a Miss Bradford, of Keene. Children of Thomas and Mary Redington. 1st, Charles, birth not known. He went to Charlestown, S. C. to recover his health, but died of consumption. 2d, George, b. Nov. 27, 1799, and is still living at Littleton, N. H. 3d, William. 4th, Henry. 5th, Mary, m. a Mr. Ely, of Littleton, N. H. 6th, Frances, d. unm.

ROLLINS, WILLIAM, the son of William, of Dublin, N. H., was born there, Jan. 1, 1803, and came to Walpole early in the present century and married Clarissa, the sister of Gardner Dodge, Oct. 10, 1825, who was born in Marlow, Aug. 11, 1803. Ch. I. William G., b. May 10, 1827; m. Mrs. Eliza Dorr, of Wells, Me. II. Sarah J., b. May 17, 1828; m. Henry R. Chase, of Vermont. III. Reuben Christopher, b. Dec. 26, 1829; m. Frances, dau. of Gardner and Fanny (Graves) Dodge, of Walpole. IV. George H., b. Jan. 19, 1839; m. Marcia Sabin, of Vermont. Mrs. Rollins died July 23, 1865, and he then married Fanny Bidwell, of Langdon—she died Feb. 14, 1879, aged 74 years.

ROYCE, JONATHAN, came from Connecticut to Marlow, N. H.,

about the time of the exodus of families from that state to the settlements on Connecticut river, which was between 1775 and 1780. He drew his household goods upon a hand sled and was guided on his way by marked trees to the above mentioned place. He built himself a cabin in the wilderness; but did not remain there only one year before he removed to Walpole and pitched on the farm now owned by Oliver Hall, where he remained for a while, when he removed to the Valley, where he located permanently. He owned at one time more *poor* land than any man living in Walpole, the number of acres being two thousand, twelve hundred lying in Walpole, and the remainder in Essex, N. Y. His name first appears on the town records in 1787, as one of the selectmen, and he was elected to that office more years than any other man in town. He was for many years Justice of the Peace and is generally remembered as Squire Royce. In the first years of the present century, he embraced the political sentiments of Thomas Jefferson and lent his aid in the establishment and support of a political newspaper, known as the Political Observatory, published here. He was born in 1735 and died July 10, 1826. He married Sarah Marvin, b. 1749; d. Aug. 27, 1809. Ch. I. Marvin, b. 1770; d. July 22, 1841; m. Prudence Stiles, of Lunenburgh, Mass., b. 1771; d. June 15, 1843. Ch 1st, Betsey, d. unm. 2d, John S., m. Mary Brooks, of Chester, Vt. Ch. (1) Merriam, m. Almarian Griggs. (2) John Jackson, went West. (3) Benjamin Brooks, m. Jane Bixby and lives in town. (4) Jasper. 3d, Jonathan. 4th, Hiram. 5th, George. 6th, Jesseniah. 7th, Isaiah, m. and had 2 ch. 8th, Susan R., b. Oct. 11, 1811; m. William Watkins. (See Watkins). II. Abigail, m. Levi Harris, of Langdon, N. H. III. Abner, m. a Lovell and removed to the state of New York. IV. Jonathan, jr., m. Polly Emory and went to Illinois and had a large family and became wealthy. V. Sally, m. a Mead. VI. Lois, m. a Harvey, of Surry, N. H. VII. Elisha, m. Betsey Reed. VIII. Phebe, m. John Cross, of this town and had 9 ch., one of whom, John jr., m. Eunice Beckwith, of Acworth, N. H. IX. Polly, m. her cousin, Nehemiah Royce. (See Nehemiah Royce.)

ROYCE, NEHEMIAH, came from Lyme, Conn., and settled in
the Valley, about 1810, the exact time not being known. He
married Polly, the daughter of Jonathan Royce, Esq., his
cousin, and had the following children: I. Eliza, m. Elijah
Mack, of Rockingham, Vt., and had 3 ch. II. Mary, m.
Thomas Fortune, of Essex, N. Y.,—issue 2 ch. III. Cyrus,
b. Jan. 8, 1814; m. Laura, daughter of Timothy Lovell, of
Rockingham, Vt., b. Nov. 19, 1821. Ch. 1st, Cyrus, jr., m.
Ida, dau. of Albert and Cordelia (Boyden) Richardson and
an adopted dau. of one Boyden, of Brattleboro, Vt. 2d, La
Fayette, m. a daughter of Rev. A. B. Flanders, of Chester,
Vt.,—issue 1 ch. 3d, Grace S., b. Sep. 10, 1849; m. Lucius
Wellington, of this town. 4th, Laura Ella, b. Aug. 7, 1852.
IV. Samuel, b. July 25, 1815; m. Nancy S. Mack, of Charlestown, N. H.,—issue 1 ch., d. young. V. Nehemiah, jr., b.
1823; m. Sarah Ann, dau. of James and Lucy (Locke) Benson, d. Nov. 31, 1874. He came to his death from injuries
received by falling down an embankment near his house a
few days before he died. He was a quiet, unobtrusive man in
his intercourse, and was highly esteemed by his townsmen.
He was one of the selectmen of the town at the time of his
death, and had served as such for several years preceding.
VI. Sarah Amanda, b. Nov. 30, 1826; m. Joshua Collins Quinton, b. Dec. 23, 1834,—issue, 3 ch.; 2 living. (See Ap.) Nehemiah Royce, sen., d. Feb. 10, 1838.

RUGGLES, WILLIAM, came to Walpole from Reading, Mass.,
it is said, about 1818 or 20, and married Betsey Lawrence,
Oct. 7, 1821. He had no children, but adopted a daughter of
one of his sisters, whose name was Elizabeth G. Stratton: she
married George H. Cole, of Westmoreland, Jan. 1, 1853. Mr.
Ruggles was Town Clerk for twenty-one years, and is remembered as very quaint in his manners and mode of speaking.
He and his wife both died in Ludlow, Vt., but were buried
in this town.

William had a brother, Samuel T., who lived in town a
number of years, in the Valley, and had the following children. I. Ira White, b. July 3, 1817. II. Cornelia, b. Mar. 4,

1820; m. Samuel Prentiss, whose former name was Hogg,[*] and moved to Reading, Mass. III. Sumner Stratton, b. Nov. 26, 1821. IV. Caroline Orpha, b. at Dorchester, Mass., Aug. 6, 1824. V. Emily, b. July 16, 1827, at Dorchester. VI. Otis Taft, b. Nov. 26, 1829. VII. Walter Wilson, b. Nov. 6, 1831, at Reading, Mass. VIII. Helen, b. at Reading, Nov. 17, 1833. IX. Gould Grant, b. at Dorchester, June 6, 1836. X. Laura, b. at Reading, June 4, 1839. This family all moved to Reading, Mass.

RUSSELL, JAMES, and his wife, Lucy, came to this town at an early period, from ·Wellington, Ct., and were among the early members of Rev. Thomas Fessenden's church, which they joined in 1770. He was born in 1710, and died Oct. 8, 1784; she was born in 1718, and died April 24, 1791. He settled on a plot of land, now known as the Ezra Hall place, which was held by himself and his descendants till the present year (1879). James and Lucy had six children, but it is impossible to name them in their order of succession. Thomas was the oldest of the three sons belonging to the family of James, and was born Oct. 22, 1751, and died Nov. 27, 1845. He m. Eunice Alexander,—b. Sept. 8, 1769, Jan. 25, 1785; she d. Jan. 11, 1857. He first settled on the place now owned by J. W. Taggard, and then on the place owned by William B. Mason, which was the home of the Russells for three-fourths of a century or more. In connection with his farming interests he used to make flaxen ropes and halters during the winter season. His children were as follow: 1st, Thomas, jr., b. Sept. 3, 1785; m. widow Hannah (Flint) Wellington, b. June 11, 1782. He d. March 28, 1872; she d. Jan. 5, 1866. Ch. (1) Amos, b. Sept. 11, 1818; m. Elizabeth Ann Clark, of Concord, Mass., March 7, 1843; issue, four ch., three daughters and one son. (2) Franklin Flint, b. May 6, 1822; m. first, Jan. 19, 1845, Ellen Hyne, of Rochester, N. Y.; m. second, Sophia Knott, Dec., 1875,—issue, one dau. (3) Levi Alexander, b. April 18, 1823, and is alive, unm. (4) Sarah Amanda, b. July 10, 1825; m. James H. Phelps, May 2,

*The former name of the Prentiss families in Walpole was Hogg.

1848,—issue, one daughter and one son. (5) Josiah Quincy, b. Oct. 19, 1830; m. Nov. 22, 1864, Ella Abby Murphy,—issue, one dau. 2d, John, d. in Ohio, Oct. 1, 1845; had nine ch. 3d, Richard, b. Jan. 15, 1790: m. Tirzah, dau. of David Hall, July 22, 1795. Ch. (1) Thomas, b. Dec. 24, 1813; m. Oct. 2, 1845, Pamelia Leonard,—ch., two sons and two daughters. (2) Almira, b. Oct. 15, 1815; m. O. H. Williams, Nov. 3, 1834, and had six ch. (3) Sophia, b. March 17, 1817; m., Dec. 23, 1826, A. Buck, and had ten ch. (4) Lydia H., b. Dec. 29, 1820; m. Isaac Bartholomew, July 30, 1867. (5) Levi F., b. Nov. 5, 1823; m., Feb. 14, 1853, Eliza Cotton,—two ch. (6) Rhoda, b. Nov. 23, 1825. (7) Henry, b. April 25, 1830; m., Feb. 12, 1857, A. C. Baker,—issue, four ch. (8) Mary J., b. May 19, 1836; m., June 25, 1855, J. R. Piper,—issue, two ch. 4th, Sally, b. Aug. 30, 1796; d. June 5, 1875; m. Elisha Angier, b. Dec. 6, 1787. (See narrative, for death.) Ch. (1) Silas, b. April 30, 1812; d. Dec. 14, 1878; m. first, Caroline F., dau. of John Emerson, Nov. 8, 1838; m. second, widow Mary Long, dau. of John Marshall,—issue, five sons and three daughters. (2) Amanda, b. April 3, 1814; m. Stephen Fay, April 6, 1837, and had several ch.; d. Aug. 13, 1877. (3) John, b. Dec. 18, 1815; m. Mary Rochafella, Nunda, N. Y. (4) Emily S., b. March 12, 1819; m. Sala P. Webb, M.D., Jan. 1, 1850, and has two sons. (5) Sophia, b. Feb. 5, 1825; lives unm. (6) Mary Philena, b. Nov. 20, 1820; m. Lewis Lane. (See Lane.) (7) Sarah, b. Aug. 15, 1829. (8) Geo. H., b. Aug. 31, 1831; m. Adeline Smith. (See Ap.) (9) Harriet M., b. Aug. 31, 1831: m. Sylvanus Titus, of Keene, Sept. 7, 1858. (10) Andrew Jackson, b. April 18, 1834; d. Nov. 11, 1864. 5th, David, b. Aug. 30, 1796; d. June 5, 1875; m. Mary A. Wheeler, Dec. 25, 1817: b. July 1, 1796. Ch. (1) David Allen, b. Oct. 16, 1818; m. first, Nancy, dau. of Jacob B. Burnham, b. Jan. 13, 1824: d. June 6, 1860; issue, one dau., d. in infancy; m. second, Helen L., dau. of Dr. Jesseniah Kittredge, Sept. 19, 1865, b. Aug. 7, 1837. (2) John B., (See Ap.) m. Lucy, dau. of Elisha and Jemima (Ormsby) Hooper,—issue, three sons and two daughters. Ch. [1] Ella F., b. March 10, 1843; m., May 20, 1862, William H.

Fuller,—issue, one dau. [2] George II., b. July 4, 1844; m. Minnie Kurch, March 1, 1870. [3] Charles M., b. Oct. 23, 1846; m. first, Emma A., and second, Janette M. Messer. (See Ap.) [4] J. Edward, b. Jan. 8, 1848; unm. He is a clergyman and teacher. [5] C. Clarissa, d. in infancy. (4) George II., b. Nov. 14, 1824; d. Sept. 16, 1828. (5) Mary E., b. Sept. 26, 1828; m. George S. Wilder, July 1, 1862. (6) Martha P., m., Jan. 1, 1855, Albert Derby, b. July 4, 1822,— issue, one daughter, Minnie F. 6th, Levi, b. 1800; m. Elizabeth Waldo; d. Sept. 21, 1831. Ch. Ira W., b. May 17, 1825; m. Harriet A. Ballou, Sept. 3, 1850, and has four ch.,—and had two that d. in infancy. 7th and 8th. Elvira and Philena. Philena (See P. Foster). Elvira (See Jennison). 9th, Eunice, b. March 7, 1808; d. Oct. 23, 1852; m., April 20, 1830, Orlando Frink, b.April 20, 1803, and had three ch., Mary E., Henry O., and Sarah E. 10th, Betsey P., b. May 5, 1810. (See Dickey.) II. Hannah, m. Luke Fletcher, July 23, 1784. At one time she lived in a little one-story house that stood some fifty rods south of Henry Fletcher's. She is said to have been intellectually vigorous. She got into some controversy at one time with one Bailey, a Baptist clergyman living in Westmoreland, on some religious points, and wrote a long disquisition, in the form of a dialogue, defending her position, and got Henry Fitch to revise it for publication; but the cost of publication was not within her means, and it never took form in printer's ink,—a great disappointment to many of her friends. III. Priscilla, m. David Pulsipher, of Rockingham. IV. Lucy, m. John Fletcher, of Westmoreland. V. Aquila, m. Abigail, dau. of William Glazier, and had eight children, which number he deemed not sufficient for a poor man, but adopted two more. He lived at one time where Allen Dunshee now lives, and was for many years sexton for the town. Ch. 1st, Elijah, b. Jan. 18, 1781; m. Sally Griffin, Feb. 23, 1808. 2d, Abner, b. Nov. 20, 1782; d. young. 3d, James, b. Jan. 27, 1785; m. Eliza P. Houghton, March 8, 1807. 4th, Thomas, b. Jan. 27, 1786; m. in Dummerston, Vt. 5th, Lucy Farmer, b. Sept. 3, 1787; m. in Troy, N.Y. 6th, Gideon, b. Sept. 28, 1791; m. Sarah Plant, of Weathersfield, Vt. 7th,

Ruth, b. Sept. 29, 1793; m. Elias Williams, Nov. 21, 1813. 8th, Sarah Glazier, b. April 19, 1799; m. a Thomas, in New York. The family all left town, and not any of the blood of that branch remains. VI. Jeduthan was the second son, and lived on the homestead of his father,—the Ezra Hall place. He was born in 1744: several years before the Russells came to Walpole. He married Hannah, the daughter of William Glazier, one of the early settlers of the town, Nov. 28, 1772, when he was twenty-eight years old. His wife died Sept. 8, 1799, aged 44. Whether he married again or not is unknown. He was killed at the raising of a barn, which is now standing on the place owned by John W. Taggard, by falling from the plate to the ground, May 13, 1813, aged 69. Ch. 1st, Martha, age unknown; m. a man named Dudley. 2d, Eli, b. March 13, 1775; m. Hepsibah, dau. of Benjamin Floyd, Jan. 5, 1803, and lived in Westminster, Vt. She had six ch., two of whom are well known music publishers in Boston. 3d, Lucy, b. April 13, 1777; m. John Graves, of this town. 4th, Lydia, b. Oct. 18, 1779; m. a Kendall. 5th, Hannah, b. Aug. 6, 1782; m. Amos Graves, of this town. 6th, Jeduthan, jr., b. March 14, 1785; m. Rhoda, dau. of David Hall, and was a miller at Saxton's River. 7th, Joseph, b. July 6, 1787; m. first, Lucy Angier, and second, Harriet Robinson, and went to Nunda, N.Y. Ch. (1) Priscilla, m. Seranus Britton, and had three ch. (2) Charles. (3) William. (4) Sophia. (5) Almira. He had ch. by his second wife. 8th, Priscilla, b. May 13, 1790; m. Ezra Hall, July 19, 1807. (See Hall.) 9th, Susanna, b. Jan. 11, 1793; m. Erasmus Wellington: lived first in Westmoreland, but subsequently went west. 10th, William, b. Aug. 7, 1795; m. in Rochester, N.Y., where he went to live. 11th, Martin, b. Aug. 20, 1799.

SCOVILL, FREDERICK, came to Walpole in the early part of the century, which is infered by the birth of his oldest child, who was born at that time. He settled on land in the east part of the town, and remained on his first purchase during life. He was a quiet, good citizen, and was content to reap the fruits of honest labor. He married Sarah Howard, by whom he had children as follow. I. William Howard, b. Nov. 14,

1809; m. Elsie, dau. of Amasa Carpenter, and had fourteen children, three only of whom are now living, viz. 1st, George, a music teacher, now a resident of Westmoreland, N. H. 2d, Frank, resides in Massachusetts. 3d, Ella A., m. Edward A. Watkins, of this town. William Howard, d. May 19, 1877. II. Frederick Willard, b. Dec. 28, 1813; m. first, Mary Ann Dinsmore, of Alstead, N. H. by whom he had children. She d. and he m. again, wife's name unknown, residence California. III. Sarah Ann, b. Nov. 19, 1815, m. George Coffin, residence, Massachusetts. IV. Harriet Eliza, b. Aug. 18, 1817. V. Mary Louisa, b. Apr. 19, 1819. VI. Martha Maria, b. Apr. 3, 1821. VII. Amos, age unknown; he married and went to the state of New York, and died there.

SEAVER, THOMAS, came to this town about the year 1803, from Northboro, Mass., and married Eunice Redington, a sister of Thomas and Isaac, who were for many years merchants in the place. Mr. Seaver soon commenced trade, and continued business for more than forty years. He kept various kinds of goods for sale, but his principal business was the compounding and sale of drugs and medicines, and among other things he made a liniment which was very popular for a time, and met with a ready sale. He was one of the early pillars of the Orthodox church and for many years one of its deacons. He was proverbially a pious and peace-loving citizen and a constant attendant on public worship. He was from a long-lived family and he reached the ripe old age of ninety years and five months, Dec. 5, 1862; his wife d. Jan. 9, 1850, aged 72. Ch. I. Harriet, b. June 15, 1804 II. Almira A., b. 1807, m. Samuel Prentiss, of Langdon, and had 5 ch. III. Susan, b. June 5, 1809; m. Leonard Worcester, who was an educated man and once taught an academy in this town. She had one child. They died in New Jersey. IV. Mary E., b. Oct. 1810, m. Francisco B. Lopez, and went to South America —4 ch. V. Hannah L., b. 1811; m. John C. Weir, moved to Alabama, and had six children. VI. Eunice Rebecca, b. Dec. 24, 1813; m. Wm. T. Matthews, and went to Alabama. VII. Thomas Henry, b. 1818. He was a merchant, and, at one time, was in company with his father, in town, but subsequently went to Alabama, where he died. He married Julia, dau. of Chester and Phebe Wier, of this town. She d. 1878.

SHERMAN, EPHRAIM, the first settler by the name in Walpole, was a descendant of John Sherman, who was born in Durham, Eng. 1613, and came to America and settled in Watertown, Mass., in 1834. Ephraim Sherman, the fourth by that name in America, settled in Grafton, Mass. and had five children, viz. Elizabeth, Lydia, Martha, Thankful and Ephraim, who was born July 9, 1767, and was the father of the Sherman family which follows. His four sisters married four brothers—a circumstance, perhaps, without a parallel. The sixth, Ephraim, came to Walpole from Grafton, Mass. in 1803, and his parents came with him. His father died Mar. 6, 1818, and his mother soon after, Sep. 19, 1820. Ephraim Sherman, sixth, settled on the place now owned by Eli W. Graves, once owned by Manoah Drury. He married Remember Cook, of Tiverton, and had fourteen children, as follow: I. Mary, b. June 24, 1790, in Grafton, where nine of the family were born; m. Alexander Watkins jr. (See Alexander Watkins' family.) II. Ruth, b. Aug. 17, 1791; m. Sampson Drury. (See Drury family.) III. Remember, b. June 3, 1793; m. Frederick Onstine, of Newburgh, Ohio, and had 9 ch. IV. Patty, b. Feb. 6, 1794; d. in infancy. V. Nancy, b. June 7, 1695; m. William Williams, of Newburgh, Ohio, and had 8 ch. VI. Ephraim jr., b. Mar. 17, 1796; d. Sep. 1853, unm. VII. Martha, b. Aug. 17, 1798; m. Charles Watkins, of Charlestown, N. H., and had 4 ch. VIII. Amy, b. Nov. 27, 1799; m. Charles Watkins of this town. (See Watkins family.) IX. Betsey, b. June 26, 1801; m. Russell Wheelock, of Grafton, Mass.—issue 3 ch. X. Clarissa, b. Sep. 2, 1802; m. Ariel Harris, of Vermont. XI. Harriet, b. July 10, 1804, the first child born in the family after they came to Walpole, m. Wm. Stafford and went to Concord, Mass. and had 6 ch. XII. William C., b. Sep. 26, 1807; m. first, Fanny, dau. of John and Lydia (Graves) Maynard, Oct. 8, 1832, who d. Feb. 8, 1834—issue 1 ch.—d. in infancy; m. second, Lorinda H., a sister of his first wife, Nov. 28, 1837—issue one dan. Helen Rebecca, b. July 15, 1841. William C. Sherman, at one time, in middle life, was engaged in the manufacture of sale shoes, in the firm of Allen, Maynard & Sherman. After the firm dissolved, he was for several years, an employee of A. K. Maynard & Co., in the same business, and was also assistant postmaster, during the eight years that Mr. Maynard held the office. In 1861, he was appointed Postmaster and held the office, with the exception of about three months, (when Philip Peck held the appointment,) till 1869.—Since that time he has lived in retirement. XIII. Maria, b. Apr. 5, 1809; m. first, Strong Jones, and had one son Joseph—resides in Chicago, Ill.; m. second, Lincoln Brooks, and had one dan. who m. a Van Black, and lives in Lodi, Ill. Ephraim Sherman, d. Oct. 11, 1819; his wife, Remember, d. July 17, 1841.

SPARHAWK, GEORGE, Dr., was born in 1757, graduated at Harvard in the class of 1777, studied medicine, and came to this town some time between 1780 and 1790, and commenced the practice of his profession. He built the house where A. H. Bellows now lives, and kept "bachelor's hall" till December, 1802, when he married Polly, the daughter of Aaron Allen, and bought and removed to the place now owned by George B. Williams. There he lived till the time of his death, 1847, aged 90. He made additions, from time to time, to his first purchase, till his landed estate was one of the largest in town. He had no children, but adopted John Black Sparhawk, a son of his cousin Hull, who had a large family. John Black married Phœbe Carlisle. (See Hull Sparhawk.) The doctor was a man of superior natural and acquired abilities, had an extensive practice, and accumulated a large fortune, for the times, always appropriating the "lion's share" to himself when an opportunity presented itself.

An anecdote has been told of the doctor and one Thomas Messer, who was the son of Timothy, the first settler on the Ramsay place. It appears that Thomas Messer was a neighbor of his, living in a house just west of Oliver Hall's. The doctor had a large drove of swine, which gave Messer trouble by breaking through Sparhawk's fence and destroying Messer's crops. The doctor had been repeatedly importuned by Messer to take care of his hogs, but he paid little heed to his importunities. At length Messer caught him in the vicinity where the hogs broke through, and pointed out to him the hole. "A hog go through that hole?" said the Dr. "No hog can go through so small a hole as that: it is all nonsense!" Messer was of Herculean strength and frame, and, being provoked, seized the doctor and thrust him through the hole, and exclaimed, "There! I'll take my oath I saw one hog go through." The doctor's hogs never troubled Messer afterwards.

SPARHAWK, HULL, was the cousin of Dr. George Sparhawk, and came to this town about 1785 or 1786. The Christian name of his wife was Elizabeth. He moved to Barre, Mass., about twenty years after he came to town. Ch. I. George, b. 1786; d. in infancy. II. Charlotte, b. Feb. 6, 1789. III. Mary, b. Jan. 10, 1791. IV. Elizabeth, b. March 27, 1793. All three of the girls married and moved to Hadley, Mass. Mary m. Harvey Dickinson, but who the husbands of the other two were is unknown. V. Nathaniel, b. March 27, 1795. VI, John Black, b. April 10, 1798; m. Adeline Carlisle, Sept. 7, 1818. He d. March 31, 1846, aged 48; she d. Sept. 2, 1870, aged 70. John B. was adopted by his father's cousin, Dr. George Sparhawk, and lived with him till he died. His heirs inherited the doctor's property. He had a taste for keeping tame animals about his premises, and also for fine horses. It was not an uncommon thing for one to see, on visiting his home, a tame bear, two or three monkeys, tame coons and foxes, and numerous other animals. Ch. 1st, Mary, m. Charles Capen, and resides in Dorchester, Mass. 2d, Phœbe, m. Reuben Hatch; resides in Illinois. 3d, George C., m. Johanna G. Capen, and had one son, George. 4th, John, was drowned on his way to California, at the breaking up of the steamer Independence, Feb. 15, 1853, off the Gulf of California. VII. Guy, b. March 3, 1801; d. Aug. 2, 1825. He never married, and lived alone when he died, having become estranged from his connections.

SPARHAWK, THOMAS.—The Sparhawk family in Walpole are the descendants of one Nathaniel Sparhawk, who came from

England, and settled in Cambridge, Mass., early in the settlement of the town. The original spelling of the name was *Sparrowhawk*. Thomas was the ninth child of Thomas of the second generation from Nathaniel, and was born in Cambridge, Mass., March 24, 1737, and graduated at Harvard College in the class of 1755. He married Rebecca Stearns, 2d. of Lunenburg, Mass., July 10, 1758, and came to this town in 1769. Where he first located is unknown, but he was not here long before he purchased a large tract of land, comprising, in part, what is now the Sparhawk homestead, and built for himself a substantial dwelling, on the site of the residence of Mrs. B. B. Grant, which was burned a few years since. Here he lived till he died.

In 1760 the people of Walpole bought their necessary store supplies in Northfield, Mass., of Aaron Burt, an ancestor of the Burt family in town; but soon after Mr. Sparhawk established a store here, and probably was the first merchant in town, and Amasa Allen the second. Barnabas, a negro child "belonging to Thomas Sparhawk, Esq.," was baptized, Jan. 20, 1778, and was probably one of the two slaves enumerated in the census of 1767. Mr. Sparhawk was the first man to represent the town in the N. H. Assembly, held at Exeter, in 1775, and was, for many years, Judge of Probate for the County of Cheshire, and Clerk of the Court. He was a leading man of the town, holding some responsible office yearly till his usefulness was impaired by the infirmities of age. By what information has been obtained, it is inferred that he was a man of influence, affluence, and strict integrity. He died Oct. 31, 1803; she died May, 1807. Ch. I. Thomas, jr., b. June, 1761; d. 1848; m. Octavia Frink, by whom he had nine ch.: two Henrys d. in infancy; the other seven lived beyond middle life, George being the only one who ever married. Thomas, jr., was a man of sterling worth, and held an esteemed position with his townsmen. He held many town offices from year to year during the active period of his life, and was honored with a seat in the General Court in 1795, 1796, 1798, 1801, and 1803. He was also a member of the Constitutional Convention of 1783. He

lived and died a man of strict integrity, piety, and good works.
His wife died Dec. 22, 1843. Ch. 1st, Thomas, 2d, b. Feb. 6,
1791 ; graduated at Dartmouth and became a lawyer, and
practised in town for a few years, and died in 1839. 2d, Rebecca,
b. Aug. 28, 1793; d. Aug. 28, 1851. 3d, Octavia, b. Oct. 7,
1795; d. May 22, 1850. 4th, George, b. April 24, 1797; m.
Eliza Parker Hammond, of Newton, Mass., March 7, 1822; b.
Nov. 25, 1798; d. Aug. 28, 1872. He d. Nov. 10, 1865. Ch.
(1) Rebecca Eliza, b. Jan. 31, 1823; d. June 1, 1851; m. Chas.
Sargent, of Boston, Mass., April 24, 1850, and had one son,
Charles Edward, who m. Annie E. Lewis, of Watertown, Mass.,
June 7, 1875. (See Ap.) (2) George Henry, b. Feb. 1, 1825;
d. Feb., 1851; m. Fanny A. Webb, March 26, 1848, and had
four sons : [1] Arthur George, b. Jan. 1, 1850; d. Feb. 26,
1871,—a model young man. [2] Rollin Webb, b. June 15, 1852;
d. May 6, 1879. He was engaged at the time of his death as a
school-teacher in the village; was stricken with pneumonia,
and lived but a few days. His death was lamented by all who
knew him. (See Ap.) (3) and (4) Emily Augusta and Mary
Octavia, b. May 14, 1830. Emily Augusta m. George R. Jennison. (See Ap. and Jennison.) 5th, Charles, b. April 2, 1799;
d. April 1, 1859, unm. 6th, John Stearns, b. Jan. 7, 1801; d.
April 3, 1842. 7th, Mary, b. Oct. 4, 1802; d. May 7,1869, unm.
II. Rebecca, b. 1797; m. Josiah Bellows, April 13, 1788; d.
1791. (See Bellows.) III. Oliver Stearns, b. 1771; m. Hannah
Stearns Whitney, Nov. 30, 1800. He built the house where
Harrison G. Barnes now resides, and had a large family of
children, but what became of some of them it is difficult to ascertain. He was a thrifty, stirring business man during his comparatively short life, and much respected. He d. July 6, 1824; she
d. Aug. 25, 1818. Ch. 1st, Marietta, b. Aug. 12, 1801. 2d,
Oliver, b. June 16, 1803, and went to Greenfield, Mass., where
his widow now lives. 3d, Julia Anna, b. Sept. 4, 1804. 4th,
Hannah Stearns, b. July 2, 1806. 5th, William, b. May 12,
1808. 6th, Lucius, b. Oct. 11, 1810; d. 1813. 7th, Rebecca
Stearns, b. 1811; d. 1813. 8th, Sarah Whitney, b. Sept. 15,
1812. 9th, Sophia Ann, b. Dec. 4, 1816. IV. Mary, b. Sept.

30, 1773; m. Josiah Bellows, Oct. 28, 1798; (See Bellows.) d. July 31, 1869. V. John Stearns, b. Aug. 12, 1775; d. at Andover, Mass., 1799. VI. Jonathan Hubbard, b. Feb. 7, 1781. He left Walpole early, and married at Windsor, Ct. VII. Samuel, b. 1787; m. Sophronia Brown, and was a merchant in Keene for a number of years, and died Feb. 8, 1838. He is said to have been a man of rare business qualities, and much respected as a citizen. Ch. 1st, Samuel, jr., b. Nov. 6, 1805. 2d, Sophronia, b. Sept. 22, 1810. 3d, Henry, b. Dec. 25, 1812. 4th, Eliza, b. March 24, 1816; m. George Hitchcock, and lives in Ashby, Mass. 5th, Harriet, b. May 1, 1818; m. Roger Fenton. 6th, George, b. May 22, 1820. 7th, John Hubbard, b. May 10, 1822; m. Martha Watkins, and lives in Richmond, N. H. 8th, Edward, b. Aug. 27, 1827.

STARKWEATHER, LEMUEL, came to this town early in the present century (1815) from Mansfield, Ct. He was born in 1792, and, after coming here, married Almira, daughter of Elisha Eldridge, and first commenced keeping house on what is known as the old Carlisle place, but subsequently purchased the farm lying north of the Isaac Jennings place. Here he lived during life. In his early days he was considered a famous school teacher for winter district schools. Where other teachers failed to secure order, in turbulent schools, his services were much in demand. An instance is related of a school where the large boys made it a pastime, winters, to carry out teachers, and *three* teachers had been made to yield to their united strength on this occasion in one winter. The ring-leader of the clan was a large, burly negro. Mr. Starkweather's services were sought, and he was not reluctant in engaging the school, feeling that his physical strength, which was not feeble, and his moral courage, were adequate to any emergency that might arise in the school room;—in fact he courted the opportunity of having a little (to him) coveted sport with the boys. It was not long after he commenced the school, at the appointed time, before he saw that mischief was brewing, but he kept perfectly quiet, not seemingly noticing what was going on. At the forenoon recess the boys all formed in a line, each with a billet of wood in his hand, with Sambo for captain. Various military orders were given by Sambo, which were skillfully and promptly obeyed by those under his command, all of which, were noticed by Mr. S., through the window. A signal was given for a return of the boys to the school room, when Sambo ordered his company to "shoulder arms!" They then all filed and marched for the door, the negro taking the lead. He had no sooner stepped over the threshold of the door than the teacher yelled out with all his strength of voice "Ground arms!" at the same time dealing an unmerciful blow with the palm of his hand on the side of Sambo's head, which brought him to the floor, helpless and quivering. The rest of the boys, seeing their captain fall, beat a hasty retreat, disbanded their forces, and returned quietly to the school-room, viewing as they passed in one by one their chieftian prostrate and pale with fright, as a negro could be. This was the last act of the drama; rebellion was totally silenced for that winter. Mr. Starkweather was considered by his townsmen a man of good practical judgment, and was chosen several years one of the selectmen of the town. He was also honored by a seat in the State Legislature in 1834, '7, '8. He at last succumbed to that scourge of New England, consumption, in 1844, aged 52, which disease he transmitted to several of his posterity. His wife died in 1866, March 28. Ch. I. George Freeman, b. July 7, 1815, in Mansfield, Ct.; m. Pamelia S., only dau. of Dr. Eber Carpenter of Alstead, by whom he had nine children of promise, seven of whom died, soon after arriving at their majority. The surviving children are 1st, Dr. C. F. Starkweather, residence Hartford, Ct. 2nd, Edward S., Insurance agent, Rockford, Ill. 3d, Katie C., resides at Keene. He and his wife are still living in Keene. For many years he has been an insurance agent. II. Edna Augusta, b. July 20, 1817; m. George Wilson, of this town. III. Ashley Gardner, b. Aug. 18, 1819; d. March 21, 1864. IV. Persis Marilla, b. Dec. 24, 1821; m. a Haskell. V. Almira Amanda, b. Mar. 29, 1824. VI. Sophrona Eliza, b. Mar. 21, 1826; m. Silas Hills. VII. Charles O. Mera, b. May 10,

1828. VIII. Henry Augustus, b. July 1830. IX. Otis Lemuel, b. Apr. 27, 1885; m. Harriet Kingsbury, of Keene, he d. Sept. 5, 1873. X. Leonard Bisco, b. Oct. 11, 1838, and at his majority, went to Chicago, Ill. XI. William H., b. in 1841, d. Nov. 14, 1871.

STARKWEATHER, RICHARD, married Sally C. Crossman and came to Walpole, from Mansfield, Conn., in 1821, and moved on to the farm now owned by Dolphus Booth, lying just east of his residence. He was a brother of the late Lemuel Starkweather of this town, and a farmer by occupation and also a fine singer. Ch. I. Ephraim Crossman, b. Nov. 18, 1819, and m. Catherine Russell, of Boston. The fruits of their marriage were six ch., three living II. Celia, b. Nov. 9, 1821, m. Henry Amerage, of Malden, Mass., and had two sons. III. Adeline, b. Nov. 28, 1823; m. Moses Fisher. (See Fisher.) IV. Archibald, b. Oct. 28, 1825; m. Abby A. Taylor, of Boston, and resides in Brookline, Mass. 2 ch. V. Josiah, b. Nov. 20, 1827; m. Jennie Wyman, of Boston, where he lives, by trade a paper-hanger. VI. Sarah, b. July 5, 1830; m. Lemuel W. Spear; 1 ch. VII. Mary J., b. Jan. 1833; d. unm. VIII. Phebe Augusta, b. Sept. 1835; m. W. J. Swift, of Coventry, Conn., ch. 2 sons. IX. Julia, b. Dec. 1837, d. young. X. Harriet Isabella, b. Apr. 13, 1842; m. Clinton W. Hatch, of Coventry, Conn., 1 ch.

STEARNS, MOSES. Isaac Stearns, the American ancestor of the Stearns family in Walpole, came from England in the ship Arabella, and landed at Boston in the summer of 1630, and subsequently settled in Watertown, Mass. He was of the old Puritan stock which might be inferred by the Bible names given to the family for more than eight generations. The line of descent from Isaac to Moses Stearns, who settled in Walpole, is as follows; a son of Isaac was Samuel, who married Hannah Manning; 2d, John, who married Abigail Fisk and had thirteen children; of these the fifth was *Abigail*, who married Col. Benjamin Bellows, the founder of Walpole. The fifth son, David, was for many years, a pastor at Lunenburg, Mass., while the first son, John jr., was the father of Moses, he

being the fifth generation from Isaac, and a nephew of Mrs.
Benj. Bellows. Moses Stearns married Ruth Houghton, June
13, 1754, and settled in Westminster, Mass., on a farm at the
base of Wachusett mountain. He and his son Ephraim came
to Walpole, and purchased the old Stearns place of Col. Benjamin Bellows—the deed bearing date Feb, 1773. The land
had been previously *occupied* by Constantine Gilman, who took
it up in 1759, and was probably one of the first settlers in town.
He built a house on the opposite side of the road from the old
Stearns dwelling, near the brook, on the place now occupied by
the old orchard, and brought his family to Walpole in 1760,
from Newmarket, and lived there four years, when his wife
died and he returned to Newmarket. On his way thither he
stopped over night at an inn in Peterborough, kept by the
grandfather of Gen. James Wilson, of Keene, and there left
his daughter Molly, a child then four years old, where she remained till she was eighteen, when she returned to Walpole,
her father, who was then living on the George Jennings place,
having previously returned.

STEARNS, EPHRAIM, married Molly Gilman, Dec. 30, 1781.
Soon after the battle of Bennington he joined the American
army; but whether as a regular soldier or a "minute man" is
not known. He was stationed at Fort Edward to prevent the
retreat of detachments of Burgoyne's army. Here he had a
narrow escape, it being brought about by having a skirmish
after dark, with a party of Hessians, when a bullet discharged
from one of their guns cut the skin of his throat, and as he
used to tell the story, "he thought it cut the *jug*-ular vein;
but in putting his hand up to stop the out-pouring blood, he
found it was *dry*. It was in a batteau taken from the Americans that night that Lathwood, (the father of aunt Sally, so
well known to the older citizens of the town, was captured.
He, (Stearns) served one year under General Thomas, in the
Canada campaign, at Montreal and Quebec, where he had the
small pox. When he returned to Walpole he settled down on
the old Stearns farm, where he lived until his death, which
occurred Oct. 19, 1843, aged 88; Mrs. Stearns died Oct. 27, 1850,

aged 90. Ephraim's father, Moses, died Sept. 24, 1808, aged 80 years; his wife, Ruth, died Feb. 27, 1815, aged 82. Ephraim was a man of genial disposition, fond of company and enjoyed in his old age living his life over again, in telling his youthful exploits. In stature, he was about five feet five inches, and in the times of cider and cider brandy, turned the beam at 206 pounds, but after he abstained from the use of alcoholic drinks he weighed about 150 pounds. Ch. of Moses and Ruth Stearns. I. Ephraim m. as above stated; ch. 1st, Simon, b. Feb. 26, 1783; m. Sarah Noyes, in 1815. 2d, Calvin, b. Jan. 24, 1794; m. Deborah Allen; d. Apr. 27, 1840. 3d, Stephen, b. April 27, 1786; m. first, Harriet, dau. of Deacon Jonas Hosmer, and had one child, Josiah W., b. Aug. 15, 1823; m. Abby Martin, Apr. 25, 1850. Ch. (1) Henry C., b. May 11, 1851; graduated at Union College, Chicago, in 1876; the first in his class, and has recently (1879) been admitted to the bar in the state of Illinois. (2) Harriet H.; b. Nov. 4, 1857, 3d, Martin P., b. Mar. 4, 1862. Stephen Stearns was born, lived and died on the old homestead. He was one of the old, solid, reliable and much esteemed citizens of the town. He was a member of the legislature in 1839, and again in 1842. He buried his first wife, aged 31, Dec. 20, 1827, and married widow Lora Burroughs, Apr. 27, 1830. He died Jan. 28, 1855; she survived him fifteen years, and died Jan. 22, 1870. Josiah W. abandoned the old homestead in 1863, which had been held by the Stearns family 90 years, and went west, and now lives in Watseka, Ill. 4th and 5th, Ephraim and Molly, b. June 2, 1788; Molly d. in infancy; Ephraim was drowned in Connecticut river, under the following circumstances. He and Avery Ware were in the river, bathing, and young Stearns from some cause required assistance, being in imminent danger of sinking. Ware swam to his rescue, and was seized and discommoded with so firm a grasp that he could not swim; when, in order to save himself, he had to strike poor Stearns a violent blow upon his head, which stunned him to that extent that he loosened his grasp and sunk, and Ware saved himself. The Stearns family, although the death of their son and broth-

er was a severe blow to them, thought that Ware acted wisely.
6th, Polly, b. Aug. 16, 1790 ; m. Zephaniah Kidder, July 7,
1823. (See Kidder.) 7th, Lyman, b. Aug. 13, 1792; d. Mar.
27, 1803. 8th, Curtis, b. Jan. 23, 1794; m. Rebecca Baron, of
Alstead. He d. May 2, 1868 : she d. Aug. 30, 1874, aged 69
years. Ch. (1) Mary, b. 1831 , d. 1852. She was endowed by
nature with more than common abilities, and possessed a gentle and lovely disposition and grace of person seldom seen.
She possessed also, a poetic genius, and many of her effusions
are kept treasured in the family. (2) Frances A., b. Mar. 25,
1839; m. Silas M. Bates, and has two children, a son and a
daughter, Edward and Mary. (See Ap.) Mrs. Bates and her
children are all that remain in town of the numerous descendants of Moses Stearns, who settled here more than one hundred
years ago. They have made their entrance, acted their little
part on life's stage, and passed into the shadow, like the dissolving scenes of a magic lantern. Such is life ! 9th and 10th,
Willard and Wilder, b. June 6, 1796. Wilder m. Hannah
Wier, Feb. 5, 1823, and Willard m. Harriet P. Mitchell. 11th,
Elijah, b. July 27, 1798; m. Sarah Blanchard; d. Sept. 29,
1828. 12th, Harvey, b. June 3, 1800; m. Rebecca Brown.
13th, George, b. May 10, 1802; m. Mrs. Gibson, and is the
only one of the family now living. (1879.) II. Esther, b. Apr.
11, 1757; m. James Eastman, and removed to Newfane. III.
Reuben, b. Sep. 11, 1757; went to Shrewsbury: d. Apr. 26,
1791. IV. Relief, b. Mar. 8, 1762; m. Simon Farmer, of Herkimer, N. Y. V. Elizabeth, b. Sep. 9, 1764 ; m. John Adams,
of Walpole. VI. Lois, b. Aug. 1776 ; m. James Knapp, Nov.
26, 1789. VII. Benjamin, b. Oct. 11, 1768; m. Esther Simonds,
of Kingsborough, and removed to Trumbull, La. VIII. Lucy,
b. Jan. 14, 1771 ; d. Nov. 29, 1796. IX. Abigail, b. Feb. 27,
1775 ; m. Isaac Gibson, of Grafton, Vt.

The old Stearns homestead has been under cultivation 120
years, and the original part of the house now standing, was
built in 1774; the east and west part have been added since.

STEARNS, AARON, was a brother of Moses, and lived in Walpole " Valley." There is but little known of the family. He

had seven children, but where most of them went is unknown. Probably the family removed from town. Ch. I. Zenas, died in Vermont. II. Levi, died in Acworth. III. Jesse, lived in town some forty years ago, and is remembered as a lame shoemaker. He had a family of children, one of whom, Lyman, b. Mar. 11, m. Rhoda Ann, dau. of Anson Graves, and was also a shoemaker. He had another son, named William, b. July 1, 1810. IV. John. V. Lydia. VI. Esther, m. Simeon Mead. of Langdon. VII. Rhoda.

STONE, DAVID, came to Walpole a short time before the year 1800, and formed a co-partnership in trade with Josiah Bellows 3d, which was continued nearly a quarter of a century. The firm occupied the old brick store, after 1806, and had a branch house in Cincinnati, Ohio. They were largely engaged in the Western fur trade, which caused Mr. Stone to be absent from Walpole a large share of his time picking up furs in the West. He was Postmaster at Walpole in 1816, and his compensation was $240.55. In 1817 Oliver Allen had the office, but in 1820 Mr. Stone was re-instated and held the office till 1826. His compensation in 1824 was $208.42. In 1828, he, with his family, moved to Dayton, Ohio. In 1799, July 4, he married Frances, the dau. of Col. John Bellows, by whom he had 2 ch. I. Maria, who d. in 1802, aged one year. II. Frances, who d. in infancy. His wife d. Aug. 13, 1803, aged 23, so that he was then without wife or children. He married again, Aug. 22, 1805, Hannah, the sister of his first wife, and had 5 ch. III, Fanny, b. May 29, 1806; m. Francis E. Phelps, of Windsor, Vt. IV. Sophia, b. Mar 20, 1808; m. a Sears, of Buffalo, N. Y. V. Hannah, b. Nov. 4, 1810; m. a Richards. VI. William Bainbridge, b. June 7, 1814. He went West with his father. VII. Nathaniel Edward, b. Feb. 23, 1820; m. Laura, dau. of Hubbard Bellows.

STRATTON, CHARLES, was a descendant of Peter Stratton, who immigrated to this country from England with the colony under John Winthrop, numbering about three hundred, and landed at Salem, Mass., in 1630, where he settled. He had a numerous family, and the descendants of his children were also numerous, furnishing more or less men to every military expedition that was fitted out from the old Bay State, for many years. They were all of genuine Puritan stock, large in size, Herculean in strength, and tenacious of life, many of them dying at the age of four score years. It is said that one of them, at the siege of Louisburg, in 1745, carried a *mortar* from a vessel to the shore, on his back, there being no other way of landing it, on account of shoal water. One of Peter's numerous family named Ezra, removed to Concord, Mass., and settled there. One of his children, named, John was born Feb. 3, 1740, and m. Mar. 1, 1768, Ruth Wright of Concord, who bore him four children. The oldest, named Abigial, b. Jan. 30, 1769; m. Paul Faulkner of Lancaster, Mass., and had five children, two of whom died in infancy, one in middle life, and two, Augustus and Horace, are now living. She died in 1809, and Mr. Faulkner subsequently m. her sister, Hannah, b. Feb. 26, 1771, who died leaving no children.

Charles Stratton, was born in Concord, Mass., Jan. 24, 1775. It is said that John Stratton's family were startled, early on the morning of the memorable 19th of April, 1775, by hearing the report that the British soldiery were marching on the town. The wife immediately took her infant, Charles, in her arms and his brother John, jr., by the hand and fled to a distant part of the town for safety, while the two elder children (girls) drove the cow. The husband spent the day in defending his home and pursuing the retreating enemy. Mr. Augustus Faulkner has in his possession an old gun barrel which did good execution that day.

When the Continental army was raised, John Stratton became a soldier, and continued in the service of his country till he was taken prisoner, in a skirmish near New York, and confined in the prison ship "Jersey," lying in New York harbor, where, with many others, he died of starvation. Soon after his wife died, and the four orphans were tenderly cared for till of age, by a maiden sister of their father, who also took charge of her brother's farm. John jr., b. Oct. 21, 1772, lived to manhood, and is supposed to have been murdered in Chittenden,

Vt. Charles learned the trade of a cooper, a business he followed during life. He married Mary Jones, of Acton, Mass., May 10, 1803, and removed to Walpole, influenced to do so, by Hon. Thomas Bellows. He purchased himself a home, where he lived with his wife nearly fifty years, enjoying more domestic happiness than is shared by most married people. He was a plain, unobtrusive man in demeanor, and filled well the description given by the poet Pope of an honest man. He was one of the six corporators of the new Congregational church and society, a consistent member of the church, and an efficient supporter of the society. His wife died Aug., 1852, and he died Aug. 18, 1858. He was the last of Ezra Stratton's descendants bearing the name—a family that had occupied a place in New England more than two hundred years. He had two children. I. Mary, d. early. II. Harriet, m. Augustus Faulkner, Oct. 1, 1829. Ch. 1st Charles Stratton, b. June 29, 1836; m. Mary E. Abbott, of Boston, Sep. 11, 1856. 2d, Ann L., b. Aug. 7, 1835. Mrs. Faulkner d. Aug. 25, 1861. (See John Maynard.)

THOMPSON, DAVID, was born in Franklin, Mass., in 1771, and married Betsey Clark, of the same place, for his first wife, who died in 1848, and he married her sister Esther, when he was more than seventy years old. He moved from Franklin, to Alstead in 1799, and from there to Walpole in 1801, having purchased the place now owned by Andrew Roy. Here he remained till 1812, when he purchased the place now owned by Alonzo Jennings, known as the Thompson place, where he lived till he died. By his first wife he had the following children. I. David Clark, b. Nov. 1, 1799, who m. first, Mary P., dau. of Thomas Moore, one of the first settlers on Derry Hill. 2d, Lurancy, dau. of Jonathan Jennison jr. His children by his first wife were, 1st, Warren, b. Dec. 2, 1835; m. Mrs. Wealthy M., widow of Ira Graves, and has had 2 ch. (See Ap.) 2d, Eliza Jane, b. Sep. 2, 1837. 3d, Mary Emma, b. May 10, 1842; m. Myron D. Clark and resides in Alstead. 4th, Frances Adeline, b. Jan. 6, 1847; m. John L. Hubbard and lives in town. Mr. Thompson is now in his eightieth year and has always lived in town. As a townsman, he has always been honored for his uprightness and probity of character. For several years he held the office of Justice of the Peace and was chosen representative, two years, to the General Court, besides being entrusted with the concerns of the town as one of the selectmen. His occupation has been principally farming, although in his younger days his winters were spent in school teaching. II. Adeline, b. Mar. 3, 1803; not m. III. Hiram, b. June 1, 1806. IV. Eliza, b. Jan. 1809; d. unm. V. Samuel, b. July 30, 1814; m. Eliza M. Chandler, of Westminster, Vt. He went West and now lives in Appleton, Wis. and has one son. By his reputed character, he has not dishonored his native town. VI. Lewis, b. Dec. 21, 1818; lived and died in town, within a short period, unm. David Thompson died April 15, 1857.

THURSTON, LUKE, was born in Franklin, Mass., Feb. 7, 1785. His wife, Olive Clark, was born June 25, 1785. They were married in Dec. 1810, when they moved directly to Walpole, and bought the farm now owned by Andrew Roy, of David Thompson. Here he lived twenty years and sold out to Luther D. Knowlton and purchased the farm now owned by Edwin Guild, of Albert Locke, where he lived till he died. He was an industrious, unobtrusive citizen and at the time of his death had accumulated a handsome property. Ch. I. Esther, b. Oct. 10, 1811; m., first, Samuel C. Underwood of Westminster, Vt., Mar. 13, 1850. He d. Nov. 4, 1865 aged 47; she then m. Willard Witt, Dec., 17, 1873, and resides in Westminster, without issue. II. Willard C., b. Jan. 29, 1815; d. Apr, 10, 1852, unm. III. Emeline, b. Oct. 31, 1818: m. Henry J. Watkins, Nov. 10, 1842, and had 3 ch.—2 living, (see Ap.) IV. Harriet, b. Dec. 24, 1821, d. July 13, 1865. unm. V. Eliza Ann, b. May 30, 1824, m. Eri Richardson, Jan. 13, 1859. Luke Thurston died Jan. 1, 1862; his widow d. Apr. 3, 1875.

TIFFANY, AMASA, came to Walpole, from Ashford, Conn., in some of the last years of the eighteenth century. He married Sally, the sister of Dr. Stephen Johnson, and had three sons and one daughter, who came with their parents. He was born in 1764, and died April 17, 1850. His wife was born in 1771, and died Feb. 8, 1868, being 97 years old. He was a butcher, it is said, and lived at one time in the Walton Mead house, and owned the rabid dog that bit David, the son of John Livingston, mentioned heretofore, in 1815. Stephen, the oldest of his children, was born Feb. 22, 1792, and died Aug. 19, 1877. He married Maria, dau. of Dr. Stephen and Percy (Webber) Johnson, Oct. 18, 1818, who was born April 13, 1795, and died March 31, 1872. Stephen Tiffany was a soldier in the war of 1812, and went to Portsmouth, N. H., in the company that went from Walpole with Col. Josiah Bellows; he was also captain, at one time, of the rifle company organized here. He lived to be eighty-five years of age, possessing a robust constitution, although he never in his lifetime ate but a very small quantity of meat. His course of life was smooth and even, and he died without an enemy. Ch. 1st, Harriet M., b. Nov. 26, 1821; m. Ephraim A. Watkins, March, 1841, and has two children living. 2d, Sarah Ann, b. Jan. 22, 1826; m. Frederick Watkins, September, 1845, and has two daughters. 3d, Stephen Johnson, b. May 16, 1830; m. first, Mary S., dau. of Levi and Susannah (Foster) Hall, who d. May 29, 1864; m. second, Emily Buffum, of Keene, N. H. (See Ap.) 4th, Percy I., b. June 10, 1834; m. William Hall, Jan. 27, 1852; d. Jan 24, 1866.

TITUS, SYLVANUS.—Capt. Sylvanus Titus came to Walpole, about 1775, from Connecticut, and was a soldier in the Revolutionary army. He settled on the hill north of the residence of Caleb Foster, and the remains of the old house where he used to live are still to be seen. His children were as follows: I. Mary, m. Nathan Newton. II. Lavinia, m. John Gates. III. Asa, m. Rebecca, dau. of John Graves, jr., and lived with his father. Ch. 1st, Comfort, d. young. 2d, John, m. Susan, dau. of Ebenezer Wellington. Ch. (1) Ebenezer, m. Sophronia Ballou. (2) John, m. Almira Ballou. (3) Asa, d. in California. (4) William, m. and lives in Hancock, N. H. (5) Sarah M., b. Oct. 18, 1836; m. William Warn. 3d, Charles, lived to old age, and d. in town, unm. 4th, Margaret, m. Calvin Graves. 5th, Preston, b. Oct. 12, 1801; m. Vashti, dau. of Ebenezer

Wellington. Ch. (1) Louisa, d. when about twenty years of age. (2) Caroline, b. May 19, 1830; m. first, Lewis Dunshee—issue, three ch.; m. second, Ora W. Dwinnell. (3) Rhoda M., m. Curtis B. Wilbur: lives in town. (4) Emily, m. a Norris. (5) Dora, m. George Clark, of Springfield, Mass. 6th, Sylvanus, m. first, Lydia Martin, and second, Harriet, dau. of Elisha and Sally (Russell) Angier, who bore him one child. 7th, Asa, jr., m. Sophia, dau. of Jeduthan Russell, of Saxton's River, by whom he had two ch., Jane and Charles, neither of whom is living. 8th, Almira R., b. Nov. 26, 1817; m. Frederick A. Wier. (See Wier.) IV. Sylvanus. V. Samuel. VI. Mary. VII. Asahel. VIII. James. The five last named were all baptized by parson Fessenden in 1788. Capt. Sylvanus brought up two sons of his brother *James*, whose names were Sylvanus and James. Sylvanus—great *Venc*, as he was called—m. Harriet Snow, by whom he had four ch. He went west. James m. Maria Dennison. James, Sylvanus, and their cousin John, were persons of great physical strength and endurance. It has been said that John Titus had a physical organization which, for perfect development, harmony of parts, and pleasing *contour*, was seldom seen. Sylvanus and James, nephews of Capt. Sylvanus, are remembered by the old citizens as famous drummers.

TOWNSLEY, NICANOR, was a resident of Walpole as early as 1785, and lived in the old house now standing opposite the residence of Clement S. Dickey. His occupation was that of a "Jack at all trades." He had a small shop which stood just east of his house, where he used to employ a portion of his time in repairing various articles of furniture for the townspeople, which he did very neatly, he being a man of uncommon ingenuity. From 1795 to 1817 he was town clerk, with the exception of one year, 1807, when Daniel W. Bisco was chosen. Mr. Townsley wrote a good hand and discharged the duties of his office very acceptably to the town. It was his duty to cry the banns of matrimony before church service, from year to year, and his voice was so peculiar that once heard it was not easily forgotten. He held some town office every year for more than twenty-five years, and was often chosen one of the selectmen, on account of his good ability and sound discretion. He died, Oct. 26, 1830, aged 75; his wife died Dec. 13, 1847, aged 83. Ch. I. William, son, of Nicanor and Orrel Townsley, b. Aug. 31, 1786. II. Orrel, b. July 31, 1788, and died July 19, 1867, aged 79. She never married, but lived and died alone in the old house where her father had lived before, with no living human being in the house to close her eyes. Her cares and affections in her last days were centered on a bevy of cats, although she was social and pleasant with her neighbors when they called. For many years she cared for the wants of an insane mother with true womanly devotion. III. Sally, b. July 20, 1791; m. a man by the name of Reed, and resided in Newfane, Vt. IV. and V. Luther and Calvin, b. Nov. 3, 1795. Calvin was for many years a merchant in Brattleboro, Vt. VI. Frances, b. Mar. 20, 1803; m. Chester Pomeroy, of Brattleboro, Vt. She was one of the victims of the terrible catastrophe in St. Louis, several years since, where a public building was insufficient to sustain the hundreds that had gathered within its walls, on the occasion of a floral celebration on the first day of May. VII. Caroline, b. July 10, 1807; m. Prescott White and went to Littleton, N. H. She now resides in St. Paul, Minn., with her children.

VOSE, ROGER, was born in Milton, Mass., in 1763, graduated at Harvard in the class of 1790, and came to this town soon after completing his law studies, which was about 1793–4; when he commenced the practice of his profession, and continued it till he was incapacitated by paralysis, which was several years before his death. In 1801, he married Rebecca, daughter of Col. John Bellows, one of the foremost men in town at that time. When first married he lived in the house now occupied by the Maynard sisters. It was a one story house then. He subsequently purchased the homestead once owned by Thomas Sparhawk, sen., where he lived to the time of his death, which occurred in 1841. He had no peculiar qualities which would distinguish him from others at the bar.

He is remembered more on account of his fun-loving nature, ready repartee and colloquial witicisms, and also, from being the only member of Congress who ever hailed from this town. He was familiarly called Judge, which title came by his holding, at one time, the office of Judge in this State, before the county of Sullivan was taken from Cheshire. He was also, Judge of Probate for many years in Cheshire county.

Following are a few instances of his ready wit. On one occasion when in Congress, he was sitting at a window of the Capitol pleasantly conversing with one of his southern friends, a member, when a drove of mules chanced to be passing by which arrested the attention of his southern friend, who thought the opportunity a good one to rally the Judge. He gave the Judge a gentle nudge and said: "Look Judge, look! there goes a drove of your constituents," "Yes, yes," was the ready reply, "going south to teach school and run for Congress." At another time, after removing to the Sparhawk place, which commands a near birds-eye view of the cemetery, and a beautiful distant view beyond, some one asked him if he was not lonely at his new home; "O no, no," he replied, "Plenty of neighbors, and all very quiet, and, moreover I can look beyond the grave." "Whom are you mourning for?" asked the Judge of one of his students, who came into his office one morning dressed in black: "My sins only," answered the student: "I did'nt know you'd lost any," sympathisingly responded the Judge. He was the originator of comparing a thing to the size of a piece of chalk.

He had five children born as follows: I. Frederick, b. Nov. 2, 1801. He graduated at Harvard college in 1822, and, after studying the law, commenced practice in his native town, where he continued for more than forty years. In 1833, he was elected a member of the legislature of New Hampshire, and, in 1847 and 1848, a member of the State senate. He also held many important offices of trust and honor in the town, county and state, being for many years Judge of Probate, Bank commissioner, &c. As a lawyer he had a general reputation: being considered one of the soundest and

best read lawyers in the State. He seldom argued a case of
much importance before a jury; but employed others to do so,
on account of a constitutional *timidity* which he was never able
to overcome. As a citizen of the town, he was public spirited,
and in his private benefactions, liberal,—never allowing his left
hand to know what his right hand was doing. Many have
been the comforts the deserving have received at his hand.
He always manifested a lively interest in the cause of public
education. In his habits he was very retiring and unobtrusive, seldom ever appearing at social gatherings,—books and
numerous newspapers, being the society he valued most. In
social intercourse, he was a perfect gentleman. Conversation
never lagged when he was with one alone; but when several
were present, he preferred rather to listen than talk. He inherited some of his father's wit, as the following anecdote will
show. On one occasion several gentlemen were sitting upon
the steps of his office, when he was temporarily absent, discussing the subjects of geology, with which the Judge, as he was
familiarly called, was somewhat familiar. The conversation
became animated in reference to the *kind* of stone that formed
his office steps. Disagreeing, it was agreed by the company to
leave the decision to the judge, who was seen approaching, of
what kind of stone it was. As he came near, one of the party
said, "Judge, we have had some controversy about the kind
of stone forming your door step, and as we are unable to agree
we thought to abide your decision." The judge very demurely
looked at the stone, with a peculiar twinkle of his eye, and
said: "It's a *door stone* I suppose,"—not allowing a muscle of
his face to change, when the company burst into a roar of
laughter. Although a peculiar man in some respects, still he
had the esteem and confidence of his townsmen, and his loss
was keenly felt and generally lamented. He died in Nov.
1871, in the city of New York, where he had gone to transact
some important business. The County court was then holding
its fall session at Keene and the excitement incident to his
business in court, and his being unexpectedly called to New
York, produced apoplexy, which was the immediate cause of

his death. II. Sophia Bellows, b. Oct. 29, 1803, d. unm. Feb. 12, 1869. III. William, b. July 20, 1805; d. young. IV. Rebecca Hubbard, b. Sept. 26, 1807; m. Hon. John S. Marcy, of Royalton, Vt., and was the mother of several children; she is not living. V. Catharine, b. Dec. 19, 1809; d. unm. Sept. 2, 1875. She was the last of the blood of Col. John Bellows remaining in town.

WATKINS, ALEXANDER, came to this town from Pomfret, Conn., about 1777–8, and settled first on the Stephen Johnson place; but soon after purchased the place where Benjamin E. Webster now resides, of Samuel Parker, Antipas Harrington and one Mc Laughlin. He built the house now standing on the place, and lived there till the time of his death, which occurred in 1824, aged 68. He was a lame man and a tailor by trade, and worked in a shop that stood near the present highway, a short distance from his house. The latter part of his life, he kept a public house, which was the resort of a class who wanted a merry time. His house was also the resort, at noon, of those who attended church at the old meetinghouse near by, for the purpose of *warming up.* He had by his wife, whose maiden name was Hannah Ruggles, eight children, seven sons and one daughter. I. Ruggles, b. Jan. 11, 1782; m. Sarah, dau. of Thomas and Elizabeth (Boynton) Nichols. He lived on the old homestead, and was a stirring, active business man, in various pursuits through life. For many years he was deputy sheriff. He d. June 27, 1839; she d. Jan. 6, 1866. Ch. 1st, Lyman, b. Sep. 14, 1807—was a carpenter by trade, and a much esteemed citizen. He m. Abigail, dau. of Jonathan and Catharine (Dorr) Livingston; d. Sep. 4, 1861. 2d, Sumner, b. Sep. 12, 1809: d. Apr. 1, 1820. 3d, William, b. Feb. 6, 1813; m. Susan Royce and had a family of 7 ch., 4 of whom are now living, viz. (1) Mary Ann, m. Lucius B. Wright. (2) Frederick, m. Mary Ball. (3) Warren F., m. Nellie Davis. (4) Jennie, m. Charles Chickering. William jr., d. Dec. 2, 1866, aged 20, and two d. in infancy. 4th, Henry Jackson, b. Feb. 10, 1815; m. first, Nov. 10, 1842, Emeline, dau. of Luke Thurston, and had two children that survived, Albert and Emily.

His second wife was Mary French, of Westminster, Vt. 5th, Andrew, b. Oct. 18, 1816, went West. 6th, Sarah Nichols, b. Sep. 5, 1819; m. Otis B. Arms, of Bellows Falls, Vt., Aug. 16, 1842. 7th, Stella, b. Nov. 28, 1822; m. George W. Graves. (See Ap.) 8th, Alexander Sumner, b. Dec. 5, 1824; m. first, Helen, dau. of Jonathan Livingstone, second, Martha E. Wells, of Westminster, Vt. Ch. one dau. 9th, Thos. Foster, b. Sep. 9, 1826; m. Martha W. Taft, of Putney, Vt.—issue 3ch. II. George, b. Jan. 28, 1784; m. Rebecca, dau. of John Wier. He always lived in town and pursued the occupation of a butcher. He d. May 13, 1851; she d. Oct. 29, 1864. Ch. 1st, George Dana, b. Feb. 1, 1817; m. Sabra A. Stevens, of Plainfield, N. H. He resides in Troy, N. Y., where, by industry and economy, he has accumulated a competency and become one of the solid men of the city. He has three children. 2d, Harriet Rebecca, b. June 22, 1822; m. Christian B. Locke, of Richmond, Va., Dec. 11, 1843—one child living, Gustavus. 3d, Frances A., b. Nov. 9, 1828: m. May 12, 1863, Asa H. Carpenter. 4th, Mary, b. Nov. 4, 1827, m. Silas M. Bates, d. Nov. 29, 1858. III. Alexander jr., b. May 5, 1786; m. Mary Sherman, He lived in town, had a large family of children, many of whom, and their descendants, are living in town at the present time. (1879.) Ch. 1st, Sherman, b. Oct. 3, 1809; m. Harriet, dau. of Nathan Smith, and had two sons and two daughters. (1) Isabella, m. —— Lamphere. (2) Mary, m. John Farr, of Westminster, Vt. (3) Martin, m. Louisa Pierce. (4) Lewis. 2d, George, b. Mar. 15, 1811, m. Emeline, dau. of Isaac Jennings, and had 6 children, most of whom are living in town. (See Ap.) 3d, Mary Ann, b. Dec. 3, 1812; m. Frederick Kilburn. (See Kilburn.) 4th, Adeliza, b. Dec. 13, 1814; m. Alonzo Jennings. (See Jennings.) 5th, Ephraim Alexander, b. Jan. 10, 1817; m. Harriet M., dau. of Stephen Tiffany. 6th, Wm. Cook, b. May 15, 1819; m. Maria L. Onstine. 7th, Frederick, b. July 2, 1821; m. Sarah A., dau. of Stephen Tiffany. 8, Harriet Maria, b. June 28, 1823 ; m. Thomas Beal. 9th, Luke Thurston, b. Oct. 14, 1825 ; d. 1828. 10th, Frances Caroline, b. Nov. 13, 1828, m. Nathaniel Adams. 11th, Hiram, b. March 20, 1830; m.

first, Louisa B. Onstine : second, Mary J., dau. of George Bundy. 12th, Rebecca, b. Apr. 30, 1834; d. unm. IV. Ralph, b.
July 28, 1788; m. Hannah Quimby. Ch. 1st, George, b. Apr.
5, 1811. 2d, Andrew, b. Mar. 16, 1813 : 3d, Foster, b. Aug.
19, 1815. 4th, Martha Eleanor, b. Oct. 16, 1816 ; m. Wm. J.
Shipman, of Westminster, Vt., had 1 ch. 5th, Moses Q., b.
Mar. 13, 1820; m. Mary A. Spaulding. 6th, Holland B., b. July
16, 1821; m. Mary Tuttle, 3 ch. 7th, Roxana Quimby, b. July 27,
1823; m. Sep. 13, 1841, Azro B. Bishop. 8th, Mary Jannette,
b. Sep. 26, 1826; d. Sep. 19, 1836, of tetanus. 9th, Nancy, m.
George Fairbanks and has 1 ch. 10, Hannah, m. Charles
Towns of Bellows Falls and has one son, Charles. V. Nancy,
b. Mar. 13. 1791; m. Holland Burt. (See Burt.) VI. Charles,
b. Aug. 7, 1793, m. Amy Sherman, and purchased the old Kittredge homestead, where he lived till he died. He was a successful farmer, making sheep husbandry a speciality. Ch. 1st, Marietta Louisa, b. Apr. 19, 1821 ; m. Oliver Hall. 2d, Oliver Haz-
zard Perry, b. Aug. 5, 1822; m. Mary P. dau. of William and
Naomi (Moore) Arnold. 3d, Alfred, b. Sep. 3, 1825 ; m. Isabella Leonard. 4th, Clarissa, b. Nov. 4, 1827; m. Alonzo Jennings. 5th, Charles Edmund, b. Dec. 10, 1829; m. Frances
Church. 6th, Sophia, b. Sep. 16, 1831; m. Daniel Gilbert. 7th,
Helen, b. May 22, 1833; d. 1869. 8th, Amy Elnora, b. Aug.
12, 1837; m. Henry F. Lawrence. The descendants of
Charles are mostly living in town and their ages will be found
in the Appendix. VII. Alfred, b. Sep. 7, 1798. He studied
medicine with Dr. Ebenezer Morse, of this town, and, in 1816,
went to Troy, N. Y.. where he completed his studies and practised his profession during life. He became eminent in his
profession and a man of affluence and influence in the city of
Troy, being at one time its mayor. For some reason he changed the spelling of his name from Watkins to *Wotkyns* which
has been followed by some other members of the family. He
m., for his first wife, Mary Augusta Williams, by whom he had
three children ; by his second wife, Elizabeth Braley, he had
five. VIII. Hiram, b. Sep. 27, 1801. He studied the medical
profession with Daniel Gilbert of this town, and completed his

studies with his brother Alfred, in Troy, N. Y., about 1828; after which he commenced practice in the city and continued till 1858, when he returned to the Mecca of his early days to spend his declining years with his kinsfolks and old townsmen. He is the only one of the family now living, and although born in 1801, *time* has been generous with him, as his carriage and appearance do not indicate the frosts of more than three score winters. He married Sarah Dauchy, of Troy, by whom he has one daughter, Helen. A large majority of the family of Alexander Watkins, and their descendants have lived, and are still living in town, being generally thrifty, well disposed and energetic citizens.

WATKINS, NATHAN, came very early to this town, but, at precisely what time is unknown. He was a boatman on the Mohawk river, in his younger days, and on his way home to Ashford, Ct., he stopped over night with Col. Benjamin Bellows. He was a black-smith by trade, and the colonel, seeing the need of skilled workmen of all trades, in forming a new settlement, persuaded Watkins to make trial of a settlement in town : but after a few days he became homesick, and, unbeknown to the colonel, started for Connecticut. Mr. Bellows, missing him, mounted his horse, followed, and overtook him in Westmoreland, and offered him such inducements that Mr. Watkins was persuaded to return. He settled on the place now owned by the Kingsbury brothers, and built himself a shop on the south side of Kingsbury hill. At that time he was about thirty years old, but whether married or not is not known. He brought the apple-trees now standing on the Kingsbury place, a little south of their residence, from Connecticut, on a horse's back, and set them out there, more than a century ago. The ancestors of this branch of the Watkins family were from Wales and Scotland, and their descendants settled in New England and Virginia, and can be traced back to 1513. Nathan was born in 1732, and died in Walpole, Oct. 6, 1805: his wife, whose maiden name was Esther Lyons, was born in 1756, and died Jan. 4, 1824. He had eight children ; I. Chloe, m. Daniel Dennison, Feb. 28, 1781. (See Dennison.)

II. Polly.   III. Rhoda, m. Aaron Hodskins, June 16, 1791.
(See Hodskins.)   IV. Elizabeth, m. Horace Floyd.   V. Allen,
m. Patty, dau. of Manoah Drury, Sep. 10, 1797.   He used to
boast, as his mother was a Lyon, that he had Lion's blood in
him, which gave him the *sobriquet* of "Tiger" Allen.   Certainly,
one needed some brave blood in his veins, to lead to the altar
a girl who could fling a barrel of cider into a cart with as
much apparent ease as an ordinary woman can pick up her
lap-dog.   He had two sons, Gardner and Mason; and two
daughters, Fanny and Sally.   VI. Edward, m. Keturah, dau.
of Daniel Dennison, Oct. 3, 1786.   Ch. 1st, Royal, b. Oct. 1,
1788; m. a Carpenter, from Swanzey.   Ch. (1) Freeman C.,
m. in Michigan, where he went early in life, and is still
living there, in the town of Norvell, a man of influence and
affluence.   (2) Elvira.   (3) Ruth; and one or two more born
in Michigan.   2d, Miriam, b. Mar. 7, 1781; m. John Dennison, Nov. 18, 1806.   3d, Ira, b. Apr. 19, 1793.   4th, Alpheus,
b. May 29, 1797.   5th, Charlotte, b. July 21, 1769; m. Levi
Leonard.   Tradition says that Edward Watkins possessed
great physical energy, a strong native intellect, and some
literary taste.   He accumulated quite a respectable library of
books agreeable to his taste; such as various works on Theology and History.   Royal, his son, inherited his vigor and
tenacity of life.   He died in 1876, aged 86.   VII. James, never
married: he died at the house of his sister, Mrs. Aaron Hodskins.   VIII. William, m. Olive Shattuck, Feb. 4, 1774, and
had fourteen children.   The death of two has been mentioned
heretofore, in the narrative portion of this work, and six died
in infancy.   Those that survived were, 1st, William, m. Hannah Hodskins, and had five or more children, and went west.
2d, Elizabeth, m. Dean Ray, Dec. 23, 1825, and had five ch., 2
girls and 3 boys: 3 children survive.   3d, Ira, married at the
west.   4th, Philinda, m. Alpheus Clark, and had five girls and
one son.   5th, Nathan, m. Harriet Carpenter, of Swanzey.   6th,
Harriet, m. William T. Ramsey.   Mrs. Dean Ray is the only
descendant of this family now living in town, bearing the
Watkins name.

WEBBER, CHRISTOPHER, COL., was one of the earliest settlers and seems to have been one of the leading men in the town's early settlement. He lived on the place which was subsequently owned by William Guild, and is now owned by George Jennings, and brought up a numerous family. He represented the town at Exeter in 1776–7, in the most trying times of its history, and was captain of a company in General Bellows's regiment when he went to Saratoga. He held some office of trust and honor in town yearly for more than twenty years. The oldest citizens in town remember very little about him, and his descendants living, being of the fifth and sixth generations, have treasured up little or nothing worth recording. He was married twice, his first wife's name being Hannah ———, and his second, Lucy ———. Ch. I. Persis, b. April 19, 1769; m. by Andrew French, Esq., to Dr. Stephen Johnson, Dec. 31, 1793. II. and III. Sarah and Elizabeth, b. Feb. 18, 1771. Sarah m. Winslow Warren, Sept. 10, 1789. IV. Christopher, jr., b. May 7, 1773; became a physician; located in Cavendish, Vt., and was married four times. V. Hannah, b. Feb. 19, 1775; m. Moses Cutler, of Stockbridge, Mass., Feb. 21, 1805. VI. Ebenezer Sumner, b. June 22, 1778; d. 1782. VII. by 2d wife, Lucy, Richard Mayo, b. Aug. 7, 1782. VIII. Amos Sherman, bap. 1785. IX. Melzar, bap. 1787. X. Alathea, bap. 1789; d. same year. XI. Samuel Ruggles, bap. 1790. XII. Lucy, bap. 1793. XIII. Orlen, bap. 1795. Col. Christopher Webber d. Feb. 28, 1803, aged 63; his wife, Hannah, d. Feb. 28, 1781, aged 43.

WELLINGTON, EBENEZER.—The Wellington family were originally from Sturbridge, Mass., where the progenitor of the following family was born, in 1765, and died in this town in 1851. The maiden name of Ebenezer's wife was Rebecca Levens, also from Sturbridge, by whom he had fourteen children, twelve of whom lived to advanced age and had large families. After leaving Sturbridge he resided in Westmoreland a few years previous to his coming to Walpole, which was about 1800. Ch. I. Eleanor, b. Nov. 5, 1783; m. James Hooper, May 18, 1802. (See Hooper.) II. Erasmus, b. Aug. 28, 1785; m. Eunice Russell; went west and died there. III. Abel, b.

Dec. 19, 1789; m. Elizabeth Spear, April 7, 1814. IV. Susan,
b. Nov. 10, 1791; m. John G. Titus, Jan. 1, 1815. (See Titus.)
V. Ebenezer, b. Aug. 24, 1793; m. Mary, dau. of Roger Wolcott, Jan. 1, 1822. VI. John, m. Julia, dau. of William Guild,
May 4, 1821, and went to western New York, where they both
lived till they died. He died 1879. VII. Rebecca, b. May 5,
1797; m. Caleb Paschal Graves, Dec. 25, 1823. (See Graves.)
VIII. Sally, b. Aug. 20, 1799; m. Adolphus Fletcher, Nov. 4,
1817. IX. William, b. Oct. 22, 1801; m. Aesah, dau. of Abiah
Kidder. Ch. 1st, Martin, b. Jan. 7, 1837, and was drowned in
Connecticut River, June 14, 1860. He was studying law in the
office of Frederick Vose at the time his death occurred. He
went to the river to bathe, and is supposed to have slipped
from a shelving rock into deep water, and, being unable to
swim, lost his life. He was a young man of fine promise, and
was expected to speak the next day at a political gathering to
be held in town, in the campaign of 1860. His death was a
heavy stroke of affliction to his parents and kindred, and a
source of sorrow to all who knew him. 2d, Irena, b. July 19,
1838; m. Charles H. Camp, Aug. 27, 1864, and went to Michigan. 3d, Edward, b. July 24, 1839; m. Nellie B., dau. of
Jacob B. Burnham; d. 1872; she d. 1873, aged 30. 4th, Diana,
b. Sept. 7, 1840; m. Horatio N. Fletcher, April, 1866, and lives
in Westmoreland. 5th, Leonard, b. Sept. 12, 1842; m. Hattie
N. Chandler, Jan. 19, 1870, and is a practising lawyer in Keene.
6th, Scott, b. March 5, 1848, and lives on the old homestead.
7th, Lucius, b. May 18, 1849; m. Sarah G., dau. of Cyrus
Royce, of this town, June 1, 1875; he also lives on the old
place, a farmer, although a lawyer by profession. 8th, Narina.
X. Maria, m. Amos Philips, April 17, 1822. XI. Vashti, b.
April 10, 1805; m. Preston Titus. (See Titus.) XII. Almira,
b. 1807; m. Jesse Graves; d. March 4, 1868. (See Graves.)
Ten of the family have died, two within the past year (1878-9),
most of them having lived to old age; but what is quite remarkable, they have all died suddenly—heart disease being the
immediate cause; a circumstance worthy of the notice of med-

ical men.   This family is also remarkable for being prolific in progeny, having in the aggregate *ninety-three* children.

The Wellingtons have been noted for their powers of physical endurance.   The following are instances: William, now living in town, dug *one hundred and forty bushels of potatoes* in one day, and stored them in the cellar, for William Jennison. He also laid *twenty-nine rods of stone wall* for Charles Watkins in the same length of time.   He is now seventy-eight years old ; but every few weeks he walks to Keene and back the same day, a distance of not less than twenty miles.

WHIPPLE, DANIEL, came to this town from Grafton, Mass., in its very early settlement.   He was an iron-founder, and had a foundery on the brook, west of the meeting-house, in the "Hollow," where he had purchased a large tract of land. When he came to town, that portion where he settled, was one dense forest, and his wife always kept a stock of fire-brands ready to drive away bears from the premises, as that kind of gentry have an instinctive dread of fire.   He married very young, Martha Adams, a cousin of John Adams, the second president. A silver spoon made from a tankard once belonging to President Adams, is now in the possession of one of Daniel Whipple's grand-daughters, Mary Robinson.   When they came to Walpole they were mere children ; but they forced their way through all the hardships and privations incident to frontier life, living in a small hut that once stood near the Wellington place, getting their milling done somewhere near the Merriam place, and attending church in the first meeting-house that stood near J. W. Hayward's residence.   She, it is said, was a woman possessing great force of character and personal worth —always sympathizing with those in affliction and ready to lend a helping hand.   He was born in 1750, and died Dec. 29, 1796.   Ch. I. Daniel, b. Jan. 18, 1777; m. Zerviah, dau. of Nathan Bundy, Sep. 25, 1800   He had a son, Daniel, who m. Elizabeth, dau. of Thomas Moore, and went to Lyndon, Vt. II. Adams, b. Sep. 13, 1779 ; m. Huldah Howard, b. Sep. 3, 1780 : d. in 1843.   Ch. 1st, Harriet H., b. June 23, 1804 ; d., of spotted fever, in 1812.   2d, John Adams, b. Dec. 17, 1805 ;

m. Ellen Carpenter, of Keene.   3d, Martha Adams, b. Jan. 22, 1808; d., of spotted fever, in 1811.   4th, James Duncan, b. May 16, 1810; d., of spotted fever, in 1812. 5th, Maria, b. May 24, 1813: m. Edwin Hosmer, of this town. (See Hosmer.) 6th, Nathaniel Grout, b. Feb. 18, 1815; m. Eliza Bickford, of Boston, and now lives in Belvidere, Ill.   7th, George Washington, b. Mar. 20, 1818; m. Emily, dau. of George Bundy, and has 3 ch., two daughters and one son.   III. Andrew, b. Sep. 29, 1782; d. 1790.   IV. Polly, b. Sep 19, 1785: m. first, James Duncan, and had one child, Adeline, who m. Charles G. Livermore: m. second, Elisha Parks, and had 4 ch.   V. Luthera, b. Nov. 24, 1788; d. 1790. VI. Betsey, b. July 18, 1791; m. Isaac Duncan, and went to New York State.   VII. Eben Waters, b. July 24, 1793, and is now living in Owego, N. Y.

WIER.   The history of this old family is involved in much obscurity, as there are no public nor private records extant. It appears, from what information can be gathered from the old citizens of the town and from distant relatives of the family, that one JOHN WIER came to this town from Hampstead this State as early as 1780, or perhaps before, and that he had a family of four sons and one daughter certainly, and it is thought more than one. Ch. I. Robert, who settled on the place now owned by John L. Houghton, and kept a public house there.   He was a man of good natural abilities, but set the laws and customs of society wholly aside.   He was convivial in his habits and his house was the rendezvous of men of his own stamp.   Three of his guests are remembered Roll Hall, Pel Hall and Quinton, who, when together, were as happy as flip could make them.   II. John, an own brother, (John, sen., had two wives) m. Rebecca, dau. of John Livingston, sen., and lived on Boggy Meadow.   He was known as Capt. John, and d. June 5, 1837. aged 84.   His wife's age was 89 when she died. Ch. 1st, John, who never married but cared for his parents in their infirm years.   He d. at the age of 62.   2nd, Rebecca, (see Watkin's family.) 3d, Jane, m. Aaron Day of Gilsum. 4th, Mary, m. Theodore Phelps, and had three sons and three daughters. 5th, Betsey, d. Nov. 13, 1815,

aged 20. 6th, Ann, never married. 7th, Fanny, m. Benj.
Bixby and had the following children; (1) Ellen, m. Samuel
Spear. (2) Frances, m. Henry Davis. (3) John, m. Cornelia,
dau. of Asahel Hodgkins. (4) Jane, m. Benj. B. Royce. (5)
Esther, m. Albro Bean. 8th, Almira, b. Jan. 21, 1805, and is
the only member of the family now (1879) living. III. William, a half brother of the above; m. first, a White of this
town, and settled on the place now owned by Henry E. Houghton. His wife died and he married Betsey a sister of Danforth
Clark, to whom he sold his farm and removed to Vt., where he
run a grist mill. There was an incompatibility of feeling
between himself and wife, she tantalizing him to such an extent
that he ducked her in the mill-pond, when she left and he
subsequently married again. IV. James, m. Catherine White,
and had two children. She d. and he m. Submit. dau. of Moses
and Submit (Ross) Burt, and had the following children; 1st,
Sarah W. b. July 15, 1823, m. Lewis Wilbur. 2d, Eliza S., b.
Dec. 13, 1824; m. Nelson H. Van Driezen. 3d, Hannah, b.
Sep. 25, 1826; m. James Wilbur, and has 2 ch. V. Betsey,
d. unmarried. Frederick A. Wier, of this town, the man who
introduced the Morgan breed of horses here, was the grandson
of John Wier sen., and was born Apr. 12, 1812; m. Almira
R., d. of Asa and Rebecca (Graves) Titus. Ch. (1) Geo. A., d.
1845, aged 2 yrs. (2) Frances R., b. June 8, 1838; m. Palmer
D. Brown, of Peterborough, N. H. (3) Alma A., b. Feb. 24,
1840; m. Wm. A. Craig, of Keene, N. H., Nov. 1869, 1 ch.
(4) Mary K., b. Nov. 31, 1847. (5) Geo. F., b. Jan. 31, 1850;
d. Sep. 23, 1878. (6) Fred A. jr., b. Feb. 26, 1852; m. widow
Julia A. Lovell, dau. of Lyman Chandler of Alstead. (7) Rowe,
b. July 7, 1844. (8) Edd., d. Oct. 20, 1873, aged 15 years.

WIERS, SAMUEL, was born in 1746. His father was an English soldier, and after the close of the war in which he was engaged he went back to the mother country, leaving two children, a son and daughter. Samuel was cared for by one Maj.
Stratton, of Northfield, Mass., and the girl married Samuel
Marshall, the grandfather of John W. Marshall, of this town.
In 1775, Samuel surreptitiously helped Mary, the daughter of

Aaron Burt, a merchant of that place, out of the window of
her father's house and they were clandestinely married, when
he and his wife made their way to Walpole. He took possession of some valuable land in the south west corner of the
town ; but of whom he obtained his title is not known. There
he lived for several years unmolested ; but at length his title
was disputed by one, Mrs. Norman, the daughter and heir of
an Irish lawyer, by the name of Brush. The case was in court
some twenty years, the proceedings of which will be found in
the historical part of this work. Samuel Wiers died at Charlestown, in 1802, while attending court there. He requested that
he might be buried on his claim, saying, " I can hold my *length*
and *breadth* at any rate. " His request was granted, and a
modest stone slab marks his resting place on the farm now
owned by Lyman Chickering. He was married twice. By the
first wife he had five children, viz: I. Samuel M., b. Aug. 4,
1776; d. Sep. 1, 1859; m. in 1795, Rachel Chaffee, of Westminster, Vt., b. Dec. 16, 1772; d. Nov. 9, 1852. The issue of
this family was ten children. 1st, Chester, b. Mar. 26, 1796;
m. first, Laurinda, dau. of Hugh Dunshee, in 1826, and went
to Stockholm, N. Y. Ch. (1) Lewis. (2) Diana C. (3) William
A. He married for his second wife Diantha, a sister of his first
wife. 2d, Annette, b. June 28, 1797; m. John Dunshee. (See
Dunshee.) 3d, Hannah, b. May 22, 1799; m. Wilder Stearns,
of this town. 4th, Persis, b. Mar. 30, 1801: m. Harry Gates,
of Lyndon, Vt. 5th, Samuel, b. Feb. 12, 1803; m. Isabella
Baron, of Lyndon, Vt., and had six ch., viz : (1) Jarville C.
(2) Sylvania. (3) Calvin. (4) Perry. (5) Almina. (6) Ezra
C. All born between 1825 and 1832. 6th, Fanny, b. May 11,
1806 ; m. Benjamin Dwinnell, of Keene.   7th, Livonia, b.
Aug. 4, 1807. 8th, Nancy, b. July 5, 1810. 9th, Hiram B., b.
Mar. 2, 1814. He enlisted into the U. S. service, and what
became of him is unknown. 10th, Mary Melissa, b. Mar. 21,
1817; m. Reuben Farmer, of Herkimer, N. Y. II. John H.,
b. Jan. 2, 1778; m. Sarah White, of Northfield, Mass.; lived
in Westmoreland, and died Mar. 7, 1857, without issue. His
widow afterward married Larkin Baker, Esq., of Westmore-

land. III. Chester, b. 1780; d. 1849; m. Effie Lombard, and had seven children. 1st, Hiram. 2d, James. 3d, Fanny. 4th, Chester, m. Phebe, dau. of Ephraim Lane, of this town, and had three ch. (See Lane.) 5th, Maria. 6th, Samuel. 7th, Louisa. He married, for a second wife, a widow by the name of Aldrich. IV. Fanny, b. 1782; m. Jacob Locke, of this town. V. Samyra, b. Feb. 22, 1782; m. Harlon Simmons, of Westmoreland, when advanced in life. Samuel Wiers' second wife was Thankful Lombard, b. 1760; d. 1846. The issue of this marriage was four children. VI. Vice, (probably Lovisa,) b. 1796; m. Levi Lyman. (See Lyman.) VII. Dilate, b. Jan. 7, 1798; m. Alvin Chickering, of Westmoreland, and has two sons living in town, Lyman and Charles. VIII. Sally, b. Dec. 12, 1799, died unm. at Alstead, July, 1847. IX. Moses, b. May 52, 1801; m. Betsey Rich, of this town, and had five children, only one of whom, Mary, b. 1831, survived and lived to maturity; m. William White, but died young.

WIGHTMAN, SAMUEL, Deacon.—The Wightmans have mostly disappeared from town, there being but one family bearing the name now residing here. The following imperfect account is given, owing to the want of proper data in relation to the succession of births. Samuel Wightman came to this town when somewhat advanced in life, from Rehoboth, R. I., in 1801, and purchased, of Isaac Redington, three hundred and fifty acres of land, lying in the vicinity of the mouth of Cold River. The land had been owned previously by Col. John Bellows, and he had erected, on the site of the residence of Thomas N. Keyes, a public house—since burned—for his son Josiah. To this house Mr. Wightman moved his family, and remained there two or three years, and in the mean time built what is now known as the Carpenter stand, near the railroad station at Cold River; removed soon after its completion, and spent the remaining portion of his days there, living with his son-in-law, Zachariah Carpenter, to whom he had deeded that portion of his property. He died Dec. 26, 1827, aged 89; his wife, Amy, died March 12, 1837, aged 98. Deacon Wightman's family consisted of eight children,—three sons and five daughters,—of whom Israel was the oldest, who died March 21, 1838, aged 74 years. Ch. I. Israel. The father gave his son Israel the place on the plain, which was the largest portion of his estate, where he lived during life, after coming to Walpole. He m. Frances Allen, of. Providence, R. I., and had ten ch.: 1st, Samuel Allen, m. Matilda, dau. of Salmon Bellows, and went to Ashtabula, Ohio. 2d, John, m., first, Laura Guild, of Rockingham, Vt., and had three ch.,—two living,—one of whom, Henry G., m. Harriet E. Gates, May 1. 1851. (See Ap.) John m., second, Martha E., dau. of Henry W. Hooper, of Charlestown, N. H., who was the widow Philips. 3d, Herman, d. young. 4th, Herman, m. a Lovell, of Claremont, N. H. 5th, Sarah, m. Nathan Walker, April 15, 1811, but did not settle in town. 6th, Maria, m. first, John Drown, of Providence, R. I., who left her, and she m. a Sherman. 7th, Hannah B., m. Capt. Aden Henry, Sept. 5, 1820, by whom she had a daughter, Mary R., who m. Loren C. Frost, of Keene, Sept. 29, 1847. Mrs. Henry afterwards m. Elisha Mayo. 8th, Pamelia, m. Dea. Amos Wood, and d. in town. 9th, Content, m. Stephen Johnson, of this town, April 23, 1823. (See Johnson family.) 10th, Frances, m. Gardner Philips, and settled on the homestead of his father-in-law. II. George, m. and went to Chester, Vt. III. Samuel, m. and settled in Providence, R. I. IV. Betsey, never m. V. Lydia, m. Zachariah Carpenter, of Providence, R. I., and lived there a few years, when she, with her husband, came to Walpole and spent their days caring for her aged parents at the old Wightman stand. VI. Nancy, m. Almarian Parker, and d. in town, without issue. VII. Frances, m. Joseph Bridge, of this town, who was by trade a hatter, and had a shop in the building now occupied as a dwelling by Mrs. Kendall. He had two sons who married two daughters of Nathaniel Holland, both of whom went to St. Louis, Mo., and became very wealthy. (See Holland.) Mr. Joseph Bridge subsequently removed to Arlington, Vt. VIII. One daughter, whose Christian name is unknown, m. a lawyer by the name of Kennicut, of Rhode Island, by whom she had a son who became eminent in the profession of his father. Many anecdotes are related of the doings at the old Carpenter stand during the lifetime of Dea. Wightman. The following is given as a specimen: During the time deacon Wightman was keeping the Carpenter tavern, at the foot of the mountain, several lumbermen were boarding at his house, who were cutting timber on the mountain. When it came night they amused themselves by playing pranks on each other or some one else. After supper, one night, one of the party told the deacon that he had found a partridge's nest that day with sixteen fresh eggs in it, and had brought them down; and if he would find rum and sugar the company should be regaled with *egg-nogg*, to which proposition the deacon not reluctantly assented. In the mean time one of the party went to his barn and purloined hen's eggs sufficient for the occasion. The party contrived to break the eggs unseen by the deacon. When the *nogg* was duly prepared, foaming in the mug, the deacon was presented with it first, in deference to age. He was not loth to accept the proffered courtesy, and grasped the mug and began to sip and taste, sip and taste, till the company began to think that he was imbibing the lion's share, when he placed the mug upon the counter, at the same time 'smacking' his lips. One of the party then asked him how he liked *partridge-nogg*, when he replied, "Amazing good! *Amazing good!* but I think it tastes a l-e-e-t!e of the wild!"

WOLCOTT, ROGER, was born in Weathersfield, Conn., Nov. 1746; m., first, Mary Slater; second, Esther Wilson. He came to Walpole in 1774, and bought the place where Philip Thomas now resides, which is known as the Wolcott place. Mr. Wolcott took his deed under the Crown of Great Britain. When he bought the place, there was standing a small hut upon it. He immediately went to work making clearings, and being an industrious pioneer, and a carpenter by trade, soon had his land under cultivation, and respectable buildings upon it. He was at work in his field the day the battle of Bennington was fought, and distinctly heard the booming of cannon. He, with many other Walpole men, was at the surrender of Burgoyne. Mr. Wolcott was a distant relative of Oliver Wolcott, who was one of the signers of the Declaration of

Independence. At the close of the 18th century his first wife died without issue. By his second wife, he had four children, all daughters. I. Mary, m. Ebenezer Wellington. II. Esther, m. Increase S. Guild. III. Clarissa, m., first, Harvey Foster; second, Philip Thomas. IV. Alzina, m. John Eams. Mr. Wolcott died in April, 1828, aged 81; his widow, Esther, d. in Dec. 1852, aged 86.

WYMAN, UZZIAH. Two large families by the name of Wyman, at one time lived contemporaneously in this town; but exactly where is not known. The progenitor of one of these families, was Uzziah. He was born in Townshend, Mass., May 18, 1764. When he was sixteen years of age, he joined the Revolutionary army, and continued a soldier until the war was closed. In 1787 he married Lydia Nutting, and immediately removed to Walpole, and, it is thought, took up a residence somewhere on Carpenter Hill. He had a family of ten children, all of whom were born in Walpole, except the oldest and youngest, the latter being born in 1811, which circumstance would seem to indicate that the family had removed from town about that time. His children were: I. Lydia, b. May 7, 1787, d. 1862. II. Uzziah, jr., b. Apr. 28, 1789, and is still living in Vermont. (1879.) He m. Orpha, dau. of David Britton, of Westmoreland, and had the following children: 1st, Elmira. 2d, Oren, who was for several years a resident of Walpole, and a member of the "Walpole Band." 3d, Elliot, now living in Westmoreland, by occupation a farmer, and an occasional contributor to the county press, on various matters. 4th, Mary. 5th, Loring. 6th, Harriet E. 7th, Emily S. III. Thomas, b. Feb. 17, 1791; m. Huldah, dau. of Ebenezer Gilbert, of Walpole, and removed to Vermont, and died there Sep. 17, 1879. One of his children, Andrew A. is a man of some prominence in business circles at Cambridgeport, Vt., and also possesses some scholarly attainments. Another of his sons was a music teacher of considerable celebrity. He once taught vocal music in Walpole, with good success. He resided in Keene at the time, when, in the prime of manhood, he was stricken with disease, and lived but a few days. He was much respected, and his death was lamented by a numerous acquaintance. IV. Joseph, V. Olive; both d. young. VI. Sybil, b. July 23, 1799; d. Aug. 14, 1845. VII. Livonia, b. 1800; d. young. VIII. Richard, b. Jan. 11, 1801; d. aged 11 years. IX. John, b. Oct. 3, 1804,—still living at Cambridgeport, Vt. X. Rhoda, b. Mar. 31, 1811; is still living.

WYMAN, WILLIAM. In the records of the town are found the following memoranda: Susannah, daughter of William and Polly Wyman, born Jan. 10, 1783. William, jr., b. Mar. 1785. Frances, b. May 17, 1787. Polly, b. June 3, 1789. Sally, b. Jan. 23, 1792. Thomas, b. May 1, 1794. Willard, b. Dec. 10, 1796; was killed by a fall from a tree. Elnathan Winchester, b. Jan. 30, 1799. Gibson, John, and George. Where the foregoing family lived in town is not known; but there was a family by the name of Wyman, that lived in the Valley, near a place known as Wyman's Hill, and this may be the one.

APPENDIX.

List of the inhabitants of Walpole, taken in the summer of 1878, including every person living in town on the first day of April of that year. The date of birth in some instances could not be ascertained. The place of birth is Walpole, and the state New Hampshire, unless otherwise specified. Abbreviations are w for wife and c for child of the foregoing.

DATE OF BIRTH.	NAME.	PLACE OF BIRTH.
	ADAMS.	
1815, Jan. 10,	Addison K.,	Andover, Vt.
'17, July 25,	Lucia A., w	Springfield, Vt.
'41, Mar. 29,	Dorr H., c	Rockingham, Vt.
'45, Sept. 21,	Helen B., c	"
	ALDRICH.	
'16, Apr. 24,	George,	Westmoreland.
'45, Jan. 17,	Mary J., w	
'51, Sept. 27,	Mary L., c	
'55, July 22,	George T., c	
'29, Mar. 11,	Niles,	Westmoreland.
	ALEXANDER.	
1794, Apr. 16,	Ezra,	
	ALLEN.	
1821, Mar. 6,	Henry,	Winchester.
'23, Oct. 18,	Marcia E., w	Cavendish, Vt.
'51, Jan. 23,	Henry P.,	
'53, Apr. 29,	Bell E., w	Acworth.
'76, Jan. 25,	Geo. H., c	
'78, Feb. 26,	Florence J., c	
'78, Feb. 26,	Fannie B., c	
'48, July 7,	Fred Lyman,	W. R. Junction.
'07, Apr. 13,	Mary R.,	Surry.
'48, May 22,	Henry T.,	
'48, May 16,	Sarah W., w	Vermont,
'52, Oct. 14,	Frank P., c	

DATE OF BIRTH.	NAME.	PLACE OF BIRTH.
1799, Aug. 29,	Henry S.,	
" July 7,	Ruth, E., w	
1836, Feb. 29,	Stephen,	
'55, July 15,	Dolly A., w	Dublin.
'74, Nov. 30,	Lucella J., c	
'41, Sept. 25,	Geo. W.,	Surry.
'18, Jan. 24,	Mary E., w	Keene.
'43, Nov. 12,	William W. c	Keene.
'68, May 13,	Ernest S., c	"
'70, Oct. 8,	Miron H., c	Swanzey.
'74, Dec. 19,	Cora L., c	Keene.
'78, Mar. 28,	George D., c	
	AMES.	
1846, Feb. 26,	Hattie F.,	Orford.
	ANGIER.	
'31, Aug. 31,	Geo. H.,	
'37, June 4,	Adeline, w	Westmoreland.
'61, May 7,	Chas. E., c	
'70, Dec. 14,	Lizzie, O., c	
	ARNOLD.	
1795, Sept. 14,	Naomi M.,	
1826, Dec. 26,	William,	Pawtucket, R. I.
'33, Feb. 20,	Mary S., w	Barre, Mass.
'55, May 9,	Cora J., c	
'63, Oct. 5,	Fred W., c	

BACON.
1805, Feb. 9, Elizabeth, Boston, Mass.
BAINE.
Edward, Chicago, Ill.,
BAKER.
'55, Aug. 8, Abbie,
'19, May 7, Eliza A.,
'14, Mar. 15, Hannah,
'45, July 19, Kesiah,
BALL.
'21, May 28, Ransom L., Alstead.
'19, Nov. 14, Phebe, w
'50, Aug. 5, Jennie M., c
'59, Aug. 1, Elnora H., c
'02, Oct. 24, Levi, Alstead.
'07, Feb. 27, Caroline, c
'43, Nov. 6, Sarah J., c
'18, May 1, Harding, Alstead.
'21, Jan. 19, Thankful H.,w
'52, May 18, Henry E., c Merrimack.
'55, Oct. 30, Sumner A., c "
'58, Aug. 21, Eliza J. F., c "
'60, Apr. 25, Fred W., Winchester.
BALLAM.
'42, Feb. 25, Solomon, England.
'45, Jan. 18, Mary, w "
'64, July 15, William A., c "
'67, Mar. 28, George, c "
'68, Aug. 4, Anna M., c "
'70, Mar. 1, Charles, c "
'72, May 6, Lizzie B., c "
'74, Sept. 12, Sherman F., c
BARDWELL.
'29, July 16, Harriet O.,
BARKER.
'44, Aug. 6, Ephraim W., Granby, Mass.
'50, Dec. 16, Emily L., w Acworth.
BARNES.
'26, Jan. 31, Harrison G., Jamaica, Vt.
'32, May 6, Eliza L., w Boston, Mass.
'55, Mar. 25,Jeanie L., c "
'56, Dec. 9, Charles H., c Brooklyn, N. Y.
'59, Jan. 26, Alida M., c Newark, N. J.
'73, July 1, Edwin G., c
1799, Dec. 23, Emily,
BARNETT.
1845, Jan. 22, John,
'19, Aug. 17, Emily P., w Weathersfield,Vt.
'44, Jan. 1, Winslow G.,
'58, Aug 5, Maria K., w
'99, Jun. 27, Harriet G.,
'21, July, George G., c
'33, June 8, Harriette E., c
'58, Mar. 30, Carrie A., c
BARRETT.
Martin, Ireland.
Margarette, "
'57,Mar 31, Edward,c Fitchburg, Mass.
'59, Apr. 20, James, c "
'61, June 10, John, c
'65, July 16, Mary, c
BATCHELDER.
'21, Apr. 21, Josiah W., Sutton, Mass.
'23, May 27, Almira M., w
'55, June 12, Harry E., c
BATES.
'45, Nov. 12, Silas M., Fairfield, Me.
'39, Mar. 25, Frances A , w
'61, Mar. 10, Mary G., c
'65, Dec. 3, Edward S., c
BEAN.
'49, Sept. 23, Henry E., Burlington, Vt.
'52, July 8, Mary E., w Cavendish.
'76, Sept. 21, Alice M., c
BECKWITH.
'27, Feb. 11, Alvin A., Hadley, Vt.

1830, Jan. 11, Nancy A., w Alstead.
'54, Mar. 8, Chas. E., c
BELLOWS.
'41, July 24, Josiah G.,
'41, Jan. 29, Katharine H. W., w
'07, Sept. 23, Thomas,
'21, May 8, A. Herbert, London, Eng.
Julia A., w Boston, Mass.
'62, Nov. 15, Blanche H., c Concord.
'64, Nov. 8, Herbert G., c
'68, Mar. 2, Arthur B., c
'51, Feb. 22, Charles L.,
'66, July 2, Filetta, Washington.
Mary Nichols, Cooperst'n, N.Y.
'42, May 29, Henry Nichols,
Georgianna
Lumie, w New York.
'75, Aug. 27, Stewart, c San F'cisco, Cal.
BENSON.
'65, June 19, Lucy, Stoddard.
BIXBY.
'42, Nov. 20, Edward,
'54, Mar. 20, Thankful, w
'70, Feb. 17, Rosetta W., c
BLAKE.
'28, Apr. 4, Geo. Albert, Raymond.
'30, Apr. 2, Margarette H., w
'58, Jan. 22, Charles E., Westmoreland.
BLANCHARD
'22, Sept. 29, Roswell S.,
'64, Sept. 26, Albert E., c
'67, Jan. 8, Ella F., c
'18, Oct. 11, Willard T.,
'45, May 18, Louisa L.,
BOND.
'19, Mar. 27, Wm. A., Washington.
'26, May 24, Louisa M., w Philadelphia.
'24, Aug. 17, Chas. B.,
'49, Oct. 16, Edward F.,
'53, Dec. 25, Edwerta P., w Macon, Ga.
'75, Mar. 1, Mamie L., c
'77, Nov. 14, Mattie E., c
BOOTH.
'26, Sept. 26, Dolphus S., Lempster.
'51, May 6, Sarah P., w "
'61, Aug. 31, Emma, c "
'64, Nov. 24, Fred, c
'69, Aug. 7, Alice, c
'75, Dec. 11, Edwin,
BOVIER.
Joseph, Vermont.
BOWEN.
Cornelius, Ireland.
Katharine, w "
'53, Sept. 5, John, c Massachusetts.
'55, July 14, Mary, c
'60, June 5, Timothy, c
'57, Oct. 21, Nellie, c
'62, Apr. 16, Patsy, c
'64, July 22, Hannah, c
'67, Aug. 11, Michael, c
BRITTON.
'17, Dec. 22, Major J., Surry.,
'21, Aug 1, Jane M., w Adams Mass.
'55, Aug. 17, Emma Jane, c
'61, Nov. 10, Arthur A., c
BROOKS.
'56, Dec. 16, Frank E., Illinois.
BROWN.
'33, Nov. 11, Herod W.,
'41, Dec. 31, Mary A., w Rockingham, Vt.
'63, Mar. 7, Lizzie M., c
'65, Apr. 8, Grace M., c
'67, July 7, James R., c

1874, Mar. 30, Ethel S., c
'77, Apr. 22, Clifford A., c
'38, Sept 10, William, Rev.,Concord, Mass.
'37, Feb. 29, Salome, S., w Taunton, Mass.
'66, July 15, Cornila C., c Shelburn, Mass.
'68, Mar. 7, Wm. C., c "
'74, Sept. 20, Ophelia S., c "
'31, June 10, John C., Acworth.
'39, Feb. 22, Jennette, w Wilmington, Vt.
'62, Dec. 6, Annette, c Langdon.
'67, June 1, Orr W., c
'73, Feb. 18, Ashton B., c
'74 Feb 1, John C., jr., c
'76, May 3, Florence M., c
'21, Dec. 15, Isaac, Acworth.
'28, July 25, Frances L., w
'55, June 19, Geo. D., c Surry.
'61, Sept. 28, Mary L., c "
'65, Sept. 26, Fred A., c "
Charles,
'42, Apr. 15, Mary, w
'70, Aug. 28, Harry E.,
'30, June 16, Daniel N., Antrim.
'41, Apr. 17, Jane, w Rockingham.
'38, Apr. 17, Benj. F., c Perkinsville, Vt.
'21, Jan. 25, John, Ireland.
'28, Apr. 1, Honora, w "
'61, May 20, William, c "
'55, May 20, John, jr., c
58, Apr. 1, James, c
'61, Oct. 17, Margarette, c
'61, Oct. 17, Kate, c
'63, July 5, Mary, c
Julia, c
BRUCE.
'06, Dec. 24, Nellie S., Newfane, Vt.
BUCKLEY.
'27, Margaret, Ireland.
'75, June 12, Grace, Boston, Mass.
BUFFUM.
'03, Aug. 11, Mary Ann D., Sterling, Ct.
'22, Apr. 11, Wm. G., c
'32, Sept. 4, Sarah A. H., c
'26, Feb. 8, Joseph H., c
'05, Apr. 15, David, Westmoreland.
'06, Mar. 5, Mary Hubbard, w
'34, Aug. 29, Ann Reynolds,
'30, Sept. 8, Thomas B.,
'36, July 24, Ann R., w
'69, Dec. 13, Thos. B. jr., c
BUNDY.
'50, Apr. 23, Geo. H., Beverly, Mass.
1798, June 26, Jane,
'52, May 29, Amasa P., jr., Beverly, Mass.
BUNTING.
'20, Sept., James, England.
'36, May 24, Mahala, w "
'64, Apr., Charles W., c .
BURK.
'27, Jan. 27, David, Ireland.
Honora, "
BURNHAM.
'61, Jan. 27, Hannah, Williamst'n, Vt.
BURT.
'12, May 12, Levi,
'12, Aug. 27, Mary, w
'27, July 22, Henry,
'25, Jan. 22, Charlotte E.,
'54, Nov. 10, Edna J., c
'17, Dec. 9, Alfred W.,
'18, Aug. 29, Caroline, w Alstead.
'55, Dec. 9, Chas. S., c
'52, Mar. 26, Geo. F., c
BUSKY.
'63, Moses,

CALAHAN.
1858, Jan. 19, Hannah, Westmoreland.
CAPEN.
Josiah, Dorchester, Ms.
CARPENTER.
'24, Nov. 9, Frances A.,
'44, Jan. 10, Albert,
'41, Mar. 26, Mary M., w N. Y.
CARR.
'35, July 14, Clark C., Washington,N.H
'40, April 4, Isabella R., w Marlow.
'62, July 24, Walter C., c Sutton.
'64, July 21, Nellie B., c Keene.
'71, May 23, Fred L., c Keene.
CARROLL.
Patrick, Ireland.
Catherine, w "
'59, Jan. 6, James H., c
CARTER.
'56, Nov. 8, Fred A., Bradford, Vt.
CATER.
'51, Oct. 30, Charles E., Alstead.
'52, Mar. 28, Nancy C., w Sullivan.
CHANDLER.
'42, Aug. 28, Henry H., Alstead.
'42, Mar. 27, Alma, w "
'64, Feb. 28, Edwin H., c "
'68, May 2, Herbert G., c "
'61, Sept. 26, James, "
'06, April 21,Mary B., w Rockingham, Vt.
'52, Mar. 10, William, c Alstead.
CHAPIN.
'45, Aug. 30, Warren P., Westmoreland.
'47, Dec. 13, Helen A., w Keene.
'67, Jan. 15, Edward H., c
CHAPPELL.
'18, Dec. 14, William, Lyme, Ct.
'19, April 13, Alvira, w Goshen.
'48, Oct. 20, Juliette, c Lempster.
'51, Aug. 20, Abbie E., c "
'58, Dec. 11, Clara Bell, c
CHICKERING.
'40, July 23, Charles, Westmoreland.
'49, June 15, Jennie A., w
'74, Dec. 10, Ethel J., c
1798, Jan. 7, Dilate,
1829, Feb. 10, Lyman J., Westmoreland.
'75, July 29, L. J., w Chesterfield.
'76, Feb. 29, Jessie L., c
CHURCH.
'26, July 21, Cyrus, Hinsdale.
'27, Sept. 7, Mary A., w
CLARK.
'64, July 25, Willie, Keene.
COBB.
'42, Jan. 19, Samuel D.,
'42, Jan. 3, E. Josephine, w Lexington, Ms.
'95, Feb. 24, Joseph, c
1799, Feb. 25, Jerusha,
1833, Aug. 25, Ellen,
COCHRAN.
'12, Dec. 10, Samuel,
'22, Feb. 6, Relief W., w
'50, April 30, Mary C., c
'54, Feb. 4, Ada L., c
'56, Feb. 23, Lucy J., c
'58, July 17, James B., c
'60, July 30, Frances S., c
'62, Mar. 13, Robert J., c
CODIER.
'30, May 5, Peter, Ireland.
'32, Jan., Julia, w "
'62, Jan. 5, Mary E., c
'65, July 26, Julia A., c
'66, July 26, Elizabeth, c

COLBURN.
1829, Aug. 15, Albert, Alstead.
'29, Jan. 24, Angeline, w England.
'53, Nov. 12, Alice A., c
'58, Nov. 7, Willis A., c
'61, July 12, Warren H., c
'64, Mar. 18, Alvin E., c
COLLINS.
John, Ireland.
Johanna, w "
'67, April 8, Jeremiah, c
'59, June 28, Mary, c
'61, Oct. 8, John, c
Bartholomew, "
'44, March 3, Sarah, w Canada.
'55, Aug. 12, Mary, c
'77, Nov. 29, John, c
COMSTOCK.
'68, April 23, James, Sullivan.
'17, April 28, Eliza, w Dublin.
'51, Oct. 26, Charles, Westmoreland.
'47, Aug. 7, James M., Jaffrey.
'45, April 18, Antoinette, w
'63, Dec. 6, Nellie S., c
'71, July 18, Ole Bull, c
'76, Aug. 6, Dolly May, c
'78, April 2, Geo. H., c
CONNELL.
'13, John, Ireland.
'15, Catherine, "
COOK.
1796, Nov. 6, Sarah, Grafton, Vt.
1858, La Fayette, N. Y.
'42, March 4, Ellen, w
'59, May 19, Ellen R., c
'64, Aug. 26, Chas. L., c
'66, Oct. 1, Flora A., c
'68, April 14, Herbert J., c
'74, July 1, Salinda E., c
'76, May 18, Mary E., c
COPELAND.
'29, July 26, Sarah,
'55, June 8, Frank H., c
'59, Oct. 1, Mary A., c
CORBIN.
'53, Nov. 16, Pamelia P., Ashford, Ct.
'64, May 12, Frederick E., Warren, O.
'44, Nov. 16, Persis L., Wellington, Ct.
CORLISS.
'57, Milan D., Lempster.
COWDERY.
'21, July 3, Geo. W., Westmoreland.
'25, Sept. 13, Selina, c Springfield, Vt.
CRAM.
'53, John, Ireland.
CRAY.
'38, John, Ireland.
'53, May, Maggie, w "
'74, Nov. 6, Hannah, c Vermont.
'76, Jan. 13, Eugene, c
'77, June 6, Patrick, c
CROSS.
'00, Nov. 16, John,
'41, Feb. 21, Charles W., Burke, Vt.
'40, Jan. 30, Abby, "
CROWELL.
'34, Oct. 23, Curtis R., Westminster, Vt.
'35, June 1, Mary J., w "
'62, May 1, Flora May, c "
'68, July 8, Walter G., c "
'05, Nov. 27, Christopher, "
'08, Sept. 29, Annie G., w "
CROWLEY.
'59, Oct. 7, Cornelius, Vermont.
DAME.
'60, May 15, George, Lawrence, Mass.

1841, Mar. 19, Eunice, Ashburnham, Ms.
DARBY.
'59, June 17, Mary E., New Haven, Ct.
'62, June 24, Edward I.,
'60, Dec. 9, Mabel J., B. Falls.
DAVIS.
'18, March 2, Sarah G., Marlow.
'44, Aug. 16, Charles C., Woonsocket, R.I.
'42, Feb. 3, Carrie L., w Fall River, Mass.
'69, Nov. 29, William R., c
'72, Oct. 1, Mary C., c
'75, Mar. 28, Thomas C., c
'77, Feb. 6, Arthur P., c
'49, Aug. 7, Charles A.,
'56, Mar. 21, Abby L., w Keene.
'74, April 5, Mabel A., c
'75, Sept. 15, Abbie G., c Keene.
'78, Feb. 9, Frank A., c
'24, April 21, Marshall A., c Rockingham, Vt.
'27, Dec. 2, Rebecca, w "
'58, Feb. 23, Frank M., c "
'62, Oct. 15, Abbie M., c "
'29, Nov. 4, John L., Washington.
'57, May 4, Mary E., w Northfield, Vt.
'70, Mar. 20, Geo. F., c
DE LANY.
'42, Oct. 27, Dennis, Stockbridge, Ms.
'53, Mar. 27, Katherine, w Boston, Mass.
'64, Sept. 11, Lawrence, c
'72, Feb. 7, William, c
'75, Sept. 12, John, c
'76, Nov. 6, Katie, c
DENNIS.
'20, July 8, Anna R., Newfane, Vt.
'53, June 25, Chas. F., c Rutland, Vt.
'55, April 19, Helen L., c "
'58, Jan. 18, Willie C., c "
'60, Nov. 4, Fred F., c "
DE WOLF.
'20, June 2, Dares A., Deerfield, Mass.
'23, Sept. 12, Lucinda, w Rhinebeck, N. Y.
'60, Sept. 11, Maggie B., c Westminster, Vt.
DICKEY.
'06, Mar. 12, Clement S.,
'12, May 5, Betsey P., w
'48, Dec. 8, Albert C., c
'20, Nov. 1, Lewis,
DODGE.
1798, April 18, Phebe,
1841, July 8, Gardner, Marlow.
'49, Aug. 19, Fannie, w
'47, Aug. 11, Henry R., c
'49, Nov. 30, Charles W., c
'52, April 28, Frank A., c
DORNEY.
'26, Nov. 9, James, Ireland.
'26, Mary, w "
'54, Aug. 6, Morris, c
'55, Dec. 19, Sarah, c
'57, May 30, James, jr., c
'58, Feb. 11, Ellen M., c
'63, Aug. 6, Maggie, c
'65, June 14, Mary, c
DORSON.
'02, Oct. 8, Jane, Ireland.
DRISCOLL.
'35, May 2, Bartholomew, Ireland.
'43, June 24, Helen, w "
'65, Feb. 6, Nora, c
'66, July 28, Morris, c
'68, Mar. 17, Bartholomew, jr., c
'70, Oct. 15, Nellie, c
'72, July 3, David J., c
'76, Mar. 14, Michael, c
'78, Feb. 25, Frank, c
'22, Dec., Eliza,

DRISLANE.
1824, Mar. 17, Patrick, Ireland.
'26, Nov. 1, Margaret, w "
'65, April 12, Lizzie M., c
'71, June 12, Geo. J., c
'57, Jan. 1, Catherine L.,
DUNHAM.
'14, Dec. 8, Elisha, Westminster, Vt.
'15, Aug. 24, Adeline M., w Athens, Vt.
'45, July 25, Lora, c Westminster, Vt.
'49, Dec. 21, Ella, c "
DUNSHEE.
'14, June 10, Allen,
'46, Feb. 3, Herbert A., c
'54, Sept. 9, William L., c
'52, July 14, John L.,
'54, Feb. 17, Annette,
'57, Dec. 27, Frank,
'59, Jan. 25, Carlos E.,
'35, July 2, Sarah A., w
DUNSMOOR.
'26, Oct. 27, Stansbury, Townshend, Vt.
Abigail, w
1861, July 16, Mattie J., c
'62, June 13, Idella L., c
'63, Aug. 25, Nettie, c
'64, Sept. 24, La Fayette, c
'65, Dec. 24, Willis, c
'68, Aug. 4, Joseph S., c
'71, June 5, Hattie, c
DWINNELL.
'40, Aug. 10, Benj. F., Andover, Vt.
'41, June 12, Lucy A., w Grafton, Vt.
'62, Mar. 24, Benj. F., jr., c Westminster, Vt.
'12, Sept. 27, Oris W., Andover, Vt.
'59, May 19, Caroline M., w
'19, May 13, Benj. H., Andover, Vt.
'18, Mar. 11, Luceba, w "
'45, April 29, Alvin, c "
ELLIOTT.
'22, Sept. 26, Moses, Mason.
'30, Dec. 5, Mary E., w Alstead.
'49, May 30, Ferdinand S.,c Marlow.
'09, Nov. 1, Mary E., c N. Y.
'59, Dec. 1, Edward L., c Marlow.
'67, Feb. 1, Joseph A., c
ELLIS.
'48, Sept. 22, James W., Dublin.
'49, May 12, Sarah J., w Alstead.
'68, Dec. 3, Nellie M., c Langdon.
'70, Aug. 8, James F., c Keene.
'06, Dec. 4, Samuel, "
ELWELL.
1821, May 24, Samuel K., Langdon.
'35, Oct. 30, Emily E., w Alstead.
'49, June 9, Geo. G., Langdon.
'72, Nov. 4, Charles, c "
'74, May 30, Harry, c S. Charlestown.
EMERSON.
'50, Dec. 19, Mary F., Westminster, Vt.
'72, Sept. 9, Charles E., c Alstead.
'74, Mar. 28, Jenny G., c "
'23, Oct. 12, John C.,
'36, July 7, Urana C., w
'57, June 19, Geo. M., c
'58, Sept. 29, Franklin B., c
'63, Aug. 3, Harriet U., c
EMORY.
'03, May 28, Fanny,
'35, Feb. 27, Edwin, c N. Y.
ESTABROOKS.
'43, April 30, John W., Westminster, Ms.
'59, Jan. 8, Sarah A., w Dunbarton.
'70, Aug. 16, Fred W., c
'78, Mar. 12, Ella A., c

FARNHAM.
1820, Sept. 3, Martha,
FARNSWORTH.
'39, April 12, John S.,
'40, Mar. 12, Ellen, w Cavendish, Vt.
'80, Mar. 14, Mary L., c
'61, Dec. 6, Nellie J., c
'65, May 23, Charles E., c
'68, Sept. 8, James B., c
'72, April 19, John, c
'75, July 20, Lizzie D., c
FARR.
'24, Sept. 7, Justin, Windham, Vt.
'28, Dec. 29, Abby E., w Andover, Vt.
'56, Aug. 20, Carleton L., c Windham, Vt.
FAULKNER.
'06, Feb. 27, Augustus, Lancaster, Mass.
'17, Oct. 20, Mary A., w
'35, Aug. 7, Ann L., c
'65, Oct. 24, George M., c
FAXON.
1800, Dec. 18, Mary D., Needham, Mass.
FAY.
'52, Aug. 19, Fred H., Alstead.
'53, Oct. 2, Addie M., w Springfield, Vt.
'77, Nov. 9, Lucy A., c
FELCH.
'22, Oct. 14, Thomas F. S.,
'38, July 17, Lucy R., w
'56, April 25, Augustus P., c
'59, April 20, Irvin W., c
FETTERMAN.
'45, Dec. 12, Samuel, Pennsylvania.
'45, Aug. 15, Julia, w New York.
'64, April 6, George, c
FIFIELD.
'20, June 20, Joseph, Canaan.
'22, Feb. 26, ——, w Lyme.
'59, Feb. 19, Carlos, c Keene.
'85, Mar. 24, Emma, c
FISHER.
'54, May Ornstus, Hinsdale.
'29, Nov. 1, Charles,
'35, Feb. 14, Emma J., w
'35, Feb. 28, Frank M., c
'58, Sept. 19, David, c
'61, April 1, Oliver, c
'15, May 16, Moses,
'23, Nov. 28, Adeline, w
'50, Jan. 4, Henry W., c
'45, Jan. 19, Emily C., c
'46, Dec. 12, Frances A., c
'17, Mar. 28, Joseph,
'22, Feb. 6, Adeline, w Danville, Vt.
'55, June 10, Fred, c
'50, Aug. 25, Andrew J.,
'29, April 9, Clarissa, w Dorchester, Ms.
'57, Mar. 15, Ada M., c
'62, Aug. 22, Katie M., c
'72, Feb. 25, Albert L., c
FLANNERY.
'18, Jan., Bridget, Ireland.
'40, Dennis,
FLEMING.
'40, Jan., James R., Canada.
'43, Dec. 5, Sarah, w "
'75, Feb. 12, Frank Geo., c
'77, Mar. 24, Maud M., c
FLETCHER.
'02, Mar. 24, Mary, Vermont.
'43, Feb. 2, Mary J., New York.
'59, Mar. 21, Mary F., c "
'64, June 2, Frank, c "
'66, Sept. 1, Virginia, c
'55, April 29, Curtis J.,
'41, Sept. 25, Diantha, w New York.

1865, May 3, Fannie D., c
'74, Feb. 3, Carlos E., c
'50, Jan. 28, Alma E., , New York.
'27, July 28, Henry H.,
'35, Nov. 16, Mary E., w Jamaica, Vt.
'55, Dec. 12, Marcella M., c
'63, March 4, William H., c
FLOYD.
'01, March 6, Eliza,
FOLYER.
'43, John,
'38, Mary, w.
'71, Jan. 1, Mary, c.
'75, Jan. 8, Ellen, c.
'70, Oct. 8, Anna, c.
FOSTER.
1799, Feb. 1 , Levi H.,
1808, Sept. 26, Mary S., w Keene.
'25, Mar. 22, Caleb,
'26, Sept. 11, Isabella E., w
'52, Sept. 21, Edward P., c
'56, Aug. 13, Wesley C., c
'59, Feb. 10, Alfred M., c
'62, Dec. 4, Hiram M., c
'26, Oct. 15, Henry T.,
'31, Aug. 11, Hannah M.,w Westmoreland.
'54, Jan. 6, Frank H., c
'58, Oct. 6, Willis C., c
'59, Nov. 7, Velmer E., c
'61, Sep. 28, Adine P., c
'69, July 20, Florence J., c
'70, Aug. 10, Annie R., c
'01, July 5, Eliza
'45, Feb. 22, Katie J., c
FRINK.
'16, Jan. 3, Louisa A.,
FULLER.
'43, Aug. 13, Jane L., Waterville, Vt.
'49, Jan. 4, Henrietta S., "
'63, June 9. Mary L.,
'24, July 31, Catherine, Marion, Mo.
'56, Aug. 12. Mary L., c Boston, Mass.
'65, Dec. 25, Benj. W., c Roxbury, Mass.
GASSETT.
'24, Nov. 17, Geo. H., Pepperill, Mass.
'19, Apr. 2, Sarah C., w Townshend, Vt.
'55, Aug. 17. Geo. W., Marlow.
'60, June 9, Jos'ne S., w Wethersfield, Vt.
'63, Feb. 3, Abby F. L., Langdon.
'69, Feb. 16, Walter C.,
GATES.
'39, Apr. 14, Charles,
'63, Nov. 18, Lilla A., c
'65, Aug. 7, Minnie O., c
'68, Aug. 12, Benj. F., c
'49, Jan. 11, Sarah A.,
'12, Mar. 26, Adeline, Westminster, Vt.
'39, Dec. 13, Andrew J.,
'51, Oct. 29, Angie S., w Alstead.
'76, Nov. 21. Idella, c "
GEER.
'21, Dec. 20. Mary, Charlestown.
GENSER.
'22, Mar. 8, Loring, Germany.
'14, Aug. 3, Frederica, w
GILBERT.
'92, Dec. 21, Asa, Surry,
GOODWIN.
'50, Feb. 7, Geo. W., Charlestown.
GORDON.
'05, Dec. 12, George D., Sterling, Ct.
GOWING. "
'31, Aug. 14, Calvin C., Dublin.
'64, Mar. 28, Clara, c
'25, Mar. 16, Betsey Maria, "
'01, Nov. 27, Lucy, "

GRANT.
1812, Apr. 16, Geo. W.,
'44, Oct. 1, Helen E., c
'56, Herbert C., c
'58, Jan. 20, Mary Bellows,
GRAVES.
'05, July 5, Martha,
1800, July 14, Mary,
'24, Sep. 13, Charles H.,
'28, June 23, Lucinda M., w.Newport.
'54, Mar. 18, Fred D., c
'57, Feb. 9, Josiah H., c
1800, June 21, Saphrona,
'02, Aug. 31, Calvin,
'30, Sep. 22, Isaac M.,
'35, Apr. 28, Esther A., w
'55, Oct. 26, Ella L., c
'57, July 27, Minnie E., c
'61, Oct 19, Hattie L., c
'34 Mar. 27, Andrew A.,
'33, Aug. 25, Martha A., Westmoreland.
'50, Nov. 2. Fredr'k A., c Billerica, Mass.
'92, May, 9, Lizzie J., c Westmoreland.
'63, Aug. 20, Frank O., c "
'68, July 22, Ida M., c "
'76, Nov. 13, Charles W.,c
'34, May 30, Eli W.,
'55, Aug. 5, Edna A., w
'67, Dec. 15, Walter E., c
'36, Dec. 27, William C.,
'59, July 9, Geo. H.,
1797, May 5, Rebecca W., Acton, Vt.
'12, Apr. 5, Geo. W.,
'22, Nov. 28, Stella, w
'54, Nov. 10, Francis H., c
'59, Nov. 13, John W., c
'62, Jan. 21, Russell G., c
'66, Oct. 12, Nellie M.,
GREEN.
'32, Dec. 13, Silas B., Stoddard.
'54, Jan. 20, Carrie L., w Ludlow, Vt.
'60, Feb. 8, Jennie A., c New York.
'68, Nov. 28, Molly J., c "
GRIFFIN.
Dennis. Ireland.
Catherine, w "
'59, Mar. 5, Mary E., c
'61 Aug. 14, Anna J., c
'64, May 28, Thomas E., c
'66, Dec. 17, William, c
'67, Apr. 11, Dennis G., c
'73, Feb. 17, Frances J., c
'75, Sep. 25, Maggie, c
'77, Oct. 16, Andrew, c
'77, Oct. 16, Arthur, c
Thomas, Ireland
'44, Feb. 26, Bridget, w "
'66, June 17, Maggie, c
'68, Apr. 21, Thomas jr., c
'70, Apr. 8, Cornelius, c
'72, June 23, Edward, c
'74, Mar. 1, Ellen, c
'76, Mar. 12, David, c
'78, May 21, Mary, c
GRISWOLD.
'34, Jan. 1, Henry W. S., Ft. Moultrie, S.C.
'51, Nov. 12, Eliza A., w Lowell, Mass.
'54, Oct. 5, Anna A., c Norwich, Vt.
GUILD.
1800, Jan. 17, Increase S., Rutland, Mass.
'63, Sep. 18, Esther, w
'27, Aug. 23, William W., c Bethel, Vt.
'31, Nov. 20, Eliza J., c Troy,
'58, Aug. 20, Flora L., c Fitzwilliam.
'65, June 26, Warren W., c
'68, June 17, Elwin E., c

1871, Jan. 28, Helen M., c
'74, Apr. 10, Sylvia M. c
'43, Jan. 6, Maria J.,
'29, Oct. 24, Edwin, Bethel, Vt.
'58, Oct. 4, Sophia, w Concord, Vt.
'60, Aug. 2, Arthur E., c Dummerston, Vt.
'71, Feb. 7, Norman. c
'74, Jan. 12, Esther M., c
'75, Apr. 19, Eva A., c

HALE.
'20, Feb. 24, Moses J., Ohio.
'22, Aug. 22, Sarah G., w
'48, Mar. 6, Chas. B., c
'58, Nov. 11, Dudley P., c
'63, Nov. 18, John E., c

HALL.
'18, Apr. 13, Martin J.,
'15, Jan, 2, Maria. w
'53, Aug. 43, Melissa C., c
'42, Sep 24, Levi A.,
'44, Jan. 18, Estelle M., w
'67, Mar. 21, Alfred A., c
'74, Oct. 2, Clifford F., c
'26, June 4, William,
           Louisa P., w
'67, May 26, Percy L., c
'15, July 5, Hall, Mary, Surry.
'52, Mar. 26, Hall, Otis A., Westmoreland.
'59, Aug. 28, Ellen G., w
'09, Sept. 12, Gardner E.,
'27, Sept. 14, Arabella A.,w Windsor, Vt.
'30, Sept. 27, Chas. B., Surry.
'31, Oct. 20, Sarah J., w Westmoreland.
'50, Aug. 3, Horace H., c "
'58, Sept. 15, Addie K., c "
'60, Sept. 3, Emma J., c "
'62, Sept. 13, Lucy C., c "
'71, June 7, Albert H., c
'73, Sept. 13, Benj. H., c
'27, Oct. 19, Henry P.,
          Caroline, w
'16, Dec. 4, Oliver,
'35, Sept. 7, Ellen A., w
'64, Aug, 7, Oliver E., c
'69, June 30, Bell M., c
'54, Mar. 27, Albert L.,

HARNETT.
James, Ireland.
Margarette, "

HARRIMAN.
'19, May 23, Leander, Claremont.
'44, Apr. 20, Nellie M., c "
'57, Apr. 17, Clarence L., c "

HARTY.
'23, May 18, Margarette, Ireland.
'42, Dec. 26, David, "
          John, "
'29, Dec. 20, Joanna, w "
'54, Nov. 2, James, c "
'56, Nov. 12, John, c
'58, Feb. 10, Maggie, c
'60, Aug. 2, William, c
'61, Mar. 17, Cornelius, c
'63, July 15, Anna, c.
'65, Mar. 1, Michael, c
'67, May 27, Johanna, c
'69, Nov. 26, Thomas, c
'72, Feb. 18, Patrick, c

HARVEY.
'49, Dec. 14, Sarah, Westmoreland.

HASTINGS,
'26, Mar. 18, Harriet M.,
'58, Feb. 1, Edward H., c Cambridge, Ms.,
'59, Feb. 23, Thomas N., c "

HAYWARD.
'31, Dec. 26, Waldo Flint, Wayland, Mass.

1828, July 5, John W., Wayland, Mass.
'26, Mar. 19, Esther C., w
'56, Feb. 28, Frank M., c
'64, June 19 Louisa B., c
'67, April 3, John W. jr., c

HEALD.
'19, Apr. 19, John E, Lynesboro.
'35, Oct. 2, Ann, w Ireland.
'53, July 18, John, c Australia.
'53, Sep. 25, Robert D., c "
'57, July 18, Amos J., c Washington.
'61, Jan. 15, Letitia L., c "
'62, Sep. 24, George W., c "
'64, Nov. 13, Ida M., c "
'66, Oct. 15, William C., c "
'69, Nov. 15, Millie E., c Lempster.
'47, July 24, James H., Fort Ann, N. Y.
'46, Nov. 21, Anna E., w. Grafton, Mass.

HEALY.
1829, Patrick, Ireland.
Margarett, w "
1860, Nov. 4, Jerry, c N. B.
'33, John, c
'64, June 16, Patrick, c
'66, June 29, James, c
'69, Jan. 20, Thomas, c

HENNESY.
'47, May, James, Ireland.
'49, May, Fannie, c "
'76, Feb. 28, Dennis, c
'78, Jan. 6, Nellie, c
Eliza, c Ireland.

HERSCH.
1865, Dec. 30. Frank C., Keene.

HICKS.
'42, Jan. 19, Hiram G., Jefferson.

HINDS.
'19, Nov. 14, Jarvis D., Hubb'dston, Ms.
'19, Dec. 22. Mary E., w England.
'59, Dec. 18, Arthur D., c
'44, July 13, Jarvis H.,
'46, May 7, Emma G., w Alstead.
'74, Jan. 13, Geo. Rust., c
'77, Sep. 7, Clifford J., c
'13, Jan. 10, Woodward, Hubb'dston, Ms.
'02, Oct. 15, Elizabeth, w Woonsocket, R.I.

HITCHCOCK.
'15, Sep. 11, Henry A., Claremont.
'19, Oct. 24, Jane, w. Woodstock, Vt.
'50, June 12,Anna J., c
'52, Apr. 29, Lizzie S., c
'21, Sep. 1, Chloe, Claremont.

HODGKIN.
'49, Sep. 9, John E., Putney, Vt.
'46, Mar. 31, Frances C., w
'66, Nov. 6, Lizzie C., c
'72, Apr. 5, Nellie J., c
'77, May 3, Nettie F., c
'37, Jan. 30, Harriet,

HODSKINS.
'38, Jan. 22. George H.,
'47, Mar. 11, Sarah A., w Gilsum.
'76, Mar. 16, Clara F., c
'08, June 26,John N.,
'08, Sep. 10, Emily, w
1799, Aug. 23, Cynthia,

HOLDEN.
1838, July 29, George H., Langdon.
'48, May 15, Jane M., w
'70, May 14, George N., c
'72, Mar. 16, Charles H., c
'04, Mar. 30, Asa, Langdon.
'51, Apr. 21, Edward M. "
'50, Jan. 26, Lora F., w

HOLLAND.
'34, Apr. 11, Leonard B.,

1835, Aug. 9, Elnora, w
'58, Apr. 27, Mary M., c
'60, June 26, Nath'niel W. c
'62, Mar. 26, Henry D., c
'63, June 6, Ada R., c
'66, May, 6, James L., c
'69, Dec. 22, Isabella B., c
'71, Jan. 24, Charles S., c
'73, Aug. 2, Emma, c
'76, Jan. Abbie, c
'77, Oct. 9, Lenora, c
1798, Mar. 8, Nancy M.,   Alstead.
1838, Mar. 17, George R., c
'28, Feb. 12, Edward M., c
'55, Oct. 6, Charles H.,   St. Louis,
HOLMES.
'48, Oct. 31, Hannah,   Mt. Holly, Vt.
'21, Feb. 16, Ira,   Stoddard.
'23, Sept. 24, Cath. R., w   Chester, Vt.
'54, Apr. 13, Emma F., c   Lempster.
'58, Nov. 24, John P., c   "
1791, Mar. 8, Augustine,
HOLTON.
'56, May 30, Abbie,   Westminster, Vt.
HOOPER.
1809, Dec. 10, Charles,
'11, Jan. 11, Almira, w
'24, Oct. 12, Harriett,
'04, Jan. 24, Harriett,
'63, Apr. 7, William F.,
'53, Sep. 4, George D.,
'52, Mar. 28, Elbra M., w   Bethel, Vt.
'76, Feb. 6, Ellen, c
'77, Feb. 9, Hayes, c
'12, Feb. 21, William,
'16, Mar. 7, Elvira, w   Rockingham Vt.
'18, June 22, John,
'22, Mar. 10, Agnes.   Scotland.
'59, Sep. 27, Marion L., c
HOSMER.
'05, Mar. 7, Edwin,
'13, May 13, Maria, w
'42, Feb. 14, Ellen,
'68, Sep. 13, Ethel, c
HOUGHTON.
'43, Sep. 21, Charles W.,
'47, June 25, Josp'ne F., w   Winchendon, Ms.
'69, Sep. 13, Phebe L.,
'52, Oct. 22, Mary E., c
'38, Apr. 19, Henry E.,
'37, May 19, Abbie M., w   Fairlee, Vt.
'59, Nov. 13, H. Leslie, c
'60, Oct. 31, Everett L., c
'62, Dec. 4, Frank M., c
'66, Oct. 19, E. Orin, c
'68, Mar. 10, Algion E., c
'70, Sep. 24, Clara B., c
'72, June 5, Mary L., c
40, Apr. 16, John L.,
'38, Aug. 2, S. Augusta, w, Chesterfield.
'65, May. 13, Emma A., c
'68, Apr. 11, Geo, L., c
HOWARD.
'35, Mar. 23, Roselvo A.,   Andover, Vt.
'35, Aug. 25, Katie E., w   Weston, Vt.
'57, Oct. 30, Willis A., c   Chester, Vt.
1786, Dec. 5., Mary,   "
'11. Jan. 5, Mary,   Andover, Vt.
HOWE.
'25, Jan. 26, Albert N.,   Londonderry, Vt.
'29, Aug. 19, Emeline E., w   "
'54, Aug. 12, Albert W., c   "
'60, Oct. 8, Ella E., c   "
'66, Oct. 6, Fred A., c
'34, June 26, Lucius S.,   Grafton, Vt.
'43, Apr. 8. Lucy, w   Royalston, Mass.

HOWLAND.
1800, May, 18, Hublah,   Rockingham, Vt.
HURBARD.
1799, May 8, Catherine,   Surry.
'38, Aug. 23, Frederick J.
'40, Feb. 8, Julietta F., w
'60, Dec. 20, Walter F., c
'74, Aug. 7, Alfred S., c
'08, Dec. 28, Clarissa A.,
'43, Nov. 17, Oliver J.,
'45, Feb. 19, Serena J., w   Chesterfield.
'70, Apr. 22, Ola A., c
'72, Oct. 28, Ira S., c
'21, Sep. 21, Willard,
'21, Nov. 19, Elvira, w   Grafton, Vt.
'38, Dec. 13, John L.
'47, Jan. 6, Frances A. w
JEFTS.
'12, Sep. 10, James L.,   Townshend, Vt.,
JENKS.
'60, Oct. William W.,   Newport.
JENNINGS.
'19, Mar. 17, Geo.,
'25, Sep. 26, Lydia S., w   Acworth,
'60, Apr. 5, Minnie A., c
'52, Jan. 22, Clara L., c
'55, Apr. 16, Ida L., c
'13, Aug, 7, Alonzo,
'27, Nov. 4, Clarissa, w
'55, Oct. 28, Charles A., c
'57, June 10, William A., c
'64, Feb. 24, Amy W., c
'64, Feb. 24, Alice W., c
JENNISON.
'67, June 14, John,
'63, Apr. 23, Alvira, w
'44, Mar. 28, Warren H. c
'34, Jan. 13, Geo. R.
'30, Nov. 14, Emily A., w
'52, Sep. 24, M. Rebecca, c
'65, Jan. 27, Frances E., c
'66, Feb. 28, Emily M., c
'69, Aug. 20, Marion S., c
'40, Aug. 10, Josiah H.,
'48, Feb. 9, Sarah J., w   Charlestown,
'67, Jan. 15, Frank W., c
69, Oct. 12. Warren E., c
'70, Dec. 2, Emma B., c
'73, Aug. 12, James H., c
'75, Dec. 15, Geo. F., c
JONES.
'38, Nov. 14, Frank,   Sutton, Vt.
'48, Apr. 17, Laurinda, w   Franklin.
'72, Jan. 17, Lizzie W., c   Vermont.
'75, Jan. 21, Anna F., c   Vermont.
'77, Feb. 17, Louisa M., c   "
JOSLIN.
'37, May 16, Geo. H.,   Surry.
'40, Dec. 24, J'phine A., w   "
'60, Sep. 24, Charles H., c   Millbury, Mass.
'67, Sep. 23, Edith L., c   Worcester, Mass.
'77, Sep. 7, Catharine M.,
'55, Jan. 4, Frank M.,   Surry.
'58, July 20, Lizzie C., c   "
'62, July 9. Jessie F., c   "
JOSLYN.
'08, Mar. 11, Joseph,
'36, Dec. 24, Oliver T.,
'40, Aug. 5, Abbie C., w
KEEFE.
'50, James,   Ireland.
'53, Jan. 1, Mary A., w
'75, Aug. 6, Arthur J., c
'77, Nov. 6, Anna, c
'58, Feb. 26, David,   Ireland.
'51, July 16, Hannah,   "

KELLER.
1841, Sep. 19, Charles, Germany.
'51, May 10, Rosa, w "
'71, Mar. 13, George, c "
'73, Nov. 24, Charles jr., c "
KEMP.
'54, Aug. 22, John P., Alstead.
KENDALL.
'22, Apr. 16, Isaac F., Bangor, Me.
'28, May 13, Mary E., w Langdon.
'62, Dec. 26, Frank E., c Charlestown.
'73, Feb. 6, Lillian M., c Boston.
'16, June 22, Catharine M., Boxboro, Mass.
'42, Aug. 14, Charles W.,c Manchester.
'46, Apr. 29, Amos G., Chester, Vt.
'44, Jan. 27, Gertrude A.,w Vermont.
'70, Apr. 21, Nellie E., c Townshend, Vt.
'72, Nov. 12, Dorr E. T., c Springfield, Vt.
'78, Jan. 27, Fred A., c "
KENRICK.
'62, Sep. 10, Charles T.,
KENT.
'42, Nov. 29, Samuel E., Acworth.
'48, Aug. 6, Aurora L., w "
'77, Apr. 19, Geo. R., c "
KEYES.
'07, Jan. 29, Thomas N., Cambridge, Vt.
'15, Oct. 26, Mary A., w Randolph, Vt.
'45, June 21, John V., c Combridge, V.
'42, Nov. 26, George A., "
'52, Oct. 25, Carrie W., w Bethlehem.
'75, Apr. 27, Fannie C , c New York.
KIDDER.
'25, July 25, Joseph,
'26, Sep. 10, Susan, w. Alstead.
'67, Oct. 17, Edward H., c
'69, June 17, Benjamin F., c
KILBURN.
'09, Apr. 4, Frederick,
'13, Dec. 3, Mary A., w
KINGSBURY.
'25, Aug. 16, Ellen A.,
'50, May 28, Asahel H.,
'49, Oct. 15, Maria L., w
'74, Apr. 12, Walter W., c
'55, May 2, George W.,
'57, May 24, Frances C., w
KINTRY.
John, Ireland.
'30, Margarett, w "
'55, June 6, William H., c
'56, Nov. 11, James, c
'58, May 15, John jr., c
'61, July 15, Nellie, c
'52, Feb. 1, Bartholomew, Ireland.
'38, Ellen, w "
'58, Sep. 2 Nora, c
'62, Oct 11, Barthol. jr.,c
'65, Jan. 8, John, c
'67, Jan. 1, Daniel, c
'68, May 27, Thomas, c
'71, Nov. 23, Frank W., c
KNAPP.
'09, May 4, Richard, Brattleboro, Vt.
'15, Aug. 12, Rhoda A., w Stoddard.
'20, May 29, Francis B., Roxbury, Mass.
KNIGHT.
'27, Mar. 13, Alfred, England.
'24, Aug. 10, Elizabeth, w "
'49, Dec 21, William E., "
'50, Jan 15, Eliza, "
'61, June 15, Leonard, "
'43, Mar. 2, Ellen, Ireland.
'76, Oct. 17, Thomas E., c "
KNIGHTS.
'25, Sep. 25, Moses H., Coventry, Vt.

'29, Apr. 30, Emeline L., w Athens, Vt.
'55, Apr. 29, Sarah M., c Langdon, Vt.
'57, July 4, Viola, c Chester, Vt.
'57, July 4, Viona, c "
'66, Jan. 23, Allen L. c "
68, Oct. 3, Herbert E., c "
'22, Apr. 27, J. William, Farmington.
'32, Jan. 22, Gracia J., w Springfield, Vt.
KNOWLTON.
'06, Apr. 6, Luther,
'34, July 13, Chauncy E.,
'60, Apr. 7, Susie G., w
'11, Oct. 8, Elias W.,
'23, Feb. 4, Emeline W. w Seekonk.
'60, June 17, Edward A., c
'62, Oct. 5, Warren D., c
KNOX.
'63, July 14, Eleanor M., New York.
'17, Aug. 4, Maria, Callas, Vt.
LANDON.
'77, Dec. 14, Cora L.,
LANE.
'44, Dennis, Ireland.
'43, Hannah, w "
'74, Aug. 1, William, c
'14, Sep. 28, Lucy W. Bradford.
LARABEE.
61, July 21, Frank, Jamaica Plains.
LATHROP,
1799, Hope, Tolland, Conn.
LAWRENCE.
'37, Apr. 16, Henry F.,
'37, Sep. 12, Amy E., w.
'81, Nov. 3, William H., c
'85, Oct. 7, Arabella E., c
'59, June 18,Willie L.. c Worcester, Mass.
LAWTON.
'51, July 3. George F., Newfane, Vt.
'52, May 25, Nancy E., w Springfield, Vt.
LEBOURVEAU
'25, Nov. 27, Jerome, Keene.
'29, Aug. 25,Betsey F., w Sullivan.
'51, Feb. 27, Fred A., c Keene.
'59, June 6, Lillie F., c "
LEONARD.
'21, Aug. 20, Rufus,
'28, Sep. 8, Sarah E., w
'53, Feb. 3, Willie G., c
'55, Mar. 3, Clara E., w Westmoreland.
'77, Mar. 20, Wallace C., c
'20, Dec. 29, Levi S.,
'26, Aug. 26, Lucy,
LIVINGSTON.
1793, Oct. 10, Polly,
1834, July 31, Charles, Vermont.
'43, Jan. 8, Colborn, Canada.
'44, Sept. 16, Millie H., c N.Springfield,Vt.
'67, Mar. 26, Fannie M., c
LOCKWOOD.
'27, July 21, Lorenzo D., Springfield, Vt.
'27, Oct. 11, Elizabeth, w
'54, July 10, Charles, Springfield, Vt.
'56, Oct. 15, Ida L., w "
'73, June 8, Edward, c Charlestown.
'76, April 3, Ernest, c "
'30, June 16, Daniel, Chester, Vt.
'37, Aug. 13, Esther A., w Sherburne, Vt.
'58, July 5, Cora A., c Springfield, Vt.
'58, Dec. 4, Franklin C., Chester, Vt.
LONG.
Mary, Ireland.
Mary, c "
'54, Nov. 16, Geo. S., Alstead.
'58, Oct. 15, Mary M., w
LOUARE.
'42, May 10, Raymond, Canada.

1850, Jan. 17, Delia, w   Vermont.
'67, Nov. 18, Mary, c   "
'71, Jan. 9, Charles, c   "
'77, May 14, Nelson, c   "

LOVEJOY
'13, June 5, Mary H.,

LOVELL.
'44, Nov. 24, Julia A.,   Alstead.
'72, Dec. 22, Willard L., c

LUCKE.
'22, Feb. 9, Christian B.,   Richmond, Va.
'21, June 22, Harriet R., w
'46, Feb. 2, Gustavus, c

LYNCH.
'38,   Thomas H.,   Ireland.
'33, May,   Abbie, w   "
'60, Dec. 4,   Henry, c
'63, Aug. 20, Daniel, c
'65, June 10, Thomas, c
'68, April 4, Jane, c
'70, Mar. 10, George, c
'71, Mar. 10, William, c
'74, Jan. 6, Edward, c
'76, June 14, John, c
'33,   Anna,   Ireland.
'50, May 6, Ellen,
'60,   Bridget,
   Maggie,
'64, Aug. 6, Johanna,
'69, Nov. 14, Julia,
'52, March 5, David,   Vermont.

MARCH.
'36, April 14, William,
'38, April 15, Frances S., w   Woodstock, Vt.
'03, Nov. 26, John S.,
'19, Feb. 27, Abby G., w
'49, April 27, Abby, c
1799, Sept. 13, Rebecca G.,
1815, April 2, Hannah M.,

MARSH.
'15, May 1, Farnham,
'48, July 11, Julia A., w   Newark, Vt.
'64, May 21, Ellen J., c
'65, Nov. 25, Albert F., c
'67, Sept. 13, Nellie A., c
'70, Jan. 6, Emma M., c

MARSTON.
'39, April 27, Thomas R.,   Claremont.
'38, April 7, Jane M., w
'67, July 13, Grace, c   Rutland, Vt.
'68, Oct. 5, George G., c   "
'75, Dec. 8, Inez A., c   Canada.
'76, April 9, Clara E., c

MARTIN.
'07, Feb. 25, Oliver,
'24, July 7, Louisa M., w   Windsor, Vt.

MAYNARD.
'46, Sept. 28, Charles G.,   Boston.
'59, Nov. 29, Mary G., w
'27, Mar. 24, Sarah J.,
'24, Sept. 17, Lydia A.,
'21, Mar. 15, Susan A.,
'45, Mar. 27, William A.,
'46, July 5, Frances A., w
'14, Dec. 19, Amherst K.,
'23, May 5, Maria G., w   Charlestown.
'52, May 17, Lizzie M., c
'58, Jan. 25, Mary E., c
'19, March 5, Augustus F.,   Holden, Mass.
'19, Nov. 8, Fannie H., w   Claremont.

MARSHALL.
'35, Jan. 22, John W.,
'36, Feb. 22, Louisa P., w
1794, April 9, Hannah,

MARVIN.
1854, July 30, Noble C.,   Alstead.

MASON.
1801, June 31, Holland,
'03, July 10, Susan V., w   Braintree, Mass.
'16, Sept. 18, William B.,
'27, Feb. 21, Sarah A., w
'52, Oct. 30, William C., c
'54, May 2, Harriet I., c
'56, Dec. 16, Charles E., c
'62, May 1, George B., c
'64, Oct. 16, Walter C., c

MEAD.
1789, Dec. 18, Amy,
1829, July 8, Samuel O.,   N. Cambridge, Ms.

MELLISH.
'26, Sept. 10, Mary A.,
'68, April 13, Julia W., c
'44, July 31, Charles B.,
'52, June 25, Elvira M., w   Stoddard.
'76, Oct. 26, Sarah E., c   Orange, Mass.
'04, Mar. 30, Henry,
'04, Feb. 23, Sarah, w   Dorchester, Ms.

MERRIAM.
'10, Feb. 28, Daniel,
'18, Mar. 17, Emily E.,
'07, Sept. 22, Eliza,

MESIAH.
'58, Nov. 21, Henry,   Vermont.

McCARTY.
'28,   Eliza,   Ireland.
'33, June 24, John, c   "
'56, Mar. 18, Michael, c
   Daniel, c
   James, c
   Lizzie, c
   Alice, c
'54, January, Patrick,   Northampton, Ms
'54, Aug. 30, Mary J. T., w   Vermont.
'78, June 29, Mary A., c

McDONALD.
'21, Dec. 23, Thomas,   Ireland.
'34, April 30, Jane, w   "
'55, Jan. 22, James, c   "
'58, Mar. 22, Thomas, c
'59, May 31, William, c
'61, April 1, Ellen, c
'64, May 4, Mary, c
'66, July 20, John, c
'68, April 25, Edward, c
'73, Sept. 27, Charles, c

McGEE.
'57,   George C.,

MILLER.
'23, Sept. 17, Addison,   Marlow.
'26, Nov. 27, Asenath S., w   Lempster.
'22, Aug. 14, Mary H.,   Concord, Mass.
1794, Jan. 24, Irene L.,   Alstead.
1834, Sept. 12, Ellen,

MITCHELL.
1788, April 28, William,   Westmoreland.
1821, Nov. 9, Sarah L., c
'61, Aug. 4, William, 2d,
'64, June 14, Martha E.,

McLAUGHLIN.
'59, July 13, Ida,   North Carolina.

McMANARA.
'28,   John,   Ireland.
'34, August, Julia, w   "
'58, May 19, James, c   Vermont.
'61, Jan. 2, Morris, c   "
'63, Aug. 6, Mary, c   "
'67, April, Michael, c   "
'70, Feb. 14, Julia, c
'53, Mar. 21, William,
'77, Nov. 5, Edward,   Vermont.

MORAN.
'43,   Edward,   Ireland.

1842, Mar. 17, Catherine, w   Massachusetts.
'66, June 3, George, c
'70, Mar. 11, Ellen, c   Vermont.
'74, July 12, William, c

MOORE.
'54, June 13, William M.,   Amherst, Mass.

MORAN.
'43, Sept. 26, Dana A.,   New York.
'48, Dec. 23, Lena M., w   Windsor, Vt.
'72, Feb. 28, Gardner E., c

MORIARTY.
1809, July 4, John H.,   Ireland.
'15, Johanna,   "
'48, Nov. 3, Weston, c   Massachusetts.
'51, Jan. 27, Frank, c

MORSE.
1791, Nov. 4, Esther C.,

MUNROE.
'18, Jan. 14, Nathaniel,   Marlow.
'19, Jan. 1, Susan, w   Stoddard.

MURDOUGH.
'27, July 9, George W.,   Holden, Mass.
'18, Apr. 27, Ch'rlotte B., w. Tyngsboro, "

MURRAY.
'28, Mar. 14, Patrick,   Ireland.
—, w
'57, Sept. 10, William J., c
'59, Oct. 7, Thomas, c
'36, Richard,   Ireland.
'40, Mary, w   "

MURPHY.
John,   Ireland.
Margarett,   "

NASH.
'48, July 16, C. Walter,   Stoddard.
'56, Apr. 27, Susan A., w   Sullivan.
'74, Apr. 22, Alice A., c
'76, Jan 27, Henry H., c
'77, Oct. 25, Oscar W., c
'17, Aug. 27, James P.,   Gilsum.
'62, Feb. 1, Emma J., c   Hartland, Vt.
'67, May 6, Ida M., c   Westminster. Vt.
'36, Aug. 8, Andrew,   Gilsum.
'47, Feb. 6, Susan E., w   Massachusetts.
'65, Nov. 24, Beulah R., c   Gilsum.
'66, Apr. 25, Andrew E., c   Nelson.
'69, Jan. 5, Charles P., c   "
'77, Oct. 15, Perry, c   "

NEWTON.
'30, June 15, Hubbard B.,
'40, Dec. 25, Fannie, w
'64, Dec. 4, Harry H., c
Mary.

NICHOLS.
'05, Mar. 29, Alura,   Stoddard.
'07, May 13, Louisa,
'40, June 26, Freeman,   Braintree, Vt.
'41, Jan. 23, Eliza E., w   "
'66, Aug. 10, Cora B., c   "
'75, Aug. 25, Sadie I., c   Randolph, Vt.

NIMS.
'54, Nov. 6, George A.,   Keene.
'38, Apr. Albert F.,   Sullivan.
'32, July 26, Cynthia, w
'71, Oct. 23, Mary C., c

NOURSE.
'05, Apr. 10, Isaac,   Keene. *

OBER.
'18, Nov. 21, Herekiah,   Vermont.
'30, May 15, Sarah, w   Canada.
'63, Sep. 15, William G., c
'66, Apr. 12, Geo. W., c   Rockingham, Vt.
'68, Mar. 14, Mary A., c   Charlestown.
'70, June 5, Alice J., c   "
'49, June 11. Isaac,   Vermont.

O'BRIEN.
1825, May 15, Daniel,   Ireland.
'34, Dec. 23, Kate, w   "
'51, Oct. 12, William, c
'56, July 10, Michael, c
'60, Nov. 7, Timothy, c
'63, Mar. 23, Anna, c
'62, Feb. 17, Daniel, Jr., c
'68, Aug. 11, Thomas, c
'73, May 18, James, c
Patrick,   Ireland.
'52, Katie, w   "
'76, May 16, Mary, c
'78, Apr. 20, Katie, c

O'CONNOR.
1793, Bridgett,   Ireland.
1838, Aug. 15, John,   "
'64, July 18, Mary E., c
'30, Mary,   Ireland.
Michael,   "
Julia,   "

ORDWAY.
'33, Dec. 1, D. W. Clinton. Hillsboro.
'40, Oct. 22, Helen M., w
'70, June 22, Lee Clinton, c

OWEN.
'34, Dec. 27, Byron P.,   Enfield, Conn.
'35, May 6, Chloe S., w   Milton, Vt.
1797, Feb. 12, Gen. Geo. C.,   Windsor, Conn.

PARKINSON.
'45, May 31, Charles jr.,   Boston, Mass.
'42, Aug. 29, Mary D., w   Mt Holly, Vt.
'70, Sep. 17, Alice M., c   Alstead.
'19, Oct. 12, Charles,   Dunbarton.
'20, June 4, Julia A., w   Merrimack.
'43, Aug. 27, Geo., c   Charlestown, Ms.
'49, May 5, Sarah M., w   Templeton, Mass.
'71, Apr. 1, Geo. H., c   "
'72, July 14, Edward E., c   Winchendon, Ms.

PARKS.
'55, Aug. 13, James,   Canada.

PERCY.
'44, Jan. 6, Warren E.,   Vermont.
'43, Jan. 28, Lois A., w   New York.
'71, Feb. 26, Emma L., c   Tilton.
'72, Sept. 22, Alta L., c
'73, July 24, Walter W., c
'74, Jan. 30, Myrtie M., c
'77, Nov. 30, Arthur E., c

PERRY.
1841, Feb. 15, Horace A.,   Bethel. Vt.
'44, Jan. 18, Sarah J., w   Westminster, Ms
'64, Dec. 9, Carrie A., c   Westminster, Vt.
'72, April 6, Fred J., c

PLAISTRIDGE.
'09, Jan. 7, Joseph,   Cornish.
'18, Mar. 10, Harriet A.,   Ashburnham, Ms

PIERCE.
'29, Aug. 20, Mary,
'64, June 26, Hattie E., c
'38, April 16, Hattie,   Ashburnham.
'60, Sept. 28, Albert,   Newark, Vt.

PODWIN.
'46, Jan. 5, Henry C.,
'39, Jan. 7, Nancy, w
'74, Feb. 20, George H., c

PORTER.
'35, June 23, George P.,
'38, Jan. 8, Sarah J., w   Albion, N. Y.
'64, May 1, Mabel A., c
'23, Nov. 20, Winslow B.,   Morristown, Vt.
'20, Mar. 31, Laura M., w
'30, Sept. 27, Warren W., c   Alstead.
'54, Dec. 18, Mary B., c   "
'25, Nov. 20, Samuel H.,   Morristown, Vt.

1826, Dec. 16,	Harriet A. E., w	Alstead.
'64, July 2,	John Lincoln,	"
	POTTER.	
'44, Aug. 1,	Charles W.,	
'54, Mar. 11,	Christine C., w	
'75, July 17,	Sarah E., c	
	POWERS.	
'43,	John,	Ireland.
'43,	Elvira, w	"
'68, June 14,	Katie, c	Vermont.
'70, July 14,	Patsy, c	"
'70, July 14,	Maggie, c	"
'72, June 27,	Mary, c	"
'74, July 14,	Ellen, c	"
'75, Dec. 20,	Thomas, c	
'77, Feb. 28,	John, c	
'49, Aug. 17,	Elmer W.,	Marlow.
'53, Nov. 28,	Flora R., w	Alstead.
'74, Mar. 19,	Winfred A., c	
'77, Aug. 11,	Harry E., c	Marlow.
	PRATT.	
	Kate,	Boston, Mass.
'61, Mar. 17,	Thomas W.,	
'63, Mar. 14,	Andrew E.,	
'40, Jan. 27,	Isaac,	
'52, October,	Esther C., w	Gilsum.
'75, Oct. 5,	Flora R., c	
1778, January,	———	
1848, Nov. 2,	Asa,	
1795, July 25,	John,	
1860, April 1,	Elbert H.,	Vermont.
	PRENTISS.	
'10, Oct. 10,	John W.,	Alstead.
'24, Oct. 14,	Emeline, w	"
'57, Nov. 20,	William J., c	
'68, June 15,	Fred P., c	
	PRESSY.	
'46, May 19,	Eugene E.,	
'49, Sept. 23,	Maria L., w	Randolph, Mass.
'17, May 22,	Lorenzo D.,	Sandown.
'22, Nov. 28,	Mary S., w	
	PRIEST.	
'10, January,	Belinda,	Waterford, Vt.
'34, April 22,	George W., c	"
'36,	Merrill J., c	"
	PROCTOR.	
'45, April 18,	John E.,	Alstead.
'50, Mar. 13,	Emma J., w	New York.
'05, Nov. 17,	Ebenezer,	Alstead.
'12, Jan. 11,	Anna K., w	Watertown, Ms.
	PROCTY.	
'39, Oct. 14,	Elbert L.,	New York.
'47, April 27,	Abbie S., w	"
'49, Jan. 28,	Herbert F.,	"
'46, Jan. 1,	Ruby E., w	"
'72, Sept. 10,	George E., c	"
'74, Jan. 3,	Charles K., c	"
'77, April 12,	———, c	
	PUNT.	
'32, Nov. 25,	David,	England.
'31, Aug. 31,	Sarah M., w	
'56, Dec. 26,	George E., c	
'62, Dec. 12,	Arthur E., c	
'54, Aug. 23,	William L.,	
'55, Jan. 15,	Rose, w	
1797, June 1,	James,	England.
1805, Aug. 12,	Amelia, w	"
	PUTNAM.	
'28, Sept. 4,	Henry E.,	
'32, Jan. 7,	Clara P., w	Willington, Ct.
'56, Sept. 8,	Susie,	Charlestown.
	PUTNEY.	
'24, July 4,	Jonathan H.,	Winchester.
'24, Sept. 22,	Betsey M., w	
7'61, May 24,	William H., c	
'62, Mar. 30,	Minnie E., c	

	QUINTON.	
1806, Sept. 17,	Elizabeth,	Marlow.
'49, May 8,	Horace, c	
'34, Dec. 24,	Joshua C.,	Fair Haven, Vt.
'26, Nov. 30,	Sarah A., w	
'62, July 8,	Mary E., c	
'63, Aug. 22,	Nancy S., c	
'65, June 19,	Thomas C., c	
	RADFORD.	
'69, Jan. 21,	Carrie L.,	New York.
	RAMSAY.	
'17, Aug. 4,	William T.,	Springfield, Vt.
'26, July 22,	Harriet E., w	Concord, Vt.
'61, Oct. 29,	Frank R., c	
'63, Oct. 24,	Sarah E., c	
'65, Nov. 21,	Fred A., c	
'69, May 20,	Bertha F., c	
'69, May 20,	Bell F., c	
'72, May 24,	Ira W.,	
'57, Dec. 3,	Retta M., w	
	RAWSON.	
'33, Mar. 25,	Henry C.,	Alstead.
'33, April 9,	Mary H., w	Stonington, Ct.
	RAY.	
'63, April 25,	Elizabeth,	
'27, Sept. 2,	George H., c	
	REDDING.	
'04, Dec. 13,	Jonathan,	Surry.
'34, Dec. 13,	Louisa,	Alstead.
'38, June 21,	John,	"
	REYNOLDS.	
'11, Oct. 11,	Peter,	Ireland.
'24, Jan. 14,	Bee K., w	"
'54, Nov. 5,	Ellen, c	
	RICE.	
'07, Aug. 7,	Charles,	
'06, Sept. 8,	Lavonia, w	Northfield, Vt.
'24, May 29,	Mary A.,	
	RICH.	
'37, July 3,	Nellie E.,	
	RICHARDSON.	
'34, Feb. 14,	Abel P.,	Lempster.
'44, July 12,	Sylvia F., w	Marlow.
	RILEY.	
'53, Mar. 24,	George A.,	Lyndon, Vt.
	ROBIE.	
'35, Sept. 24,	Thomas S.,	Gorham, Me.
'37, Mar. 22,	Virginia D., w	Camden, Me.
'61, Apr. 24,	Thos. S., jr., c	Waldoben, Me.
'63, Jan. 24,	Lewis P., c	
'69, Oct. 12,	Virginia, c	Salmon Falls.
'71, Oct. 18,	Geo. P., c	Scituate, Mass.
	ROBINSON.	
'35, Jan. 6,	Abba R. P.,	Woodstock, Vt.
'46, July 20,	Cornelia A.,	Sherburne, Vt.
'76, Feb. 42,	Byron A., c	Lebanon.
	ROGERS.	
'42, April 18,	Hoxie C.,	Mt. Holly, Vt.
'47, March 1,	Theresa R., w	Brandon, Vt.
'68, Feb. 6,	Grant, c	Michigan.
'69, June 26,	Orie R., c	"
'73, April 24,	Rebecca T., c	
'74, Sept. 8,	Helen C.,	
'76, Feb. 18,	Euphronia, c	
'77, Oct. 30,	Eugene H., c	
'43, July,	Oscar W.,	Langdon.
'43, June 14,	Mary F., w	
	ROLLINS.	
'05, Jan. 1,	William,	Dublin.
'06, July 16,	Fanny, w	Charlestown.
	ROSS.	
'35, Nov. 4,	Martin A.,	Ludlow, Vt.
'34, Aug. 26,	Selinda, w	"
'58, Jan. 25,	Norris F., c	'
'61, Nov. 13,	Emma M., c	Plymouth, Vt.
'06, Nov. 19,	Daniel,	Lyndon, Vt.

1834, May 10,	Eliza, w	England.
'38, July 1,	Lizzie M., c	Windham, Vt.
'34, Mar. 16,	Levi A.,	Lyndon, Vt.
'44, July 4,	Lizzie M., w	Bath.
'64, Nov. 22,	Geo. F., c	Canada.
'75, Aug. 11,	Nellie M., c	
'66, Feb. 17,	Diana L.,	

ROY.

'14, June 18,	Andrew,	
'56, July 17,	Sarah J., c	
'55, Oct. 10,	William E.	
'55, June 1,	Mary A., w	
'75, Sept. 17,	Mary L., c	
'77, Nov. 12,	Edith M., c	

ROYCE.

'02, May 22,	George,	
'14, June 8,	Cyrus,	
'21, Nov. 19,	Laura, w	Rockingham, Vt.
'52, Aug. 7,	Laura E., c	
'52, June 6,	Sarah A.,	
'18, July 25,	Samuel,	
'18, Apr. 9,	Nancy S., w	Charlestown.
'57, Mar. 20,	Ella C.,	
'39, Mar. 18,	Benjamin B.,	
'56, June 4,	C. Belle, c	
'76, May 30,	Benj. B., jr., c	

RUSSELL.

'46, Oct. 28,	Charles M.,	
'46, Aug. 43,	Jean'tte M., w	Alstead.
'69, Jan. 1,	John B., 2d., c	
'70, Nov. 9,	Ines E., c	
'70, Nov. 9,	Avis E., c	
'73, Sept. 20,	Mary A., c	
'76, Dec. 10,	Frank M., c	
1796, July 1,	Mary A.,	Deerfield, Mass.
1820, Mar. 22,	John B.,	
'20, Sept. 19,	Lucy, w	

RUST.

'25, Aug. 24,	Elizabeth S.	Heath, Mass.
'52, Jan. 26,	Mary E., c	Burlington, Vt.
'55, Jan. 3,	Ella L., c	"

RYAN.

'20,	John,	Ireland.
'25,	Fanny, w	"
'52, Jan. 1,	William, c	
'53, Nov. 28,	John, jr., c	
'56, Dec. 24,	Nellie, c	

SABIN.

'16, May 12,	George,	Westmoreland.
'25, Oct. 29,	Julia A , w	
'47, Jan. 10,	Frances M., c	
'82, Dec. 22,	Emma J., c	
'69, Apr. 30,	Lydia,	Dummerston, Vt.

SARGENT.

'51, Apr. 22,	Charles E.,	Boston, Mass.
'52, July 2,	Anna A., w	Massachusetts.
'76, Mar. 13,	Charles, c	Watertown, Ms.
'78, Feb. 14,	Robert L., c	

SAXTON.

'52, July,	Thomas,	New York.
'52, " 6,	Ada M., w	"

SEABURY.

'12, Dec. 2,	Edwin,	Yarmouth, Mass.
'42, Apr. 2,	Edwin K.,	
'41, June 14,	Helen Maria, w	
'68, Apr. 29,	Maria Elizabeth, c	
'72, July 20,	Mary Hosmer, c	
'74, " 2,	Geo. Edwin c	
'76, Feb. 27,	Samuel Mason, c	

SELKIRK.

'73, Feb. 11,	Lizzie R.,	
'44, Sep. 9,	James,	Canada.
'50, July 13,	Mary E., w	Woodbury, Vt.
'74, Dec. 6,	James S., c	Surry.
'76, Oct. 6,	William R., c	
'40, Feb. 21,	John,	Canada.

SEAVER.

1804, June 15,	Harriet,	

SEWARD.

'52, Apr. 26,	Fred E.,	
'62, Aug. 19,	Charles E.,	

SHAWNESSY.

'48,	Thomas,	Ireland.
'45, Apr. 3,	Catherine, w	"
'78, Mar. 26,	Thomas jr., c	

SHERIDAN.

'46,	Charles,	Ireland.
'57, Aug. 10,	Delia, w	Vermont.
'70, Aug. 1,	Charles, c	New York
'73, Jan. 8,	Nellie, c	Vermont.
'55, May 3,	Mary,	

SHERMAN.

'07, Sep. 26,	William C.,	
'12, Feb. 2,	Lorinda H., w	
'41, July 15,	Helen R., c	

SHIPMAN.

'15, Jan. 8,	Wm. J.,	Westminster, Vt.
'16, Oct.	Maria E., w	
'50, May 28,	Emma C., c	

SINEFF.

'17, June 17,	Joseph,	Germany.

SHORT.

'40, Feb. 18,	Albert H.,	England.
'53, Apr. 15,	Almira L., w	Derby, Vt.
'51, June 9,	John,	England.
'16, May 26,	Catherine,	"

SLADE.

'22, Mar. 1,	Stillman,	Alstead.
'52, Sep. 12,	Abbie S., w	Brookville, Me.
'61, Mar. 8,	Elmer S , c	
'63, June 5,	Addie V., c	
'68, June 12,	Edward J., c.	
'70, Oct. 12,	Lizzie A., c	
'74, Mar. 22,	Allen E., c	

SMITH.

'27,	Franklin,	
'44, Nov. 5,	Stella, w	
'76, Feb. 11,	Fred E., c	
'72, May 6,	Ada M., c	
'28, Feb. 27,	Daniel W.,	Needham, Mass.,
'00, Mar. 24,	Esdras,	Langdon.
'23, June 17,	Alice M., w	Lempster.
'54, Jan. 12,	Edgar E., c	Langdon.
'55, July 26,	Arthur A., c	"
'57, Mar. 2,	Alice M., c	"
'59, Nov. 1,	Herbert W., c	"
'16, Mar. 4,	Nelson C.,	Fairlee, Vt.
'25, Mar. 19,	Mary J., w	Lebanon,
'65, Jan. 23,	Nellie B., c	
'70, June 9,	Lizzie, c	

SPARHAWK.

'30, Mar. 17,	Geo. C.,	
'26, May 7,	Fanny M.,	Rockingham, Vt.
'52, June 15,	Rollin W., c	"
'59, Aug. 2,	Thos. C., 2d.,c	"
'61, July 14,	Carleton E., c	"
'29, Feb. 14,	Thomas C.,	
31, Nov. 14,	Mary,	

SPACK.

	Michael,	Ireland.
'30, June,	Ellen, w	"
'57, Feb. 21,	Michael, c	
'61, July 12,	Maggie, c	
'65, Sept. 29,	James, c	
'69, Dec. 26,	Lizzie, c	

STARK.

	Mary	Ireland.
'69, Jan. 25,	William, c	
'70, Feb. 6,	Christopher, c	
'73, Dec. 24,	Henry c	

STEARNS.

'08, May 2,	Dolly H.,	Winchester.

STEVENS.

1828, May 23,	Gilbert T.,	Warwick, Mass.
'23, May 22,	Elizabeth, w
'55, Mar. 4,	William N., c	Warwick, Mass.
'58, Aug. 2,	Jane C., w

STEWART.

'21, June, 24,	James,	Washington.
'37, Sept 6,	Lizzie, w	Alstead.

STILL.

'48, Mar. 5,	Don.
'53, Jan. 1,	Mary N., w	Alstead.
'76, Mar. 14,	Leland D., c

STODDARD.

'23, Dec. 6,	Harriet M.,
'50, Oct. 31,	Stella M., c

STONE.

'53, July 31,	Charles W.,

STOWELL.

'37, Sept. 27,	Charles P.,	Windham, Vt.
'47, Oct. 11,	Helen E., w.	Peru, Vt.
'67, Sept. 16,	Harry J., c.,
'69, July 9,	Nellie, c
'71, Oct. 26,	William G., c.
'11, Jan. 24,	Ebenezer E.,	Lyndon, Vt.
'09, Jan. 11,	Sarah K.,

STREETER.

'59, Jan. 29,	Geo. H.,	Dana, Mass.

SULLIVAN.

	James,	Ireland.
'48, Feb. 28,	Ellen, w	"
'68, July 10,	Hannah, c
'70, Jan. 17,	Mary, c
'72, Aug. 6,	James, jr., c
'74, April 17,	Eugene, c
'76, Feb. 25,	William, c
	Cornelius,	Ireland.
'41, April 12,	Hannah, w	"
'61, Dec. 16,	Kate, c	Vermont.
'63, Oct. 1,	James, c	"
'65, Dec. 12,	William, c	"
'71, Feb. 11,	Cornelius, c	"
'76, May 17,	Annie, c
'30, Mar. 17,	Patrick,	Ireland.
'32, June,	Margaret, w	"
'55, Aug. 12,	James, c
'60, June 5,	Jerconiah, c
'62, Oct. 15,	Lizzie, c
'63, Oct. 27,	Cornelius, c

TAGGARD.

'27, Dec. 25,	John W.,	Hillsboro' Bridge
'32, June 24,	Anna, w	Swanzey.
'52, Dec. 17,	Charles H., c	Marlboro.
'59, Oct. 21,	John W., c	Swanzey.
'66, Sept. 17,	Willie A., c
'70, March 3,	George O., c
'73, Jan. 30,	Edward S., c

TAUNT.

'14, May 8,	Thomas,	Canton, Mass.
'11, Nov. 23,	Mary A., w	Northfield, Mass.

TAYLOR.

'39,	Mary E.,	Lisbon.

THAYER.

'19, July 16,	Denzel R.,	Jamaica, Vt.
'27, April 7,	Dulcina L., w	Wardsboro, Vt.
'53, Dec. 15,	John K., c	Jamaica, Vt.
'55, Sept. 18,	Dorr M., c	"
'59, April 24,	Frank D., c	"
'62, Aug. 24,	Carlos F., c	"
'65, Aug. 15,	Edwin A., c	"

THOMAS.

'06, May 28,	Philip,	Westmoreland.
'05, Dec. 6,	Clarissa F., w

THOMPSON.

1799, Nov. 1,	David C.,
1835, Dec. 2,	Warren,
'47, July 26,	Wealthy E., w	New York.

1875, Oct. 1,	Lillie M., c
'77, Sept. 20,	David L., c
'83, March 1,	Adeline,
'50, Sept. 16,	Herbert H.,	Marlow.

THURSTON.

'62, Oct. 22,	Andrew H.,	Vermont.

TIFFANY.

'30, May 16,	S. Johnson,
'38, Nov. 24,	Emily W., w	Keene.
'70, May 16,	Katie M., c
'73, Feb. 20,	Geo. B., c
'78, Jan. 15,	Clara J., c

TIMOTHY.

'42, July 22,	Alonzo,
'43, Oct. 9,	Ellen M., w	Vermont.
'61, Feb. 11,	Frank K., c
'66, Aug. 14,	Edward L., c
'68, Oct. 14,	Ida J., c
'74, May 13,	Herbert A., c	Vermont.
'76, Jan. 8,	Charles F., c

TITUS.

'15, Feb. 24,	Sophia R.,	Saxton's Riv., Vt.
'66, Jan. 16,	Emma,
'01, Oct. 12,	Preston,
'55, April 10,	Vashti, w	Westmoreland.
'37, Aug. 4,	Ozro W.,	Plainfield.
'42, Aug. 9,	Martha P., w	Stratford, Vt.
'61, June 7,	Harvey O., c	Plainfield.
'63, June 19,	Mary F., c	Lebanon.
'83, June 19,	Marion E., c	"
'75, Sept. 24,	Charles F., c	Hartford, Vt.
'11,	Ellen,	Ireland.

TOBY.

'65, Oct. 9,	Carrie Gardner,	New York.

TOLE.

'32, April 24,	John,
'35, Mar. 23,	Katie,	Ireland.
'56, Nov. 8,	Edward, c
'58, Aug. 14,	John, jr., c
'60, Nov. 23,	Henry, c
'62, July 10,	Ellen, c
'64, June 14,	Margaret, c
'73, Aug. 3,	George, c
'28, March 7,	Matthew,	Langdon.
'33, Jan. 25,	Margaret, w	Ireland.
'56, Dec. 12,	Mary, c
'68, May 16,	Sarah, c
'75, July 24,	Grace M., c
'98, July 23,	Julia,	Ireland.
1846, Mar. 26,	Charles W.,
'30, Mar. 27,	Mary E.,
'20, June 19,	Margaret A.,
'41, July 24,	Julia,
'59, Aug. 15,	Thomas,
'61, Aug. 20,	Charles S.,
'65, June 13,	Sarah,
'67, Aug. 5,	William,
'71, Dec. 5,	Lillie,
'73, Nov. 6,	Frank,

TOWNE.

'41, Aug. 10,	Haskell,	Alstead.
'45, July 28,	Lizzie F., w	Keene.
'74, Jan. 18,	Gertie M., c
'77, June 3,	George S., c
'14, Jan. 30,	Salem,
	Emily, w

TUFTS.

1798, Sept. 1,	Jonas,	Charlestown, Ms.
1766, May 1,	Sarah, w	Charlestown.
1841, Sept. 29,	Susan, c	"

TURNER.

'24, Mar. 16,	Jane,	Langdon.
'14, Sept. 9,	William J.,	Claremont.
'27, April 16,	Julia A., w	Swanzey.
'57, Aug. 14,	Fred W.,	Reading, Vt.

TUTTLE.
1857,   Anna,   Alstead.
'30, Nov. 29, Oratha,   "

WALTON.
1795, Jan. 3, Nabby,   Hillsboro.

WARN.
1788, June 22, Elizabeth,
'35, Mar. 26, William,
'36, Oct. 18, Sarah M., w
'73, Oct. 8, Charles R., c
'76, Mar. 4, William W., c

WATKINS.
'13, Feb. 6, William,
'11, Oct. 11, Susan R., w
'17, June 10, Ephraim A.,
'21, Nov. 26, Harriet M., w
'57, Apr. 17, Herbert J., c
'26, Mar. 13, Moses Q.,
'37, Sep. 14, Mary A., w   Port Hope, Can.
'30, Mar. 20, Hiram,
'34, Mar. 27, Mary J., w
'66, Feb. 1, Eva M., c
'70, June 5, Jennie M., c
'74, Mar. 28, Katie H., c
'15, Feb. 10, Henry J.,
'33, Aug. 24, Mary E., w   Keene.
'44, Apr. 9, Emily A., c
'71, Mar. 15, George,
'12, Jan. 13, Susan E., w
'52, July 9, Sumner S., c
'57, Oct. 4, Louisa, c
'55, July 28, Alonzo J., c
'21, July 2, Frederick,
'26, June 22, Sarah A., w
'48, May 22, Albert H.,
'45, May 3, Nellie, w   Bangor, Me.
'43, Oct. 22, Leonard G.,
'44, Mar. 13, Elizabeth M., w Hartland, Vt.
'72, July 12, Carrie S., c   Westminster, Vt.
'29, Dec. 19, Charles E.,
'34, Apr. 3, Frances, w   Westminster, Vt.
'57, Aug. 10, Minnie R., c
'59, Feb. 9, Chas. H., c
'62, Aug. 27, Winnie F., c
'64, Nov. 22, Bessie C., c
'67, July 29, Norman E., c
'69, July 28, Elmer A., c
'72, Aug. 12, Louisa A., c
'74, Oct. 3, Della L., c
'76, Sep. 21, Hattie M., c
'23, Aug. 5, Oliver H. P.
'24, Sep. 27, Mary P., w
'50, Jan. 10, Charlie A., c
'55, June 1, Lizzie N., c
'54, May 22, Edward A.,
'33, July 10, Ella A. w
'25, Sep. 3, Alfred,
'30, Jan. 6, Isabella, w
'65, Apr. 18, Frederick H., c
'07, Feb. 2, Abby F.,

WEBER.
'20, Aug. 29, Andrew,   Germany,
'23, July 20, Elizabeth, w   "
'57, Nov. 20, John A. c
'61, May 11, Lizzie E., c
'64, Mar. 13, Carrie E., c
'65, Sep. 27, Ricka, c
'33, May 7, George,   Germany.
'51, Dec. 9, Tena, w   "
'76, June 6, Theresa, c   New York.
'78, May 4, Mary, c

WEBSTER.
'15, June 6, Benj. E.,   Gilsum.
'15, Feb. 19, Abigail N., w Keene.
'51, Oct. 10, Daniel E., c   Boston.
'55, Jan. 13, Lillie E.,   "

1857, Mar. 27, Benj. F., c
'37, Apr. 22, Edwin E.,
'42, Oct. 1, Emily E., w   Putney, Vt.
'63, Nov. 1, Carrie E.,
'69, Mar. 22, Albert E., c
'63, Mar. 8, Eunice,

WELCH.
'53, Aug. 6, Thomas,   Ireland.

WELLINGTON.
'01, Oct. 24, William,
'49, May 18, Lucius,
'49, Sep. 10, Sarah G., w
'48, Mar. 5, Scott,
'04, Sep. 20, Mary A.,   Concord, Mass.

WELLS.
'38, Apr. 17, Edward,   England.
'42, June 31, Elizabeth, w   "
'62, Dec 25, Elizabeth A.,   "
'68, Sep. 25, Catherine, c   "
'70, Apr. 17, Sarah, c   "
'73, Mar. 1, Ada, c
'77, Nov. 13, Katie, c
'14, Sep. 18, Julia,   Thompson, Ct.
'50, Jan. 27, Julia M., c   Bellows F., Vt.
'60, Feb. 4, Arthur E., c

WETHERBEE.
'34, Dec. 6, Levi K.,   Ludlow, Vt.
'37, Aug. 8, Mary E., w   Guildhall, Vt.
'64, Aug. 31, Minnie M., c   Reading, Vt.
'59, June 7, Walter L., c   "
'72, May 14, Irus L., c   "
'74, Oct. 28, Clarence A., c   "

WEYMOUTH.
'31, July 28, Henry,
'44, Apr. 5, Mary E., w
'63, Nov. 20, Harry A., c   So. Vernon, Vt.
'70, July 22, Henry W., c   "
'72, June 16, Frank E., c   "
'72,   Fred S., c   "
'32, Sep. 20, Geo. W.,   Woodstock, Vt.
'47, June   Kate, w   Ireland.

WHEELER.
'14, Oct. 20, Harriet A.,   Acworth,
'50, Dec. 25, Henry C., c
'54, Oct. 8, Frank M., c
'19, Nov. 5, Orrin,   Lempster.
'21, Oct. 9, Mary T., w   New Ipswich.
'50, Sep. 17, Charles F., c   Lempster.
'53, " 16, Orison T., c   "
'57, Oct. 23, Frank O., c   "

WHITNEY.
1798, May 4, Mary,
1838, Dec. 14, Lewis,

WHITTIER.
'47, June 2, Henry M.,   Newport.
'51, Aug. 8, Anna M., w   Indiana.

WICKER.
'22, Feb. 20, Mary,   Leicester, Mass.

WIER.
'10, April 12, Frederick A.,
'17, Nov. 26, Almira R., w
'47, Mar. 31, Mary K., c
'50, Jan. 31, George F., c
'52, Feb. 24, Frederick A., jr., c
'54, July 7, Rowe, c
'65, Jan. 21, Almira,

WIERS.
'30, Sept. 1, Diana C.,   Stockholm, N. Y.

WIGHTMAN.
'28, July 12, Henry G.,   Westport, N. Y.
'33, Oct. 15, Harriet, w
'54, Oct. 5, Carrie L., c
'59, Jan. 6, Geo. H., c
'66, July 12, Walter B., c   Bellows Falls.

WILBUR.
'38, Jan. 9, Curtis B.,   Westmoreland.

1838, Mar. 19,	Rhoda M., w		
'66, Sept. 6,	Edward, c		

WILDER.

'26, June 30,	George S.,	Keene.
'29, Sept. 26,	Mary A., w	
'52, July 25,	Helen A.,	Boston, Mass.
'51, Aug. 30,	Herman M.,	Lempster.
'53, Nov. 22,	Octavia, w	
'78, March 2,	Allen H., c	
'53, Nov. 22,	Octavia,	

WILLARD.

'27, Nov. 25,	Linus R.,	Northfield, Vt.
'36, Sept. 13,	Hattie H., w	Hudson, Mass.
'55, Jan. 7,	Ida H., c	Cavendish, Vt.
'56, Oct. 18,	Julius L., c	Claremont.
'59, July 12,	Everett G., c	Littelton.
'65, July 11,	Newell H., c	Westminster, Vt.
'65, July 11,	Nellie Mary, c	"
'76, June 9,	Emma J., c	Putney, Vt.
'76, June 9,	Etta M., c	"
1798, Dec. 6,	Sophia,	Westmoreland.

WILLIAMS.

1798,	Eliza,	
1824, Aug. 13,	George B.,	Petersham, Mass.
'25,	Martha J., w	Damarascotta Me
'57, Dec. 1,	Mary J., c	West Newton, Ms
55, Dec. 31,	George B. jr., c	"
'26,	Asenath,	Petersham, Mass.

WILLSON.

'17, Sept. 12,	Henry R.,	Langdon.
'21, April 15,	Roxana, w	"

WILSON.

'19, Sept. 6,	George W.,	
'27, Dec. 7,	Jefferson,	Claremont.
'31, June 26,	Melissa, w	Thetford, Vt.

1865, Nov. 7,	George J., c	Claremont.
'66, Aug. 22,	Eliza,	Keene.

WITT.

'26, Oct. 22,	Charles,	Chesterfield.
'33, Jan. 18,	Sarah F., w	Orange, Vt.
'63, Mar. 24,	Ella G., c	Charlestown

WOLCOTT.

'53, Aug. 15,	Frank P.,	Claremont.
'59, July 30,	Jennie M., w	"

WOODWARD.

	Ora,	
'52, Mar. 17,	John M.,	Lowell, Mass.
'54, Mar. 15,	Vina, w	New Jersey.
'77, Mar. 18,	Lista, c	New York.

WORCESTER.

'13, Nov. 24,	Charles, C.,	Stoddard.
'19, June 7,	Harriet, w	"
'45, Oct. 27,	Charles C., jr.,	"
'52, Oct. 23,	Mary A.,	

WOTKYNS.

'01, Sept. 27,	Hiram,	
'08, Oct. 22,	Sarah U., w	Troy, N. Y.
'49, July 16,	Helen A., c	

WRIGHT.

'19, Nov. 26,	David,	Keene.
'27, May,	Anna, w	Woodstock, Vt.
1797, June 14,	Moses,	Surry.
1804, July 23,	Fidelia, w	Keene.
'61, July 14,	Harry, A.,	"

YOUNG.

'46, Jan. 30,	Edward O.,	Vermont.
'47, July 19,	Edna M., w	"
'75, Oct. 22,	Florence c	
'78, Mar. 21,	Ira M., c	

ERRATA.

Page 273, sixth line from top, for Jonathan, read Jeduthan.

Page 211, after Robert Barnett, read June 16, 1836.

Page 336, 3d line from top, read, 1st, William James; 2nd, Eleanor Farnham; 3d one d. young.

Page 209, 5th line from top, for Eleanor, read Elenora.

Page 389, 9th line from top, for Acsah, read Achsa.

www.ingramcontent.com/pod-product-compliance
Lightning Source LLC
Chambersburg PA
CBHW032305280326
41932CB00009B/710